D1826599

EVERYTHING IN STYLE
HARRIETT LOW'S MACAU

Hong Kong University Press thanks Xu Bing for writing the Press's name in his Square Word Calligraphy for the covers of its books. For further information, see p. iv.

EVERYTHING IN STYLE
HARRIETT LOW'S MACAU

Rosmarie W. N. Lamas

Published in conjunction with

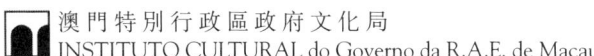
澳門特別行政區政府文化局
INSTITUTO CULTURAL do Governo da R.A.E. de Macau

香港大學出版社
HONG KONG UNIVERSITY PRESS

Hong Kong University Press
14/F Hing Wai Centre
7 Tin Wan Praya Road
Aberdeen
Hong Kong

© Hong Kong University Press 2006

Hardback	ISBN-13: 978-962-209-788-9
	ISBN-10: 962-209-788-X
Paperback	ISBN-13: 978-962-209-789-6
	ISBN-10: 962-209-789-8

British Library Cataloguing-in-Publication Data
A catalogue record for this book is available from the British Library.

Secure On-line Ordering
http://www.hkupress.org

Printed and bound by Kings Time Printing Press Ltd., Hong Kong, China.

Hong Kong University Press is honoured that Xu Bing, whose art
explores the complex themes of language across cultures, has written
the Press's name in his Square Word Calligraphy. This signals our
commitment to cross-cultural thinking and the distinctive nature of our
English-language books published in China.

"At first glance, Square Word Calligraphy appears to be nothing more
unusual than Chinese characters, but in fact it is a new way of
rendering English words in the format of a square so they resemble
Chinese characters. Chinese viewers expect to be able to read Square
Word Calligraphy but cannot. Western viewers, however are surprised
to find they can read it. Delight erupts when meaning is unexpectedly
revealed."

— Britta Erickson, *The Art of Xu Bing*

Contents

Acknowledgements

I wish to thank the following individuals and institutions for having, in one way or another, supported this project:

The Cultural Institute of the Macau Special Administrative Region, for the scholarship that allowed me to see the original diaries of Harriett Low at the Library of Congress in Washington, D.C.; Beatriz Basto da Silva, for having accompanied the genesis of this work; the late Monsignor Manuel Teixeira, whose publication on Harriett Low was the first longer extract from the journal that I read, and who was always willing to receive me to discuss God, Harriett Low and the affairs of the world; Staci Ford Hosford for having read the whole manuscript and given me valuable advice throughout; both Nan P. Hodges and the late Arthur W. Hummel (Sr.), co-editors of the first integral version of Harriet Low's journal, for their expert editorial work — I am very aware of how much this book has benefited throughout from their work and most grateful for being able to build on their excellent foundations — and Nan Hodges especially for her prompt and exhaustive answers on my e-mails; Colin Day for his enthusiasm, patience and sense of humour; Phoebe Chan for her careful editing of the manuscript; the Institute for Tourism Studies (IFT) in Macau, my former employer, for granting me a month's leave to go to the USA; the suppliers of the illustrations of this book, for their sympathetic and non-bureaucratic treatment, namely Patrick Conner from Martyn Gregory Gallery, London; Helen Swinnerton from the Hongkong and Shanghai Banking Corporation, Hong Kong; the Peabody Essex Museum in Salem, Massachusetts; Anne McIntyre, who proofread the manuscript thousands of kilometres away from Macau, in tranquil Ireland; the Library of Congress, for providing a splendid environment for studying and friendly attendance everywhere. Finally, I want to thank my husband Luís for insisting that I look for a publisher for this book and for his support and patience over all these years. I also must say "sorry" to my children Tomás and Clara, whose playtime both with their

Mama and at the computer was often cut short by this book. But, at least, they will have something substantial to connect them with their birthplace, Macau, when they are old enough to ask.

Preface

This book is yet another attempt at dealing with the journal left by Harriett Low (1809–1877), together with the particular circumstances and places, in which it was written. Considering that the first full and annotated edition of her journal was published in 2002,[1] after abbreviated impressions in 1900 and 1953,[2] the question why so soon another book on the same topic should disturb the quiet rhythm of 50 years in-between publications is fully justified. A short glimpse at the previous editions, however, will show that this book diverges from them substantially in content and structure. The most obvious difference is that it does not follow the chronological order as a journal would. Instead, it is divided into chapters, each focusing on a topic that I found worthwhile exploring in the context of her era. Harriett Low is, no doubt, the heroine in this work, but in a more attenuated way. Although still in the centre of attention, the social and physical environment in which she moved, is subject to analysis too. By accompanying her during five extraordinary years (1829–1834) of an otherwise rather normal life, she serves as a window to the past, which brings me to the main motivation for writing this book.

My interest in Harriett Low was aroused when looking for books for my History of Macau classes for undergraduate students in Macau. Taking on a generation that hails everything audio-visual and tends to consider books as an anachronism, I needed something with a pinch of edutainment, a kind of History Channel in book-form, to get them reading. Thus, after having heard about Harriett Low at a conference and having skimmed excerpts from her journal, I found her life worthwhile to be used and abused for my purpose. The fact that she was a woman, though a *gwei lo* ("foreign devil"), was important too, to create empathy with my overwhelmingly female students. Guided by the vivid impressions and animated descriptions from the journal, I wanted them to feel some of the drawing power of historical documents written by ordinary people. With Harriett Low as their guide, they can stroll through Macau's narrow pathways and admire its former beauty with their inner eye, to get acquainted with its motley inhabitants and their manifold occupations, thus feeling the thrill of connecting with those who lived decades or centuries ago.

However, the information contained in the journal had to be presented in a different way, because reading the unabridged version may prove somewhat tedious. There are obviously many repetitions of situations that occur over the years, which invariably provoke similar reactions. Besides, witty remarks or interesting thoughts are more easily forgotten or not even noticed when skimming a book. Hence I tried to extract in context her more original ideas or points of view and offer a more accessible version of the journal, without being superficial. The thematic chapters shall allow the readers to select certain topics according to their interests and to skip others, if they wish. As a consequence some people may even become interested in reading the integral version! Although this book had its origin in the grove of Academe and is published by an academic press, I endeavoured to present the topics in such a way as to appeal to the interested traveller and even to the general reader. Contemporary inhabitants, who live in the places that are described in more detail in the journal, namely Manila, Cape Town, St. Helena, London and, above all, Macau, may also be attracted by what this book has to tell.

In my understanding, the continuous appeal of Harriett Low's journal is based on the fact that it describes the living conditions of the China trade community from an entirely female point of view. The male position is well known through official historiography and books written by China traders, artists, priests, seamen and others, as well as through letters to their business partners and families. Her journal gives us a clearer picture of the daily life of foreign women on the China Coast and of their joys and sorrows. It tells us about the colonial lifestyle led by the foreign community and their relations with both the Portuguese colonialists and the native Chinese. Besides, many people that Harriett Low saw on a regular basis were individuals who were already well-known, such as the painter George Chinnery, the Protestant missionary Robert Morrison, and the surgeon Dr. Thomas Colledge, or who would achieve fame at a later stage, such as the Swedish consul and historian Sir Anders Ljungstedt or John Francis Davis, sinologist and governor of Hong Kong. Through her journal, we know the reason why they became famous, but as a novelty we also see them as human beings in their daily lives, betting on horses, quarrelling with their wives, cracking jokes and so on. We become acquainted with some of their idiosyncrasies, which make them more human in our eyes. Thus, it is certainly the most comprehensive report of this particular period in Macau's history, shortly before the Opium War.[3] The latter would bring about great upheavals in the traditional trading system between China and Western nations, which had already existed for about a century and in which Macau played an important role.

The journal is also interesting, because it was written by a person with a great liking and power for introspection. It tells us about the challenges that await those who leave their usual environment behind, in physical, intellectual-cognitive and emotional terms, and how the individual deals with them. A further advantage of the journal lies in the fact that it was written without any literary pretensions of publication, unlike most of the books of Harriett's male contemporaries. Besides, it was written down in an almost daily routine, and not from memory several years or decades later, where sometimes the past can be "gilded" or certain details forgotten. Later on in her life, when living in England, Harriett Low was even offered the chance to publish her journal by none less than the accomplished writer and early sociologist Harriett Martineau, whom she knew from frequenting the same church.[4] But her reaction was not that of an authoress, as is evident in a letter to her father.

> *Miss Martineau called to see me the other day & what do you think she proposed? how I laughed! Why nothing more or less than to make an authoress of your daughter, which she would insure would put me in possession of 300£, and for what you will say or how. She heard me say last winter that I kept a journal while I was in Macao. She is very anxious to see it and take it into her own hands and make it up for the publisher. Fortunately for me, it is locked up in America. She thinks it would be highly interesting as it would be such a new subject. So you see I have a resource, when we all fail.*[5]

Harriett Low's reluctance is understandable, because the journal was a very personal and often intimate reflection of her life in China and the great majority of the main characters in it were still alive. Besides, she did not like Martineau's style of writing and probably feared some negative impact on the book. In the same letter Harriett also admitted that "it would be hard to hear all the newspaper criticisms," assuming that unlike Martineau, she would not be *"callous"* towards them. Therefore, Harriett Low died without fame.

Arthur W. Hummel has put a quotation by Virginia Woolf from *The Common Reader* at the beginning of his transcription of the journal:

> *Should you wish to make sure that your birthday will be celebrated three hundred years hence, your best course is undoubtedly to keep a diary. Only first be certain that you have the courage to lock your genius in a private book and the humour to gloat over a fame that will be yours only in the grave.*

Although we are far from celebrating Harriett's birthday, fame came to her nevertheless and much earlier than the quotation predicts. Ironically, some of her famous contemporaries have fallen into oblivion, but are being resurrected thanks to their mention in the journal of an innocent writer.

Facts and Editorial Method

The first integral transcription of Harriett Low's journal was prepared by Arthur W. Hummel (Sen.; 1884–1975), a former missionary to China. In 1945, when Harriett Low's original diaries were handed over to the Library of Congress by her granddaughter Elma Loines, together with many family letters of the Low clan, he was the chief of its Asiatic (now Orientalia) Division. The transcription of the nine journal volumes amounts to 947 pages and his comments consist of 520 footnotes over an additional 128 pages. This work was completed in the early 1950s. However, his labour never paid off in the form of a publication of the integral version of the journal, or even by an enlarged, annotated edition of it. As a result, Hummel's initiative passed unnoticed by the general public.

The feat of publishing the whole journal was accomplished by Nan P. Hodges, who *"took up where Arthur W. Hummel left off"*.[6] Consequently, Hodges includes the name of Arthur W. Hummel as co-editor, thus doing justice to his labour that had begun more than half a century earlier. In her role as co-editor, Hodges tried to restore, as much as possible, the original punctuation, paragraphing and idiosyncrasies of style, which had been modernised in Hummel's transcription. She also endeavoured to give answers on questions that Hummel had not asked, apart from having taken into account important literature published on the China trade and related topics since the completion of Hummel's work. Without entering into too much detail here, references to the joint Hodges/Hummel edition of the journal will be made throughout this book.

All the quotations from the journal in this book are based on the joint edition. I have made some minor changes, however, which have become necessary for a better understanding of the story. For instance, Harriett Low often abbreviated the names of people who appear more frequently in the journal, or spelled them wrongly at the beginning of their acquaintance and correctly at a later stage. In both cases I have spelled out the names fully and correctly, because this study is not organised in a chronological way and reproduces excerpts only. Furthermore, the dates of the journal entries in this book appear in parentheses after the quotations, which I found more agreeable to the eye than when they were placed before the quotations originally. For the same reasons, I have also kept the dates to a numerical day-month-year scheme. By force of habit, I write Macau with a "u" at the end, although Harriett Low and some other English-speaking authors spell it with an "o". Both forms are used in English and in this particular case in the same book.

1
A Passage to China

U ntil the beginning of the 19th century, women rarely had the opportunity to travel much beyond their country of residence. In general, the proverb "a woman's place is in the home" characterised the prevailing ideology, which was subscribed to by both sexes. If women travelled at all, it was in their function as domestic beings, namely accompanying a male member of their family as spouses, daughters, or sisters. At that time, each journey was an arduous task, considering the slow and uncomfortable means of transportation, the poor standard of hygiene in public inns and taverns nor to mention the dangers of robbers and impostors of all kinds. There was no possibility of insuring one's health, life or luggage. Furthermore, the confrontation with different beliefs and customs abroad was seen as potentially harmful to a woman, especially if she was still young and impressionable.[1]

Since the 1820s, the traditional view of women primarily as domestic beings was challenged in many Western societies, due to the increasing industrialisation and expansion of commerce and all the social changes it entailed. The continuous progress in the development of faster and safer means of transportation encouraged more and more women to accompany their loved ones to virtually any place on the globe, or to hit the road on their own in the search for adventure, erudition, excitement, or self-realisation. A few decades later, travel was seen as a status symbol and an indicator of economic power. The experience of having travelled abroad was then regarded as an asset for a young, middle-class lady at the age of marriage.[2]

Although Harriett Low's journey took place in the shelter of kinfolk and thus can be considered under the traditional motives for travelling, she cannot be denied a good sense of adventure in view of the potential dangers and uncertainties that such a long voyage entailed. In the latter sense, Harriett Low and other travelling wives, sisters and daughters can be seen as true pioneers of their country and kind.

*   *   *   *

A momentous invitation

Harriett Low was born and raised in Salem (Massachusetts), as the second child among twelve of Seth Low (1782–1853) and of his wife Mary Porter Low (1786–1872).[3] Her father was a trader, importing medicinal drugs and other goods from overseas. The family belonged to the early 19th-century North American bourgeoisie, White, Anglo-Saxon, and Protestant, with all their beliefs and habits. Harriett had visited a school for young ladies in Salem, where she learnt what girls of her social position had to know, including a basic knowledge of French. At the same time, however, she also had to assist her mother with the daily chores:

> Before her departure for China, Harriett Low's life had been defined more by hard work than dancing. Her role in the large and economically pinched household had been that of seamstress — constantly making button holes or mending clothes for herself and seven brothers and three sisters.[4]

The opportunity for a change from the daily routine came, when her uncle William Henry Low (1795–1834) was invited to go to Canton as partner and head of the American company Russell & Co., in order to substitute Samuel Russell, one of the founding members, who wanted to retire.[5] Since he would be living mainly in Canton, a city that was off-limits for Western women, he challenged Harriett, who was his favourite niece,[6] to stay with his wife Abigail Knapp Low (born in 1800) in Macau to keep her company, as the couple had no children. Thus, in order to feel always close to home, she decided to write a journal for her elder sister Mary Ann, who also kept a diary to be exchanged with her.[7]

Harriett Low and her aunt became a part of the first generation of North-American women who ventured beyond the borders of their country. This process started in the 1820s and it proved to be irreversible:

> In an unprecedented female exodus, they fanned out around the globe on the waves of ideological, economic, political, and technological developments. … Travel was transforming women from private into public actors on the world stage.[8]

Two months after their departure in May of 1829, this branch of the Low family moved from Salem to Brooklyn (New York), where several members and descendants would assume important public positions. Since the opening of the Erie Canal in 1825, New York had rapidly turned into a navigational centre, while the harbour of Salem, due to problems of silting, could no longer receive large vessels.

These Lows were remarkable people. Everything they became involved with on the sea turned to gold, but they kept up their cultural interest as well.[9]

First impressions of a long voyage

The Sumatra *and her crew*

As regards the characteristics of the ship on which the Lows travelled to the Far East, the first editor of the journal, Harriett's daughter Katharine Hillard, who lived in the golden age of ocean steamers, wrote:

> *It is hard to realize that it then took four or five months, at best, to reach China, and that nearly a year must elapse before an answer could be received to a letter sent from there. In those days a ship of seventeen hundred tons was considered a marine marvel, and its accommodations were spoken of as "magnificent".*[10]

The Lows travelled to Macau on board the *Sumatra*, a sailing boat of 287 tons. She was commanded by Captain Charles Roundy (1794–1864), who regularly sailed between Salem and the Far East. It was not very common for ships to have many passengers, because at that time only those people who wanted to do business in China, to convert the heathen or to heal the wounded, travelled there. Apart from the three Lows there was merely one other passenger listed, Philip Ammidon Jr. (born 1804),[11] whose father was the co-founder of the firm Russell & Co., which Harriett's uncle was going to join. Only at a later stage in the journal we learn that the Lows had also taken a maid, Nancy, with them. However, her name does not appear on the passenger list.

A very important element on these long intercontinental voyages was the crew on board. Individuals with criminal and violent tendencies, or alcoholics, could easily put the success of a journey at risk. In this respect, the men on the *Sumatra* were exemplary, just like their captain.

> *They are all orderly in their deportment and you hear no swearing, see no fighting or anything of the kind. The greatest harmony prevails through out. The Captain first <u>chop</u>, the officers excellent, the sailors all good, the Cook good, and <u>sanctified</u> enough in his appearance. Seems as though he thought it a sin to <u>smile</u>. The Steward <u>active</u> and <u>attentive</u>. Uncle William <u>kind</u>. Aunt Low <u>ditto</u>. Mr. A. agreeable. Myself the same <u>fascinating</u>, <u>engaging</u>,*

enchanting, _sweet tempered_, _obliging_, _passive_ creature _that_ I _ever_
was. (3.6.1829)

Thus, all the conditions for a harmonious voyage seemed to have been present.

Before the anchor is lifted: travel preparations and food supply on board at the time of the big sailing boats

The journal does not tell us much about Harriett Low's personal preparation in terms of clothes and books taken, but Katharine Hillard mentions the following in her introduction, giving us an idea about some crucial supplies:

> As there was no possibility of having anything washed on board,
> an enormous amount of linen had to be carried, a lady was obliged
> to provide herself with at least six dozen of every kind of under-
> clothing, not to mention the variety of other garments that were
> needed for a voyage that took the traveller from the temperate to
> the torrid zone and back again to the temperate.[12]

35 days after leaving the United States, the _Sumatra_ crossed the equator, and then the inversion of the seasons on the southern hemisphere could soon be felt:

> [The weather is] tolerably pleasant, though we are now in cold
> weather. We are glad enough of woollen stockings, and shut up
> the cabin. (13.7.1829)

But even the woollen socks were not enough, to prevent the appearance of chilblains, "_my old complaint in the winter season_" (12.8.1829).

As regards the food supply on board, Hillard wrote:

> There were no such things then as canned meats, fruits, and
> vegetables, or condensed milk; and we can readily imagine that
> provisions for the table, on so long a voyage, must have been
> somewhat monotonous.[13]

Harriett confirmed the truth of this observation with the following entry:

> I should not know the days of the week were it not for our dinners.
> Methinks I hear you say a novel way for noting time. But every
> Tuesday and Friday we have _Bean_ _Soup_ which I depend upon,
> and anticipate them from one to the other. It tastes more like what
> I eat at home than any thing else we have, though every thing is
> cooked in the best manner. Yet there is that relish wanting that
> you never can get any where but at _Home_. (27.6.1829)

The boats used to supply themselves with fowl and pigs before their departure. The latter, apart from serving as foodstuff, also represented a source of distraction for the passengers:

> By the bye, the pigs are a great amusement to us. They quarrel so. Mr. Johnson sometimes makes caps for them to keep them from biting. (11.6.1829)

During the voyage, the sea obviously also served as an important source of food, supplying fish and train-oil.

> Mr. Johnson caught a porpoise last night. It was very large — he judged it weighed 300 weight [sic]. This morning we had the pleasure of seeing it dissected. Was a very interesting exhibition. It was about 2 yds long. The outside contains blubber which they get considerable oil from. The meat looks like beef, is very good eating. (18.8.1829)

But fresh fruit was a rarity. Only three months after their departure, on arriving in Malaysia, they ate fresh fruit again, the hitherto unknown fruits of the tropics.

Sad feelings at the beginning of the voyage and a difficult acclimatisation to the ship

The first entry in Harriett's journal dates from 24 May 1829, the day she left the house of her parents in Salem, bound for Macau. However, in a marginal note she informed that

> this journal was commenced a week after we sailed. It then appeared like a month. (24.5.1829)

Both leaving her family, as well as the change from land to sea, demanded a lot of energy and resolution:

> Embarked on board Ship Sumatra bound to Manilla from thence to Macao where I shall probably take up my residence for the next 4 years and for you my Dear Sister shall this journal be kept. I left home at 5 o'clock with feelings not to be described, nor imagined, but by those who have been placed in a similar situation. We were escorted out, as far as Baker's Island by a few friends from Salem which made it rather pleasanter for me, though I cannot say that I enjoyed any thing that took place that day. The morning was delightful as it could be, a delightful breeze that soon wafted

*us beyond the sight of our native land. About 9 o'clock our party
left us. However I behaved like a <u>heroine</u>, as I had resolved to be
— at 10 o'clock was taken sick and remained so for the next day.
Suffered nothing in comparison to what some people do, though
enough to feel that state of <u>utter</u> <u>hopelessness</u>. Such prostration of
<u>strength</u> and <u>spirits</u> as <u>I</u> never before knew or desire to feel again.
Remained on deck most of the day but cared neither how, or where,
I was going — continued pleasant throughout the night.
(24.5.1829)*

*Becalmed today, low in spirits. Think a sailor's life the worst of
all others. Tolerably well in health though have not felt bright yet.
Cannot relish coffee or tea without milk. Lead a listless sort of a
life, not having energy to do, or say any thing. (27.5.1829)*

The state of absolute weariness, indifference and weakness lasted for about
one week. On the Saturday after their departure, Harriett was already sewing
with pleasure and walking on deck, as well as eating and drinking without
problems and she was even singing at night. The search for a new rhythm of
life had begun, as well as for diversions in order to interrupt the monotony at
sea. Harriett warned her sister of the dullness of her life, which would inevitably
reflect in her journal:

*You must excuse me my Dear Sister if in this you find many things
uninteresting, but I give you free permission to omit reading any,
or the whole of it. I write as much for my own amusement as any
thing. So few are the incidents in this place, that I am obliged to
put in more about myself than I otherwise would. A less partial
eye than yours however must never see it, that I strictly enjoin.
We have some jokes, which if I could tell them would excite your
<u>risibles</u> but will not have the effect coming from paper. (27.5.1829)*

When finally feeling herself again, Harriett decided to orient her life according
to the following motto:

*To be resigned when ills betide
Patient when favours are denied
And pleased with favours given. (2.6.1829)*[14]

Some inconveniences of sea travel

The powers of Nature

Having overcome an attack of seasickness did not guarantee immunity against it. On the contrary, feeling seasick was a complaint made with a certain regularity, depending on the state of agitation of the sea, which could turn very simple tasks such as walking and eating into huge problems:

> *Strong wind and squally. Pitching, tumbling and tossing, very much to the annoyance of the Bean soup. Oh the ... exercise, the skill, that is required to make sure of a dinner at such a time — and more especially to sit down with a good appetite. It is as good as a play however for a spectator. (14.8.1829)*

Many of these violent movements of the ship happened without previous warning. They did not grow from a light agitation to a more severe one, but surprised everybody on board.

> *After dinner I was seated in the cabin at work, when I was suddenly taken from my chair and thrown over the other side, by the sudden lurch of the ship, and as unceremoniously thrown back again, with all violence, but fortunately escaped without any broken bones, which is quite miraculous. Begin to think however that I must have some of the qualities of Gum Elastic, as I always rebound, very much to the amusement of the company. (12.8.1829)*

> *I cannot keep the skin on my elbows — am continually bruising myself. (30.7.1829)*

These tremors were particularly dangerous when on deck, because they were frequently accompanied by a surge of water and could even throw a person over board.

But in general the *Sumatra* was very lucky with the weather, even when sailing around the dangerous Cape of Good Hope.

> *We get along pretty well. 72 days since we have seen land. But we have had most delightful weather most of the time. I cannot yet tell you what a storm at sea is. ... & My Dear Sister if you did but know it; it is a very rare thing to go round the Cape of Good Hope in the winter season and have such beautiful weather. We certainly ought to be very grateful. (4.8.1829)*

Yet there was one kind of wind hated by everybody, head wind, because it slowed down their progress, thus prolonging their stay on water. According to Harriett,

> [a <u>head wind</u>]'s worse than the <u>tooth ache</u>. It gives us all the <u>blues</u>. (2.6.1829)

However, the *Sumatra* did not completely escape all hazards. There were some dangerous incidents during her voyage.

> Capital breezes. Met with the first accident to day of consequence since we have been out. At ¹/₂ past 7 carried away our Fore Top Mast and Royal Mast. Were going at the rate of 9 knot an hour. Was no danger attending but made something of a job for <u>all</u> <u>hands</u>. We have been remarkably favoured in every respect. The Captain frequently tells us we do not know what it is to go to sea. But I think I know as much as I <u>want</u> to. (21.8.1829)

Just one week after this incident everybody on board was woken up at 4.30 in the morning with the warning to get ready for the lifeboats, as the *Sumatra* had been caught by a very strong current during a calm and was being pulled towards a reef. Only in the last minute another current miraculously prevented a disaster from happening.

> Need I say that we felt very grateful to our constant protector. The greatest danger in the Straits of Sunda and Gaspar lies in these strong currents. We are so apt to have calms here, and there are many Shoals and points to be avoided, which gives the Captain great anxiety, or rather keeps him upon the look out. (27.8.1829)

Man and his anxieties

Apart from the dangers and furies of nature other problems existed, created by the human mind, such as the occurrence of depression, frequently called the "blues" by Harriett, caused by the monotony and the restricted living space on board, as well as by homesickness.

> Have spent the day below reading. This eve spent on deck. Got a little of the <u>blues</u>. Sunday eve seems to be favourable for them. Long still eve — a beautiful moon now. Have thought much of home. (5.7.1829)

Uncle and Aunt are as happy as they can be. They have all that they wish for, but with all the rest of us, the <u>heart</u>, the <u>heart</u> is lonely still. Something wanting. (8.7.1829)

Even the captain was not exempt from an occasional attack:

Rainy to day — light airs. Captain got the blues. (6.6.1829)

Head wind today. The Captain looks blue. Lost his appetite. (9.6.1829)

An anxiety of another nature was provoked by the announcement "sail O!".

Just before tea <u>Sail O</u> was heard. We were all on deck in short time — a sound that makes us start like the cry of fire in Salem but which excites a great variety of feelings. A fear that it may be a <u>pirate</u>, though joy and hope predominate. A hope that she may be bound home, and a hope that she may have some of our friends in her. A desire to speak with her and a regret that we can not, as is <u>generally the case</u>. We watched her till dark — found she was bound to the Westward but could not speak her — how aggravating. (7.6.1829)

Fortunately the *Sumatra* never had problems with pirates, although fear of them was always latent:

Have had one severe attack of the <u>pirates</u> however which was not quite so pleasant — in my dreams. (29.5.1829)

The lack of medical support

Diseases or accidents could be fatal more easily at sea than on land, because many ships did not have a doctor on them.[15] William Hunter, for example, who travelled shortly before Harriett, describes how the ship's cook burnt himself seriously with boiling liquid, when caught by a tremor of the vessel:

His lower limbs were almost peeled and had it not been for the presence of the "doctor" [a Scottish passenger], he would have inevitably died.[16]

As regards the health of the passengers on the *Sumatra*, the journey came off without major problems. But, as we shall see on the voyage home in 1834, the Lows had to make a lengthy stop in South Africa, because Harriett's uncle was not fit to continue the journey by sea. The only health-related incident mentioned by Harriett during their voyage to Macau was their maid Nancy's toothache:

> *Mr. Johnson took out a tooth for Nancy to day. Thanks to those who persevered in my having my teeth extracted. I should have suffered enough, I have no doubt, if I had not have had them out. She did for 3 days and nights.* (3.7.1829)

It is not clear which teeth Harriett is referring to, the wisdom teeth or some decayed teeth, because during her stay in Macau she often suffered from severe toothache, and even broke a tooth.

Fighting against monotony: the pastimes on board the *Sumatra*

It is not difficult to imagine that the possibilities of entertainment on board the *Sumatra* were very restricted. The landscape, or rather seascape, was always the same, except for the changes in the colour of the sky and sea and the height of the waves. The group of passengers was very small, and the day-to-day was characterised by the same occupations: reading, walking on board, observing nature, writing letters, eating, trying to catch fish and to shoot at passing birds, sewing, playing cards, telling jokes and proposing a toast to the ones that stayed behind.

> *O what a task to find anything to write in a journal. I however write just what pops into my head. Mr. Ammidon advises me to write my dreams, which are generally <u>very</u> <u>interesting</u>, as you probably recollect. Methinks I hear Mother say, I hope she does not tell all her silly dreams. No, Mother, I do not, only once in a while when they are very witty.* (30.6.1829)

Harriett kept her promise and did not bother her sister with her dreams, which, apart from this, were not very entertaining or witty, but rather an expression of her homesickness. Instead, she liked to impress Molly with her newly gained knowledge about seafaring.

Learning to be a sailor

> *Take a lesson in the rigging of the vessel every day. I now know the <u>head</u> <u>from</u> <u>the</u> <u>stern</u> and likewise that it is a difficult matter, to <u>cut</u> <u>the</u> <u>water</u> <u>with</u> <u>her</u> <u>Taffril</u> which is more than I <u>once</u> <u>did</u>.* (29.5.1829)

As the time on board passed by, Harriett commenced using more specific vocabulary, such as the designations for the various masts and their sub-divisions or the great number of different sails, which are unintelligible for landlubbers. Hummel mentions in this context:

> Metaphors relating to the sea came easily to the tongues and pens of New Englanders. Even their womenfolk, who went to sea only occasionally, spoke the language of mariners, and possessed an awareness of wind and weather which we, in this century, no longer cultivate.[17]

An indication that often appears next to the date in the journal, like in a captain's logbook, is the position of the *Sumatra* in terms of latitude, proving her progress. It seems natural that her course was a daily topic among passengers and crew.

> My first questions in the morning are, How does she head, Captain? and how fast are we going now?. (1.6.1829)

The determination of the longitude at sea was a more complicated matter. It depended on a clock that could withstand pitch and roll, variations in humidity and temperature and keeping exact time at sea. If the clock can accurately indicate one's home time, the only thing needed is to determine one's local noon, that is when the sun has reached its zenith and the shadows are shortest. The difference between the two indicates one's longitude.[18] Therefore, when the *Sumatra* met an English ship while sailing around the Cape of Good Hope,

> the Captain agreed to stay by us till 12 o'clock to give us the Longitude, ours differing some from his as it had been some days since we have had a Lunar. (26.7.1829)

Observing nature

People who never travelled by sea cannot imagine its charms and beauty. Harriett was no exception in this respect, becoming enthusiastic about it once her seasickness had passed. Therefore nature is a frequent topic in the first volume of the journal. She describes smells that are new to her, the different qualities of the water, from smooth as glass to agitated and stormy, its tiny and enormous inhabitants, and the sunsets. Even later in Macau she would remember some of the spectacular sunsets of her voyage. Memories of this kind seemed to be more precious then than nowadays, perhaps because there were no means yet to fix them "eternally" on a photograph.

> *O Mary Ann if I could describe to you the beauty of the sunset tonight! I never saw anything half so splendid before. … I have thought two or three times before I had seen a glorious sunset, but never did I before. It was worth the whole voyage. I thought how my Dear Father would have enjoyed it, and indeed all of you — one colour in particular, and that was a beautiful <u>green</u>. The atmosphere was remarkably clear. (22.7.1829)*

But all the charms of the sea could not compensate Harriett's longing for terra firma. After having been on sea for more than three months without ever seeing land, everybody was anxiously waiting for the call "land O".

> *This afternoon about 5 o'clock heard the cheering sound of <u>land O</u>, and I'll assure you I was on deck in a short time. Christmas Island (within 4 degrees of Java head) had just opened to our view; it was 36 miles from us, but we watched it till we passed it. … If it had been in the day we should have had a fine view of the Island, passed within 6 or 8 miles of it. I should have thought it a <u>black cloud</u> if I had not known to the contrary. We shall probably see Java head tomorrow night. (24.8.1829)*

After a sleepless night because of the anticipation of seeing land the following day, Harriett got up at 6 o'clock in the morning, enchanted with seeing Java and other smaller islands.

> *You may judge of our felicity, after having but one scene for three months, to be suddenly enclosed with land covered with cocoa, pine apples, etc., in consequence of which before night my face was almost blistered. I set in the <u>long boat</u> all day, hardly spending time to eat. … We entered the Straits of Sunda in the forenoon with a delightful breeze. Had a fine opportunity to view the land as we went very near in shore — some very high land covered with an impenetrable forest. Looked very green, many bluff rocks and points — but many pleasant little <u>spots</u> I discovered. … Suffice it to say that I was pleased with every thing I saw, but I cannot say that I saw any spot on the Island of Java or any other in which I should like to take up my abode. I could not help thinking what a graveyard it has been, and still is, for all foreigners. (26.8.1829)*

Later in Macau she would hear many stories confirming the truth of this observation.

Daily and weekly rituals

> *It is tedious to be on the water so long, even to have pleasant weather so long and so little <u>variety</u>. It is a life to be <u>endured</u>, not enjoyed. Books is my only resource; cards have exhausted their charms, and almost everything else except <u>eating</u>, and that is every thing. The moment I have done my breakfast, I begin to anticipate dinner, and so on. I am now as <u>fat</u> as I <u>ever</u> <u>wish</u> to be. I have gained as much as 10 lbs since I came away from home, the weather is now so cold it is not comfortable on deck. Without great exercise, which it is impossible to take without endangering your [heads], I go <u>bouncing</u> about at a great rate. (10.8.1829)*

This was written shortly after they had sailed around the Cape of Good Hope, in full winter. Before reaching these southern latitudes, Harriett used to walk a lot on deck, alone or with whoever wanted to accompany her and measured the distances thus covered in terms of walks that she used to do in Salem:

> *Walked, I should judge, as far as Buffums Corner, two or three times, had a very pleasant walk. In imagination went with two or three of my friends. (12.6.1829)*

Or:

> *After tea took a long walk with the Captain we thought as far as the Danvers Meeting house. (17.6.1829)*

But Harriett's favourite pastime was, without any doubt, reading. It is not written anywhere how many books and journals the Lows took with them, nor whether there was something like a small library on board, but until they reached Manila, Harriett enumerated more than 20 books read by her. It can be assumed that she had read even more, because of the following remark made more or less in the middle of their voyage:

> *I am now going on a different plan with my journal. I intend to write every day and put some ideas or extracts of what I have been reading in the course of the day. It will be an advantage to me, as it will serve to impress it upon my mind. (20.7.1829)*

The choice of titles gives us a first idea of Harriett's interests and character. There are many books related to religion and faith, such as collections of homilies by Unitarian ministers, the faith that she professed. Every Sunday she would read some sermons alone, as well as listen to their proclamation by either her uncle or Mr. Ammidon. Furthermore, descriptions by missionaries, mainly in Asian countries such as India or Burma, also belonged to this group. Sometimes she even ventured into works with a more theological-philosophical character. On her list of preference followed books about history, which during the voyage were limited to biographies of English and French royalties. Only then appear romances, mainly written by English authors, and also poetry, preferably Byron. Books or articles about China were not on her reading list.

Sunday on board always felt special, not only because of its religious significance, but also because this day, like some kind of milestone, marked the beginning of a new week, thus giving a clearer idea of the passing of time and of the ship's progress.

> *4 weeks to day since we left all our dear friends, ¹/₄ of the time that we shall probably [be] on the water. The other 3 months will pass rapidly away. It really seems like Sunday even at Sea to me. I went on deck after breakfast. There all seemed still and quiet. The <u>Jack's</u> [sic] were all dressed clean, sitting with their books, <u>forward</u>. Every thing on deck nice. The heavens above and the waters below were alike serene, I stayed on deck an hour, then went below combed my hair and dressed in my <u>black</u> <u>silk</u>, and felt like a Lady, which is not the case except <u>Sundays</u>. At 10 we had our Sermon, one or <u>two</u> of Mr. Robinsons, an Englishman, ... which were very good. (21.6.1829)*

Another of Harriett's pastimes was writing and reading letters. As it was very complicated to receive or to dispatch correspondence at sea, she had wisely taken closed letters with her from family members and friends. Every Sunday she would almost religiously open one of them:

> *After sermons read Abbott's [a brother] letter, it is really very pleasant to have those letters. Only when I have one I want to open all the others but I command all my <u>self</u> <u>denial</u> on the occasion. Have not yet transgressed. Only wish that I could sit down and answer them. I have so many things I want to say to you all. I long for the time to come when I can sit down and write with a prospect of sending them. It grieves me to think how many anxious thoughts I shall occasion the best of parents — but I comfort myself with the thoughts that you will not have time to think of me. (21.6.1829)*

However, the Sunday came when there were no more closed letters left, a problem solved by Harriett in the following way:

> *Read over old letters, for the lack of any thing new. It is not the first time they have been pored over, nor will be the last. O I long for the time when I shall have a fresh supply. (28.7.1829)*

But she had to demonstrate a lot of patience before receiving the first letters from home, a fact that would still cause her lots of grief. On the other hand, they could dispatch their letters only when the *Sumatra* anchored at Anger (Anyer, on Java), on 26 August 1829, that is three months after they had left the United States.

First encounters with different peoples

An encounter with a British ship

The first opportunity to see new faces occurred two months after their departure from Salem, when they met a British vessel at the Cape of Good Hope. Harriett was quite thrilled with this encounter:

> *It was a large English ship, filled with passengers. We saw about a dozen ladies and a great number of gentlemen, <u>babies</u>, <u>servants</u>, etc. — it looking like a moving world. And you can imagine the pleasure it must have given us to have seen so many human beings and so much life on the water. (26.7.1829)*

As a gesture of attention, the English captain even sent several men over, with whom they could practise their intercultural skills.

> *He lowered his boat soon after and sent 4 of his <u>youths</u> on board the* Sumatra, *3 of the passengers and the mate, the latter the only decent one among them. The other three were dressed as fantastically as you can imagine. They appeared to think we looked on them with admiration, but I'll assure you they have been the subjects of many a joke. <u>They</u> and <u>we</u> however were very civil, and after taking a glass of wine and begging a pack of cards, inviting us to dine, offering anything they had on board, asking and answering questions, they bid us good morning. I must describe their looks a little, because we do not have such a chance very often. The first then that jumped on board was a long, lean looking chap,*

> *supporting a huge pair of <u>mustachios</u> and <u>whiskers</u>, on a pale and sickly <u>phiz</u>. He for an Englishman was very cordial, but we accounted for it by his being a <u>Mason</u>. He wore a drab coloured pair of pants, blue coat, etc. Last not least his cap. It was made of leather with a strap coming down and buckling under the lip, which gave him a singular appearance. We have had many conjectures about that strap. He endeavored to look interesting, but Uncle W. thought by the looks of his fingers he must be a <u>tailor</u>.*
>
> *The second was <u>fair</u> to <u>middling</u>. His dress consisted of light <u>pants</u>, a blue frock coat embroidered from top to the toe with cord, a military undress, and to crown all a scarlet cap. I cannot give you any idea of that — it is beyond description. But the colour was bright scarlet, drawn on one side and looked singularly I'll assure you. He was cultivating a pair of mustachios but as yet they were in infancy. He likewise endeavored to leave an agreeable impression. The third was dressed in common style but was a great buck. Indeed they all were. We conclude they are military characters, going out to join their regiment, as the vessel was bound to Madras and Calcutta. (26.7.1829)*

At this first occasion of contact with the English, Harriett's undecided and insecure attitude towards the representatives of this nation, which pervades her journal, is already visible.

> *I could not help thinking how differently we should have felt if it had have been an American. We should have been so delighted to have seen any one from our dear country. I was astonished to find that I possessed so much more love for my countrymen than any other people. To be sure, it is most natural that we should, but I always thought I could greet a strange Englishman with as much cordiality as I should a strange American. But now I know to the contrary. To be sure the prejudices we have towards Englishmen in particular influence our feelings in a measure. The cold haughty manner of the English is proverbial you know. I however will say no more upon the subject. ... However, we are much indebted to them for this day's amusement and many a <u>standing joke</u>. (26.7.1829)*

This quotation reveals another particularity of Harriett, testifying to her good nature or character: always after having made some unkind or unfriendly observations, be it about the English, Chinese or anybody else, sooner or later she tried to attenuate her remarks. In a marginal note next to the above quotation, without date however, she wrote:

> *I have again altered my opinion of the English. How often we make mistakes from ignorance. All the English I have seen are quite as cordial in their manners and even more so than the Americans.*

The first contact with Asians

On reaching the Indonesian archipelago, having left behind them the immense Atlantic and Indian Oceans, everybody on board began to cheer up at the prospect that the end of the voyage was near. Besides, a totally new world opened up to them, featuring peoples of different races, cultures and languages to their own. Already before arriving at Anger, Harriett had an opportunity to observe Malays catching fish from their *proas*, as their bamboo boats are called. Her description may still sound familiar to those who have visited these latitudes nowadays, as well as the following scene, where, however, we have to substitute the *Sumatra* for some noisy and smelly vessel full of tourists: A small Malay boat, trying to sell pineapples, bananas, mangoes, sweet potatoes and other fruits, approached the *Sumatra*, which was sailing at full speed. But after doing good business, the small boat, compared to a nutshell by Harriett, began to sink rapidly before their eyes.

> *I thought of course they were gone and it was out of our power to save them. But the men said it was as impossible to drown them as it would be to drown a fish. And I was soon relieved by seeing them astern. Two of them were swimming and holding their frail vessel up while the other baled it out. But the poor fellows lost their <u>dollar</u>.* (26.8.1829)

The voyage to Macau also offered her the opportunity to "study" the anatomy of the opposite sex, because, apart from the great differences in climate, there were also great differences in terms of decency and shame between the North American and the Malay societies.

> *I suppose you will like to know what I thought of a Malay and how my <u>modesty</u> could withstand such a shock as to see a <u>man</u> <u>unclad</u>. But I agree with Bishop Heber in thinking their colour serves as a covering. They seem like a different race of beings. Some of them had on jackets and sort of an apron, or loose petticoat. Their faces (those we saw) were bright and intelligent. They are very short. They average 5 feet 2 inches, the men; the women, 4 feet 11. Their*

teeth from the constant use of the betel become very black, which
they take great pride in. A young man, before his teeth gets well
blacked, feels quite mortified to see any one. (26.8.1829)

Manila — a "pleasant disappointment"

Before definitively setting sail for Macau, the *Sumatra* stayed in Manila for three
weeks. The Philippines were a Spanish colony then and Manila was an important
way station in the trade between China and Latin America. A nephew of Philip
Ammidon, George Robert Russell (1800–1866), had founded the house of
Russell, Sturgis & Co. in Manila in July 1828, together with Henry Parkman
Sturgis (1806–1869).[19] Harriett's commentary before disembarking seems a little
bit surprising, considering that everybody on board was already anxious to feel
terra firma beneath their feet:

> *I cannot say that I think of it [stopping in Manila] with much*
> *pleasure. I however may be disappointed agreeably in the place.*
> *(6.9.1829)*

This attitude reveals itself as a characteristic of Harriett, as the journal continues.
In Macau she often expressed negative expectations towards a certain event, for
example dinners or walks in the company of people that she did not like, which
afterwards were praised in the highest tones. Her entry on departing from Manila,
illustrates this observation very well:

> *I have got so much <u>attached</u> that I felt really gloomy. Reminded*
> *me also of the morning when I left my own dear native land. ...*
> *I never left any place except my home with so much regret. I shall*
> *always remember my visit to Manilla with much pleasure.*
> *(22.9.1829)*

Among the things that made her visit in Manila so pleasant and memorable,
were the beautiful house of Mr. Russell, the company of many compatriots, and
the excellent food. For the first time they had the opportunity to taste the
pleasures of a colonial life style in an exotic environment.

> *I really do not know what to say about Manilla. You cannot have*
> *any idea of the place by description. I am told it is like all Spanish*
> *towns. The forts, Convents and Churches take a great portion of*
> *the place. The roofs of the houses are covered with tile, mostly of*
> *one story and some of them very spacious. They have no glass*
> *windows. The sides and front of their houses are of pearl shell in*
> *little squares, and venetian blinds to some of them. The houses*

are all whitewashed, which the climate soon makes black, which gives the whole city an appearance of being smoked as though there had been a great fire. An immense number of people live on the water in Bancos, Cascos,[20] and smaller boats. We arrived at Mr. Russell's about 10 o'clock. The boats go directly to the gate. A canal runs from the river up to a lake a little beyond, which affords us much amusement in seeing the Boats continually passing. He has a fine spacious house, very airy. The rooms are all [on] one floor — very high and immensely large. Found a number of American gentlemen there after dinner. I had a most delightful ride with Mr. Russell on the Calzada[21] where we met all the nobility of Manilla. It is the fashion to ride every day about 6. No ladies walk out. Very suddenly the postillion stopped; Mr. R. told me that it was the hour of vespers, when every one was obliged to stop and say a prayer for the occasion. (9.9.1829)

Harriett did as the nobility in Manila, not walking but travelling mainly by coach. On her excursions, she was sometimes confronted with images that would have been considered completely inadequate for a young woman back home in the United States.

Saw a great many sights on our ride that would have shocked a young lady in America, but I have now got quite hardened. (12.9.1829)

Once or twice they even went to the countryside with its plantations of rice, bananas and other plants.

But it takes half the pleasure of riding in the country away, to ride through the suburbs, which are very extensive, and filled with babies and pigs which are brought up in the same style. I never knew anything like the babies, and children a little larger than babies. (15.9.1829)

Apart from this she observed and disapproved of many of the Catholic customs, a topic that would still consume lots of ink in Macau.

About 10 we rode out through the city, to visit the churches. The Cathedral was not open. We went to the Church of St. Domingo. It is a pretty church, rather gaudy in its ornaments however. There were several women there had just been confessing. They go away happy, thinking they are absolved from all sin and ready to begin a new list. (14.9.1829)

On the next Sunday, Harriett made a similar entry in her journal:

> *It is true they all go to Mass in the morning and confess, but they spend the rest of the day in frolicking. (20.9.1829)*

As we shall see later, during her first year in Macau she was unable to conform minimally to the non-observance of Sunday, in accordance with the Puritan habits of their Unitarian creed, as regards "frolicking", as she called it, both by the Catholics and by the Anglicans.

Taking course on Macau: the arrival and the first impressions of their house

The *Sumatra* left Manila on 22 September, but head wind withheld them in a bay nearby for several days, causing long faces on everybody.

> *I have felt really homesick this three days past. How shall I support 4 years absence? 4 months to day since left. (25.9.1829)*

As regards Harriett's expectations about Macau, she wrote the following during the short passage between Manila and Macau:

> *I long, yet dread, to see this place. I have heard so many different opinions about it — some in favour but more <u>against</u> — but I have determined to take no one's opinion but my own. (26.9.1829).*

Some months after having installed herself in Macau, she commented:

> *Phil [Ammidon] dined with us. ... I took much pleasure in telling him how much we had enjoyed ourselves since here. He had endeavored all the passage to make us think this a dreadful place. (25.3.1830)*

After having been on land again, in Manila, the last bit of the journey was very hard for all on board, mainly because of the torrential rains and strong winds, causing everybody to be seasick. The powerful downpours and winds may have been the effects of a typhoon, but which did not hit them fully. September coincides with the end of the typhoon season, which usually starts in late May or June. The *Sumatra* arrived in Macau on the morning of 29 September 1829. The agitation of the sea made getting ashore a little adventurous:

> *This morning all busy enough getting our loads of things out of the boat. A heavy sea which makes it very difficult for a boat to come*

*along side — indeed we were obliged to lower them over the stern.
You would have been amused to have seen us tied into a chair,
swinging over the stern of the ship, but we got along very
comfortably. (30.9.1829)*

The first impression of Macau and of their new home, the mere description
of which must provoke a sigh of envy in contemporary Macau residents, was a
favourable one:

*Macao from the sea looks beautifully. Some most romantic spots.
We arrived at Macao about 10 o'clock. Took Sedan chairs and
went to our house, which we like the looks of much. The streets
of Macao are narrow and irregular, but we have a garden to our
house where I anticipate much pleasure. There are two, one above
another. All the isles have flat stones and as smooth as a floor.
You ascend 5 flights of steps and come to an observatory from which
we have a fine view of the Bay and harbour and can see all over
the town. Round it there is a terrace and many pretty plants. It is
not in as good order as it must be soon. With this little spot and a
few birds, I shall get along very comfortably. I had no idea there
was so pretty a place here. Again I want someone to enjoy it with
me. (30.9.1829)*

*The birds are flying through the house all day. Frequently see 5 in
the hall and dining room at one time. There are some trees round
the house in which they lodge. Some fine singers among them.
(9.10.1829)*

Samuel Russell, whom Harriett's uncle was going to substitute, had prepared
the house, in which the Lows lived during the first six months of their stay in
Macau. In a later entry Harriett described the beautiful view from the
summerhouse in the garden, indicating some landmarks:

*From the front of the summer house we have a fine view of the
fort on a high hill. On another hill near stands what is called the
Gear,[22] signifying beacon. [It] is very high and it is a convent, I
believe. Below we have a view of the town and the Beach, a view
of the Church and Franciscan Green where the Ladies walk. And
every Saturday eve there is a band that plays here, which is
pleasant. I can hear them from the summer house. On the other
side we have a little view of the sea, which would be complete if it
was not for a new house built up lately which interrupts the view*

much. On the other side we have a fine view of the harbour and
surrounding hills. On the other is an ancient Church and convent.
It is really a delightful spot. I love it now, and if we remove as we
soon expect too I shall regret it much. (24.10.1829)

Since foreigners in Macau were not allowed to buy land or to own houses, they had to rent them from the Portuguese or Macanese. According to Major Samuel Shaw, who was the first American consul at Canton and who had to reside almost six months at Macau in 1787, after having lost his passage to India, the housing question gave rise to frequent disputes between the Portuguese and the foreigners.

Another instance of the injustice of the Portuguese on the one part,
and the submission of the Europeans on the other, is in relation to
houses. These are generally in a wretched condition when let to
the Europeans. As soon as a house is put in good repair, which is
done at the expense of the tenant, the proprietor, although the lease
may have been given for a number of years, demands his house
again, or else an addition to the rent. Unless one of these conditions
is complied with, the owner takes possession the moment the tenant
leaves it to go to Canton, and the latter is then obliged to look out
for another house. The Swedes' house was the best in Macao, and
for repairs and improvements had cost their company upwards of
eight thousand dollars. The governor, or rather his lady, took a
fancy to it, and the Swedes were under the necessity of consenting
to an exchange, which was in every respect unfavourable to them,
for the governor's house is not worth half the money which the mere
improvements on the other have cost. In matters where an
individual European is concerned, they do not use even the
ceremony of asking consent.[23]

There are no complaints about this matter in Harriett's journal anymore, allowing us to conclude either that the Portuguese had moderated their unreasonable demands in the meantime, or that the foreigners had become careful with their investment in the reparation of the houses. According to another testimony, many Portuguese seemed to have lived in more Spartan conditions than the members of the foreign community:

The houses of the Portuguese are mostly very spacious, but dreary
and uncomfortable, from the scanty furniture and want of carpets,
which are not used except in the houses of the richest citizens. ...
Fires are not used in the winter, although many days occur during

the season, in which a warm room is very desirable, and even
necessary, to those who are suffering from indisposition. Stoves or
grates are always placed in the houses occupied by Americans,
English, &c. but either the poverty or avarice of the inhabitants
induces them to dispense with this comfort.[24]

Foreigners arriving in Macau today have a vast range of flats to choose from, which is good news for those who want to rent or even buy, although real estate prices have risen quite a lot over the past few years. Newly built houses, especially on the Newly Reclaimed Areas of the Outer Harbour (NAPE) and on Taipa Island, are also much more spacious than the traditional flats in Macau. However, the density of construction, which is contrary to one's idea of privacy, is something that outsiders will have to get used to.

2
Macau — Then and Now, Old and Modern

Cities have always been poles of attraction for myriads of people for as many reasons. In the case of Macau, the reasons for visiting the enclave can be narrowed down to a few. As in Harriett Low's time, most people who come to this place, arrive with the expectation of making money, preferably very quickly and in large amounts — to be enjoyed elsewhere. The major difference is that opium has been replaced by another rather uncommon and addictive business, that is gambling or gaming.

Merely a tiny percentage of the millions that flood its borders every year are looking for what only Macau, as the first European-style city in China, can offer: a rich and complex history, the co-existence of different cultures and languages and the remains of an interesting Luso-Chinese culture. Luckily there is just enough left for history buffs to find their way back to the past between the high-rise buildings, with a journal like that of Harriett Low or a painting of Chinnery, or both, in one's mind. Having returned from the time machine adventure and seeing Macau's skyline again, the metamorphosis seems so unbelievable, especially because there is no hinterland over which to expand, as cities naturally do over the course of centuries. Instead, Macau had to expand upwards. The sea and the sky are the natural borderlines, but Macau continues to work hard to defy the limits of both.

In July 2005, the "Historic Centre of Macau" became China's 31st entry on UNESCO's World Heritage List, thus safeguarding many of the special places of Harriett Low's Macau for posterity.

*   *   *   *

A short history of a Portuguese settlement in China

The foundation of Macau

In 1513, the Portuguese were the first European nation to reach China by sea. It was to be a further step East in the expansion of their Asian Empire, known as *Estado da Índia*, which was administered by a viceroy based in Goa, India. Other important Portuguese possessions already established in Asia included Malacca and the Moluccas, or Spice Islands (1511). Since China had entered a period of self-isolationism, or "closed-door policy", during the early Ming period (around 1430), foreign trade had come to a total standstill and was even illegal. However, because business opportunities were very promising (silk, spices, precious metals), and increasingly so after their discovery of Japan in December 1542 or January 1543, the Portuguese could not be deterred from returning to China year after year, despite the subsequent destruction of their first settlement near the mouth of the Yangtse river. In the 1540s, the Portuguese decided to look for another base in China, although at a greater distance from Japan. They returned to their original place of landing, at the mouth of another big river, the Pearl River, and close to an important trading city with a longstanding tradition, Canton. After the opening of short-lived trading posts, first at Shangchuan Island and then at Langbaiao, both in the nearby surroundings of Macau, the Portuguese settled down on the peninsula of Macau in 1557.[1]

From now on they could trade undisturbed, having found a *modus vivendi* with the local population. Consequently, the settlement grew and prospered very fast. Its wealth was based on the Japan trade and the Portuguese role as carriers of Chinese silk to Japan and of Japanese silver to China.

> *It has been reliably estimated that at least one-half of Japan's total output of silver was exported at this period, most of it by the Portuguese of Macao.*[2]

The town was granted the privileges of a Portuguese city by the viceroy of India in 1586, and given the title "City of the Name of God of Macau in China" (*Cidade do Nome de Deus de Macau na China*), because of its growing importance, both in commercial and religious matters, among the Portuguese settlements in Asia. Travellers visiting Macau at the height of the Japan trade, and consequently at the height of its splendour, described the city and its inhabitants in colourful terms, such as Marco D'Avalo, an Italian who passed through Macau in 1638.

> *I believe that* Maccauw *or* Maccau *may justly be considered as*
> *the best, strongest and most profitable of the Portuguese possessions*
> *in the Indies, — I having visited the majority of them.*[3]

But only one year later, the Japanese decided to put an end to the trade with the Portuguese due to internal political reasons, forbidding them to ever return, or else they would be executed. Since the citizens of Macau could not imagine an existence without the Japan trade, they dared to embark on another Japan voyage in 1640. The Japanese, however, kept their word and executed 61 individuals out of the 74 sent by Macau. The other 13 had to watch the suffering and execution of their friends and were sent back to Macau as eyewitnesses, together with a warning letter that they should never return to Japan again.

This was the most important in a series of unfortunate events for the Portuguese in Asia, which left Macau an isolated territory in the 1640s. Without further prospects of trade, the city seemed doomed. Morale was very low and insecurity and violence were everywhere. Only during the first half of the 18th century, conditions in Macau improved slightly. In 1685, the Chinese had opened several ports to foreign trade and the European boats that came to China usually stopped in Macau, what had a positive impact on the local economy. In 1759, the emperor took the landmark decision to close all ports apart from Canton to foreign trade. This measure inaugurated Macau's second "Golden Era", which lasted until the end of the Opium War in 1842, when the Chinese had to agree to the opening of the so-called "treaty ports". Besides, the British settled in Hong Kong since 1839 and very soon it would overshadow and overtake Macau. As a consequence, Macau lost its century-old importance as the only gateway to China.

The question of Macau's sovereignty

As regards the Portuguese sovereignty over Macau, there was a generalised consensus among the foreigners that *"the government of Macao is only nominally Portuguese,"* as Harriett Low wrote in a letter home.[4] William W. Wood, her contemporary and compatriot, stated accordingly:

> *The long-continued and scarce-resisted insults and exactions of the*
> *Chinese, have at length reduced the Portuguese power here to a*
> *mere name, and so long a period has elapsed since these oppressive*
> *measures have been patiently endured, that it would now be almost*
> *impossible for them to resume the privileges and immunities which*
> *their imperial grant originally entitled them to.*[5]

The "exactions of the Chinese" and their "oppressive measures" referred to the existence of a Chinese customs official in Macau, called *hoppo*, and of a local Chinese mandarin, called *tso-tang*. They had existed in Macau since 1688 and 1736 respectively. Besides, the Portuguese were paying an annual ground rent to the Chinese since 1578 and were obliged to respect a series of regulations regarding the construction of houses and of shipbuilding. Obviously, Chinese interference in the administration of Macau did not escape the attention of the foreigners who visited the city, which lowered the image of the Portuguese in their eyes. These facts were also pointed out in what can be considered the first history of Macau, written by the Swede Sir Anders Ljungstedt (1759–1835), another contemporary of Harriett Low. Therefore, his book was heavily criticised and attacked by later Portuguese historians, such as Montalto de Jesus and Jack Braga.[6] And even as recently as 1997 one could read protests in one of Macau's local Portuguese newspapers against the naming of a street after Anders Ljungstedt, for the same reason.

The situation of uncertainty concerning the sovereignty over Macau resulted in a sort of disrespect for the Portuguese authorities and their orders from the side of the foreigners, evident for instance in the way residency was established. Contrary to the efficiency of Macau's modern Immigration Services, which are equipped with the latest technology and compel all foreigners to a yearly pilgrimage for the prolongation of their authorisation of residence, these matters were handled less bureaucratically at the time of Harriett Low. The following description by Wood clearly illustrates the ease with which residence formerly was established:

> Every foreigner landing in Macao with an intention of remaining, is ordered by law, to report himself to the governor, and state the time, &c. of his arrival. Owing to this, when a report has not been made, it is necessary in making the application, to assume the name of some other person who has reported himself on his arrival, but who has gone off irregularly, that is in a ship, or in a smuggler's boat, by the outside passage. No questions are asked, and of course no difficulty experienced, as I have always succeeded without the least trouble by representing myself to be Mr. ——, whose name was still on the register, although he probably was not in the country at all, having departed without reporting himself to the authorities.[7]

Ljungstedt denied the need of having to present oneself to the governor upon arrival, but added a more practical reason for doing so:

> Though there is no absolute necessity of waiting on either of them [the Governor or Minister], a gentleman, we think, will feel

> *satisfied when he complies with the custom every where observed,*
> *of calling, at least, at the Governor's. Circumstances may render*
> *protection necessary, and in that case it is surely more agreeable*
> *to meet a gentleman with whom we are acquainted, than to ask a*
> *favor of, or justice from a man we never saw.*[8]

Harriett Low, too, confirmed the usual proceeding described by Wood and Ljungstedt, and in her account a certain negligence towards the Portuguese administration is obvious:

> *Soon after we arrived, Uncle called on his Excellency, as is*
> *customary, and told him what house he had taken, and the*
> *Governor told him he must apply to the Court of Lisbon or Goa*
> *for permission to stay here. He wrote to Lisbon; but it will probably*
> *be three years before he gets an answer, when I suspect we shall*
> *be ready to go home. So much for orders, which do not trouble us*
> *much.*[9]

Macau in the first half of the 19th century: a cosmopolitan city

Two factors were decisive for Macau's economic recovery after the damage that the end of the Japan trade had inflicted on the city. One was the increasing interest of the British in trading with China, the other one was the emperor's decree of 1759 to close all Chinese ports, which temporarily had been opened to foreign trade, except Canton. Consequently, Macau's prospects increased significantly, because foreign commerce in Canton was subject to a great number of restrictions, which aimed at minimising the contact between the Chinese and the foreigners in a variety of ways. For instance, foreign residency in Canton beyond the official trading seasons, namely the winter and the summer fairs, was forbidden, and foreign women were not allowed to go there, even for a visit.[10]

But the foreign traders did not have to go far from Canton in between the trading seasons, because in 1757 a law had been passed in Macau conceding foreign residency. In this year, the Loyal Senate (Leal Senado), responsible for the administration of the city, had finally been able to persuade the governor and the viceroy at Goa to lift the existing restrictions against foreign residency. The only party not satisfied with this move was the Catholic Church, fearing for the loss of its monopoly of missionary work in China, and for competition through the inevitable arrival, sooner or later, of Protestant missionaries. The Senate's decision to open up the city to foreign residency turned Macau into the abode of all foreign traders on the China coast, some of whom even brought

their wives and children along, thus gradually transforming the city into a
cosmopolitan centre of trade.

Macau **intra muros** *and its inhabitants*

If we compare a map of Macau from the first half of the 19th century with a
modern one, we can clearly see that there is nothing left of the once delicate
shape of the peninsula, in which Chinese poets saw the likeness to a leaf of the
lotus flower, floating, with its fine and curved isthmus, on the waters of the South
China Sea.[11] There is also no justification for yet another name by which Macau
was known in Chinese official documents before the arrival of the Portuguese,
namely Hao-Jing or Hao-Jing-Ao, meaning Mirrored Waters or Bay of Mirrored
Waters. These designations referred to the aspect of the coastlines of the bays
of Praia Grande (Grand Beach) and of the Inner Harbour (Porto Interior), the
curving of which was originally more accentuated. The seemingly un-ending
land reclamation works, which commenced all over the peninsula at the
beginning of the 20th century, have totally destroyed its former beauty and have
rendered it uninspiring to anybody, except maybe to make unflattering
comparisons. Harriett Low, however, could still enjoy all the natural and man-
made attractions that Macau had to offer its inhabitants and visitors.

As regards the pattern of settlement, the population of Western origin
was concentrated in the lower and central parts of the peninsula until the
middle of the 19th century. The limits of Portuguese habitation were constituted
by the Penha Hill in the Southwest, from where a wall ran down to the Bomparto
Fortress (literally "Good Delivery Fortress"), and in the Northeast by two
walls parting from the Monte Fort (Fortaleza de São Paulo do Monte, or
Fortaleza do Monte), one connecting it with the Fortress of St. Francis (Fortaleza
de São Francisco), and the other one linking it to the Inner Harbour. The
Christian city located in between these limits was therefore designated as *intra
muros*, which means exactly "in between walls". The Chinese population lived
in small villages dispersed over the upper part of the peninsula, such as Patane
or Mongha, but there was also a settlement in the extreme Southeast, near
the A-Ma temple. Ljungstedt indicates the total number of Chinese as being
around 30,000, including those living in boats. As regards the number of
inhabitants within the walled part of the peninsula, he quotes the following
numbers:

> In 1830 the population was estimated, exclusive of the military and
> clergy, at 4628, viz, 1202 white men, 2149 white women, 350
> male slaves, 779 female slaves, 38 men and 118 women of

*different castes. The Portuguese born in Portugal and in its
dominion, residing at Macao, in 1834, did not exceed 90 persons.*[12]

Wood indicates lower figures than Ljungstedt, estimating the Portuguese, the
half-castes, which are probably the Macanese, and the caffre slaves, as amounting
to 3,000, and also about 4,000 Chinese within the walls.[13]

At the beginning of Macau's existence, all the Chinese had to leave the city
at sunset and were only allowed back in at sunrise. At the time when the journal
was written, this habit had long since ceased to exist. The Chinese servants and
coolies used to sleep on the ground floor, also called "go down", which served
as a storeroom, while the living quarters of the master and mistress were in the
upper parts of the house. But there were also many, less fortunate individuals,
who did not have a place to sleep and who had to lie down on the streets:

> *How you would stare to see the exhibitions that we see in the streets
> — they are literally lined up with Chinese and Caffres asleep. They
> make the "cold flinty rock" their pillow and lay there at the mercy
> of cockroaches and mosquitoes, tough I doubt whether the latter
> could make an impression upon their <u>well</u> <u>tanned</u> <u>hides</u>. It seems
> to us impossible that they can sleep in such situations, but they
> appear as quiet and no doubt they are enjoying as delightful dreams
> as their <u>imaginations</u> will permit. (20.8.1833)*

Another unusual and unpleasant sight were the disabled people in Macau's
streets.

> *It is not uncommon to meet 4 or 5 blind people together some days
> in the streets. The deformed people, too, about is quite shocking
> sometimes. I never saw any thing to equal the distortion of limbs
> that I have often met here. (31.3.1833)*

The second Low residence near the Cathedral

The Lows occupied their first residence in Macau for only six months. In March
of 1830, a new house was prepared for them, where they lived until their
departure:

> *We are to remove soon, as we have taken Robertson's house, but
> it must be cleaned and colour washed before we can enter it.
> (1.3.1830).*

The location of the new house is thought to be known, because Harriett, when explaining the reasons for the move, also mentioned its proximity to the Cathedral (Sé):

> This house is much better finished and more elegant than the other, and much cooler, which is a great object in summer. There are six large rooms, quite sufficient for our small family. It stands near the Cathedral, from which we see all the processions, etc., start. The back of the house opens on a large terrace, which gives us a fine view of the roads, and all the ships coming in and out, the hills all round, and the Praia [Grande]. Downstairs there is a fine entrance hall, whence a flight of dark varnished stairs and a small entry lead up to the drawing-room — a room that you would be proud of in America. It has a fine doomed ceiling, ornamented with stucco-work, a handsome marble fireplace, and three French windows, opening on to the veranda, and thence to the terrace. The dining-room faces the street. Two doors open from the drawing-room into my room, also a fine large room with a domed ceiling. Next to mine comes Aunt Low's room, very spacious, and built in the same way, and a very handsome little sitting-room beyond that. Plenty of "go-downs", large bath-rooms, etc.[14]

After a week of packing, the Lows changed to the new house at the end of March of 1830:

> I put my things all in order, and before 2 o'clock all the "topside", as the China men say, was removed. And how do you think they manage it. You know, we have no carriage of any sort for carrying. Everything is carried upon men's shoulders. It is astonishing to see what burdens they carry with apparent ease, great heavy trunks, sideboards. Now, they do not shoulder them as a man in America would shoulder an axe, but have poles, ropes, etc. You never see a China man carry anything in his hands, but always in baskets, jars, etc. … Wind blew very high — seemed as though we should blow away in this house. I shall like it, I know. (30.3.1830)

The view from the terrace of their new abode was even more splendid than the house itself.

> How [I] wished for Mr. Chinnery's talent for painting that I might sketch for you the beautiful scene before me. The church large and handsome of milk white with a splendid flight of stone steps,

> *surrounded by trees and shrubbery. Just beyond this a fort stretching*
> *itself into the Bay, this too <u>mixed</u> with green trees and shrubbery.*
> *Beyond these you can see the roads, and the little boats skimming*
> *the surface. In the distance could be discerned two islands of high*
> *land. ... A little further in was a little European boat flying along*
> *with full sail, and "<u>any quantity</u>" of Chinese boats in sight. The*
> *sun just high enough to shed a pleasant brilliancy upon all. Now*
> *can you not imagine this a pleasant view, and this is all from our*
> *terrace. It is a most lovely situation. (2.4.1830)[15]*

The location of the second house allowed its inhabitants to keep a close eye on what was happening on the quay and beyond, namely spying on the arriving ships and their passengers.

> *You would be amused to see the eagerness with which we both*
> *[Aunt Low and Harriett] get our glasses to see who has come. We*
> *made out to see Mr. Latimer, Capt. Neish and another we did*
> *not know. We have two fine glasses, and we can distinctly see the*
> *features of a person. (29.6.1830)*

Since Harriett was always anxious to receive letters from home, the hope and expectancy rose with each new arrival — only to be disappointed most of the time.

According to Teixeira, two members of the Low family, the sisters Susan and Linda Low, visited the house in 1971, under his guidance.[16] In 1979, however, it was destroyed, to give way, as so many other former residences, to an anonymous, dull office building. But the house (if it is the correct one) is clearly visible in photographs taken of the Praia Grande prior to the 1970s, or on 19th century prints, although the latter are not always accurate regarding the details of private residences.[17] On the top floor of the Museum of Macau, there is a large historic panoramic view of Macau from the sea, where some residences of famous inhabitants are identified. The Lows' house is one of them, although Harriett's name is only known to a restricted group of people in Macau.

Popular places to be, and what has become of them

For those who know Macau nowadays, one of the most densely populated territories in the world, where the people live in concrete high-rise buildings and where anything green or natural is worth its weight in gold, it may seem unimaginable that in the first half of the 19th century many foreigners, mainly English from India, came here from October onwards, in order to pass a few months away from the heat of the tropics, looking for fresh and healthy air.

> *I suppose you are now enjoying a fire, but we still find it*
> *comfortable with windows and doors all open. Most delightful*
> *weather. I wish all invalids could be transported here. This air could*
> *not [but] help restoring them. (1.11.1829)*

However, Harriett had arrived in the best season for foreigners to gradually acclimatise themselves in these latitudes. A few months later, she would begin to suffer from the humidity and heat, which are so characteristic for Macau, and complain accordingly.

Macau once possessed an immense number of gardens and other green areas, offering the opportunity for extensive walks. There were also several beaches, and from the hills in and around the city a great number of fine views could be enjoyed. Prints and paintings of Macau at this period in time still captivate modern viewers. But the first walk left the Low ladies quite breathless and with a rather negative impression:

> *We went out with the cooly, and he carried us all round the Prio*
> *[Praia] Grande, over the great hill and back through the town, a*
> *monstrous walk. And for the first walk it was terrible. It is so long*
> *since we have walked that it overcome us all. The streets here are*
> *intolerable, hilly, irregular and horribly paved. You meet no one*
> *but Portuguese and Chinese men, and they annoyed us very much*
> *by their intent gaze. (19.10.1829)*

With a little bit of training, however, Harriett rapidly gained strength and became an enthusiastic and indefatigable walker. When an American friend of hers, Caroline Shillaber, arrived at the end of 1831, she almost despaired of her incapacity for walking, while at the same time proudly emphasizing her own fitness:

> *I find it very pleasant having a companion I assure you, but I*
> *cannot make a <u>walker</u> of her. She has been so used to a <u>carriage</u>*
> *of late, that it fatigues her, and I must confess it requires a year's*
> *practice to run over these rough paths and hills. I have become quite*
> *celebrated in that way, for I go over the hills as I should over a*
> *level path. (15.12.1831)*

The Campo

One of the favourite and therefore most frequented places was the Campo (literally "field" or "countryside"), which could be reached through the St. Lazar Gate (Porta de São Lázaro), also called the Countryside Gate (Porta do Campo).

> *We went to the* <u>*Campo*</u>, *a beautiful place. The campo is out of the town some way, is between two high hills, and the sea washing up on one side. I ascended one of the hills, which is very high, and on looking round, found my party at a great distance below. They had not followed my rash steps, but I was not sorry. It was a perfect spot and I shall try it again. (27.10.1829)*

According to Ljungstedt, all the territory in the upper part of the peninsula, beyond the city walls, was considered Campo:

> *[It] extend[s] to the very boundary of the peninsula. ... The higher grounds of the Campo are used by the Chinese for burial places; the lower, comprising an extensive space between Mong-ha and Patané, laborious husbandmen render very productive; it bears rice and a great variety of vegetables.*[18]

One part of the Campo served as cricket ground for the English, a fact that constituted an additional attraction for the ladies, mainly the unmarried ones such as Harriett — at least at the beginning of her stay in Macau. Apart from this, families frequented the Campo with their children, and those who owned horses used to ride there.

> *Went out to the Campo. Stopped to speak to Mrs. Daniell — she was sitting in her chair with her children playing round her. The handsome papa was entering fully into their innocent gambols. ... It was prettier than any picture I ever saw. (12.9.1832)*

Thus we can say that the Campo was a space used in a variety of ways by all the inhabitants of the peninsula, both Chinese and Westerners.

Nowadays nothing but a name, Rua do Campo (Road to the Countryside) is left, reminding us of Macau's once agricultural past. This is the road that went from the Praia Grande in the direction of the Campo. The St. Lazar Gate has disappeared long ago, together with the city walls. The transition from the former Macau *intra muros* to the now inexistent Campo can still be seen in the straight and more orderly arrangement of the streets, compared to the crooked and narrow roads within the previously walled part. Apart from a few exceptions, the modern Campo is totally covered with asphalt and concrete, carrying the weight of thousands of habitations.

The Garden of Camoens, the Casa Garden and the Old Protestant Cemetery

Among the many gardens that once existed in Macau, two have attained particular and long-lasting fame. One of them, the Garden of Camoens (Jardim de Camões) still exists as public property. At the time of Harriett Low, however, it was privately owned by António Pereira, a wealthy Portuguese. In the garden was (and is still nowadays) one of Macau's most beautiful colonial-style mansions, known as Casa [House] Garden (Casa da Horta), which the owner used to rent to well-to-do foreigners. Soon after their arrival, Harriett and her Aunt decided to make a courtesy visit there, to see Mrs. Fearon, the lady of the house. Her husband Christopher was Hanoverian Consul and a private trader in Canton.

> It was a long ride, at the furthest end of the town, but a most splendid house and romantic situation. You go into a gate up a long circular isle, on both sides trees and flowers of all descriptions. Seems like a perfect paradise. The house stands high. You ascend an immense flight of stone steps and enter a verandah with a marble floor and filled with plants. You then enter the drawing room, which is furnished elegantly. The rooms are large, and it seems like a palace — a view of the town and the country round from the windows. (7.10.1829)

But it was the garden that enchanted Harriett more:

> The garden at Mr. Fearon's is the most romantic place. It is very extensive and abounds in <u>serpentine</u> walks. A fine view of the sea, you <u>ascend</u> <u>hills</u>, <u>immense</u> <u>rocks</u> and trees. There are several <u>temples</u> in the garden, one very high. In another part a cave in the rocks, where the celebrated Camoen[s] wrote his Lusiad[s]. A bust of Camoen[s] stands in the Cave. ... It is a wild and delightful spot. (20.10.1829)

> It is a work of art, it is true, but it resembles Nature so perfectly that you would not think but that it was originally formed in this way. It was a high hill, and the walks have been dug out. ... It is almost frightful to look up in some places and see the great rocks piled upon one another, and as if the least touch would throw them down. There are several Banyan trees, growing with their roots almost out of ground, spreading over the rocks. (21.11.1829)

Both the Garden of Camoens as well as the Casa Garden have changed a lot, but not unrecognisably. The Garden of Camoens is still one of the most beautiful spots in Macau, augmented by the weight of its history, having delighted generations of residents and visitors. On 10 June, which is the national holiday of Portugal and of Camoens, the national bard, his bust becomes the focal point for a pilgrimage by Portuguese pupils and for eloquent speeches by local Portuguese dignitaries. The Casa Garden is now owned by the Orient Foundation (Fundação Oriente), an influential private institution, which has its local headquarters there. Before that time, the former Museum of Camoens, owned by the Municipality of Macau, was housed there. The collection, which consists basically of Chinese calligraphy and ceramics and of Western paintings, has now changed its name into Macau Museum of Art and is exhibited in the new Macau Cultural Centre.

The Old Protestant Cemetery is in the immediate vicinity of the Casa Garden and worthwhile a visit. Although established by the British East India Company, it was open to Protestants of all nations and accommodates the last remains of many of Harriett Low's acquaintances and friends: George Chinnery, Robert Morrison, Anders Ljungstedt, Thomas Beale, Mrs. Fearon, Richard Turner, and three infant sons of her friends Caroline Shillaber and Thomas Colledge. The first burial there took place in 1821 and the last one in 1857. Some older tombstones that date from before 1821, were transferred to the Protestant Cemetery only after its establishment.[19] Interestingly, not a single tomb displays a cross:

> The cemetery was an extension of Georgian England, of the Protestant fear of Catholic ascendancy and general aversion to the image of the cross, to which pagan symbolism was frequently preferred.[20]

Beale's garden and aviary

The other famous garden belonged to Thomas Beale, an Englishman residing in Macau between 1791 and 1841. It was located below the Saint Lawrence's church (Igreja de São Lourenço) and does not exist anymore.[21] Beale had become immensely rich through the opium trade, but he lost everything and subsequently committed suicide.[22] Harriett always speaks of him with respect and displaying great admiration for his garden and aviary. Both of them were full of rare and exotic species.

> He has an aviary filled with the most choice collection of birds. The bird of Paradise he has, which is by far the most _beautiful_. You cannot imagine plumage more perfect. You have seen them

stuffed, but you can barely judge of its beauty. It is much too handsome for the temper it possesses. The next most beautiful are the gold and silver pheasants. Their plumage is rich and they seem conscious of their beauty. The next is the Mandarin duck which is clothed in a great variety of colours, but put on to suit the most fastidious taste. They are remarkable for their fidelity. Mr. B. gave us a history of one of them. He says the <u>husband</u> and wife always keep together and if one dies, the other never marries.

Another singular bird is what is called the dagger breasted pigeon. Its colour on the back is slate colour, the breast white with a red spot directly in front, which resembles blood. They look as tho' they had had a fresh wound. I cannot describe to you the beauty of these birds. They are too numerous. In the Aviary, which is made of wire, is a large tree, which is completely covered with birds of all descriptions. We could not think of seeing the whole in once going. He has some of the richest parrots I ever saw, magpies, mockingbird and almost every thing you can think of. After we had looked sufficiently at the birds, we walked in the garden, which is literally filled with plants and trees the most rare. In the garden he has a pond with a great variety of golden fishes. What astonished me as much as any thing was the air plant, which grows without earth. It is first put into a shell of cocoa nut till it shoots and is soon after suspended to a tree or wall and grows <u>upwards</u>. (26.10.1829)

In 1845, all moveable plants of Beale's famous garden were brought to Hong Kong and replanted at Green Bank.[23]

The subtropical climate of Macau provides favourable conditions for growing exotic plants and keeping all kinds of tropical birds. In modern times, however, the chronic lack of space on the peninsula, as well as the different interests of its inhabitants, have reduced the number of plant and animal species considerably. Besides, there are no more individuals like Beale who would invest part of their wealth and time in something as perennial as plants or birds. This is now the task of Macau's Municipality, who does its best to maintain green spaces and to open up new ones for the population to enjoy, for example on reclaimed land. The parks are intensively frequented by people of all ages and they are one of Macau's most charming and lively spots. Men walk their birds in cages and occasionally hang them in trees to compare their singing with each other. Fitness fans do their exercises in the Chinese or Western style. Old people go there to play cards or other games, to air their feet and to socialise. Children play in fountains, or with balls and their latest toy.

The Praia Grande

The once beautiful, crescent-shaped Praia Grande serving as landing beach and being probably the most famous and most depicted view of 19th-century Macau, was confined by two fortresses at its extremities, namely the Fortress of St. Francis (Fortaleza de São Francisco) in its north-eastern corner, and by the Fortress of Bomparto in the south-west. A smaller fort, St. Peter (São Pedro), was located in the middle of Praia Grande, in front of the governor's house. In Harriett Low's days, the political and economic elite of Macau had their mansions there.[24] The British East India Company occupied one of the most opulent buildings, where many formal dinners took place. Nature, too, seemed to be rivalling with the magnificence of the mansions bordering the shoreline of Praia Grande:

> *After tea Capt. R[oundy] and I went on to the Prio Grande for a short walk. I never saw a more splendid sight than then, the water rushing upon the beach wave after wave in gradual succession, and the moon shining upon each made the water on the edge of each look, like I am sure I cannot say what, but so brilliant that it made a flash like lightening and all the colours of the rainbow. All around the shore for some distance you would see this brilliant light. I never saw any thing like it before. I came home perfectly delighted with my walk. It was if *possible*, more splendid than the water at sea of a dark night. (2.11.1829)*

Apart from a few colonial-style buildings, there is not much left of the former beauty of this Grand Beach, the view of which has been thoroughly altered through extensive land reclamation and the substitution of the beautiful mansions by impersonal, dull high-rise buildings. Those, who knew it in its ancient glory, cannot forget.

> *Our heart is bleeding at the sight of the little or nothing that is left of the former lordly mansions of Praia Grande, which rivalled in age with the centenarian banyan trees — the imposing façades with their arches and their characteristic colours, their luso-oriental style and their coats of arms; all this was destroyed by the stone-mason's hammer of progress.*[25]

Some compensation is offered, however, by the Macau Tower (338 meters), which was opened to the public in December 2001, affording a bird eye's view away from the noise and exhaust fumes of the city.

Cacilhas Bay

Cacilhas Bay was a small beach beyond the fortified part of the city, in the Northeastern corner of the peninsula, where the rocks, from a bird's eye view, seemed to form a little horn or hook. It had become famous through the failed Dutch invasion in 1622, who chose this unfortified place as their landing beach, in their last and biggest attempt ever at conquering Macau. Nowadays the bay is totally covered by Macau's water reservoir. At the time of Harriett Low, it was one of the favourite destinations for people who wanted to relax, to talk or dream, while watching the waves coming in softly on the beach and on the base of Guia Hill.

> [I] had a short chat with Sir George Robinson who came up waiting upon his son on horseback — a little boy of six or seven. I do not know what papas would think at home to be trotting after children in such a manner. Every day we meet Sir George running at the side of the pony which mounts one of the children. Three times in an afternoon he trots out to Casilhas and back again. I think if he knew the value of time he would hardly be willing to spend so much of it in tending babies. But "every one to their fancy" as the old woman said. _Titles_ do not always bring _sense_, nor always _cents_, as per example in this instance. (18.7.1833)

Seemingly, not only the aspect of Cacilhas Bay has changed a lot, but also the standards according to which a man is judged as a "good father". Could there be a more exemplary father than Sir George Robinson?

The Bar and the A-Ma temple

Beyond the wall linking the Fortress of Bomparto with the hermitage of Our Lady of Penha de França, a little more further to the Southwest, was the Fortress of St. James (São Tiago), or Barra. Among the English it was known as Barfort, or the Bar. Located at the entrance to the Inner Harbour,

> ships are not allowed but with the permission of the Governor to pass this fort. Chinese junks and boats go out and in whenever they please.[26]

The fortress, or what is left of it, has been transformed into one of Macau's most charming hotels, the Pousada de São Tiago, which is open not only to hotel guests, but to visitors too, who want to see the chapel with the statue of St. James or admire the architect's design, which incorporates the original walls of the fortress.

A few hundred metres beyond the Bar, we find the A-Ma temple (Templo da Barra), one of Macau's oldest and most important Chinese temples. According to the legend, it was here that A-Ma, the patroness of fishermen and seafarers, appeared to a trader from the Chinese province of Fujian in stormy weather, calming down the waters and saving the vessel. Thankful for the rescue, the navigators are said to have erected a shrine in her honour. This shrine or temple is usually quoted as being at the origin of the name Macau: the most popular version of the etymology of the word Macau has it that it derives from *Amagau*, which in the local Cantonese dialect means Bay of A-Ma. The A-Ma temple was a very popular motif with 19th-century painters. Harriett Low passed the temple several times by boat, and occasionally walked there. Nowadays this temple still attracts large crowds of both worshippers and tourists. It is also the symbol for Macau as a Chinese city, representing it, together with the Ruins of St. Paul's as the symbol for Macau as a (former) Portuguese city, in the Palace of the People in Peking, where each Chinese province is characterised by its most well-known landmark or feature.

The Inner Harbour and the Green Island

Proceeding further north and leaving the A-Ma temple behind, one definitively enters the Inner Harbour (Porto Interior). This is the place along which the first Portuguese settlers in Macau had built their houses 300 years earlier, but which was no longer a "good address" in the 19th century, when it was chic to live at or near Praia Grande. It was flanked by various beaches on Macau's side (Praia do Manduco, Praia Pequena, and Praia do Patane). On the other side of the Inner Harbour, opposite the peninsula, we find the hilly island of Lappa, or Priest's Island. Home to a large floating population, known as *Tanka* (literally "egg people"), they gave and still give quite a unique character to this corner of Macau. Since this term has a negative connotation in Chinese, the Tanka call themselves *Soi Seong Ian*, meaning "water people".[27] There are many interesting paintings and sketches of them by Harriett's contemporaries Chinnery and Borget. Chinnery also painted two sampan girls, whose names are delivered as Assor and Alloy, in a variety of poses. Probably they were the ones who rowed Chinnery around once in a while, for example when he wanted to sketch from the sea.[28]

In the Inner Harbour, quite close to Macau, there once existed a small island, known as Green Island (Ilha Verde), because of its lush green vegetation. Although the name continues, the designation Green Hill would be more adequate for this spot nowadays, because it had already ceased to be an island in 1891, when it was connected to Macau by a dike. Since then land reclamation has continued unceasingly in this area, and whole new districts and neighbourhoods are being added to Macau. Long ago, however, it was a point for picnics or rambles:

> We went to the Isle de Verd, there landed, while the Tiffin was prepared. We then after having our refreshment got under weigh. The scenery all around us was delightful. The sun was behind us on our return, just setting behind the hills and shedding its softened beams upon the city of Macao — which added much to its beauty. As we approached, the busy scene before us was quite new and amusing. A vast number of the poor people live upon the water and appear cheerful and happy. But you would wonder that [there is] a smile upon their faces when apparently so miserable. Their dress is singular. We saw a Josh house at a distance which formed a very pretty scene. Shall visit it nearer before I pretend to describe it to you. It stands among immense rocks and trees on the sea shore, is fancifully ornamented and presents a picturesque view from the water. (14.11.1829)[29]

Where there is an Inner Harbour, there must also be an Outer Harbour (Porto Exterior). In the days of Harriett Low, it was located in a place where there is no water at all nowadays, namely on Taipa Island, or rather in-between what then were two islands, Big Taipa (Taipa Grande) and Small Taipa (Taipa Pequena). Land reclamation has joined them into one island. This location provided a better protection in the case of a typhoon than the Inner Harbour.[30] Modern Macau also has an Outer Harbour, which has nothing but the designation in common with the former Outer Harbour. It is located next to the water reservoir, in the northeastern part of the town, where the bulk of tourists who visit the territory enter.

The Barrier Gate and former racetrack

The original Barrier Gate (Portas do Cerco) was erected in 1573, more or less in the middle of the (former) isthmus connecting Macau with the mainland, representing the first territorial border of Macau with China. There was a Chinese inscription on it, which read *"dread our greatness, respect our virtue,"* and was certainly to be understood as a warning to the Portuguese. Strategically located at a very narrow point, it allowed for easy control of the peninsula, not only in military but also in economic terms, serving as a Chinese customs barrier. Throughout much of Macau's history, the Barrier Gate symbolised the dependency of the city on China: whenever the Chinese disagreed with measures proposed or undertaken by the Portuguese, they withdrew the Chinese servants from them and did not allow any foodstuff to pass through the Gate, thus "convincing" the Portuguese of the correctness of the Chinese demands.

There was a road from the Porta do Campo to the Barrier Gate and for Harriett and her contemporaries the China Gate, as it was also known in English, was a favourite destination for "long distance" walks, mainly in the cooler season, if there is any such thing as a "long distance" in Macau:

> *After dinner Mr. V[achell] as engaged called for us to walk.*
> *Accordingly we all went and voted it decidedly a barrier night. A*
> *cool and bracing air is required for this walk as it is rather long.*
> *(7.5.1830)*

Since it was located far away from the "civilised" parts of Macau and some Chinese villages had to be passed or crossed on the way, the ladies were not supposed to walk there without male company:

> *We [women] never go to the barrier, as the gentlemen say it is not*
> *safe. (7.3.1830)*

Another attraction at the Barrier was the racetrack, where the English, with their traditional inclination towards horses and betting, used to run their horses, mustering crowds of any race and colour. There are several descriptions of racing days in the journal, the first one being particularly vivid because of its novelty to the observer:

> *Called for Mrs. Turner at 2 o'clock and from thence to the race*
> *ground, but without thinking that I should enjoy myself. I cannot*
> *tell you why, but my spirits seem to have a lead attach[ed] to them.*
> *The race ground is at what is called the barrier, which prevents all*
> *foreigners from passing over that spot. The course is about 3 qrs*
> *of a mile. It is a delightful place & I was much amused at the novel*
> *scenes. There was a temporary house of bamboo built for the ladies,*
> *and I'll assure you My Dear Sis it was very interesting to look upon*
> *the motley group below us. Chinese of all descriptions, dressed in*
> *their most singular dress, some with those large basket hats. Many*
> *of them wear nothing on their heads but carry a fan, which they*
> *hold over their heads to screen them from the sun. Some of them*
> *had bags on their backs about ½ yd square in which they deposit*
> *their babies. The poor little things were knocked about in the crowd,*
> *as though it was a bit of wood. It is a very common mode of*
> *carrying children. Portuguese and Lascars[31] were mixed with*

> *Chinese, and to hear the mixture of languages, none of which I*
> *understood, made me think of the confusion of Babel but led me*
> *to wish that those foolish people had been content to live on the*
> *earth while they were permitted. Some of the races were very good.*
> *Some large bets made. (5.11.1829)*

Obviously, where lots of money is at stake and in a business as risky as gambling, not everybody can be a winner:

> *Capt. Hinz [Hine] called to day, says there was much money lost*
> *yesterday. (6.11.1829)*

The original Barrier Gate was blown up in 1849 by the Portuguese and replaced by a new one, in the form of a triumphal arch, in 1870. On top it quotes a verse from Camoens, *"Honrai a Pátria, que a Pátria vos contempla"* ("Honour the Fatherland, for the Fatherland looks to you"). Although this is a very patriotic sentence, it has escaped the post-handover cleansing of Portuguese symbols on public buildings. Anyway, the appeal is universal. This gate, now a classified monument, is still standing and worth a visit.

The existence of the first racecourse is still remembered in various street names, namely the Rua dos Cavaleiros, Beco dos Cavaleiros, and the Rampa dos Cavaleiros,[32] located in the Northeastern part of the city. The races towards the Barrier Gate started in this area, although the Chinese had explicitly prohibited them in April 1829, but apparently the races continued. In March 1927, after a series of land reclamation projects along the isthmus, Macau's first hippodrome was opened on the left-hand side of the isthmus. It is remembered in the street name Estrada Marginal do Hipódromo.[33] Four years later, the Macau Jockey Club was founded.

It is almost superfluous to say that Macau is still attracting crowds of betters, both in horse racing and greyhound racing. In the meantime, however, the racetrack and the Jockey Club have moved to Taipa island. Most of the betting fraternity comes from Hong Kong, but there are also many betting enthusiasts from Taiwan, China and from all over South-East Asia. The readiness and passion for this kind of pastime among the Chinese continues to be as bewildering for most Westerners who visit China, as it was for Harriett Low's contemporaries.

> *In China, this vice prevails among persons of every rank in society.*
> *The passion for gaming is universal, and is the principal*
> *employment of the idle hours of both rich and poor. Most of the*
> *games with which the children amuse themselves, are so arranged,*
> *as to have a stake depending on the issue of the contest, and the*

attention and eagerness with which they pursue their sport, evinces
the delight they derive from it.[34]

In Macau with its great (and steadily growing) number of casinos, this
phenomenon can be observed very well.

Guia Hill

Rising 90 metres above the sea, the Guia Hill is the highest elevation in Macau.
Since the 17th century it has been the site of a hermitage known as Our Lady
of Hope (Nossa Senhora da Esperança) or Our Lady of Guia (Nossa Senhora
da Guia). Located beyond the city wall, in "Chinese territory", the Portuguese
built a wall there in 1637 and installed a small garrison. Being the highest point
and looking out towards the open sea over the immense mouth of the Pearl River
with its many small islands, it provided an ideal point for spying on friend or
foe, and functioned as a point of reference for navigation:

> *The fort Guia, "fortaleza da Guia" — serves during day-light as*
> *a guidance for ships, steering for Macao and Canton. When a ship*
> *is descried the Governor is advised by signals of her approach, and*
> *when her flag can be discerned by a writing, the commanding officer*
> *sends down to him. On the arrival of a Portuguese vessel a bell is*
> *rung.*[35]

The signals from Guia were repeated at the fort of St. Peter in the middle of
Praia Grande.

Nowadays, Guia constitutes the largest green surface of the peninsula with
various recreational facilities for young and old. Since its summit is visible from
many parts of the town, it is one of the two places where the typhoon signals
are hoisted whenever one is heading for Macau. Yet this act seems more like a
tradition than a necessity, because people usually know about approaching
typhoons from the omnipresent TVs and radios and rarely bother to lift their
heads towards Guia or the Monte Fort, which is the other place displaying the
typhoon signals. Of course, they were very useful in the past. Next to the chapel
of Our Lady of Guia we find the lighthouse, which has become one of Macau's
landmarks. Together they figure on the one-Pataca coin. Ironically, the lighthouse
was only erected in 1865, at a time when Macau was already being eclipsed as
commercial port by Hong Kong and the treaty ports, mainly Shanghai. The
interesting views from Guia over Macau and the South China Sea attract many
tourists daily.

The Monte Fort and the St. Paul's Church

Two adjacent hills in the centre of the peninsula are the locations of Macau's most impressive defence and religious structures, the Monte Fort (Fortaleza de São Paulo do Monte, generally known as Fortaleza do Monte) and the Church of St. Paul's (Igreja de São Paulo).[36] Jesuit engineers and architects, who had started to occupy this area soon after the foundation of Macau, designed both buildings. They were completed in the first half of the 17th century, and originally also administered by the Jesuits. Located in-between the Church and the Fortress was the College of the Mother of God (Colégio da Madre de Deus), once of eminent importance in the training of generations of Catholic missionaries for China — Macau was not only a commercial hub, but also a religious centre and the only gateway to China for several centuries. In 1576, less than 20 years after its foundation, Pope Gregory XIII made Macau a diocese, elevating the Church of Santa Maria to the status of a Cathedral (Sé). Since the beginning of the 17th century, when the first Jesuit missionaries were allowed at the Court in Peking, all information about China passed through Macau, and Macau was China's only window to the Western world. However, tensions between the spiritual and political powers in Europe, church versus state, as well as tensions within the Catholic Church, led to the dissolution of the Jesuit order by the Pope, and to their expulsion from Macau in 1762. While these buildings are considered special nowadays, for Harriett Low they were just two among many fortresses and churches, although they visibly impressed her. The church was in the vicinity of the residence of one of her friends, and could be seen from its large terrace.

> *Saint Paul's Church by moonlight is a most romantic object, really magnificent. It stands very high. I think I counted 70 steps before reaching the top, the whole width of the Church. Add to all this the <u>chiming</u> of the bells, which they do very well — they have a very good set — a pleasant little party round the table, a fine cool breeze, and you will have us to a T[urner] tea party. (28.6.1830)*

As regards the Monte Fort, Harriett Low was surprised at the artillery found there:

> *After dinner went to the "Monte Fort" accompanied by Mr. Thornhill, Mr. Ibar and Mr. Huddleston. The views from it are quite perfect. Some of the guns are said to be very large and made in <u>1626</u>, and the <u>curiosity</u> of them is that they were made in Macao. After <u>inspecting</u> this fort, we walked part way to the*

barrier, and returned to Mrs. T[hornhill]'s where we spent a
pleasant evening. (3.4.1832)

Two hundred years before the time under examination here, Macau had a famous gun foundry, run by the Bocarro brothers, which supplied guns and cannons as far as Goa and even Peking. Nowadays, there are no more of these original guns in Macau, but the Tower in London possesses one.

Although devoid of their traditional functions for a long time, both buildings represented the heart and soul of Macau under Portuguese rule. Dating back to the very beginning of the city's history, they are its silent witnesses. The church burnt down in 1834, leaving only the majestic façade. It is now known as the Ruins of St. Paul's and houses a small Museum of Sacred Art (Museu de Arte Sacra). The Monte Fort was transformed into a City Museum (Museu da Cidade), a legacy to the two cultures that co-existed peacefully on this tiny peninsula for centuries. For those who cannot visit it in person, a virtual visit is highly recommended.

Penha Hill and some other attractions

Penha hill offers one of the most picturesque views of Macau, overlooking both the Praia Grande and the Inner Harbour. Consequently it was one of the favourite spots of many Macau residents for their daily walk. In 1622, the hill was topped by a hermitage dedicated to our Lady of Penha de França, the protectress of sailors. Even before taking drawing lessons with Chinnery, Harriett tried to capture the beautiful view from there on paper:

> *I had a delightful walk with Mrs. Allport this evening and Mrs.*
> *Cleveland. We went to the Pania [Penha]. I took my pencil to*
> *take a little sketch of the surrounding scenery, which is very*
> *beautiful. (1.12.1829)*

Away from the hustle and bustle of Macau, Penha hill was also a place for musing and daydreaming.

> *Caroline & I after dinner went to the Peña Church; a most lovely*
> *evening. We were above every body except a few old padres who*
> *live in the Convent. We could have a view of every part of the town.*
> *The sea; and the atmosphere was so clear that we could see the*
> *Islands at a great distance. We spent an hour in <u>meditation</u>. My*
> *thoughts were of many <u>colours</u>. All nature seemed in perfect harmony,*
> *but to look upon the busy town and to fancy the discords, the misery,*
> *the wretchedness that might be found in that little space, made one*

almost wish to be void of reflection; and then to reverse the picture
and think how delightful it might be. We stopped till the vesper Bell
had given its accustomed warning and came down. (1.8.1832)

The hermitage has long since disappeared. The latest church on this hill dates from 1935. Dozens of tourist buses make their way up the hill daily to enjoy the pleasant views.

Many of Macau's hills were (and still are) topped by churches. However, as a staunch Unitarian and declared anti-Catholic, Harriett Low did not show great interest in them. Modern visitors, independently of their creed, should not miss to visit one or several of them. They are like rocks of continuity, having resisted to the speed of transformation and modernisation around them. St. Dominic's church (Igreja de São Domingos), which often served as backdrop for Chinnery's sketches of Chinese street life, is one of the few churches that can be reached without previous physical exertion, standing right in the heart of the town. Chinnery lived in the immediate vicinity of St. Lawrence's church (Igreja de São Lourenço), which has a beautiful double staircase leading up to the churchyard. Inside, there is a gorgeous, painted wooden ceiling. St. Joseph's church (Igreja de São José) is Macau's only church with a domed roof. It is renowned for its excellent acoustics, which makes it an ideal location for concerts. The adjacent seminary trained countless priests, mainly for China, between 1728 and 1966.

Lappa Island

Lappa island on the other side of the Inner Harbour, opposite Macau, has long since ceased to be part of Macau. Harriett mentions it as being the place where the clothes for many Macau residents were washed, probably because of an abundance of fresh water, as well as being a favourite destination for walks and picnics, often in the company of a dozen or so people. Sometimes during these occasions they also had contact with local Chinese, which usually provoked a variety of ambiguous feelings:

This morning a party set off for the Lappa, composed of Mr. and
Mrs. Davis, Miss Morrison, Mr. Pierson [Pearson], Mr. Vachell,
Lindsay, Daniell "alias enigma", Mr. Wood and myself. We had
a very delightful sail and walk on the other Island. The sun was
rather hot and I did not enjoy [it] as much as I otherwise should
for it gave me a severe headache.
We were gone about three hours. Visited the Joss house which
is situated in the most picturesque manner on the declivity of a high

hill, in among a great deal of shrubbery and some fine trees. It is a sweet spot. The river runs before it at a little distance, and at one side at no great distance is a fine fall of water. The people were excessively civil and gave us tea and all the oranges they had. The tea was the best they had but I could not be tempted to taste it. They brought in some cakes and something else, a sort of nondescript. Mr. Davis called it "pig pye not sufficiently disguised" — the junks [chunks] of Pork fat were much too apparent although there were no Mahometans in the party. You would have been amused at the tea pot we had, but I cannot describe it. We set on the steps of the Joss house after having seen all that there was to see and partook of our frugal meal, and after having rested our weary limbs a little, we again commenced our journey home, and went by a different route. All were highly pleased with the excursion and even Mr. Davis who before he set out thought it "complete assassination of a day" acknowledged that he had been quite paid for it. (2.3.1831)

The coastline of this once green sanctuary facing Macau has developed into another urban space with high-rise buildings, while the hilly hinterland still looks temptingly inviting for a ramble. Unfortunately, despite its proximity, people never consider it as an excursion destination because of the trouble getting there. The trip involves queuing at two borders and foreigners also require a visa.

The climate and its hardships

Contrary to Macau's physical appearance, little or nothing has changed regarding the climate. Though initially praised by Harriett, because the Lows had arrived at a time when the weather was more tolerable, especially for foreigners from moderate climatic zones, her praise turned to complaint with the onset of the humid season in February and with the hot and humid season in April/May. These are all too familiar to everybody who has lived in Macau for a year or longer, although air conditioners and dehumidifiers make modern life much more tolerable.

Wintertime: wood by the catty[37]

Winters tend to be short in the subtropical climate of Macau, but they can nevertheless be uncomfortably cold. The coolest days are usually around Chinese

New Year, when temperatures can drop to 5°C for several days and oscillate between 10°C and 15°C a couple of weeks before and after that. The feeling of cold is exacerbated by the fact that the houses are not built for it. This was true at Harriett's time and continues to be so in modern Macau. Since many houses had only shutters instead of glass windows during the hot and humid season, in order to allow the air to circulate at all times and to create draughts, several measures had to be taken by the tenants, if they did not want to suffer too much with the arrival of the cooler season.

> *Having windows put into the hall, preparing for cold weather. No fire place in the house yet. Shall have to put a stove in the dining room. Some of the houses look quite <u>winterish</u>, carpets, fireplaces, and curtains. (13.11.1829)*

Most of Harriett's complaints about cold weather refer to the winter of 1832/ 33, which must have been the coldest during her stay in Macau.

> *Terrible cold. I do not like cold weather in this country — great barns of rooms, great <u>cracks</u> under the doors and the floors you can see through. The carpet does not seem to do much good. And it is so rainy now we cannot get a walk, and one's limbs are almost stiff with the cold. ... The Chinamen all look as thick as they are long now. So many clothes on. The Portuguese, many of them go to bed and there lay. (27.12.1832)*

Besides, the raw materials for heating were expensive, which made a nice fire even more precious.

> *Coals scarce, wood brought by the <u>catty</u>, very dear. What would you think at home of buying wood by the <u>pound</u>? But it is so in this place. Caroline & I get <u>into</u> the fire almost. (17.1.1833)*

At night time, Harriett and Caroline decided to beat the cold with the shared heat generated by their bodies.

> *A very cold night, and I was very glad to get snug in bed. Caroline & I sleep together and it reminds me so much of you, Molly, but she does not <u>flirt</u> the bedclothes as you used, for she does not think it necessary that one should know how cold it is to enjoy the comforts within. (19.1.1833)*

The most uncomfortable time starts when humidity takes over, usually shortly after Chinese New Year:

> We had two months since a little damp weather, when the water was running down the walls as though the Engine had been playing on top of the house — every thing was wet. The bed curtains seemed as though they had been dipped in water, sheets and all. But it is very astonishing people never take cold in this weather — when you would think it unavoidable. (11.4.1831)

Apart from being uncomfortable, great care had to be taken with many things, because of the destructive nature of the humidity:

> Busied ourselves with packing up and putting away new goods. They have to be all done up in oil paper. You can have no idea of the trouble it is to keep things in this climate. The new silk I had last year is almost spoiled. (12.7.1831)

Even writing became more difficult:

> It is almost impossible to write as you will see [by this journal]. The weather is so damp everything moulds. (25.5.1831)

Summertime: blistering heat and tropical humidity

As the year progresses, the temperature rises too, adding the burden of heat to the burden of humidity. Like most newcomers, Harriett found the first year in Macau particularly difficult:

> The sun has shone more to day than this long while, but the air [was] so close that it took my strength away & I have been on the couch reading or working all day, and feeling so languid that it was burdensome to speak. (11.3.1830)

Therefore, any activity outside one's own four walls, may have seemed rather intimidating:

> Tremendously hot today, not a breath of air, and a scorching sun. ... Oh the thoughts of dressing for a party this evening is quite shocking. (15.6.1830)

One of the best ways to combat the heat was by sitting "en déshabille" (5.8.1831), as she often wrote in summertime.

> *Set in the verandah with as little on as I could be decent in. We*
> *told the servant to say "No could see" and made ourselves*
> *comfortable. (26.6.1833)*

No wonder, therefore, that Harriett often felt *"in a melting mood,"* with her *"too solid flesh … fast dissolving" (24.8.1830)*. Even a year after her first summer in Macau, Harriett wondered whether she would ever get used to the climate:

> *Weather is hot, and I do not feel as though I had strength for any*
> *thing. Begin to think it not a good plan to get up early.*[38] *Have*
> *already had one doze in my chair, shall have several more I dare*
> *say. However when I get accustomed to it, if I ever do, I may feel*
> *better. Now come my Spanish lesson and I am too stupid for study.*
> *The idea of lifting a Dictionary to day is quite dreadful. Oh, Molly,*
> *people do get lazy in this climate. (21.4.1831)*

But still people in Macau considered themselves lucky compared to those living in Canton, because the air in Macau was fresher and purer owing to its proximity to the sea.

Harriett also experienced two droughts, in 1830 and 1831, which adversely affected the local agriculture:

> *Last night we had a most refreshing shower and now a cool north*
> *wind is blowing, it had become quite serious. The ground was*
> *parched and dry as it could be. The wells were dry and they [the*
> *Chinese farmers] could find no water to wet their grounds; the rice*
> *requires a monstrous quantity of water. The Chinese have fasted*
> *and prayed for rain & hired the Portuguese to pray for them. We*
> *have now only had enough to wet the Surface. I hope we shall have*
> *more before long, for we cannot have our little garden dug till we*
> *have more, the Comp[radore Apew] says "all the same dry two*
> *feet thick". (11.4.1830)*

It would be interesting to know who were the Portuguese "rainmakers" hired by the Chinese. Although this observation sounds rather fantastic, it illustrates the seriousness of the situation and the despair of the Chinese. Exactly one year after this entry, Harriett observed:

> *Rained violently most of the day, which quite delights the*
> *Chinamen, they had become quite anxious about their rice crop.*
> *The earth seemed quite parched, for we have not had a soaking*
> *rain for six or eight months. (11.4.1831)*

An impressive spectacle of nature in these latitudes are the sudden downpours during the summer monsoon season, although sometimes the rain may become rather depressive if lasting days and weeks, due to its density, power, and often, unexpectedness:

> When we got about ¹/₂ way home, a black cloud poured forth its contents upon us, and those who had not [sedan] chairs, myself among the number, were quite drenched, the first <u>regular</u> <u>ducking</u> I have had here. Equestrians and pedestrians all alike, poor Mrs. Davis on horseback looked ¹/₂ drowned. (5.8.1831)

A typhoon

Perhaps the most feared natural events in these latitudes, then as nowadays, are typhoons. In modern times, however, major damage can be prevented with the help of satellites and weather forecasts, informing and warning everybody way ahead of the course of the typhoon. But people in those days were often taken by surprise, although a sudden fall of the barometer was generally a safe indication of foul weather to come.

> This morning threatens a Typhoon. The wind is blowing a <u>gale</u> ... The wind increased till about 2, the tide coming in at the same time, it made the sea quite tremendous. We could see it from our windows washing over the tops of the houses on the Quay. It has completely destroyed the Praya Grande, rooted up 10 ft. pieces of granite and thrown them into the halls of the houses. Capt. Whitehead kindly called in after dinner to see if we were alive, Mrs. Davis in too. A little boat was anchored in front, at last they cut their cables thinking it was their only chance and let her drive, it was a dreadful sight. It seemed impossible that she could live in such a sea. We watched her till it seemed as though she must with the next wave dash on to the point — but I have since heard with the assistance of Capt. Whitehead the men were all saved. The boat [was] completely dashed to pieces. (23.9.1831)

As the days passed by, more unpleasant discoveries about the typhoon's fury were made:

> Nothing but a scene of destruction this morning — our verandah is quite unroofed, our mats all gone. Proceed to the point of the terrace. Where is the Quay? Gone! Completely demolished!

> *Houses without roofs! A large piece taken quite out of the Company's! from the roof to the ground. Immense masses of granite thrown up. Look a little further. Several Chinese houses at the end of the Quay quite levelled. Look at the Peña church — much damaged. Now come back to this side. On the point near the Franciscan church is a large fishing boat, a complete wreck! Look into the roads. There is the hull of a large ship that only a few days since I saw come into the roads with their towering masts filled with canvass. Now it is levelled to the hull, not a stick standing. This is what meets our eye. But alas I fear that is not all. I hear during the gale masts of ships with men on them in numbers were floating about calling for assistance, but the ships could render them none. How horrid. Many ships are expected now, but I am afraid we shall hear of much damage.*
>
> *After dinner Mrs. Davis called for us and we went out to see all the ruins. … Went into Mrs. Whiteman's on our return in the evening. She was obliged to take to the "go downs" during the gale as part of her roof came in. (24.9.1831)*

One week after the typhoon, people feared the occurrence of another one:

> *A dreadful rainy day. … The rains ceased about dark, but the wind began to blow and we feared another Typhoon. The Chinese call it the "Typhoon's wife". (30.9.1831)*

Luckily for everybody, it was a false alarm. But it would not be the last typhoon experienced in Macau, though it was the most powerful one.

The last story about the typhoon was written down two weeks afterwards, telling of the fate of an English lady, Mrs. Baynes, who had had a baby three days prior to the typhoon:

> *She was giving us a history of her troubles. … She happened to be alone for a minute, the people were all busy fastening doors — and a gust came, burst open her windows and took all the tile off her room so that she could see the sky through. She rushed out of bed with her infant and a sheet, knowing not where to fly to, thinking the whole house would go. Bare feet and painted floors — she fortunately escaped all colds and is now quite well. (7.10.1831)*

Imagine the worries of Mr. Baynes, and all the men in Canton, who had wives and children in Macau!

Little, big troublemakers: cockroaches, mosquitoes & co.

One of the less attractive sides of tropical and subtropical climates is the world of insects that it accommodates, except for entomologists perhaps. In these latitudes not only are they more dangerous, capable of transmitting many and sometimes deadly diseases, but Nature has also exaggerated their size. People who are only used to European-style cockroaches, spiders or beetles, usually get a profound shock at the sight of their first tropical-style cockroach, characterised by an immense, black-brownish body with feelers, often of the length of the body itself, and capable of flying and moving very fast. Some people may never get used to them. Harriett was such a person, and therefore each successful hunt on cockroaches was triumphantly described in the journal, a satisfaction that is perhaps only fully understood by those who abhor these insects as passionately as she did. At present we have a whole industry dedicated to eliminate pests in a more elegant way, but in those days the only means against them were mechanical:

> *Now I must go to bed. But I must tell you what I have just done. I thought I heard something moving behind me. I turned round to see what and lo and behold an enormous cockroach crawling on my clothes that hung upon the stand. I screamed out, awoke Uncle and Aunt in the next room, but courageously took off my shoe and beat his brains out, and am now astonished to think I did it. It was quite two inches long. (18.4.1830)*

Other more troublesome and painful pests were the mosquitoes. In Macau, where lights have to be switched on at 7 pm at the latest, even during summertime, people suffered immensely with their buzzing and biting and mainly when under one's bed curtain:

> *Last night I was kept awake most of the night, by a little insignificant mosquito, who without license or invitation found his way under my curtains, very much to my annoyance. But had he been still, he might have had a comfortable night's lodging, but he was so delighted with his situation, that he kept an incessant singing, but his notes were too discordant to afford me any pleasure and I persecuted him with a little whip (made of horse hair on purpose) but he was too small to be killed, and I was vexed with myself that so trifling a thing could annoy me. But so it is, "trifles you know make the sum of human things". (24.3.1831)*

Their presence was also annoying in other situations, such as writing or reading at candlelight:

> And now here I sit fighting mosquitoes — every half second my pen is put into my mouth while I attempt <u>murder</u>. I have given myself several severe blows upon the ear (not <u>tender</u> boxes either), and the little tormenters still keep on singing. Have killed one however to my joy. Think they must be alarmed in the next room, for my hand frequently makes a sad noise pouncing generally unsuccessfully on the table. (2.4.1830)

A few pages further there is even a blood stain in the journal, with the following remark:

> Blood of a mosquito, some of mine I dare say. Have blotted my book to killing him. No matter, there is one less. (5.4.1830)

Other pests about which Macau residents complained and still complain, such as book-eating insects or wood-eating white ants, as well as rats and mice, did not provoke the same strong reactions as cockroaches and mosquitoes and don't appear very often in the journal.

3
The Power of Religion

Religion has come a long way in human history and is as diverse as human culture itself. To the question why has it always been, and still is, man's companion on Earth, despite the exclamations of "God is dead" from various camps, Harriett Low's journal offers many answers. When reading her reflections and observations on religion and on the religious practices of the Westerners and the Chinese in Macau, one is tempted to subscribe to almost any theory that was ever formulated on religion. Both functionalists and Marxists can find arguments in favour of their analysis of religion in the journal.

Being a profoundly religious person, she reflects on existential hopes and anxieties, death and afterlife, faith and reason, always from the perspective of her Unitarian creed. In times of misfortune and distress, religion is her comfort. Going to church service on Sundays, despite the theological differences between Anglicans and Unitarians, is a means of being accepted by the wider community. At the same time, however, Harriett Low describes how religion can be a manipulative tool in the hands of the clergy or an instrument of self-delusion.[1]

As to the personal happiness of the people in societies that differ so widely in their interpretation and practice of religion as the Christians, Buddhists and Taoists for instance, God alone knows …

* * * *

The importance of religion in the challenges of everyday life

Harriett Low, her uncle and aunt belonged to a Protestant creed known as Unitarianism. The central belief of this faith has its roots in the very beginning of Christianity, in the discussion about the nature of Jesus Christ,[2] namely if he was really a divine being or merely human with a special relation to the divine. Unitarian ideas were revived during Reformation, when theologians in many European countries began to question the doctrine of the Trinity. The designation

Unitarianism started to be used more currently in the USA in about 1815, and mainly in the region of New England.

Harriett's father was a minister of the Unitarian church. Therefore, it is not surprising that he was very preoccupied with the temptations, mainly in matters of faith, that awaited his daughter abroad. In a letter written previous to her departure, he cautioned:

> Positions which you may consider invulnerable, because you have never known them attacked, may be overthrown by surprise. ... If you are not prepared with arguments for a defence at all points, your strongest fortresses may be demolished and you may be driven from one place of defence to another, till you lose confidence in your own mind and you come to every successive trial with less courage and decision and finally yield your faith and principles as indefensible.[3]

Harriett kept this particular letter very well and re-read it once in a while. One year after its receipt, she sighed:

> Every time I read it I find something new. Would I could have another such. (30.5.1830)

The function of religion as panacea in all adverse circumstances is very apparent throughout the journal. Her faith helped Harriett to face the stormy sea, lover's grief and homesickness. The most impressive example is the description of her uncle's last hours, both regarding his way of facing death as well as her own feelings towards this event:

> On the 18th he told me it was impossible for him to live, that he had hoped to see me safely in my native land, but that it was the will of heaven that he should leave us in this strange land [South Africa], but that God would take care of us, and he did not doubt it was all rightly ordered. ... He seemed to wish to have his whole thoughts devoted to his Maker, and regretted that he must take opiates, as it stupefied and rendered him unfit to watch at the last hour. ... He said he had prayed to be forgiven and trusted he had received pardon. He was so happy too in having a firm and full faith. He said it was the greatest comfort to him and he often spoke of it with tears, so grateful was he that it continued firm and unshaken to the last. ... It was delightful to sit by him, to hear his thoughts expressed and witness his patience through all his sufferings, the calm and sweet smile with which he would tell us

he should soon die and that God would protect us. ... He says "Make religion your study, my child", and then said it had always been a source of consolation to him that I had a well grounded faith. Never till his illness have I seen its value. It is such a source of consolation and comfort to him that I shall, I trust, think more than ever of it. ...

I asked him if he feared to die. He said "No, I long to die and be with my father and Jesus my intercessor". ... I never saw greater humility, greater calmness, and every feeling appeared so purified. His worldly feelings were all subdued. Such complete resignation and submission to the will of God, and such confidence that all was right, was very consoling to us. (30.3.1834)

After having praised her aunt's conduct and dedication during the long months of her uncle's sickness and having described her aunt's strong faith, Harriett wondered:

My dear Sister if I am not made better by such lessons as these, what am I made of? Oh God, grant that each may make a <u>deep</u> impression, let not the remembrance <u>ever</u> be obliterated, and may they serve to make me wise unto Salvation. (30.3.1834)

Two weeks after her uncle had passed away, immortality became a more "tangible" idea:

Was in my own room by myself all day thinking much of my dear departed Uncle, and fancy him enjoying a Sabbath in heaven, with angels and the Spirits of the just made perfect. What a delightful thought! How dreadful it would be to be deprived of the hope of immortality. What misery it would be to suppose our friends, both soul and body were annihilated at death, how foolish indeed it would seem to form ties today which tomorrow were to be burst asunder and leave us today on a wearysome life, without the hope of being reunited. But thanks to our Father in heaven and our Lord Jesus Christ, we have that hope to lean upon and which <u>will</u> support us in the hour of adversity and urges us to press onward in a moral and <u>religious</u> life that we also may be ready when we are called. (6.4.1834)

Although we may smile at Harriett's ideas about a Sabbath in heaven, they certainly are as true or false as our own in this respect.

The English-speaking clergy in Macau

When the Lows arrived in Macau, there were two English ministers, both employed by the British East India Company. One of them, Robert Morrison (1782–1834), was the first Protestant missionary ever in China, having come to Macau in 1807. Due to the strong opposition of the local Catholic clergy, however, who feared for their monopoly of missionary work, Morrison was immediately sent away to Canton. Two years later, the British East India Company hired him as their translator, and in this function Morrison was able to establish residence in Macau. His merits are well known. Apart from his translations to and from Chinese of the Bible or on religious topics, he also published works on Chinese grammar and vocabulary and wrote on China. His major achievement was being able to print the entire Scriptures in Chinese, in 23 volumes, in 1823. As regards his success as missionary among the Chinese, however, *"after 25 years of labour, the converts were ten in number."*[4] Despite their reduced number, they attended church services once in a while. *"He made a prayer in Chinese as there were two China men there" (24.6.1832)*. His name is still known in Macau, namely through the Morrison chapel and the Old Protestant Cemetery, which he founded and where he lies buried.

Morrison's professional merits, however, seemed to have surpassed his personal qualities. Harriett never got really warm with him, although she showed herself impressed with his intellectual achievements.

> *We ... passed the evening with Mr. Morrison. We were entertained by looking over his immense labours. His translations into Chinese are beyond all account, an immense Chinese dictionary that he has compiled, 4 large folio volumes of that with several small ones introductory to that, the Bible and many other things. His whole heart and soul is bound up in religion. He has resolved to give his whole life to the Chinese. Though I think he is an excellent man, I do not like all his plans. When the clock struck eight he brought the Bible and read the chapter and had prayers, in the midst of conversation. Now I think it would be much better to have family prayer at 10 o'clock when strangers have retired, for I am sure he took us all by surprise, so much that it was difficult to compose ourselves to attend, but it made me think of my beloved home when I last assembled with our own dear family to offer up prayers to our constant Protector and Preserver. But he thinks it right, and perhaps it is, but a person should be prepared for such things, I think.*[5]

During her stay in Macau, Harriett's liking (or dislike) of Morrison did not change much, nor do other authors show a particular fondness of him.[6] Two months after their arrival, she wrote:

> *Went to Dr. Morrison today. I do not like him very well, though it is better than nothing.*

Perhaps she felt sorry for criticising such an important person, and a minister above all, because she added: *"I believe he is a very good man"* (22.11.1829). This amendment, however, does not seem to be totally honest. One year later, her impressions about Morrison were quite unaltered:

> *I am thinking of going to Dr. M[orrison]'s today, but do not want to a bit, for I neither like the man nor his sermons.* (20.6.1830)

Another disturbing trait in Morrison seemed to have been his incapacity for music.

> *Wish he would not sing, for he don't know how. You never heard such a noise as he makes; it quite discomposes one's gravity.* (23.10.1831)

On the previous Sunday Harriett had made an enigmatic observation, which most probably also referred to his singing:

> *Went to church. Quite a large congregation. Did not feel as I ought while there, for there was an event that quite disturbed my gravity. My naughty muscles would not keep in place.* (16.10.1831)

But, once in a while, Morrison could satisfy Harriett's exigencies with respect to a good sermon and to the special "Sunday feeling" thus created: *"Went to Dr. Morrison's church to day, had a very good sermon"* (6.12.1829). Anyway, if she was not pleased with what was preached at church, which was almost invariably the case with sermons of a more dogmatic nature, afterwards Harriett would read one or several sermons at home from her beloved collection of homilies by Unitarian ministers. At other times she made up any excuse in order to justify the non-compliance with her Sunday duties:

> *Did not go to Church today, for Aunt Low was going and I thought I had better read a sermon at home than pay $1/2$ a Dollar to go to Church.* (10.6.1832)

According to the journal, there was one more reason why people, or rather some "gents", would not go to Church in Macau:

> *Latimer did not go to Church this morning because he lent his coat to Mr. Allport — an odd reason and would astonish people out of this place, but it is very common here. They are obliged to wear a coat to Church and wearing a jacket at all other times, they often leave their coats in Canton. (9.6.1833)*

The other English minister in Macau was George Harvey Vachell (1798–1839). He arrived in 1828, as chaplain of the British East India Company. Although he did not leave his name to posterity, he left deep impressions in the journal, because he was one of Harriett's most persistent suitors. According to the majority of her descriptions about him, he must have been a good preacher and pastor, and, above all, an interesting and cheerful person, without the artificial gravity characteristic of many clergymen. Their first encounter illustrates very well the relaxed manner of Vachell:

> *Had a number of calls to day. English [East India] company's minister [Vachell] called to see us. Through some mistake of the servant we did not see his card untill he left, and I was much astonished. There was nothing ministerial in his looks, indeed I thought him a great buck, and treated him accordingly. (2.10.1829)*

A few weeks later, we can read a similar commentary:

> *You would have no idea to see him that he was a clergyman, though he behaves very well for all that I know. (17.11.1829)*

But exactly this apparent normality and simplicity of Vachell's in his dealings with people and life was sometimes criticised by Harriett, in a little proselytising way:

> *Aunt Low has just gone to Church at Dr. Morrison's. I thought I would not go. If I go to Mr. Vachell's, when I look at him and think the last time I saw him he was betting at a horse race, or dancing with him, that I lose all reverence for him or what he says. I resolved to stay at home and read my own sermon, and I think I shall feel quite as well satisfied with myself as by going to Church, and I sincerely hope a little better. (8.11.1829)*

Apart from not putting on airs of superiority because of his vocation, Vachell also seemed to have possessed a sense of humour:

> Mr. Vachell has just sent his watch here for Aunt to set hers by.
> We were late at Church several times and he said he should _preach_
> _at us_ if we did not come earlier. Every Sunday now he very kindly
> sends us the right time. I should like to have you know him, he is
> one of the oddest mortals that ever inhabited this globe, I believe.
> (27.6.1830)

Besides, he was also a passionate sailor and once in a while used to sail around the islands near Macau in his little boat. Vachell left Macau temporarily for England in October 1832, and was substituted by Charles Wimberley, another Englishman imported from Calcutta and _"rather a severe muster"_ (12.9.1832), as Harriett observed after their first encounter. At the beginning she was quite favourably disposed towards him:

> Heard Mr. Wimberley preach for the first time — liked him very
> well. Seemed to feel what he read, which is more than the other
> [Vachell] did. (7.10.1832)

However, after the break-up of her friendship with Vachell, which was a long and painful process and turned her mood and judgement quite against him, as we shall see later, even a bad preacher would probably have received her praise. But her opinion of Wimberley changed dramatically with the following incident:

> Now Mr. W[imberley] is supposed to preach his own sermons, but
> last Sunday or a few Sundays since he preached one of Dr. Paley's.
> It was found in a printed volume word for word — he had it in
> _manuscript_ too. If he had have taken the book into the pulpit and
> give people to understand he was not preaching his own sermons
> every one would praise him — being assured he cannot write so
> well as many others — but it is literary theft and dishonourable,
> I think. (3.3.1833)

Obviously, from now on, people would be very careful in their assessment of Wimberley, even though it might have been a single lapse.

Apart from the two English ministers there were also two American missionaries, David Abeel (1804–1846) and Elijah Coleman Bridgman (1801–1861). However, they spent most of their time in Canton and came only sporadically to Macau. Harriett heard them several times at the Morrison chapel, clearly preferring Abeel:

> *Went to Dr. Morrison's this morning, heard Mr. Bridgman. He preached very well, but does not equal Mr. Abeel. ... Went to hear Mr. Abeel in the evening, for the last time in Macao this year. Gave us a very elegant sermon. He is a young man of uncommon talents. (8.8.1830)*

A few days earlier she remarked:

> *Mr. Abeel is a cheerful pleasant young man, and I should think superior to those generally sent on these [missionary] expeditions. (4.8.1830)*

Checking out missionaries and missionary work

Harriett Low never seemed to have become fully convinced of the missionary endeavours of her time.

> *I do not think they send the right kind of people to be missionaries, and I think they do not act on the best plans; further I will not judge them. I pray for them, that they may be guided aright. (13.6.1832)*

This remark is interesting, because it comes from the mouth of a young woman of her time and also because it reveals a certain contempt towards these mostly well intentioned, but very often immature and inexperienced young fellows, the missionaries. They are expected to convert people and be their spiritual and moral guides, at a time when their own personality is still under formation:

> *Mr. Abeel is a very amiable pleasant man, is much liked in Canton. Bridgman was just out of the [mill] when he left, and is as green as a leaf. He knows nothing of the world. (22.7.1830)*

In his book *The Golden Ghetto* Downs compares the geographical, social and educational background of the American merchants and missionaries in China. The members of both groups were usually young and rather inexperienced, but in terms of education and geographical representativeness of the USA, the missionaries ranked above the merchants. Missionaries also showed a greater tendency to return to China after personal tragedy or illness and were more frequently accompanied by their wives who actively engaged in all kinds of enterprises, notably in education, health care and charitable deeds.[7] It shall be remembered here that Arthur W. Hummel Sr. was a China missionary at the beginning of his professional career too, which led to a lifelong fascination with Chinese culture and civilisation.

In the first decades of the 19th century, many missionary societies came into existence, representing the extension to overseas of a variety of Christian churches in Europe and Northern America. They frequently competed with each other in their effort to convert "heathens". Morrison, for example, was sent out by the London Missionary Society, Abeel worked for the Dutch Reformed Church, and Bridgman was sent out by the American Board of Commissioners for Foreign Missions. The faithful at home would be reminded regularly to support the missionary endeavours not only through prayers, but also financially. Yet there was very little accountability from the missionaries for their handling of the money and other eventual mistakes committed by them. Instead, home went heart-breaking descriptions of personal sacrifice, of adventures among primitive or dangerous peoples, and of the conversion of pagans. The great majority of the donors at home had no chance to verify the content of these reports critically. They probably did not even feel the necessity to do so, because of their trust in the missionaries.

But one group of people who regularly visited both worlds, such as the crews of ships or traders, got a clearer picture about their actuation. Through some of these accounts, Harriett seemed to have become more cautious in her judgement about the work and usefulness of missionaries. The following entry is based on the report of Capt. Little, who had come to Macau via Hawaii:

> Every one that comes from there gives sad accounts of the Missionaries there. I have heretofore endeavoured not to listen to them, thinking they were prejudiced, but this Capt. Little I should depend upon. He says they are converting from the simple and as it were innocent life that God in his mercy intended them to lead, to Idleness, drunkenness, and treachery and deceit of all kinds. They have treated a little band of Catholics there was there as no <u>Christian</u> certainly had any right to treat a fellow being.[8] He says their accounts that they send home are very <u>incorrect</u> and so it goes. For my part I do not believe those who call themselves <u>ministers</u> & missionaries are generally so good as other people. But I will not judge, there is one who can and will judge the hearts of us all. It certainly seems very much against them that they do not teach them to be industrious, for Idleness, you know, is the mother of vice. I am half inclined to think they are better as the Almighty

placed them. I do not see that civilisation produces either goodness
or happiness. (4.4.1832)

Alarmed by reports such as these, Harriett felt obliged to share her knowledge with her family in the USA, to make them aware of the perversions committed in the name of Christianity:

I know the feelings of my dear father on this subject. But I would
prevent him if possible from assisting such people. It is not the
religion of Jesus they are teaching my dear father — depend upon
it. And you are not spreading his gospel. You are only converting
them from the errors of their own ways to the errors of Christians
— which are neither few nor small. (11.6.1832)

Happiness, or what is so called, is I believe pretty equally divided
all over the world. For my own part I should have some severe
qualms about enlightening them. And as to their happiness hereafter
I think their chance of happiness quite as good as ours, for will
they be punished for what they do not know to be wrong? And if
they live up to what their principles of goodness dictate, will they
not also receive their reward? We shall not be called to an account
for what we have never possessed. ... You may think my ideas
very strange, but they sprang up and I now think them correct.[9]
(13.6.1832)

Harriett's ideas about whether being a Christian was necessary for salvation, which she denied in her rationalist Unitarian argument, are interesting, because they make conversions, and therefore the main justification for missionary activity, superfluous. How many missionaries, originally convinced of the righteousness of their actions and of the uniqueness and superiority of their Christian creed, may have reached the same conclusions, but continued to convert (and still do so), even though going against their conscience? This is a dark chapter in the history of Christianity.

As regards the encounter between the early Protestant missionaries and the Chinese in particular, Downs observes:

The cultural gap was enormous, and it was made still wider by
the extraordinary ethnic chauvinism of both the Chinese and the
missionaries.[10]

In this context it is interesting to remember the acculturation strategy adopted by the early Jesuit missionaries in China (and in other places overseas), more than 200 years before the time under discussion here, when Macau played an important role in the cultural exchange between East and West. In the end, however, the Catholic Church could not cope with the Jesuits' progressive ideas of missionisation and the pope extinguished the order in 1773, which signalled the end of the Catholic China mission. After its restoration in 1814, China would no longer be the undisputed field of the Catholic Church, due to the arrival of Protestant missionaries, of whom Morrison was the first.

During her stay at Macau Harriett also knew Karl Friedrich August Guetzlaff (1803–1851), a famous German missionary, whom she called *"my recherché admirer" (5.9.1832)*. Why he should have admired her, however, remains unclear. Because of her physical attributes, her ability to make small talk, her passion in debating and defending her religion, or because of all these factors — we do not know. He was a very dazzling person himself.

> *I have this morning been to Church to hear a German Missionary preach. He has been traveling towards Pekin, indeed, beyond that place, à la Chinoise.[11] He is quite an enthusiast as you may imagine a preacher ought to be to enter such a field. And is there a more glorious or a more worthy cause for an enthusiast? I am sure not. He speaks 12 different languages. He must be very eloquent in his own, I think. His sentiments were very good, and I was much pleased with him.[12]*

Guetzlaff tried to convince Harriett that the story of her own religious struggle could serve some missionary purpose:

> *He wished me to write a little history of myself and compare it with the degraded state of the thousands of poor degraded beings in this vast Empire. He said he would publish it among them. … But, alas, I told him that I was too feeble a creature, and incapable even of writing anything. "But try," he says, and there our conversation ended.[13]*

If Guetzlaff had known that Harriett was such a passionate writer, he would probably have been more insistent. Hodges speculates that Guetzlaff

> *may have had more in mind than religion since he married three English wives in rapid succession.[14]*

This may have even been the case, but it can be assumed that neither Harriett nor her caretakers would have given him the slightest chance of succeeding ...

Apart from doing missionary work, he acted as a translator to Chinese for the British, both before and after the foundation of Hong Kong, where he became

Chinese Secretary to the Government of Hong Kong. Like many missionaries he also had some basic medical skills.

> *Dr. Guetzlaff in his journeys up and down the China Coast practised medicine among the Chinese with considerable success.*[15]

Arthur Waley sheds light on Guetzlaff's less known activity as an information officer and his troop of Chinese agents, or *han-chien* (Chinese evil-doers), as the Chinese called them. His characterisation of Guetzlaff as

> *a cross between parson and pirate, charlatan and genius, philanthropist and crook*

is probably the one that describes him best.[16]

Unitarianism versus Trinitarianism

Unitarianism — a rational religion

Unitarianism has changed a lot since Harriett Low's time, mainly because of its gradual move away from the Christian Church. Nowadays Unitarianism constitutes a so-called "liberal religion", as which it is explained on their homepages in the Internet for example. It accepts and incorporates beliefs from various religions and philosophies. Therefore, many of Harriett's observations about her faith may not be subscribed to anymore by modern Unitarians, nor would she, probably, agree with these changes and the estrangement from Christianity. The central point of this creed is revealed in the designation adopted in order to refer to their belief: they reject the idea of Trinity. On the one hand, it is considered as being against the teachings in the New Testament, where the word "God" is almost exclusively used in order to refer to the Father, and, on the other hand, as irrational, because when we speak of Father and Son, one of them was the creator and the other one the created, one of them is superior and the other one subordinate. Thus they cannot be equal in all respects. Consequently, the Unitarians contest the divinity of Christ. Besides, they don't believe in the expiatory sacrifice, in original sin or eternal condemnation. They celebrate the Eucharist, but merely as a commemorative act of Jesus' death and not as a sacrament. Harriett's rejection of the idea of Trinity as contradictory to reason is very well visible in the following comment:

> *It was today what is called Trinity Sunday and the creed of St. Athanasius*[17] *was read, which I cannot fancy that a man in his*

> senses could have <u>written</u> in any age, and much more a man of
> his senses read in this enlightened age. I believe it is not common
> to read it, but Mr. W[imberley] is [a] thorough going Church man.
> (2.6.1833)

But even then, and mainly outside the USA, there seemed to have been a
certain ignorance regarding the meaning and precepts of Unitarianism, as the
following episode demonstrates:

> Daniell [an Englishman] wanted to know if I ever went to Dr.
> Morrison's church, what church I had attended at home, or to what
> sect I belonged? I told him I had been in the habit of attending a
> <u>Unitarian</u>. He would hardly believe it, says you are <u>not</u> a Unitarian,
> how can you go to our Church? I answered his questions — he
> seemed to have a great horror of U[nitarians] — said they were as
> different as possible from the Church of England, and indeed the
> only sect that did not come within the pale of their Church. He said
> they did not believe in the <u>Divinity</u> of Christ, nor of <u>any</u> of his
> <u>institutions</u>, the Sanctity of marriage, of Baptism, nor indeed of any
> thing. I told him they were a different sect altogether in America
> — that they did believe in <u>them</u>, that I had been baptized, that they
> did believe in the sanctity of marriage, that the Sacrament was
> administered every month. He was quite astonished at the difference.
> Says the Unitarians are not called Christians in England. In short
> they are I should think what we call Deists which are as different
> as possible from Unitarians. I endeavoured to explain as well as I
> could the difference, but did not think at the time the equivalent in
> America to <u>their</u> Unitarians. (10.4.1831)

As in other Protestant churches, each individual is responsible for his or
her salvation, without the possibility of human or spiritual intermediaries. The
best way of staying firm in one's faith, the *sine qua non* in order to be saved,
consists in regular, ideally daily, reading of the Word of God. Harriett also
practised this habit:

> My little Bible given me by my Dear Father ... is read every
> morning and evening. I regret much however that it is not larger
> print, as it is very hard to read at night. (28.2.1830)

Due to this tradition, Protestant girls used to receive some basic schooling, more
so than was the case with their Catholic peers. But female education aimed
mainly at enabling girls to read the Bible and to take care of their salvation,

and not at teaching things, which could be used for a professional career out of the home. In this respect, the attitude of the Protestants did not differ significantly from that of the Catholics. In both cases, a woman was seen as the "assistant" of her husband.[18] The traditional division of work attributed to her the care for the home and its members, but totally barred her from participating in the public life. Profoundly imbued with Puritan values, such as self-discipline, introspection and a rigid observance of the "Sabbath", the living together with other Christian traditions and other religions was a constant challenge for Harriett.

A disagreeable habit of the Trinitarians: the non-observance of Sunday

The first chance for Harriett to have a closer contact with Catholicism occurred in the Philippines, where the *Sumatra* stopped for several weeks. Some of the observations, or rather complaints, about this religion would become a constant entry in the journal, at least during the first two years in Macau, when she was confronted with Catholicism as something new. Later, her fury against it was unleashed only once in a while, for example when observing a procession or listening to stories about the power abuse committed by the Catholic clergy. The same is also true with respect to the religious manifestations of the Chinese.

One irritating habit of the Catholics, which she noticed for the first time in the Philippines, was the fact that people socialised on Sundays, instead of fully dedicating themselves to religious matters and meditation. In Macau, this "bad" habit was also practised by the Anglicans, a fact regularly lamented in the journal:

> *I endeavored to pass the day as it should be, but you have no idea how difficult it is to keep alive religious feelings or to spend the day in a proper manner. I read one of Buckminster's excellent sermons aloud. Had no sooner finished it, feeling some what disposed to be serious, but Mr. and Mrs. Fearon and a Mr. Griffith called. Soon after, Mrs. Turner. They go to church and on their return make calls. Thus you see there is no country like ours for religious privileges. The Chinese pay no sort of regard to the Sabbath, go on with their work as usual. (11.10.1829)*

Thus, *"that holy stillness ... which pervades the air at home"* (28.3.1830) would remain only a dream in Macau. But Harriett was not alone with her objection:

> *Business always came first with the traders. The missionaries universally complained about the common violation of the Sabbath.*[19]

In New England, the observance of Sunday began already on Saturday evening. Therefore, any entertainment for fun or distraction, such as playing cards for example, was seriously frowned upon. The following passage was written after a visit to the Casa Garden:

> *Cards were introduced in the evening, the same as any other eve. It did not suit our Yankee notions however. We had a little supper and returned in our chairs about 10, not pleased with the evening altogether. Have resolved to avoid Saturday evening visits in the future, as we know not what will take place among people who think but little of Sundays. (21.11.1829)*

The bulwark of Unitarian faith and sentiments

Harriett's father was right in warning his daughter about the dangers awaiting her in foreign countries concerning her faith. The greatest challenges to her Unitarian creed were provoked through the contact with the Anglicans, and probably intensified because of her friendship with Vachell. One year after her arrival, Harriett expressed the wish to partake in communion:

> *Went to Dr. Morrison's this morning, communion day there. How sincerely I wished that I could partake with them, but I do not know at present what would be necessary, or how to join — but I mean to think more of it and enquire. For I do most seriously think it the duty of everyone, and a privilege. It raises such holy feelings. I left the house feeling melancholy that I could not be a partaker. I returned and read one of Buckminster's sermons on the subject which more fully convinced me that it should not be neglected. (1.8.1830)*

But it took her one year to follow this matter up:

> *This morning Vachell sent me several books ... giving some explanations of the Trinity, and a kind letter from him with some observations on the subject — and pointing out some passages which he thought would convince me of the truth of the Doctrine of the Trinity — and the Divinity of Jesus Christ — all of which I shall peruse with attention and pray to god to enlighten my understanding. I went to Church and heard an excellent sermon, read much today ... and feel convinced that I could conscientiously partake of the Holy Communion — although I cannot bring myself yet to believe in the Trinity. How much I wish I could converse a*

> *little with my dear Father. Arguments strong on both sides quite*
> *puzzle me. Everybody here believes in the Trinity, and who can I*
> *go to, to question on the other side. Would that I could feel*
> *satisfied, and I <u>do</u> feel satisfied, I do believe in <u>one</u> <u>Supreme</u> <u>God</u>,*
> *<u>most</u> <u>firmly</u> believe it — but how to answer some of the staggering*
> *verses pointed out to me I know not. But can it be so important*
> *to our salvation? Would our heavenly Father have left any thing*
> *in such hidden mystery, had it have been so very necessary to us?*
> *Would he not have explained to us, if of such vast importance?*
> *(10.4.1831)*

This is one more rationalist argument in matters of faith, which unfortunately cannot be explained by reason only ... Poor Vachell must surely have shaken his head gravely when being confronted with Harriett's arguments. After some more time reading and reflecting on Trinitarian literature, Harriett confessed to being decidedly Unitarian:

> *Did not go to Church, was on my couch all the morning reading*
> *the <u>Unitarian Advocate</u> and Masillon's <u>Sermons</u> in French. I feel*
> *quite convinced now that I shall never be any thing but a Unitarian.*
> *It appears to me now after reading much and thinking upon the*
> *Subject, that it is plainly told in the Scripture and there is hardly*
> *a ground for the Doctrine of the Trinity. It appears to me too*
> *absurd for any one to believe. In one of the Books there were 100*
> *texts cited which appear to prove plainly to me that there is but*
> *one Supreme God and that Jesus Christ is inferior, that he is not*
> *a divine Being, though endowed with unlimited power from his*
> *father, whom he expressly says is "<u>greater</u> than he". Yes my dear*
> *Sister I feel that there is hardly a doubt. These books have explained*
> *most of my doubts and if I cannot be permitted to approach the*
> *communion table till I can say I believe in the Holy Trinity, I must*
> *defer it (though I think it a great privilege as well as a duty) till I*
> *return to my own dear country, where privileges are greater. I have*
> *read Mr. Vachell's Books but they do not convince me at all.*
> *(24.4.1831)[20]*

However, after an exchange of letters with Vachell on the subject of Trinity, Harriett finally decided to participate in the Communion, an event that rose great expectations in her:

> *For the first time I approached the altar and partook of the Holy*
> *Sacrament, instituted by our Lord and Saviour Jesus Christ — and*

> *in remembrance of him are we commanded [to] do likewise. May*
> *it be the commencement of a new life in me. (29.5.1831)*

More or less at the same time as Harriett, her father seemed to have been troubled by similar questions.

> *I am glad to hear, my dear Father, that you still hold your*
> *Unitarian views. I had heard you had changed your sentiments. I*
> *could hardly believe it and I did not wish to, for after all your study*
> *I could not bear to hear you had changed — not but that I think*
> *there are as good Trinitarians as Unitarians. Far be it from me to*
> *be so uncharitable.*[21]

Like his daughter, Seth Low continued to be a Unitarian.

Reading all these doubts and questions that were aroused in the head of a serious young woman, one may understand why the Catholic Church, during most of its existence, forbade laypersons direct access to the Bible. Otherwise it is difficult to imagine that it could have survived in its present constitution until nowadays, presenting rather the same picture of fragmentation as exists among the Protestant churches. On the other hand, the Protestant freedom to think and to question the Bible is like a testimony of trust in each individual, something that seems to be lacking in the Catholic Church, where institutional survival appears to be the ultimate goal.

Observation and rejection of Catholic practices

Catholic holy days and processions

The first Catholic procession described in the journal is not very rich in details, but the way in which it was announced to them by Apew, the Chinese *compradore*[22] of the Lows is interesting, because it illustrates the difficulties in communication between the newly arrived and the Chinese:

> *Apew, our Compradore, came in this afternoon. Wanted to know*
> *if we wanted to see a* <u>*walky*</u>. *We could not divine what he wanted,*
> *but he wished us to go with him. We did. He led us up on to a*
> *terrace that looks into the street. We stayed some time, and saw*
> *nothing. He then thought it "<u>more better</u>" that we go in, and he*
> *would call us again. (11.10.1829)*[23]

But the Easter preparations of the Catholics in Macau provided plenty of events for Harriett to get excited about:

> *Tomorrow is good Friday when there will be much ceremony at the churches. They have been all opened today, and all the women in the place visit them, going from one to the other, staying 5 or 6 minutes in one and then leaving it. Just before night there was a procession from the Cathedral — Christ bearing the cross. But I was at the back of the house and did not see it. But I understand there is to be another tomorrow. Mr. Otaduy says he went to the misericordia today, and Mr. Pereira was performing the office of our Saviour washing his disciples' feet, twelve old men for the disciples.[24] I cannot bear the idea. It appears to me sacrilegious. This evening Mr. Beale had some flowers brought in called the passion flower because it blooms in passion week. These bloomed today. It is a most beautiful flower of a dark purple. In the middle of the stamen (I think it is called) seems to form a cross. It is a very deep flower. (8.4.1830)*

The observation of a procession, which left the Cathedral in the morning of Holy Friday, caused feelings of both approval and rejection:

> *First there was the Cross. The padres and friars followed. Then a coffin covered with black and an image to represent the body of our Saviour just taken from the cross — behind that was his mother and two other women. There were many other banners in a long procession, a fine band of music, and I certainly never heard any thing more solemn. They played softly and slowly, the drums muffled with black. All hats off, and the priests chanting at the same time — the street was thronged with people. I cannot bring my mind to think it right to perform this ceremony, it appears to me too solemn to be made a farce of, but I suppose they think it right. But it seems horrid to me to see an image made to represent so divine a person. They returned again to the Church after parading round the town. They were going to church all day; we went in just at night. They were singing and going through some ceremony. The church was hung with black and yesterday was seen at one end of the Church was a representation of Calvary. The virgin Mary was also in black.[25] (9.4.1830)*

As already with Holy Friday, the Catholic Easter celebrations were acclaimed by Harriett only in their musical version.

> *Was awaked from my sleep this morning by a band of music playing in the most spirited style. It sounded perfectly. This day early in the morning the women went unto the sepulchre and the body of Jesus was not there. He had risen. They will sing nothing but Hallelujahs now. I immediately thought of this, and it did seem solemn Mary Ann. Grand Mass was performed this morning and a procession then went from the Church, the priests chanting as usual, the crosses and banners, the little priests burning incense. There was one man with one each side of him to imitate Christ risen from the dead. The music was fine. I could not help thinking then: How can any man that represents the Saviour ever sin more. Only think what could have been his feelings when walking through the streets, to say to himself that he was representing that divine person. It makes me shudder. Today they all begin to eat meat, having fasted 40 days, or lived upon fish. (11.4.1830)*

Two episodes illustrating the Catholic absolutism

The following two episodes are, on one hand, typical examples of the mentality of many a member of the Catholic clergy and their relationship with simple people, apart from illustrating how many Catholics are impaired in their judgement by blindly obeying them. Harriett's reaction, on the other hand, when confronted with these examples, illustrates a certain intellectual snobbery that is typical of the Protestants when referring to their Catholic brethren and sisters.

Angry because of not having been woken up in time by their maid Josepha, probably a Macanese woman or a converted Chinese, Harriett wanted to know the reason from her:

> *Asked Josepha why she let me sleep so long. She said she went to <u>Misa</u> [Missa] or [M]ass at <u>5</u> o'clock and she did not come home in time — said she thought it was Sunday and Miss Harriett would not want to <u>study</u>. You may think her getting up at 5 to go to Church is an instance of piety, but I think far otherwise. Much as she goes to Church and as many prayers as she says there is no more religion in her than there is in a <u>Bamboo</u>. As to <u>virtue</u> among them there is no such thing. The other night I came home late and I asked her if she went to sleep evenings when we were out. She said No. I said what do you do evenings. She said she read prayers.*

> *Said I do you read prayers two or three hours? She said sometimes*
> *she did not get time to read any for two or three days and then she*
> *made up for lost time. I said "do you like to read them, Josepha."*
> *She says "Must, liky, no liky!" She give me to understand that it*
> *was not at all agreeable but she was accountable to the padre for*
> *a certain number, which she must either read or suffer the*
> *consequences! Oh, it is a vile system! (16.6.1833)*

The rationalist in Harriett was obviously disturbed with this Catholic way of settling accounts with God. In her eyes it meant belittling the greatness of God by representing him as some kind of angry teacher who can be satisfied with empty exercises. The following example of the abuse of power by the Catholic clergy was written down after having observed, incidentally, a Catholic burial in the Franciscan church.

> *The priests, as in all Catholic countries, exact large sums from those*
> *who are able to pay for their prayers and extort grievously from*
> *the poor I am told. They have great power over the minds of these*
> *poor ignorant creatures, and from all accounts many of them are*
> *very unworthy of their charge. I was told the other day by Mr.*
> *Colledge, who knows more of them than any one else, that he was*
> *called to visit a woman who was very ill indeed and had quite lost*
> *her reason, and the father confessor had been the sole cause of it.*
> *It seems she has received great kindnesses from the English residents*
> *here. She is a poor woman and they had assisted her and one day*
> *some of her friends were abusing the English as they are in the habit*
> *of doing, and this woman said she thought them very good people,*
> *and expressed her gratitude to them. The padre either heard her or*
> *was told of it. Whereupon he thought it necessary to chastise her*
> *and for this heinous sin as he pretended to consider it he told her*
> *she must confess her sins, going back to her seventh year, (she was*
> *now 40). The poor woman thought it impossible I suppose, and it*
> *preyed so upon her mind that she actually went mad and Colledge*
> *says it will no doubt be the death of her. Is it not horrid? Many*
> *such instances of oppression occur and it seems dreadful that such*
> *creatures should have such power. (17.2.1833)*

At the end of this entry Harriett wrote in a marginal note: "*The woman has since died.*"

As regards the practice of confession, which does not exist among the Protestants, Harriett commented the following in Manila, where she saw some women returning from confession:

> *They go away happy, thinking they are absolved from all sin and ready to begin a new list. (14.9.1829)*

Veil taking by a Catholic nun

Renouncing this world and entering into a convent is not a very frequent event. Therefore, it is not astonishing that such a ceremony attracted many people, even non-Catholic foreigners. Harriett had already read about it in sentimental French novels, which however are not the best introduction to this serious matter. Consequently, her description is full of the typical stereotypes associated with women who decide to become the "brides of Jesus".

> *After church Mrs. Davis came to us and told us there was in the afternoon a nun to take the <u>black</u> <u>veil</u>. I agreed to go with her. … At 4 I set out with Mrs. Davis and went to the Chapel of Santa Clara — a neat chapel belonging to the convent — the entrance to it is rather magnificent. After reading <u>Matilde</u>[26] one is apt to fancy all just like that. I had prepared myself for a very imposing ceremony, but I was exceedingly disappointed. Indeed I might have known that it would not be, for some of their most solemn and imposing ceremonies are performed without the least degree of solemnity. We had a good stand near the altar and could see the whole, and as it is a novel thing I shall give you all the particulars. At the appointed hour the lady walked into the Church accompanied by the padres and the boys with lighted candles. She kneels before the altar and an old padre (a wicked looking creature) chants something in Latin, and is responded by the other padres. The lady then mounts another step, he chants again, sprinkles her with holy water or incense, they burn the frankincense, then give[s] her an immense embroidered candlestick or rather decked with all kinds of tinsel, she takes it and walks out of the church and is then lost to the world. The band played a dancing tune as she entered the Church to remind her, I suppose, that she must lose all that — the folly of the world & etc.*
>
> *From the Chapel she went into the nunnery. At the end of the Chap[el] is a grate where there was a general rush to get to see the rest of the ceremony. I should hardly have ventured myself, but Mrs. Baynes preceded me (who cannot bear a squeeze so well*

*as I can) and I ventured, but never (I hope) my curiosity shall
lead me into such a scrape again — to see a portuguese nun at
any rate. There was I in a crowd of these nasty people, black, white
and grey, could not move an inch. Fortunately Mr. Vachell
protected me as much as he could, but he had to take Mrs. Baynes
out, when Mr. Young took care of me. But after all this squeeze
you will wish to know if I was paid for it. I can hardly feel satisfied
that the account was balanced, but I will tell you what I saw, and
you shall judge. We see at first behind the grate the nun as in the
chapel dressed in her splendid dress of white Lace trimmed with
pink satin, over [a] white Satin underdress, diamond necklace,
headdress of diamonds, fingers covered with diamond rings, and a
white veil thrown over her head. She casts all these aside, renounces
to the world and all its vanities. Has her hair cut off. Comes again
to the grate. The padre chants again, the organ plays and much
singing, being all in Latin no one could understand what was said.
She then embraces and salutes all her sister nuns who are ugly old
creatures who are behind the grate, covered with their long black
dresses. She then puts on her nunnery dress which is of something
dark Blue with a rope <u>round</u> the <u>waist</u>, covers herself with this black
thick veil, face and all, walks to the grate, and is seen no more.
To make this all very interesting and touching you will fancy her
young, beautiful and engaging, but lest it should make too deep
an impression on you I will just undeceive you on that point and
tell you she is excessively ugly, and it is said, not under 32 years
of age; I suppose despairs of ever getting [a] husband to please her
mind. She gives 1500 dls [dollars] to get in there and conceals her
charms from the world forever. The <u>gents</u> <u>made</u> <u>no</u> <u>attempts</u> <u>to</u>
<u>rescue</u> <u>her</u>. They are there as novices for 1 year and a day before
they take the black veil. During that time they can retract if they
please. If at the end of that time they conclude to remain, the bells
send forth a merry peal and there is great rejoicings. I'll assure you
I was most happy when the ceremony was over and delighted to
find myself in the fresh air. (10.7.1831)*

Harriett Low's description deserved the following commentary by Teixeira:

*Being Protestant and having a knife instead of a tongue in her
mouth, she criticises everything, the priests, the nuns and the
believers who assisted, even the Latin. ... However, we forgive*

> *her the harsh words, because it is the only existing description of*
> *the profession of the former Poor Clares.*[27]

Generally, Father Teixeira's comments on Harriett's mostly depreciatory attitude towards Catholicism make an amusing reading, because he retaliates in the spirit of a devout believer.

On the future of Catholicism

The Catholic religion presented no threat to Harriett's Unitarian faith, as some other, more liberal creed might have done. On the contrary, the more Harriett saw and knew about Catholicism, the stronger her aversion towards it became. Her fervour intensified over time, making her appear as intolerant as the intolerance of the creed so much criticised by her:

> *I wonder if the time will ever come when this Catholic religion (if*
> *we can call it so) will be done away. Yes by degrees I think it will;*
> *think of the time when all Europe was in the same state, but as*
> *the world becomes enlightened, this bigotry and superstition will*
> *be done away. The mighty fabric is gradually decaying — the*
> *foundation will soon be undermined and a new one will be erected.*
> *The religion of Jesus Christ will overspread the earth. The mild*
> *spirit of Christian Charity is growing in America and it cannot fail*
> *of spreading itself. I should like to look upon this little planet 2000*
> *years hence and see what mind will be then. ... How different the*
> *world is now or the state of society from what it was in the 15th*
> *century and shall it not go on towards perfection? We certainly*
> *have not retrograded since then, — I prophecy it will! (17.2.1833)*

Thus, the missionary spirit of the North-American society was already evident in the early 19th century. Although restricted to a religious question here, we will see later that the Americans regarded themselves as an example in political matters too. Only America could indicate the right way to follow to the world. This attitude is designated as American exceptionalism.[28] A glimpse into our modern world confirms that this ideology continues very much alive.

Chinese converts

Harriett's negative attitude towards Catholicism extended naturally to the Chinese who had adopted this religion voluntarily.

> *Coming home we passed three Chinese padres who have it is said been converted to Catholic religion. They dress in European costume, but with the exception of their being bipeds they bear no resemblance to the* genus homo*. To meet them any where else you would be extremely puzzled to know in what species they might be classed with any propriety. I have very little respect for converts of this kind, either for their faith or their works, though perhaps and no doubt it is quite as difficult to judge of their goodness or their sincerity as it is of one who calls himself a Christian in a more civilized country. It is foolish to pretend to judge either. (7.8.1833)*

With this radical step, indicated exteriorly by the wearing of European clothes, the converted Chinese ceased to be regarded as such by their own people. The decision to adopt Christianity turned them into something like social outcasts, or members of a social no-man's land, because for the Westerners they continued to be Chinese. Wood showed a similar contempt for Chinese converts, mainly for those who embraced Catholicism. Besides, his statement is mixed with ignorance and prejudice towards the religion practised by the Chinese.

> *The greatest exertions are made by the Catholic clergy to convert the Chinese, and a few nominal Christians are to be found among them, but the indulgences of their own religion, or rather the want of any religion at all, prevent their submitting to the comparatively austere precepts of Christianity. Added to this, the prejudices of the government, which discountenances such foreign innovation, render it dangerous for a native to be known as a Christian, and if successfully detected, it almost always entails a punishment for what is called a mask, concealing political machinations with discontented foreign barbarians! ... The indulgences of the Romish church are more agreeable to the Chinese taste, as the rigid observances which are enjoined by other sects, are not likely to be favorably received among a people with such uncommonly violent prejudices, to overcome which it appears almost necessary to change their very natures.*[29]

The misconceptions and ignorance about Buddhism, one of the oldest world religions, are both shocking and interesting to the modern reader, because they clearly demonstrate how little was known about the religious traditions of the East at that time, even among the educated classes.

4

The Daily Life of Foreign Women on the China Coast

Whenever women accompany their husbands to live abroad, their first responsibility is to create a surrogate home for the couple or family. Usually, the new abode would be modelled, as close as possible, to its counterpart back home, with obvious concessions to local styles of architecture and to the availability of certain products and materials. In Harriett Low's time, Western maids were taken along to assist the lady of the house in this arduous task. As in all wealthy colonial settings, menial tasks were carried out by numerous native employees. This allowed the ladies to acquire new tastes and skills, such as drawing, playing an instrument, learning a new language or riding. And though London and Paris were far away, the latest fashion dictates were keenly observed, albeit with at least six months delay. Aside from this, a comparatively large portion of time was dedicated to corresponding with the beloved ones at home or in Canton and, often, to keeping a journal. Reading was perhaps the most important and preferred activity with many ladies and men, apart from socialising over a meal, be it a breakfast of the kind "to see and to be seen" on the racetrack, an intimate tea party at home, or a formal dinner at the East India Company's headquarters in Macau.

But despite the opulent living conditions, misery also existed. There was the heavy climate, unknown diseases, a high mortality rate among infants and young adults, as well as the superficiality of many relationships due to the high fluctuation of the population.

*   *   *   *

Home-based pastimes

Living without any financial worries in big and spacious houses, surrounded by a great number of servants, coolies, and slaves, may seem a little bit like paradise. Yet for somebody like Harriett, who was the second eldest child out of twelve and used to being an active support to her parents, the inert life was only enjoyed initially. Thus, if they did not want to die of boredom, she and the women in the same situation had to look for some kind of employment. As we will see, the ladies were quite active in a variety of ways, both individually and in groups.

Writing letters and diary

The only way of communicating with family, friends and business partners that were not within walking reach, was by writing. This was a beloved, although time-consuming activity, both for women and men.

> *Wrote a letter, make it a practice to write a letter or part of one every morning. I have 12 answered; think I have 7 more to write. (17.10.1831)*

More often, however, letters and diary were written in the evening, at candlelight. Although this may sound romantic, the quality of the paper, which often became humid due to the moist climate in Macau, and of the quills of that time, made this occupation not a gratifying one in terms of physical pleasure. It was quite difficult to produce something legible under these circumstances:

> *I am astonished to see how horribly I have written these last pages. I should think I was rolling about in a Ship instead of Terra Firma. But were you to see my apparatus: I have got $^1/_2$ a dozen stumps that I have used I believe this two months, and I forget to mend them. I have to borrow Aunt Low's knife, & I cannot get it at this hour. I have got a cologne Bottle for an ink stand, but hope to have something better before long. (18.3.1830)*

Sometimes, writing could even cause muscular ache:

> *My arm aches wretchedly, for I have written steadily ever since church this morning. (20.12.1829)*

Writing was actually much more than a pastime for Harriett, it was more like a necessity of survival in Macau. It let her forget temporarily how far away she was from her family, making her present with them in her mind.

> *After dinner wrote a long letter to you My Dear Sis — which is my greatest comfort to sit down and tell you every thing that is going on. (17.1830)*

However, a great number of letters have been lost, which is very unfortunate, because

> many of the more intimate details of that life were reserved for home
> letters ... instead of being recorded in this Journal.[1]

That this should be so is natural, because the completion of a journal volume would take at least half a year, while letters were sent on a more regular basis. They were not only talking about the joys and sorrows of everyday life, but also about more confidential and intimate matters and asking for advice. Sentences like *"this subject is reserved for a letter"* or *"but this is not something to be mentioned in the journal"* can be read with a certain frequency throughout the journal.[2] According to Dorothy Wordsworth, sister of the Romantic poet William Wordsworth, in letters we can *"see the beating of the inmost heart upon paper"*.[3]

Being such a devoted correspondent, Harriett expected to receive the same treatment in return. Throughout the whole voyage to Macau, she anticipated the joy of getting her first letters there. Knowing that a boat, the *Liverpool Packet*, had left 10 days after them, she expected her first letters with its arrival:

> If not, how wo[e]ful will be the disappointment. Do not neglect
> an opportunity. (19.10.1829)

If she had known then, how long she would have to wait to get the first words from home, she probably would have despaired. Not knowing, however, the journal testifies her growing frustration:

> I cannot get over the disappointment of not receiving letters by the
> L[iverpool] Packet. It is the strangest thing imaginable that out of
> so many correspondents I could not have <u>one</u> <u>line</u>. (28.10.1829)

In her impatience Harriett seemed to have forgotten that for those who stay behind the world changes little and therefore people see no immediate necessity for writing. Gradually, the complaints became less frequent, but did not loose their intensity.

> It is pleasant to see you in dreams and I can bear the
> disappointment better than not receiving letters by the <u>Liverpool</u>
> <u>Packet</u>. I cannot think of that without wishing to <u>weep</u>. You can
> hardly imagine the disappointment nor do I wish you to. Perhaps
> in the course of time I shall get <u>callous</u> to these things, but I hope
> I shall never have enough of them. (8.11.1829)

Unfortunately, there was much suffering still to come in this particular respect, which is understandable to all those who are friends of lazy correspondents.

Harriett's impatience with regard to letters seemed to have been a common disease among many foreign residents in Macau. The following scene describes the hustle and bustle on the Quay after the arrival of two direct ships with mail on them:

> There was <u>tout</u> <u>le</u> <u>monde</u> assembled watching the boats with anxious hearts, no doubt. ... such a scene of excitement I have not seen for many a day. The huge packets from one ship had just been delivered, they were just returning from the Chief's (where all packets are opened).[4] ... I thought if the friends could but see these poor creatures looking for a letter and the desire that was manifested, and the pleasure that was evinced by those who had rec'd a quantity, that they would deprive themselves of many an hour's sleep to give them that pleasure. No one can ever realize it till they have seen it. I almost wished myself an English woman that I might participate in the general joy. (16.8.1832)

Harriett was perhaps the person in town who craved for letters more than anybody else:

> I believe if there were letters to come from Kamschatka I should look with a faint hope of some. (23.5.1832)

Therefore, it is not astonishing that the arrival of the first bundle of letters from home, nine months after their departure, provoked a variety of feelings and reactions.

> The first thing I saw was my Father's handwriting. I then knew that he was alive. I then literally <u>grabbed</u> at the others, and hardly waited to see who they were from. One after another was torn open. I wanted to read them all at a time and was vexed that I could not read faster — one the ink was so pale it was impossible to read that first — another so much of it I must leave untill the last. I then caught up a paper which margin was filled with pencilled writing. Judging it to be something very important I read it. H. Allen is to be married to a rich merchant in Antwerp. I instantly communicated it to Aunt, but in my haste I had made a mistake. I found my letters said nothing of this important piece of information. I then gave it a more careful examination and found the truth of the story. My Dear Mother's and Father's letters were then carefully perused, and all the others in due time. Yours my dear sister were read the last but with not the least interest. It was

> *a great treat to me. They all carried me directly home, in the midst*
> *of you. But we are now anticipating earlier dates, as you mention*
> *sending by several Ships before. And you may judge how happy I*
> *felt to know how well and happy you all seemed there. (26.2.1830)*

The arrival of letters was such an important event, that the doors were open day and night for the messenger with the desired news.

> *Mr. Vachell brought us our letters from Lintin this morning at 1*
> *o'clock — I mean in the night. I took them into my room but*
> *postponed the pleasure of reading them untill morning, though I*
> *suspect it would have been otherwise had they have been new. I*
> *started a[t] 6 after dreaming of them and read them with much*
> *pleasure though they were very old. She [the ship] is 212 days from*
> *England. (18.5.1830)*

The worst thing that could happen to Harriett was having to listen to the people bringing the much desired letters, who were often young men desperate for some female company and a little conversation after several months on sea.

> *A Mr. Burridge from Ship* Howard *handed me a little bundle of*
> *precious letters, which give him a welcome. Cannot say much for*
> *[his] agreeable manners however. In spite of my longing looks at*
> *my letters, he was determined I should have patience; he stayed*
> *an hour and my politeness would not let me open them. I had quite*
> *a treat, but I believe I am a most ungrateful being. The more I*
> *have the more I want — and whenever I get letters I am sure to*
> *feel* homesick. *(11.19.1831)*

Harriett was so consumed with receiving letters, that her Aunt took the following generous decision:

> *Aunt Low kindly permits me to read all hers so that I have a double*
> *share, & I take as much interest in them as my own, almost.*
> *(22.3.1832)*

But receiving a letter from home was often not enough. In Harriett's eyes, few of her correspondents satisfied her demands regarding content and length:

> *Yours my dear sis is not full enough, I want you to tell me little*
> *longer stories. You just give me a few words and leave it to my*
> *brilliant imagination to picture the rest. Now I think you are*
> *mistaken in its capacities. (25.8.1830)*

Although Molly seemed to have tried hard to live up to Harriett's expectations, the latter would never be fully satisfied with her sister's writing:

> *Your letter my dear sister give[s] me great pleasure; it is just what I want, and you branched out a little more than usual. That is generally your great fault I think, you confine yourself too closely to facts, and do not give me your opinion so much as I should like generally. I always want some of your remarks on every thing.* (7.3.1831)

Poor Molly never received a mark better than "*quite satisfactory*" (11.8.1832).

Molly's diaries, however, which she sent to Harriett as agreed on between the two sisters before her departure from Salem, found greater approval. Though probably mainly home-based and with little variety, as we may judge from the following quotation, they offered plenty to read at least and, apart from this, Harriett knew all the actors described:

> *Your interesting journal, I followed you through all the operations of cleaning with great interest I assure you. The different arrangements are all noted, and I think I know just how every thing is placed.* (25.11.1832)

Harriett's journals also found Molly's approval:

> *I am quite encouraged about writing in my journal, now you tell me it interests you. Suspect I shall be more "copious" than ever. A little praise sometimes does an immense deal of good.* (22.3.1832)

With the arrival of a new desk, Harriett's enthusiasm for writing reached new heights:

> *Uncle had a new secretary from France yesterday, and he has transferred his old desk to me, so that I am now quite magnificent — and quite at the height of my ambition — with room enough for every thing and my arms beside. Suspect I shall be more eloquent than ever.* (5.9.1832)

Reading

Another dear and very important activity in Harriett Low's daily life in Macau was reading.

> *What should I do if it were not for books! I am sure I should get quite sick of my own company.* (13.4.1831)

Often she read late into the night:

> *Read till ¹/₂ past 11, when the tempting pillow could no longer be resisted. Beside my eyes ached. I am afraid to try them too much for if I was to lose them what would become of me. <u>Little</u> as they are, they add more to my happiness than any of the other senses I am sure. (22.5.1833)*

Harriett was not alone in this passion, as Downs's remark on the Western male community at Canton shows:

> *Reading was probably the most important single recreational activity. … Canton merchants were remarkably bookish in comparison with their late nineteenth-century counterparts.*[5]

It was also very common for people to read to each other, for example William H. Low would read while Harriett and her aunt were sewing, and a discussion usually followed. As she habitually mentions the title of the books in her journal, frequently accompanied by a small commentary of approval, criticism or disappointment, we are left with an impressive list of hundreds of books at the end of her journal, which reflect her interests and personality.[6]

First of all, there were religious books and books about religion. This type of reading corresponded probably both to a feeling of duty as well as inclination. The Bible constituted daily lecture and homilies by her favourite preachers, such as W. E. Channing, J. S. Buckminster and C. W. Upham, were regularly read on Sundays, and whenever the need to do so was felt. Sometimes, Harriett Low also ventured into more theoretical fields about religion and philosophy, for example by reading Beattie's *An Essay on the Nature and Immortality of Truth* or Paley's *Natural Theology*. Nature as an emanation and reflection of the Divine were popular topics then.[7]

Second on her list of reading preferences were works about history, including books about historical personalities such as Napoleon or Nelson and royalties from all major European dynasties, as well as descriptions of historical events, from the Fall of Jerusalem to the French Revolution and the history of her own country.

> *I do <u>love</u> history better than any kind of reading, and I should much sooner go to sleep over a novel than in reading history. (18.10.1832)*

However, books about history rarely provoked feelings of pleasure or satisfaction, making this kind of lecture, more often than not, a tiring and frustrating exercise:

> *What a series of crimes and wickedness one reads in reading history, what contrasts in Character. One cannot help wishing when reading of a man of great talents that they are hereditary, though the men of the greatest talents seem to do the most mischief. You seldom meet with a <u>great</u> and <u>good</u> man. They seem incompatible almost. I am exceedingly fond of reading history, but yet it always disgusts me with human nature. What a strange propensity we have to admire men of great and powerful mind even if every page of their history is blotted with crimes. (23.3.1833)*

But there was one kind of books providing the desired elevation of feelings:

> *After dinner read History a while. I have now reached the reign of George the Second of England. I turned from this to St. Pierre's Studies of nature. I love to contrast the discords of man with the harmony of <u>Nature</u>. History lessens your respect for men, the study of nature leads you to admire more the author of all. (22.5.1833)*

Travel literature, a genre enjoying great popularity in general, constituted another type of reading. There were travel accounts from all corners of the world, written by missionaries, aristocrats, traders and adventurers. Some of Harriett Low's contemporaries in Macau, such as the Americans W. W. Wood, W. C. Hunter and the German K. Guetzlaff had already or would in time produce books about China and other places in the Orient. Once she was invited to read a manuscript:

> *Read part of Mr. Inglis' journal this morning, of his expedition in India. Was very dry and [un]interesting. Put it by in despair of ever accomplishing it. He has come down today and we thought we must say we had read it, as he lent it to us some months since. (27.7.1832)*

Contemporary descriptions about Great Britain and the USA were most prevalent among the English-speaking community in Macau, engendering fierce discussions in which each party defended their own country with the utmost patriotic zeal. In this respect, Fanny Trollope's *Domestic Manners of the Americans* created furore, not letting Harriett's pen come to a rest for several months. The book and its impacts will be discussed later, when we take a closer look at the relations between the British and the Americans in Macau.

But after all this serious and rather down-to-earth reading, Harriett would not have been a normal young woman, if she had not enjoyed reading novels too. One of her favourite authors was Sir Walter Scott, a master of the historic novel. Sometimes novels even served as a kind of real-life substitute. When feeling deprived of friendship, love, and adventures, the identification with a literary figure "who has it all" offered some consolation in this respect:

> *I am getting into a bad way of reading novels. It is the only*
> *excitement we have; we are all miserably stupid. (24.1.1833)*

A few months later she made a similar observation: *"I allow myself a novel now and then as sauce piquante" (22.5.1833)*. These remarks coincided indeed with a difficult time in her life, when she found herself a lonely spinster again, after the marriage of her friend Caroline Shillaber and the break-up of her own secret engagement with William Wood, and above all she tired of Macau. In spite of her criticism, however, novels constituted a regular reading. Only occasionally she lashed out at them, depending very much on her state of mind:

> *Vachell sent me a novel after dinner which I spent the evening in*
> *looking over but have read it before, and am glad for I don't want*
> *novels. I hate to see them come into the house, for they are*
> *bewitching. One must, however, read the novels of the days for*
> *small talk. (14.8.1832)*

But since Harriett Low was very cross with Vachell at that moment, this observation must not be taken too seriously.

Many of the authors read by her have faded into oblivion in the meantime or are known only to a specialised public, although they may have enjoyed a large readership at their time. With a few exceptions, they were all British authors, because the USA, though politically independent from Great Britain for more than half a century, were still deeply influenced by it in cultural matters, and had not yet established a strong literary tradition of their own.[8] The few American authors of lasting renown on her reading list were Washington Irving (1783–1859) and James Fenimore Cooper (1789–1851).

Harriett was deeply impressed by Byron (1788–1824) for his poetry, especially his *Childe Harold*, which she read several times and whence she quoted some of her favourite verses for her sister. However, she did not at all sympathise with Byron's personality and lifestyle, which perhaps contributed as much to his fame as his writing:

> *When reading his poetry you wish almost that nothing of his*
> *character had ever been known. He was a creature of impulse and*

> *no principles at all, and therefore you cannot respect him, or think*
> *with any pleasure of the man, but mourn that he did not make*
> *himself all that he might have been. (15.5.1833)*

His poetry even inspired her to initiate herself in this art, but without much
success:

> *Forgot to tell you after reading Lord Byron last night and after*
> *taking the Expenses of the day, I filled the paper with <u>poetry</u> which*
> *has just afforded Aunt Low a good laugh, says she shall send it to*
> *Canton. Perhaps it will adorn a <u>column</u> in the Canton register.*
> *She told Mrs. D[avis?] and she has given me the name of <u>Byrona</u>.*

Still at the same day, a small gift was at the origin of some more poetry:

> *Mr. Vachell in and brought me a beautiful <u>rose</u> which about 10*
> *o'clock produced some more poetry, I think of a <u>higher</u> <u>order</u>, have*
> *some hopes of myself, think in the course of time I may be a*
> *<u>POETESS</u>. (13.4.1831)*[9]

As this was the only time when she expressed such hopes, we can assume that
she recognised her own lack of talent in this respect and sooner or later gave up
trying. As already mentioned, she also read Shakespeare, though not for his verse
but his drama.

Since Harriett Low studied French and Spanish, she also read popular works
in these two languages. In French, she read plays by Molière and Racine, and,
among others, books by fashionable and accomplished female authors such as
de Staël (1766–1817), Cottin (1770–1807), de Sévigné (1626–1696), and de
Genlis (1746–1830).

> *I was reading this morning de Genlis' Palais de la Vérité. People*
> *were put into a Palace of Truth where they spoke all their thoughts*
> *and their real thoughts. They were all diverted of politeness and*
> *dissimulation of all kinds when there, and appeared in their real*
> *characters, undressed and unadorned by art. It is very good and*
> *very well told, and gives a very good idea of what the state of affairs*
> *would be if every one spoke the truth and the whole truth.*
> *(14.8.1833)*

She read comparatively less in Spanish, one of the works being Cervantes's *Don
Quixote*. This was mainly due to the low availability of Spanish literature in
Macau.

A great majority of the books did not belong to her or her Uncle, but made
their round among friends or were borrowed from the British East India

Company's Library at Macau, which was established in 1806. According to a catalogue of 1832, it contained some 1,600 different works in about 4,000 volumes.[10]

> *Sent to the Library for some books but could not get them, and so had to read Molière. There are very few French books in the Library. (17.6.1833)*

Another attempt at getting the desired books failed, too, although the librarian tried to offer an alternative:

> *Wanted a French book. Sent to the Library for the Memoirs of "Cardinal de Ritz". They sent me ¹/₂ a dozen old worm eaten vol[ume]s which I am sure I shall never read. Beside I do not care about knowing about all the intrigues, I am not enough of a politician. I am sure by the looks of them they must be very tedious, so I shall send them back forthwith. (26.6.1833)*

Sometimes it was even difficult to get the desired books in English:

> *I am very anxious to read an Embassy to Pekin but they have carried all the best to Canton. (19.10.1833)*

As regards newspapers, one English-language newspaper existed when the Lows arrived at Macau, the weekly *Canton Register*. It was founded by James Matheson and William W. Wood in 1827. After the foundation of Hong Kong it was transferred there, becoming the *Hongkong Register*. Other English-language newspapers were born (and died) and their success is registered in the journal. One of them was the *Canton Miscellany*, which appeared in May of 1831.

> *Oh by the bye, this morning was born to the city of Macao a book entitled* Canton Miscellany, *an anonymous production. No one is known to write for it, it springs up no one knows from whence. I devoured it instantly, glad to get any thing new. Some capital pieces in it. (9.5.1831)*

It was printed at the Company's press in Macau, but apparently a mere five numbers were published.[11] Only two months later, a new periodical made its debut:

> *The first number of the* Chinese Courier *edited by Mr. Wood reached us to day, a very spirited beginning, if he goes on as he begins. But people say there is not matter enough for two papers in Canton. I am afraid he will make himself enemies, for where*

> *there is opposition, there must be difference of opinion and they*
> *will not hesitate to let each other and every body else know it*
> *through the medium of their papers. It is a pity I think in as small*
> *a place — he already <u>fires</u> at the Chief, Ma[r]joribanks[12] and the*
> *[Canton] Register and Dr. Morrison. (30.7.1831)*

Harriett's fears would prove true, even faster than she thought:

> *Another of Wood's papers out to day, by which he has lost 41*
> *subscribers <u>smack</u> … he is too severe upon the Company. I do*
> *not think he has done right. (15.8.1831)*

Obviously, the *Chinese Courier* was short-lived.[13] The last English-language periodical to make its appearance during their stay in Macau was *The Chinese Repository*, a monthly begun by the American missionary Bridgman, with Morrison's help. The first number was published in Canton in May 1832, and the last in December 1851.[14] According to Downs, *"virtually everyone in the community subscribed it"*.[15]

Apart from the local press, Harriett was always anxious to receive newspapers from the USA.

> *This morning my first salutation was, "H[arriett], do you want to*
> *read some New York papers?" I started instantly, hoping to find*
> *in some sly corner between the papers a letter, but no. … We have*
> *had a variety of bits of new today, of one kind and another. The*
> *papers were those silly [Boston] advertisers, nothing or precious little*
> *in them except advertisements. Very glad to hear or see anything*
> *from home. (28.7.1830)*

> *Boston Advertiser, what a paper to send to China. Why did they*
> *not send some Salem papers. (3.8.1830)*

The answer to this question may be that the family had moved on to Brooklyn, where Salem papers were not easily available perhaps. While for them Salem was a finished chapter of their lives, apart from many personal ties with the friends left behind, for Harriett it was her hometown and last point of reference in the USA.

Studying foreign languages

When travelling to a foreign place with the intention to live there for several years, one might consider it natural to learn the language of the country. In the case of Macau this would be Portuguese or Chinese. While it never crossed

Harriett's mind, not even in her dreams, to study Chinese because of a number of reasons, such as the difficulty of the language and the great differences in social status between her and the Chinese surrounding her, prohibiting any contact beyond the master-servant roles, Portuguese could have been a more accessible and useful language to her. But seemingly, if we may generalise from what is written in the journal about the relations between her family and the Portuguese in Macau, there was not much socialising going on between the two groups, that is the Western foreigners and the Portuguese and Macanese. The only Portuguese family name that Harriett mentions with certain regularity is Pereira. Other Portuguese names are dropped casually, but very infrequently. Moreover, Portuguese from "good families" in Macau spoke English or some words of French, thus making the knowledge of Portuguese not an absolute necessity for her.

> *The Macaistas generally speak English, and are a kind and hospitable people.*[16]

Therefore, Harriett dedicated her efforts to the study of Spanish and French, for which she had native-tongue teachers.

> *Went to Mrs. Allport's, where we found Mrs. Turner and Mr. Otaduy, a Spanish gentleman, and to morrow we all commence taking Spanish lessons of him in Spanish. He has kindly offered to assist us; quite delighted, I'll assure you. He encourages us that in six months we shall speak. Well, time will prove.* (8.3.1830)

Harriett was an enthusiastic student:

> *I was up two hours before breakfast studying the Spanish verbs with all my might, which always gives me a good appetite.* (16.3.1830)

But the first opportunity to practise her Spanish with a Spaniard other than her teacher came too early, provoking a short blackout:

> *Who should appear but Mr. Otaduy followed by Don Gabriel Yorietta Goyenne. What do you think of that for a name. They call him however Goyenne. He is the Chief of the Spanish Factory. I knew he could speak no English and every word of Spanish I knew fled from me at the first sight of him. After he had been here a while I recollected what I knew but could not muster confidence to speak it to him. I could understand the most that he said. After a while I made out to say — he was talking of the languages —*

> *and I made out to say in reply that application was the only mode*
> *of learning and never shall I forget how smart I felt at uttering that*
> *sentence. He said <u>very</u> <u>well</u>, but I was pleased that I could*
> *understand so well what he said. (16.4.1830)*

Half a year later, after an intensive period of study, their progress was respectable:

> *Took our Spanish lesson today, wrote a letter in Spanish which*
> *Mr. Otaduy pronounced very well (muy bien). He was astonished*
> *he said. (31.8.1830)*

The Spanish lessons continued until the end of 1832, the year when the Spanish factory in Canton was discontinued, and both their Spanish teachers Otaduy and later also Joaquin Ybar, who was the last agent of the Spanish factory, left the China coast.

At a certain stage, however, the study of French took prevalence over Spanish:

> *Day before yesterday Mr. Goyenne called here and made me talk*
> *Spanish to him, but I have neglected it of late in attending to*
> *French. (2.2.1832)*

In Macau with its multilingual population, they succeeded in arranging a real Frenchman to teach them:

> *This morning Caroline came to us and young Calvo who is kind*
> *enough and hear us read French that we might get a good*
> *pronunciation. We intend to study hard now. We commenced*
> *reading the letters of Madame de Sévigné. And he is kind enough*
> *to say he will come twice a week. This took most of our morning*
> *and when we speak well we shall find great pleasure in it.*
> *(1.4.1833)*

But Calvo would be their teacher for only five months, much to the regret of his students. His leaving, as the departure of their Spanish teachers before, illustrates one characteristic of Macau that has not changed since — the transitoriness of many relations in the small Western community:

> *Calvo came this morning for the last time as he goes to Manilla*
> *tomorrow. I am very sorry as we shall lose our French lessons.*
> *... He is very discontented here and says he never shall be happy*
> *till he returns to* la belle patrie. *(13.8.1833)*

Harriett felt compelled to explain to her sister, why she spent so much time studying languages:

> You may think I spend a great deal of time learning languages and so I do, but I do not feel that I waste the time, for independently of the pleasure and benefit of learning the language, or rather of knowing it, I think it is of advantage having some fixed occupation. It fixes the attention too. I might spend a great deal of time in reading but in the warm weather one is apt to fall into a <u>dreamy</u> state over a book. You become weary of constant reading and require some stimulus to make any exertion. So I think it far better to divide the time as I do, and I always feel that I have not a moment to waste. It requires an effort at times to study, but I exert myself and I find I always fret <u>less</u>. If I think much of home and other things I become discontented & unhappy, thereby making myself uncomfortable in the present time. (13.5.1833)

Thus the study of languages functioned as yet another occupational therapy in order to combat the monotony of (unmarried) female life in Macau.

Gardening and pets

One of the pastimes enjoyed by many women in Macau, Harriett being no exception, was gardening. Two days after having moved to their second house, which had only a large terrace but no garden as the previous one, she took care of this:

> Went to the flower gardens. Bought some beautiful flowers to put upon our terrace, a beautiful white Camilla Japonica, passion flowers, and some others. One called the nun [?] flower is a very singular one. (1.4.1830)

One year later, Harriett already had a considerable number of flower pots:

> My garden is coming on, I have about 30 pots now and at this present time they are in a flourishing condition. But the situation is not good for them. The wind is too strong I believe, and from the sea too. (13.4.1831)

Although the servants could have taken care of the flowers, handling them, as every gardener knows, gives some kind of personal satisfaction:

> Have just made my bouquet. The first thing I do after breakfast is to go to the terrace, trim my plants and make up a Bouquet for the centre table. (14.4.1831)

Many gents took advantage of Harriett's interest in gardening as a pretext to give her small presents, either in the form of plants and seeds, or other paraphernalia such as rocks or seashells.

> Mr. Gordon has just sent me a root of a splendid flower. It is called a sort of white lily, but I never saw it at home. (30.6.1830)

Now and then, a gift of flowers is something special. Having a certain symbolic meaning attached to them, flowers may also be a substitute for words, where both giver and receiver understand the flower language. After the arrival of her friend Caroline Shillaber, the art of gardening reached new heights:

> Went [Harriett and Caroline] into the flower garden. Saw a China[man] making a small jet d'eau of rock, coral, etc. It struck us we could surpass him. So we told S. P. Sturgis who we met [after]wards he must find us some rocks, and that we wanted some coral. He promised to do all he could, so we shall enlist them as they come along. H. Robinson joined me soon after and I told him C[aroline] and I had an idea between us, and told him our wants. Says he will get us some coral. In the course of time we may succeed. They are very anxious to know what we are about. (18.6.1832)

Unfortunately we never get a description of the completed project, which seemed to have been quite ambitious, and mobilised a number of gentlemen too.

> Busy all the morning working upon one grotto or whatever. Set B[light] to work to get us moss etc. Get along famously. (30.6.1832)

Another pastime, thought to enhance a sense of responsibility in children and awaken maternal feelings in girls, was keeping pets. In Harriett's case, they were not bought but received as presents:

> Returned home, where I found that good man Dr. Colledge. He stayed with us an hour. Offered me a pony, but I have no place to keep and take care of it. I therefore declined the kind offer. (18.11.1829)

Yet other, less voluminous pets were accepted with pleasure:

> Mr. Beale sent me two Canary birds today. I suspect they will give me much pleasure. (19.8.1830)

But Harriett apparently had no luck with animals:

> *My poor little bird was brought in dead, much to my sorrow. Never can keep anything, only am surprised it should have lived so long.* (25.10.1831)

In an undated letter to her youngest sister Ellen, Harriett mentioned to be the owner of a dog, a fact that is never referred to in the journal.

> *I have a little dog to which I call Fidélité. he is a black terrier we want him to catch* <u>*rats*</u>.[17]

Probably Fidélité experienced the same fate as Harriett's birds, or he died from lack of rats in the Low household.

Tailoring, cutting out and sewing

As regards the domestic sphere, the only task perhaps that was not executed satisfactorily by the Chinese was cutting out female dresses and sewing them together, thus forcing the women to do it themselves. Interestingly, some of Harriett's observations on Chinese tailors may sound rather familiar to many Western women who ever tried to have clothes made in Macau, that is by private Chinese tailors.[18] While preparing a dress for a ball, Harriett complained:

> *There are none but men tailors here. We are obliged to cut and fix our own dresses, thinking them more trouble than they will do good, as it is difficult to make them understand the language.* (13.10.1829)

On another occasion she dropped a remark that continues to apply to certain present-day tailors.

> *We could not give them to the Tailor. They* <u>*smoke*</u> *[up] every thing they take and unless the article is to be washed it is not pleasant.* (18.10.1833)

Although she did not identify the smell, it must be either cigarettes or incense, burnt at the domestic altar, or both. In Macau, Harriett's clothes needed more mending than back home:

> *You must know I have to be my own tailor now. All my dresses want repairing, for the washman beats them to pieces dreadfully.*[19]

Unluckily for Harriett, sewing was an activity for which she showed little inclination, initially at least.

> *Cut out a gown and basted it, much to Caroline's amusement.*
> *She says my things <u>drop</u> together. (28.5.1832)*

Sometimes the consequences of careless needlework could be quite embarrassing:

> *We [together with her uncle and aunt] went to Casillas Bay. The*
> *tide was galloping in at a great rate. ... As I was going down the*
> *little descent I turned round and saw something white streaming*
> *upon the ground, apparently attached to me. For the first moment*
> *I could not divine what it could be. You remember a certain cord*
> *called <u>cable cord</u> that ladies put in their under petticoats to set them*
> *out. Well, by some means or other this worked itself out ¹/₂ a <u>yard</u>.*
> *The tuck got ripped (having <u>certain long stitches</u> because it has to*
> *be undone when washed). Well, what I should do with it I could*
> *not tell, but fortunately I pulled it wholly out and gave it to Uncle*
> *to pocket. I suspect this was also seen by the gentlemen upon the*
> *hill. ... I was very glad there were no other gentlemen <u>with me</u> to*
> *witness the cord <u>scrape</u>. (7.4.1830)*

But the Lows met the gentlemen of the hill on their way home. To Harriett's great embarrassment they admitted to having been very amused at the scrape, though unable to assist because of the great distance.

However, as time went by, her attitude towards dressmaking changed gradually, and a year later, after having completed a morning dress, she called herself jokingly *"an <u>experienced mantua maker</u>"* (14.3.1831). This ability was to be very useful to her, as the fair sex, then as now, is always subject to the demands of fashion:

> *Pulled out old dresses to day and find the great sleeves worn last*
> *summer will have to be cut out. Oh dear what a job. What slaves*
> *to fashion women are. (28.3.1831)*

Seemingly it would not be the last occasion for Harriett to alter the sleeves of a dress, because two years later, when Chinnery painted her portrait, we see her wearing enormous sleeves again. In 1833, the time when her friend Caroline married, Harriett felt so secure in this *métier*, that she took it upon herself to help with the wedding preparations.

Apart from dresses, Harriett also made capes, bonnets, collars and a corset for herself, as well as shirts and wristbands for her Uncle. One item that was seemingly difficult to arrange in Macau were ladies' gloves, and therefore special care had to be taken with them. After an hour or so spent in mending gloves, Harriett sighed: *"Wish I could just run into a shop in Broadway"* (14.6.1831). But she was also fortunate to receive several pairs as a gift:

> Mrs. Turner called this morning, and brought me two pair of nice gloves, too small for her — the ladies have an idea that I have the smallest hand in the place. This is the 5th pair I think that I have had given me. It is very convenient when one's stock is quite out. (5.3.1831)

And seemingly there were still other ways to supply oneself with this rare item: *"An old bet from Mr. Blight also rec[eive]d — two pair of gloves"* (1.3.1832).

Outdoor activities

Walking

Macau offered a variety of beautiful spots and scenery, providing plenty of room for physical exercise and mental distraction, to help one forget, at least for a while, homesickness or lovesickness, or both. Already at that time walking was considered as an antidote to obesity, which in the absence of both physical and mental work threatened to attack especially the ladies, who led a very opulent life-style: *"I am growing so fat that I want to walk it down"* (27.10.1833). Therefore, Harriett was always ready for a vigorous walk. The use of seamen's language and metaphors in the following quotation illustrates that her seafaring past was still very much alive in her memory.

> This afternoon Mr. Vachell called for us to walk. We went, not being aware that the wind blew very high, and foolishly ascended a high hill, where I am sure it would have been much more safe to have scud than to have gone as we did with royals and studding sails out. Although I kept crying, stand by top gallant Halyards it was of no avail. We were beating against the wind. And when at the height of the precipice my dress entangled round Mr. Vachell's legs, and in trying to extricate himself he caught his foot in the trimming which came very near throwing us both over the precipice into the sea. And great would have been the fall thereof. But after much labour we weathered the gale and arrived safely under the lee of the hill. Aunt Low and Mrs. Allport were wise enough to

*turn back. But Mr. Vachell and I are much alike in that respect;
we both dislike turning back and will persevere if possible.
(9.1.1830)*

Although the use of mariners' language subsides later in the journal, comparisons between sails and women's clothes continue to appear once in a while. Considering the amount of fabric needed to produce the dress of a lady at that time, the comparison is not too far-fetched.

Women rarely walked longer distances, even the younger ones:

*Now you must know that Aunt Low and Mrs. Allport always go
in their chairs and I am the only one that walks. (16.6.1830)*

The ladies would be carried to a certain spot and would only get out there to stretch their limbs and walk a little, before being carried home again. According to Harriett, their sedan chairs had been made in Canton. They used to be carried by two coolies, who were employed by the respective households. Yet considering Macau's climate, one may wonder who should be deplored more, the chair bearers or their freight:

*Went out in our new chairs, they are very handsome, but just like
hot houses. We have as yet no venetians and the glass draws the
sun. I was glad to get home. (2.11.1829)*

An advantage of the chairs was, of course, that their occupants could go out during rain without wetting their feet.

Apart from the more physical aspects of walking, such as for reasons of health and restoring one's psychological and emotional equilibrium through contemplating nature, walking also had social connotations attached to it. The rule most detested by Harriett was that an unmarried young lady could not go out alone, but had to be accompanied by a chaperone, usually a family member or some other trusted person:

*I have no one to walk with me and it is not proper for me to go
alone, so that I cannot have the privilege of walking when I like.
(12.11.1829)*

This situation of dependency only finished with Caroline's arrival, when the two girls could sally forth together. However, it was not always easy to come to an agreement about where to go:

*For her the Campo being new has more charms than for me, and
I am very glad not to see it for a few days. (27.2.1832)*

But a few weeks later, Harriett seemed to have reconciled with the Campo again:

> *After dinner we went out to our "<u>place</u>"; we have a place and a "<u>tomb</u>" on the Campo, which we visit as suits our disposition at the time. The tomb is a large Chinese tomb with a commanding view and where we <u>see</u> without being seen. The "<u>place</u>" is very much exposed to the <u>highway</u> and we are there seen by everyone. (27.4.1832)*

Furthermore, when walking in a group, not every gentleman could offer his arm to a lady. Conventions of social rank and age had to respected and whoever dared to challenge them, had to suffer the consequences:

> *After dinner walked out with Uncle, was joined by Talbot and Vachell. Vachell offered his arm first and I had to take it. I shall have to <u>cut</u> him yet. Uncle shakes his head and says it will <u>not do</u>. (6.7.1831)*

The British chaplain Vachell was quite desperately and unsuccessfully in love with Harriett, which had already given rise to talks between uncle and niece and to some gossiping too. Vachell should have let any of the other two gentlemen, William H. Low or Talbot, at that time the U.S. consul at Canton, offer their arm to Harriett first. Less than two weeks later, another incidental encounter between Harriett, Talbot and Vachell illustrates the complications and fears that a simple walk in Macau, involving a disobedient young lady, could provoke:

> *After dinner I went out in my chair, thinking I should meet Mrs. Allport at a little spot where we usually go Sunday eve'gs and thought I would have ¹/₂ an hour à la solitaire before she got there, a lovely eve'g. I had no sooner comfortably seated myself than who should I see at my side but Mr. Talbot. I was a little vexed at first as some people might say it was an <u>appointment</u>. We set there till it was time to go to Dr. Morrison's, and then set out to walk to my chair, and who should I come pounce upon but <u>Vachell</u>. He gave me a cold bow and we passed on. Also met Mrs. Daniell and Mat[thew]. Mr. Vachell's face said Yes, you have often refused to walk with me alone. (17.7.1831)*

Drawing, painting and to be painted

Drawing and painting seemed to have been a rather common pastime, both among men and women. Perhaps due to the absence of photography at that time more people felt compelled to develop their skills in this field, in order to be able to perpetuate a dear person, a beautiful landscape or just to illustrate letters. Apart from a few small sketches in the journal, such as of a centipede-like or caterpillar-like sea creature, of their boat *Sumatra* anchoring in a bay near Manila, or of a private residence in Macau, no graphical productions of Harriett Low appear to have survived outside the journal. But, frankly speaking, this does not seem a great loss to mankind, judging from the very basic quality of these drawings. Thus, the only interesting question, namely whether her style improved after having had drawing lessons with the great Chinnery, unfortunately cannot be answered.[20]

Before starting her lessons with Chinnery, Harriett had already visited his studio several times, in order to look at portraits and to see other people pose. At that time it seemed unimaginable that her turn to be painted would ever come true:

> *I forgot to say that I went to Chinnery the portrait painter's room yesterday. He has some fine likenesses. He is remarkably successful. How I wished that I had a little of the needful that I could put into the man's hand that he might take my <u>beautiful phiz</u> that I might transport it across the great waters into your own hands, for I flatter myself you would like it. But there, what's the use of wishing. (8.12.1829)*

Besides, a whole Chinnery-copying industry seemed to have existed in Macau and Canton, making one wonder whether all the "Chinnerys" in museums, galleries or private hands are real ones or copies ...

> *I have been employed in copying some views for Mrs. Cleveland from Chinnery's sketches. She will soon leave us, to our sorrow. (7.1.1830)[21]*

Harriett started her drawing lessons with Chinnery in April of 1830, and continued them on a rather irregular schedule:

> *Went to Mr. Chinnery's this morning ... Mr. Chinnery had a table and every thing fixed for me to go to drawing. He has been very anxious for me to draw, but I thought I might give him some trouble and I would not. (10.4.1830)*

Apparently, the lessons at Chinnery consisted mainly of copying:

> *Went to Chinnery's this morning with Mrs. Allport. Finished some*
> *very pretty sketches copied from his. (29.4.1830)*

The next mention of Chinnery only occurred two months later, when Harriett
had not seen him for a long time:

> *We concluded to go to Mrs. Turner's — a perfect evening, had*
> *tea on the terrace. The party was much larger than I expected,*
> *mustered quite strong. Chinnery was there, talking to me about*
> *sketching. I told him it was in vain for me to attempt it, I had not*
> *a pencil that would make a mark. He says why have you not called*
> *on Mr. Chinnery. Did he not tell you that he would be only too*
> *happy to supply you. We had a long confab about it. And then he*
> *asked me if he would lend me his book of sketches for one month*
> *if I would promise to show him 12 copies fit to send to America*
> *and to say they were copied from Mr. Chinnery's. I told him in*
> *return I should be only "<u>too happy</u>" so to do, and would do my*
> *best. He would supply me with pencils. (6.7.1830)*

But some information or gossip about Chinnery made her change her mind:

> *Heard something this evening which will rather prevent (if I can*
> *any way get off) my taking Chinnery's <u>sketches</u>. I am sorry for I*
> *had anticipated much pleasure in taking them. (7.7.1830)*

We can only speculate about the reasons Harriett had for wanting to withdraw,
perhaps Chinnery's fame (whether true or not) as a womaniser, or perhaps some
untold fee involved in the borrowing of the sketchbook? But Harriett continued
to visit Chinnery's studio, since many of her acquaintances had their portrait
done by him. For some time, however, she kept her distance from Chinnery and
her passion for drawing seemed to have waned.

Yet with the arrival, in March 1831, of William W. Wood, a young
American merchant from Philadelphia, whom we already know as editor of
newspapers and author, and now as amateur painter, Harriett found herself quite
interested in drawing again.[22] A week before her rediscovered pleasure in
drawing, Wood had supplied her with drawing utensils and encouraging words:

> *He [W.H. Low] brought me a <u>letter</u> from Mr. Wood with a*
> *quantity of Lithographic prints for me to copy with some very pretty*
> *engravings, a new Souvenir (a present) for 1831, some very pretty*
> *engravings — four nice pencils, a piece of India rubber, a pen knife*

> *& etc. He wishes me to draw, & I am sure I am very fond of it,*
> *and shall set about it instantly. (15.3.1831)*

Wood, who was captured by Harriett's charms before she was aware of it, considered himself Harriett's teacher in this field, thus having one more opportunity to write to her from Canton, or to see her in Macau. But two years later, after the break-up of the relations between Wood and Harriett, drawing again ceased to be one of her favourite pastimes. When sketching once more at Chinnery's studio, she became aware of this:

> *Drew a little but I do not take the same interest in this amusement*
> *as I did last year. The change of masters makes a great difference*
> *I find. Besides it recalls many circumstances which were as well*
> *forgotten. (18.5.1833)*

However, a few months before their departure from Macau, the desire to show "her" Macau to the family at home and to obtain a lasting image of its most beautiful spots, compelled Harriett to take up drawing again.

> *Took my drawing after breakfast and was employed till 2 in*
> *finishing a sketch which satisfied me and now only long for the time*
> *when I shall have the pleasure of showing it to you and bringing to*
> *your view the representation of places so familiar to my eyes. This*
> *one is a view of the barrier which I have so often spoken of. It will*
> *also recall to my mind many a long walk and agreeable*
> *conversations, as well as some dreary and desolate ones. After I*
> *had finished it I dressed and carried Mr. C[hinnery]'s book home*
> *as he is afraid to trust it to Coolies. I only went to the door and*
> *he came down to my chair, and I suspect from his appearance I*
> *roused him from a good nap — and I dare say he wished me and*
> *his book any where. He says he can do nothing the weather is so*
> *hot. It is the complaint of every one. (20.7.1833)[23]*

In the fourth year of their stay in Macau, her uncle decided that everybody would have their portrait painted by Chinnery. Harriett's description of this process is a very lively one, worthy of being quoted at length:

> *Went to Chinnery's myself this morning to have my phiz painted.*
> *Great presumption on my part I think, but it was at the request*
> *of Uncle & Aunt and the thought of the pleasure it would give to*
> *you all, that induced me. I sat there an hour looking at one of the*
> *ugliest men in existence, but he makes himself so agreeable that*

you quite forget how ugly he is. He requested my <u>mouth</u> to be open, a thing which I abominate in a picture, but he says it will never do to have it shut, for I generally have it a little open.

> *"Oh wad some power the giftie gie us*
> *To see oursel's as others see us."*

Now I am sure I was not aware that I was in the habit of it — it is the ugly formation of it. Well there I set with my head screwed and twisted in a strange manner. Then after he had finished the first sketch I looked at it. Oh ye powers! what a thing. And yet I think it must be like because I saw mother's look about the eyes, also Cousin Forster's, whom I was always said to resemble. But such a <u>fright</u> — I have laughed 51 times since to think of it. The head appeared about ready to take leave of the neck. The mouth open as though I was snoring — a little something yclept <u>nose</u> and a place where eyes should be. I suppose I must wait with patience for a few more sittings but I think it will rather lower my <u>vanity</u> though on the subject of personal appearance I never had much. Nous verons how it will turn out. (10.4.1833)

At the next session Harriett thought that Chinnery was doing even better with her portrait than he should:

> *At 11 I went there and looked at the man till 2, when I found myself in better humour with my portrait which I think will be an excellent likeness and a little paint will make it I fear better looking than I am. But if you see the likeness you can make allowances for paint. (15.4.1833)*

As regards the conditions in which painter and model worked, they seemed to have been rather sudorific, mainly considering that the large sleeves of Harriett's dress were created through the introduction of down pillows!

> *It is not very pleasant sitting there, for it is a little bit of a room and no windows open it. (20.4.1833)*

At another session, Chinnery changed something in his model, characterising her even better because of her great passion for reading:

> *He has made a little alteration, put a book in the hand, and I like it much better. (25.4.1833)*

As Harriett's portrait neared its conclusion, the story of its perfect likeness was already all over Macau and Canton:

> *It is said by every one to be perfect. They think I must have run against the canvass and left an impression — so I think of the pleasure with which you will see it and it consoles me for all the exertion I make in this hot weather. (10.5.1833)*

Her aunt's picture, which was completed before hers, was not that perfect apparently, because a few days after having come home, it returned to Chinnery's *"undergoing operations"* (8.5.1833).[24] But Harriett did not specify the nature of them.

Chinnery died in Macau in May 1852 and is buried on the Protestant Cemetery. William C. Hunter, who assisted his last hours and the post-mortem examination carried out on the same day, described this sad moment in his *Bits of Old China.*[25]

Horse Riding

For a short time during her stay in Macau Harriett took up riding. The suggestion for doing so came from a gentleman:

> *Alexander [surname] & I had a great deal of chat. Wishes me to ride his horse, a new one, a beauty, however I declined. But he said he should certainly have it decked for me some day, with side saddle, etc. (23.8.1831)*

The first opportunity for riding came soon after this conversation, although not on Alexander's horse:

> *After dinner King came in for us and we went out to our hill. Mr. Lindsay joined us on horseback, but dismounted and seated himself with us on the turf. He was walking by my side leading his horse as we were going home. I said to him if that was a side saddle, I should be for mounting. He said he thought he could make it one and he shortened the stirrup, and I actually mounted and rode home. It put me in mind of the last time I rode, which was on the "old mare" at Grandmother Eaton's. (5.9.1831)*

After that ride Harriett decided to write a letter to her uncle in Canton, asking for his permission to do so. One of her first rides, on a pony prepared for her, took her right to China, obviously against her will:

> Had a most delightful ride. Cantered and galloped. My pony not content with going to the Barrier [Gate], leaped through the gate and was unwilling to come out. I only felt afraid of the Chinese. They are not at all civil and sometimes stone people if they intrude. (16.11.1831)

After another adventure, but mainly because of Caroline's arrival the following month, riding was finally given up:

> Rode after dinner with our usual party. A splendid evening. Had a slight fall from my pony. My habit hitched on the rocks and the saddle twisted round. I fell as though I had fallen on to a bed and did not feel the least injured. Mounted again and cantered off in great style. Shall not tell Aunt Low. (22.11.1831)

Riding seems to have been quite a passion among the British, females included, and a good horse was certainly a status symbol. Sometimes, mainly when the men had come down from Canton, there even was something like a "horse jam":

> While we were there [on the hills] 18 equestrians passed, 16 of them all in a row. Made a great show for Macao. (17.4.1830)

Social life and socialising

Social gatherings: dinners, teas, parties and balls

Already in the first days after their arrival in Macau, the Lows discovered that the people in this place liked to socialise a lot and to show off their wealth.

> The ladies wear nothing but those elegant wrought dresses common in summer time. They are thought nothing of as evening dresses. The jewels they wear is beyond account. It is impossible to keep up with them at all, but I have no ambition to. All I wish is to make a decent appearance, but Uncle wishes us to have everything handsome, but I had much rather save the money to help us to get home for I cannot say that I have any desire to spend my life here.[26]

They also understood that there was no escape for them, although the non-observance of the Saturday evening, as a preparation for Sunday, and making calls on Sundays, would be criticised for a very long time. Since everybody in the foreign community was curious about the newcomers, they were virtually showered with courtesy visits and invitations in the days following their arrival.

> *Mr. Van Caneghem, Dutch Consul, and Capt. Whitehead, H[onourable] C[ompany's] S[ervice] called this morning. Invited us to a musical party on Tuesday eve. Amounts to a ball. All the ladies of Macao are to be there, but we shall decline. Macao is very gay at present, a great many strangers here. (3.10.1829)*

But the next invitation, a week later, to a Fancy Ball was accepted and marked their entry into the local foreign community.

> *Mrs. Turner came over this morning. Spent an hour and a half with us. She is a sweet woman. Brought two large books of costumes for us to choose from for the Ball. (8.10.1829)*

On the day of the ball, the Lows received no calls, seemingly everybody in town was busy preparing for the event.

> *We went at 8 o'clock to Mrs. Turner's to call for her. From there to Mr. Whitehead's where we enjoyed ourselves much and returned at 3 o'clock, the first time in my life that I was ever out so late. Every thing was elegant. The costumes of all countries and ages. … We had some fireworks in the court in front of the house. (16.10.1829)*

Life in Macau followed the Latin pace, with people staying up late, something that the Lows had to get used to. Being young, however, Harriett got into the rhythm quite fast and only one week later, after another evening entertainment we read:

> *The party broke up about 2. I thought it impossible that it was more than 12. (23.10.1829)*

As Harriett was one of the few young unmarried ladies around for some time, she was very much in demand as a partner for dancing or at the table:

> *I danced every dance but one and when I came away was engaged for the 4 next quadrilles. So you see I am coming on. They will not take no for an answer. (30.10.1829)[27]*

She had to proceed to advance-booking, in order not to offend any gentleman:

> *I danced every time and got into quite a hobble, for I engaged for*
> *four, <u>deep</u> — about the middle of the evening. And when it came*
> *to the third could not tell for the life of me who I had engaged to*
> *dance with. 2 gentlemen came and both claimed me for that one,*
> *and both were equally urgent. I however danced with Mr. Card,*
> *hoping there was time for 2, but poor Morris was deferred till the*
> *first dance the next evening — when that will be no one knows.*
> *I do not tell this with the <u>least vanity</u> Molly, for it would not be so*
> *if there were many ladies here. But you know they are scarce here.*
> *There are 20 times the number of gentlemen, only a little <u>sprinkling</u>*
> *of ladies. I have no rivals, as there is but one other spinster [Rebecca*
> *Morrison] in the place. ... We left the party highly gratified with*
> *our evenings amusement. ... It was about 2 when we arrived*
> *home. (18.11.1829)*

But soon the excitement and the novelty of these parties passed. Instead, they were increasingly accompanied by a feeling of dissatisfaction:

> *Spent the evening with Mrs. Daniell, a large party. Mrs. Kierulf[28]*
> *was there, had some good music, but I must say I come home from*
> *these parties quite wretched. I never feel half so lonely as in these*
> *mixed parties. I am sure there was not a soul there except Mrs.*
> *Davis with whom I feel the least friendship. I almost resolve to go*
> *no more. Vachell was not there. He is my only friend among the*
> *gents. (7.5.1831)*

The Lows organised only one party of this kind during their stay in Macau, although not completely by their own will but due to social coercion.

> *This morning sent out invitations for a <u>party</u> Aunt Low intends*
> *giving on Wednesday Evening. Every body has been making parties*
> *for us [Caroline and Harriett], and we find from divers hints that*
> *[it] is thought Mrs. Low ought to give one too. She has two young*
> *ladies and no children to <u>bother</u> and to them there is no earthly*
> *reason why she should not & every reason why she should. All*
> *accepted but 4, I think. (9.4.1832)*

Everything was planned with great care, in order for the party to be successful.

> *Spent most of the morning in making preparations for the party.*
> *Had everything turned out of my room to make a supper room of*

it, because it opens into the drawing room and is quite magnificent. (10.4.1832)

Most of the fuss, however, was reserved for the day of the party itself:

> *Busy as a bee all day, got every thing elegant and in good order, but tired enough before the company came. Never mind that however — must dance all night. ... At 8 we were all adorned and ready. Aunt L[ow] had a China gauze over white satin, C[aroline] Pink aerophane over white, and my ladyship blue crape over White Satin. Our hair dressed with natural flowers that some* youths *sent us for the purpose.*
>
> *Ibar was master of ceremonies. He was not well, but made every thing agreeable. Said for the House of Spain he must do his best. We had a piano from Mrs. Daniell and Mr. Paiva and Mrs. Pereira played and sang beautifully at intervals. Had the Guitar too — 4 Portuguese musicians to the grinding of whose fiddles we danced. Danced every dance, and when they broke up about ¹/₂ past 1 I could have danced as much more. I had just got so much excited that I had forgotten my fatigue. We had a handsome supper and every thing in style, I assure you. We mustered about 40: English, 4* American ladies,[29] *Spanish, Portuguese, French, & Swede & Scotch, and I am sure I don't know what other countrymen there may have been. Made the Scotchman dance a* reel *which I joined in myself — every thing went off well and handsomely. (11.4.1832)*

But dancing parties are not everybody's style, and in compensation the Lows had something like an open house. Anybody who dropped by in the morning time, were sure to be offered a "dinner", which is the word used by Harriett to refer to lunch, and usually taken at around 2 o'clock. The same was true for the afternoon, when a substantial tea with sweet and salted dishes awaited the visitors. Some people were regular guests, others appeared more sporadically. Sentences like "Mr. X, and Mr. and Mrs. Y dined with us" or "they all took tea with us" are frequent in the journal.

The same is true for "calls", namely people dropping by for a variety of reasons, such as courtesy, curiosity, chatting, gossiping, bringing letters or invitations, boredom, and many others. Having been called upon, required reciprocity of action:

> *It is according to the Etiquette of the place to return calls soon after they are made. (7.10.1829)*

Harriett sometimes accumulated calls, and then returned them all together:

> *This morning equipped myself as fashion directs, and sallied forth*
> *to perpetrate calls on the good people of Macao as I was dressed*
> *rather early. I first went to Mrs. Allport's, then to Mrs. Crockett's,*
> *then to Mrs. Neish's, where I stayed near an hour. Have not been*
> *before since her arrival. She does not look near so interesting as*
> *the last year, though she is now in what is called an "interesting*
> *situation" [pregnancy]. She was very agreeable however. I almost*
> *wished I spoke Scotch myself. I then proceeded to Mrs. Morrison's*
> *and saw the family, to Mrs. Thornhill, she looked beautifully; then*
> *to Mrs. Pereira's, also a little, big, woman — and glad was I to*
> *say go home. It is an exertion to go out in the morning when it is*
> *so warm. I felt quite fagged out before I got home. Morris and*
> *Vachell had called in my absence. (5.7.1830)*

Being thus hospitable was facilitated by the circumstances in which they lived in Macau. Colonial life was, in general, characterised by a much higher living standard than at home. In all well-to-do households the women did not have to cook, they just had to be pretty and entertain their guests. Whether there were three or nine people for lunch was the cook's problem, never that of the lady of the house. Harriett marvelled at this new situation several times:

> *The tea parties at home are so much trouble that you cannot enjoy*
> *them, but here every thing is easy. If any thing is wrong, it is all*
> *laid to the servants. The lady is not blamed as at home. (5.4.1830)*

Another characteristic of the parties in Macau much appreciated by Harriett was their informality.

> *You would like these parties much, for we do just as we like, we*
> *are not confined to a circle and allowed to speak just when a*
> *gentleman chooses to address us. We have a band of music as Mr.*
> *Majoribanks says, to make a noise, a piano. Someone plays and*
> *sings and those who have not the power of charming with melodious*
> *sounds can walk the veranda with those they like best, sit sullen*
> *on a couch if you please or take a book. In fact, you are to suit*
> *yourself, have a little bit of a supper and go home. (25.7.1831)*

Apart from the informal dinners, teas, or evening parties at the private residences, there were also formal meals to celebrate a variety of events and, with certain regularity, (evening) dinners at the British East India Company's premises on Praia Grande. Depending on who escorted her to table, Harriett described these dinners as *"rather stiff"* (11.2.1830) or even as *"the greatest of all bores"* (26.8.1830). Sometimes she was luckier and more satisfied:

> *Vachell handed me to table. Set between him and Lindsay. If I could have chosen, those would have been the ones. (21.3.1831)*

These dinners seem to have been quite impressive due to their formality and duration. Everybody was waited upon by a personal servant behind his or her chair.

> *Hot night, but had to dress for the Company's: however with 5 Punkahs it is very comfortable. Only tires one sitting so long. I think we are at the table 2 hours. (23.8.1831)*[30]

Usually the ladies left first and the gentlemen stayed behind for a more comfortable continuation of the evening, without the fair sex. Once, however, the Low ladies' chair bearers had gone home and since the air outside was a bit cool for them to wait, they were asked in again:

> *We accordingly did, and to the great surprise of its inhabitants, for Mr. Lindsay and Mr. Innis, bachelor-like the moment the ladies had quitted the room had taken their cigar and were taking <u>real comfort</u>. The cigar was gone in less time than you could speak, but it took a longer time to deposit the ponderous tongs. It is a great offence to smoke in a room where ladies ever enter — but we were quite moderate upon them. They handed chairs and we set down, and it was really the pleasantest part of the evening. But too short; the carriages came in a few minutes. Mr. Lindsay says, "Miss Low, we are just scolding about the villainous formality of this place." Upon which we had a warm discussion joined by the cheers of the party and some reiterating, "That is <u>right</u>, Miss Low, give it to them; they deserve it." (11.2.1830)*

But the fair sex were not far behind the men as regards idiosyncratic behaviour in the absence of the latter:

> *As a specimen of the comfort we take at these lady parties, I'll just tell you how we were situated tonight. We took our tea at the centre table, then had a couch on each side of the table, Mrs. Fearon on one, Mrs. Davis on another, Mrs. Low on the third, and Miss Low on the fourth. Our feet up, which is generally the custom when no gents are present. I dare say you would think it very odd, but it is the <u>custom</u>. (1.11.1831)*

Entertainment: music, games, plays, opera

By now we already know that the people in Macau, and especially the foreigners, liked to socialise a lot and to enjoy themselves. In the absence of artificial means of entertainment, such as television, radio, or game machines, everybody had to make an effort to contribute to the success of an evening, either as performer or audience, or as participant in a game. People with a pleasant voice or a good command of a musical instrument were very much admired and were sure to get an invitation to almost every party, knowing, obviously, that they were expected to perform.

> Went to Mrs. Davis's, a small party. The <u>lion</u> of the evening was Mr. Howard, and we kept him singing constantly. I could not bear to say Good Night. He is a handsome youth, elegant manners and quite unaffected, although he is caressed and courted by both ladies and gentlemen. Very obliging and good natured about singing. Says he is only too happy to have ladies to listen to him, for he only gets them when he comes to Macao. (16.9.1831)

Harriett, who as a typical Yankee only knew how to blow on a comb, became a music lover in Macau.

> Breathed a little fresh air and on our way home heard Mrs. Whiteman playing very sweetly on the piano. We went in unceremoniously and solicited a tune on the harp. She plays beautifully, it does make me wish to do something. From here went home. The sweet strains of the harp were sounding in my ears for a long time, even the constant sound of S. P. Sturgis's voice till ten o'clock hardly drowned them. (21.8.1831)

The fact that many English ladies played one or several musical instruments made her even a little envious:

> Have hardly seen an English Lady since we have been here but that plays on some instrument. I do wish I could. (19.10.1831)

In Macau Harriett was also initiated into the art of opera, the first of which seemed to have been executed by local amateurs.

> In the evening we were escorted by Higginson and Sever to the "<u>Opera</u>" where we heard <u>very</u> <u>well</u> performed the Opera of Cinderella in Spanish. The music was very good, the scenery pretty, and the acting very amusing. Cinderella was not <u>very</u> <u>beautiful</u>, being a <u>boy</u> of very somber hue. ... The company was

> *chiefly Portuguese and no beauty among them. The Opera was wholly under the direction of Mr. Paiva, who deserves great credit. He wished to let his townswomen know what an Opera was, and having travelled all over Europe and possessing great musical talents himself, he undertook it and succeeded very well. (18.10.1832)*

In March 1833, a company of 6 Italian singers, four gentlemen and two ladies, arrived at Macau, and stayed for about half a year. During that time they performed several operas and Harriett gradually started to like this musical genre. In the Puritan milieu back home operas seemed to have some kind of immoral aura associated with them, something that was and still is typical for radical Christian sects, who do not see any cultural value in this kind of performance, but put them on the same level of entertainment as any cheap musical. After having heard various operas, Harriett decidedly voted in their favour.

> *I begin to admire the Italian music very much. It is quite an acquired taste. (30.5.1833)*

A few days later, we read:

> *Tancredi was repeated. I never had a pleasanter time, that is I never enjoyed the music more, it was rich. They were all in fine voice tonight. I begin to love it. I was thinking how father would enjoy it if he would allow himself to go. I am sure I can see not the least harm in it, at least in such a place as this. The <u>effects</u> in other places I have never been able to judge. I had a book and followed them tonight. The Italian language seems made for singing, and they articulate every word so distinctly that [it] is very pleasant to hear that alone. (1.6.1833)*

The operas were performed in the great hall at the East India Company's establishment. Once Harriett gave a description of the rather limited stage:

> *You would laugh at our stage which is <u>10</u> feet high, 16 wide, and <u>20</u> deep. The tallest man, Pizzony nearly touches the <u>ceiling</u>, but the <u>music</u> is the thing, and we laugh at the rest. (18.5.1833)*

Apart from the music, going to an opera is also an occasion to make a fashion statement. For some people this may even be the prime reason for going and not the music. One evening, Harriett and Caroline decided to opt for a more exotic outfit than usual.

> *We pinned up <u>Turbans</u> to wear to the Opera tonight. … Our <u>turbans</u> were pronounced elegant. They were made of Benares*

> *muslin scarves. Hers is blue & silver, mine white and silver. They*
> *were both presents. They are such as the higher class natives (of*
> *Bengal) wear. (7.5.1833)*[31]

On the next day, the turbans were discussed by a group of gentlemen:

> *They were speaking of our Turbans. I find [mine] was not generally*
> *thought becoming. Indeed they begged me not to wear it again —*
> *the fact is the house was not lighted enough to display its beauties.*
> *Beside, it was a turban that belonged to an ancient spinster. So*
> *you see how we are deceived. I went away perfectly satisfied with*
> *myself, not having a doubt but that I should be the "observed of*
> *all observers" — that, perhaps I was, but not the "admired of all*
> *admirers". Well I don't care much. I generally have the credit of*
> *dressing with taste! Hum! "The American ladies are said to be the*
> *best dressed ladies of the place" — because we are always neat.*
> *The clothes of many of the ladies, the gents say, look as [though]*
> *they were thrown on with a pitch fork. (8.5.1833)*

It is rather difficult to believe that an impartial observer should have made the latter remark, but seemingly Harriett needed this kind of consolation, in order to get over the turban debacle.

While the performance of an opera was a rather exceptional occurrence in Macau, depending on the presence of a professional ensemble, the staging of theatre plays, employing enthusiastic amateur actors, was more common. Seemingly some of these performances were exceedingly hilarious.

> *Received or rather Aunt Low a note from Mr. Dent, one of the*
> *drollest things you ever saw. ... He requested to accompany us to*
> *the play to night, which offer we accepted. We had satin play Bills*
> *sent this morning, which I shall send to you for you to see the style*
> *in which everything is carried on in Macao. I'll assure you*
> *everything corresponds. We went to the play at 7 accompanied by*
> *Mr. Dent. You would have been amused I am sure. We had*
> *several scenes painted by Mr. Chinnery, a famous portrait painter.*
> *The play was performed very well. Some parts were admirably*
> *done, but the most amusing part was the female character. Mr.*
> *Chinnery was one, and they could not have chosen one less fit to*
> *perform a female part. But however the ridiculous appearance made*
> *much sport. He represented Miss Lucretia MacTab [McTab], and*
> *Mr. Alexander was Miss Emily Worthington, a tall lean looking*
> *man with a gruff voice, but she was breaking the hearts of all the*

young beaus, and you have no idea how ugly she was. It was so inconsistent that we could not but laugh. After the play we had a farce called Bombastes Furioso. *It was very amusing. After the farce a supper which lasted until nearly 2. We had some fine singing and enjoyed it much. (23.11.1829)³²*

Furthermore, when people came together, there would always be somebody with playing cards suggesting a variety of games. When ladies participated, they would be more for fun than money, although things were different in all-male Canton.

Fondness for competitive games of all kinds was a marked characteristic of the community.³³

A long-time favourite among the foreign community in Macau was Old Maid, a card-game in which players have to try not to be left with an unpaired queen. Some people were known for their notorious bad luck and became the subject of many a joke.

Have been playing our American game of old maid, which seems to take <u>mightily</u>. Poor Blight [a bachelor] had the queen three successive times, which quite worried him — he thinks it quite <u>ominous</u>. (29.3.1830)

Another popular game was Speculation, the objective of which is to buy or sell trump cards.

We then played <u>Speculation</u>. Mr. Colledge and I and Mr. Beale and myself went <u>shares</u> and speculated largely — but it was all in fun. At any rate I came off a winner, though almost a bankrupt at one time. We had much sport. (17.3.1830)

Other games would challenge one's imagination, such as "Aunt Cleveland's game",³⁴ as Harriett called it. At the margin she described the rules of the game to her sister:

In the first place you have a parcel of square bits of paper, each with a word upon it, any words you choose to write. Then you have larger pieces to write a question upon, and every one must write a question. Put them altogether and shake them in a box or any tray. Every one then takes out a question and a word P.T.O. [Please Turn Over] and answers the question to bring in that word, however foreign it may be to the subject of the question. The word must be concealed as much as possible because when they are all

*answered, one reads questions and answers and the others <u>guess</u>
the word that is brought in. It requires much ingenuity sometimes
to bring them in and is a very interesting game. To give you an
example of one, I will give you one that I had to answer. My
Question was "will you have a fig?" The word to bring in was
<u>Sympathy</u>. My answer, "talk not to me of figs. The exhibition at
college is approaching and my theme on <u>Sympathy</u> is not yet
commenced". That was a puzzle. ... You must always mark under
the word that the reader may know. (5.4.1830)*

After that description, who is not tempted to activate one's grey cells with an
"Aunt Cleveland's game"? It could be fun.

Gossiping and ill will

A less pleasant side of social life, but somehow unavoidable, mainly in a milieu
as small as Macau, is the emergence of rumours and the subsequent gossiping
engendered by it. The reputation of an individual could be thoroughly destroyed
through it, even if the rumour proved without any foundation in the end. The
Lows learned this soon after their arrival in Macau:

*Have heard some stories this morning which will be a good lesson
for us, I hope make us more on our guard than ever. You have no
idea how circumspect it is necessary to be in this place! Do not
think it concerns me. Not in the least, or rather only as far as it
concerns the whole sex, & I intend to learn a lesson by another's
experience. (12.11.1829)*

We already witnessed Harriett's alarm when having been seen alone with a
gentleman, for example while walking.

*Every thing flies like <u>wildfire</u> here, the more trifling the quicker it
goes. (21.6.1833)*

The rumours were not restricted to Macau, but travelled very quickly to Canton
and even to the United States, making Harriett's parents feel worried about their
daughter's integrity. Although they took more time to get there, they used this
time to inflate and to distort. The report of a captain returning from Hawaii to
Macau deserved the following commentary by Harriett:

*He says reports reached the <u>Islands</u> [Hawaii] and the <u>Coast</u>
[American continent] that I was to be married to <u>three</u> or <u>four</u>
people. I told him I thought one quite enough. It is amusing to find*

> *what a notorious person my ladyship is; really I ought to be very*
> *vain. He says my <u>fame</u> has reached from pole to pole, and all*
> *forsooth because I happen to be a <u>spinster</u> in a <u>distant</u> <u>land</u>. I might*
> *have remained in America till the end of my days and never been*
> *known beyond my own fireside. And even now should I only take*
> *unto myself a spouse, I should forthwith sink into <u>insignificance</u>.*
> *Well it is the fate of spinsters to be the subject of speculation.*
> *(28.1.1833)*

Although women are generally credited with being more gossipy than men, the examples from Macau clearly show that both sexes contribute an equal share in the creation and spread of rumours. A valuable source of gossip from exclusively male pens is the business correspondence from Canton:

> *Commercial rivalries, private animosities, and the lack of other*
> *topics of conversation led to a brisk traffic in juicy morsels of*
> *personal scandal.*[35]

Rumours reaching Macau from far could also do great harm to the people involved, as the following example shows. In August 1830, news about the brutal murder of an old and rich merchant from Salem, Joseph White, arrived at Macau and Canton. Harriett read about it in the *Boston Advertiser* and commented in her journal:

> *What a … I cannot find words to express the horrors of it. Who*
> *could it have been and what for. It is beyond all account, most*
> *shocking. That was instantly told to the great surprise, amazement*
> *and horror of all. Old White dead, not much lamented we suppose,*
> *poor old gentleman. (3.8.1830)*[36]

The speculations about the murder continued. As more information reached the Lows, probably through personal letters, the more anxiously they waited for further revelations in the newspapers, because two of the four accused were younger brothers of Harriett's aunt Abigail [Knapp] Low. They obviously feared personal consequences for their social prestige in Macau and Canton. Both brothers were hanged publicly, one in September of 1830, and the other one three months later. The actual murderer committed suicide in prison, to avoid having to testify against his brother, who was the only one to survive the investigation and was set free. As soon as Harriett was aware of the involvement of her aunt's brothers, she never referred directly to the crime in her journal again.

Without Hummel's and mainly Hodges's explanations, who presents this case in full detail, passages like the following would have remained a mystery:

> Aunt Low gave me Uncle's [letter] to read, which tells us of the fate [execution] of poor Frank [Knapp]. I did not think it could take place and even now I cannot realize it — you may judge my thoughts after that. Aunt Low was fully prepared for it, there seems to be no end to the tragedy. And tomorrow morning I shall have to get up, so contrary to my feelings, and go to a public breakfast and races and dinner in the evening. I shall get off if I can but shall go if Aunt Low wishes it, as we wish to prevent any questions being asked, and the people here are very _curious_ to know the why's of every movement … Aunt Low is under Colledge's orders and has not been out for three weeks. (6.3.1831)

What Harriett and her uncle wanted to prevent at all costs, was that people talked directly with Abigail Knapp about it, or that they would begin to avoid them socially. Harriett's reaction clearly shows the stress caused by this case.

> Called on Mrs. Morrison. Had a dreadful shock there, for she told me she had been reading a N.Y. paper and saw an account of a dreadful murder that had been committed in Salem. I was afraid I should hear the whole. She must have thought I appeared very odd I think, for I knew not what to say. The colour came into my face. But her dates were before the awful discovery. I said as little as possible about [it], endeavoured to compose myself, and changed the subject. I am very much afraid as they get all the N.Y. papers they _will_ get the whole, and if they were to mention it to Aunt Low it would be horrid. I would not tell her for any money that she [Mrs. Morrison] knew even this. (26.4.1831)

The execution of Abigail Low's brothers was used in a malicious way three years later by a fellow American, who had a personal business feud with William Henry Low. In the late summer of 1833, an anonymous "Air" was posted at the door of the East India Company factory in Macau and 500 copies left at its doorstep. It goes as follows:

> Now Joe and Frank they both are hung/And Phip is like to swing./ What horrid grief and trouble too/My thieving brothers bring.//For tho' they killed old Uncle White/They got but little plunder,/ Therefore if I'm a drop to low'/I'm sure it's no great wonder.//

*For after sticking the old Wretch/And knocking on the knob him,/
How it subdues my weaker part/To think they did not rob him
—//.*[37]

Harriett refers to this incident by talking about a "*demon*" who wanted to hurt her Aunt, again without explaining the background of this remark.

Ailments of body and soul

This morning studied and took a dose of salts, for what I cannot say. Fancied I was <u>Billious</u> or ought to be from the quantity of cucumbers I have eaten of late. It is astonishing what good health I have, and always eat just what I fancy. And other people are mincing and fearing to eat this, that, and the other. I verily believe it is of the imagination. But I suppose it is wrong for me to be so <u>uncharitable</u>. I only ought to be thankful that mine is so much better. (29.5.1833)

This observation was made in the last year of their stay in Macau, and it was true for the rest of her absence from home. Apart from a weeklong severe fever at the end of May of 1830, which even prevented her from writing journal, Harriett's major health complaints were headaches and toothaches. The latter could be particularly excruciating, sometimes lasting for several days and implying sleepless nights. As there were no dentists yet, the treatment was done by anybody brave enough to deal with people in extreme pain, by a general practitioner or by the sufferer himself/herself. The methods of treatment were correspondingly archaic.

Am almost tongue tied this few days past. I have broken a tooth and it is so sharp that [with] every word I cut my tongue, which is not comfortable. Colledge was in yesterday, said it must be a great affliction for a <u>lady</u> not to be able to <u>talk</u> and he would send me a file. (17.4.1831)

Seemingly it resulted:

Went to work this morning to <u>file</u> my teeth, and made out very well. (19.4.1831)

Harriett used to cure all her other complaints with Epsom salts (magnesium sulfate) or by rubbing the affected parts with Cologne.

Once she even tried local medicine, administered by the Lows' maidservant.

> *Josepha came to me before bedtime and said she would cure a little sort of ring worm I had on my neck if I would let her. I enquired what she intended to <u>perform</u>. In bad English she explained and I concluded I should not be quite killed and I consented. So she brought up an onion and had made it quite black, how I know not, that she rubbed upon my neck till she scraped the skin off. I was almost sorry that I submitted to such <u>quackery</u> but if it cures <u>he</u> as she tells of, I don't much care. The Portuguese and Chinese have the most singular remedies, they torture themselves with their remedies. If they have a sore throat, you see their throats all in red streaks where they have burned it with <u>hot ash</u>. I should be very sorry to be submitted to their <u>tender mercies</u>. (9.10.1833)*

But other people were not so lucky or blessed with health as Harriett. Sickness and death, even among young people, were common in Macau. For example, consumption or tuberculosis, as it is called nowadays, was a very widespread disease.

> *Mrs. Russell and her husband were at Church. She is said to be 18 only, he poor man, is in a consumption. Was coughing in a most distressing manner & I could not help feeling pity for her, poor thing. He quite disturbed my devotions. ... It is strange how people in consumption are deceived with regard to themselves. This poor man thinks himself wonderfully improved because he has a ravenous appetite, which is I believe a strong symptom of the complaint. The very <u>deceit</u> is I think a symptom of consumption. (29.4.1832)*

As regards the latter remark, Harriett could not know that a year later she would become a direct and intimate witness of a person with consumption, her uncle. Then she also would and even wanted to be deceived about his real condition, interpreting every slight change in his appearance as a symptom of improvement. Considering the relative ease by which this disease is spread, and the fact that neither Harriett nor her aunt were aware of the cause of his sickness, and therefore took no special precautions, it is astonishing that they did not catch it themselves through their daily and direct contact with him.

The average life expectancy in Western nations in the middle of the 19th century was about 40 years only. Although great medical progress was made in that century, the causes for many diseases, as well as their means of transmission, remained a mystery. Speculations in this respect make us smile nowadays, like in the following passage written while spending several weeks aboard near Lintin island, in the Pearl River Delta, in order to get a rare change from the people and the environment in Macau.

> *Some of the gentlemen of the* Peacock *went to Canton. Mr. Cunningham spent the evening with us. Invited us to come on board to Church the next day, but as he told us they had the Cholera on board and had lost 7 men with it, we were afraid to go. They got it in Manilla, they say; that Ships were laying all around them in Manilla and none had it <u>but</u> their ship. They say it was in the atmosphere, and say it is only in a particular current or draught of air, but I cannot conceive of that. They say it is not contagious, for many of the officers stood by when their men were seized with it and watched the progress of the disease, which must be <u>really</u> <u>awful</u> — but none of the officers ever took it. (10.11.1832)*[38]

Another rather common disease in these latitudes was high fever alternating with the shivers, something similar to malaria.

> *Caroline was suddenly taken with the <u>fever</u> & <u>ague</u>; I never saw anything so sudden. She was quite cold and shook like a leaf, then violent fever. Sent for Colledge. He gave her some <u>quinine</u>. (13.7.1832)*

As Caroline had stayed in the Indonesian archipelago before coming to Macau, she might have caught malaria there, but it also existed in wet and swampy areas in subtropical climates. The presence of this disease is said to have been one of the factors responsible for the relatively slow colonisation of Hong Kong, where it existed in a very aggressive form, killing many of the first settlers.

It was already mentioned that many English from India came to Macau for a few months, from October onwards, in order to enjoy the cool and fresh air. However, others had to leave this place, because the general climate was not suitable for them and put their health at risk.

> *Poor Mrs. Ploughden [Plowden] who came out in August is to leave in a few days for England; her health is so very bad she cannot stay. (7.12.1832)*

Another case was the wife of the missionary Morrison:

> *She is an invalid and going to England this year with her little tribe. Having a child a year is rather too much in a hot climate for the constitution and comfort. (6.7.1833)*

A year earlier Harriett had already observed:

> *She, poor woman, is worn to a skeleton by sickness. Her husband*
> *cut up would make 4 of her. (14.7.1832)*

But not only ladies had to leave Macau in order to restore their health. William
Hunter, for example, long-time resident in Canton and author of two well-known
books about the China trade, tried to regain his health in Macau at first, but
was then compelled to return to the USA.

Some of the English-speaking doctors in Macau have written medical
history. Dr. Alexander Pearson (died 1837), surgeon to the English Factory in
Canton, was the first one to introduce vaccination against small pox to China,
in 1805. He also instructed several Chinese in this art, who then succeeded in
vaccinating more than one million people over a period of 30 years. Many years
later, in 1816, he was the accompanying surgeon of Lord Amherst's Embassy
to Peking. On his return to England in 1832, the Portuguese community of
Macau, under the leadership of António Pereira, presented him with a letter of
thanks for his services. While Dr. Pearson is mentioned only sporadically in the
journal, the name of Dr. Thomas Richardson Colledge (1796–1879) is a constant,
though misspelled as "College" for most of the time. Only when he and Caroline
Shillaber married in March 1833, Harriett seemed to have become aware of the
correct spelling. His name appears regularly, not because Harriett or her Aunt
would have needed his services often, but because of his uniquely charming
nature and positive personality. Apart from his official duties as surgeon to the
East India Company at Canton, he founded an Ophthalmic Hospital for the Poor
in Macau in 1827, the first of its kind in China. During the first five years of its
existence, he cured about 4,000 Chinese from impending blindness. The
following praise of Colledge as a person and as a physician is just one example
out of dozens in the journal, though a bit longer than usual:

> *There is one person here who I think quite fulfils the object of his*
> *existence, and that is Mr. Colledge — he is continually going about*
> *doing good. He makes every one love him. He is so universally*
> *kind and obliging, and exerts himself to make all happy who come*
> *in his way. Every one go to him in their distresses and if possible*
> *he relieves them. He heals the sick, comforts the afflicted, and in*
> *his practice is really a Christian without any display — quietly and*
> *without ostentation he fulfils his duties. Cheerfully and happily*
> *assists all. We call him the "<u>sunbeam</u>" for every <u>thing</u> smiles when*
> *he approaches. His greatest pleasure is in doing good and his face*
> *speaks the goodness of his heart. He is open, generous, and*

possesses very noble feeling — without deceit, affable, cheerful, and entertaining. Mr. Chinnery called here after church and he was extolling him as every one does, and was speaking of his skill as an <u>optician</u>. He says a gentleman in Java hearing of his skill came here on purpose to try it. He has been perfectly miserable for two years with his eye which he had stung by some insect. He had no peace of his life and his eye was in a horrid state. He came on here despairing almost of ever having it cured, and in two months C[olledge] has performed a perfect <u>cure</u>, and now the man has gone blessing him for his kindness and attention. He sent him a most excellent letter containing every expression of gratitude, but feeling that the strongest words cannot express his feelings, he sent C[olledge] a large sum of money but it was returned (as every gift of the kind is) with [a note] saying he could not take it. He was only too happy to have the opportunity of curing him. I hardly know which must feel the happiest, the restorer or the restored, but I cannot conceive of a more heavenly feeling than this of <u>doing good</u>. (6.1.1833)

The East India Company and many of its employees, as well as a powerful group of Chinese merchants known as the *hong* merchants (see chapter 6), supported Colledge's philanthropic endeavours financially. Also, the money from the offerings at the communion table of the British chapel went to his infirmary for three years. In 1828, he opened a dispensary for natives and foreigners in Canton, with the help of two fellow physicians, Dr. Cox and the American Dr. James Hewling Bradford (1802–1859). In February 1838, Colledge was one of the founders of the Medical Missionary Society in China, acting as its President for more than 40 years, until his death. His picture was painted by Chinnery showing him exercising his profession as ophthalmologist.[39] Harriett was quite critical about his likeness, which she did not find "*so striking as many others of his pictures*" *(31.3.1833)*. Colledge returned to England in about 1841, after having lost most of his personal belongings as a consequence of the increasing Anglo-Chinese hostilities.[40] Harriett would meet the Colledges there occasionally, because she too spent most of her married life in England.

As regards ailments of the soul, "the blues" — or depression — was a frequently described condition. Usually it was caused by a feeling of loneliness, homesickness, or by the conviction of being utterly useless to society. "*Had the blues all the evening. Never felt more completely wretched*" *(1.12.1831)*. Sometimes Harriett also called this feeling "*azure spirits*" *(28.7.1831)*, or the "*blue devil*" *(24.2.1832)* or "*indigo spirits*" *(13.8.1832)*, as if by playing with this word, she could decrease its intensity. The following description characterises the symptoms of the disease in a typical way.

> *I felt in very good spirits, but all at once such a change came over me, like a flash of lightning, and I could not raise my spirits for the evening. 'Tis a very odd and most unhappy feeling, but I cannot shake it off. I have it often and cannot account for it in any way. It sometimes seizes me in my gayest humour, and I know no cause or reason why. I have been dreadfully stupid all the evening — and puzzled and perplexed. As it is now after 12 I will go to bed and endeavour to sleep off this depression. I hope I shall not get up with it. (25.7.1832)*

The most efficient antidote against this condition were letters, which however, as we know, often took a very long time to arrive. Consequently, Harriett was quite a regular victim of the blues.

> *[I] was deliberating which I had best do, read over my old letters (my constant resource) or take a dose of Salts. I finally concluded indisposition must be the cause of my gloom, so I dissolved them and was just standing before the glass in my own room thinking how interesting I looked, with the glass half up to my mouth, making faces and shuddering involuntarily, when Aunt Low came in and brought me a letter from my dear mother, one from A[biel] A[bbot] Low and one from E.W. Ward — and I'll assure you the Salts were instantly put on the table for further consideration. I read them again and again. ... I felt 6 per cent better after them. I took my salts, then my books and now I feel almost myself again. (24.3.1831)*

Occasionally, the presence of a friend could mitigate her "blue state", as in the following example with Vachell.

> *I had just had a severe attack of the "blues" and just seated myself on the verandah to relieve myself with a few drops "that from the eye relieve the heart", but his cheerful company soon dissipated them. (4.5.1831)*

Another stabilising factor in Harriett's life was her close relationship with her aunt and uncle, though sometimes she felt *de trop* in their presence as every third person or outsider feels once in a while when in the company of a couple. But it was not only ladies who succumbed to the blues, although they probably had a greater chance to become its victims, because they did not exercise any

profession, which could have helped them to overcome this condition faster or
prevent its emergence in the first place. After having walked with a young lad,
Harriett observed:

> *Poor fellow, he is pining for home. He is quite miserable I believe.
> It seems to be the general cry of youths here that they are so lonely,
> without a friend; & they want something to <u>love</u>. It is very amusing
> and I cannot help pitying them poor wretches, for I have a fellow
> feeling for them. (5.2.1832)*

But in spite of all her emotional downs, deep inside her Harriett Low knew
that all her problems were bliss compared to real suffering:

> *And perhaps the time may come when with more positive miseries
> or troubles I shall have to look back upon the time spent in Macao
> as at any rate the most quiet and most free from troubles, if not
> the happiest portion of my life — but it does not seem to be in our
> natures to enjoy the present. I bitterly sigh for home in spite of all
> my endeavours to the contrary. Time passes rapidly and yet I am
> continually wishing [it would] quicken its flight till I shall be again
> with my friends. (13.5.1833)*

Another ailment of the heart, lovesickness, will be dealt with in the next chapter,
"Matters of the Heart and of the Home".

Western female servants in Macau

One of the subjects mentioned only casually, *en passant*, and which is totally
left out in Hillard's edition of the journal, is that of the Western female servants,
i.e. the maids brought from the USA, England, or other European countries. This
attests to the fact that the world of the domestic servants was totally separate
from that of their employers, socially inferior, and as such not worth a mention.
Western maids were taken to China for a variety of reasons, namely to take care
of the wardrobe, which was much more complicated then than nowadays, both
during the voyage and at the destination, as well as for the preparation of certain
dishes and for teaching the local servants how to make a bed or set a table. The
Lows were no exception to this general rule. In a letter to her parents sent from
Manila, we can read more details about Nancy, who had been mentioned only
sporadically during the voyage:

> *The girl you got for us, Father, proves to be a bad character. She
> is good for nothing. We were in hopes we should have got rid of*

her at Manila, but it is impossible. The authorities will not allow
her to be left. She is now on board the ship. They have no female
servants in the house, except one in the morning to take care of
our rooms. Another thing, we did not want her near us. We have
no charity for her. If you see Capt. Roundy and I think you will,
he will give it to you in full. He is quite enraged. I feel sorry that
it has occasioned him so much trouble. She is the most artful girl
that ever lived. … We shall send her home the first chance, which
I fear will not be very soon.[41]

Although Harriett did not specify the nature of the problems created by Nancy, it can be assumed that she probably displayed a more permissive behaviour on board towards the crew than Capt. Roundy was ready to tolerate, thus interfering with the tranquillity on the *Sumatra*.

In the following years Nancy's name appears only irregularly. Apparently the employers and the maid had found some way of peaceful co-existence, perhaps because of the want of a better one. Nancy left Macau in July 1832. The way this event is described in the Journal allows the conclusion that Harriett had already reported it more in detail in a previous letter to her family, as well as the fact that Nancy was not with the Lows anymore. One of the reasons may be that in the meantime she had become a single mother.

I hear Nancy is going to Bombay with Mrs. Thompson. Am very
glad. She takes the child with her. I hear she is exceedingly fond of
it. I hope she will be provided for. I pity her poor thing, and would
assist her if in my power. I know she is very wicked, but when we
take into consideration the education she has had and the
temptations that such creatures have, I cannot help pitying while
I condemn. (12.7.1832)[42]

In the end, however, Nancy left without her child.

Nancy has taken her departure today in the Competitor *for*
Bombay with Mr. and Mrs. Thompson. Well God bless her, and
may she repent of her past transgressions and lead a better life. I
felt a kind of pang when I heard she had gone, not that I am not
delighted that she is out of the place, but such a feeling of regret
that she has behaved in such a manner as to be obliged to leave us
in such a manner. I hear she has left her child behind, at which I
am astonished and think there must be some foul play.
(23.7.1832)

As Nancy did not leave any money behind for her child, it was sent to an institution which took care of these unfortunate, mostly rejected, human beings since Macau's early days:

> *And it is now sent to the Misericordia, a society for all foundlings and orphans — a very excellent institution, but I should think would be overrun in this place. (25.7.1832)*[43]

These few lines and half a dozen more referring to Nancy and other Western maids only give us a vague idea about the life of Western women of the lower social classes in Macau. It would be interesting to know why they ventured so far, or to be able to see the world and some of the characters described in this journal from their perspective. However, most of them did not know how to read or write, and therefore finding written testimonies is extremely difficult. Harriett sometimes wrote letters for Nancy to her family. Even if such letters had survived, their content would have been very limited — complaints about the employers were obviously out of the question, as well as any other matters of a more profound nature. Considering the great comfort that Harriett received from her ability to read and write, we can understand that in spite of all her anger towards Nancy she could still feel sorry for her.

After Nancy's departure Harriett referred to women in a similar situation as *"Nancy case"* (14.7.1832).

> *This morning we parted with one of our family, Caroline's English servant. She was called up yesterday and told to pack up her duds, she would be off for England in the* Reliance, *starts perhaps in a few hours. She dared ask no questions having a guilty conscience. She has turned out very like our "Nancy" — not exactly a "Nancy case" but very near. She is quite notorious here, we find by a certain gentleman. European servants will not do in this place, they seldom keep their characters — deceitful creatures. (10.2.1833)*

When passing judgment on the shared predicament of Nancy and Caroline's maid, as well as on others about which she heard during her stay in Macau, Harriett was much more severe on her own sex than the seducers, a fact corresponding to the general opinion of the time. Society demanded virginity from a woman before her marriage and fidelity as a spouse, while it closed its eyes with regard to these exigencies for men, and even encouraged premarital sexual experience as well as the existence of a mistress. This is why women who erred on either count, were (and in many cultures still are) much more severely punished than their male counterparts. Yet they themselves helped to maintain these double moral standards.

> *Uncle's letter gives us a most distressing account of two young ladies in Salem. I am sure I shall be ashamed to acknowledge myself as a native of that place. … It grieves me think of the poor family, what bliss (comparatively) it would have been to have buried her. This is the error of allowing girls and boys to be <u>trapsing</u> about the streets evenings. They have a great deal too much liberty in Salem. I shall begin to be an advocate for French Seclusion almost. If girls have no respect for themselves, no power of controlling their evil propensities or if they will not use that power, they had much better be kept to themselves. … It seems quite intolerable enough for a son to offend, but a girl seems ten times worse. You know boys are more exposed to temptation and more likely to come in contact with wickedness in all shapes. And youth, thoughtlessness, and strong feelings may sometimes be alleged as an excuse and the follies of youth in a man are often forgotten in the more serious and sedate conduct of riper years. (22.8.1833)*

But after all this criticism of her own sex, Harriett came up with a good suggestion.

> *Oh wicked, heartless, cruel, sinful man to bring such misery upon a female. … How cruel it seems that he may after all his wickedness, still go into the world and by future conduct <u>may</u> make himself either respected or despised <u>as</u> <u>he</u> <u>pleases</u>. Oh that the same disgrace could be entailed on man that there is on woman. There might be fewer such instances to lament. (22.8.1833)*

Among Western women who had to earn their living in Macau, contrary to the "idle class", of which Harriett was a member, were also educators. Although literate, they do not seem to have left any more evidence of their presence than the Western maids. A casual remark in the journal, for example, tells of the existence of a governess at the Misses Pereira. We do not know anything, however, about her origin and future fate, or about other women in a similar situation.

5
Matters of the Heart and of the Home

In earlier times, female perspectives on life were clearly limited. They oscillated between marriage and motherhood, which was the socially recognised and recommended alternative, and spinster. Harriett Low, who belonged to the latter group but aspired to change to the married camp, discusses the pros and cons of the two ways of female existence repeatedly and at length throughout the journal, with a variety of feelings and emotions. The limitation also referred to a woman's living space, which was restricted to her home. This ideal was shared by the Chinese and Westerners alike, though perhaps not on the same scale. However, only the wealthier classes in both cultures had the financial means to put this aim into effect.

The "countdown" to marriage for a girl usually started in the second half of her teens and lasted little more than a decade, before she would be considered an "old maid". Males need not worry about their age or looks, because they could always find a woman desperate enough to contract matrimony in exchange for social recognition. In addition to the gender inequality, which permeated every sphere of life, different rules also applied to the members of different social classes and cultures. Liaisons between Western men and working-class women, including Chinese females, were common, but the contrary was not the case. The hypocrisy regarding morals is visible in the double standards that existed for men and women. While a mere rumour or gossip about indecent behaviour could ruin the life of an innocent female forever, the sexual escapades of males were smiled at or even encouraged.

* * * *

The engagement ruse

Knowing that Harriett Low was going to a place where men grossly outnumbered women, the prospect of being one among very few English-speaking single young ladies must have worried her caretakers. This may be the reason, why an interesting stratagem of protection, as I understand it, was contrived, in order to perplex possible suitors, initially at least. When Harriett Low came to Macau, she wore a simple plain ring on the ring finger of her left hand. This ring immediately provoked speculations among many men. The following conversation took place only a few weeks after her arrival:

> *Capt. Whitehead says Miss Low, you must excuse me, for I have got a strange question to ask you, and that is if you are engaged? Or "rather he says, is it the custom in America for disengaged young ladies to wear a plain ring on the fourth finger of the left hand?" He said he had <u>heard</u> it observed that I wore a ring on that finger, but he says I am not deputized to ask you this question nor do I intend to <u>propose</u> <u>myself</u>, but I <u>wish</u> to <u>know</u> if it <u>means</u> any thing in America? I told him I should not satisfy him, but it was a ring I <u>valued</u> highly. But he says no lady in England is <u>allowed</u> to wear a ring on that finger, particularly a plain one, before she is engaged. It made much sport for us. I did not however let him know that I felt any curiosity (though I did much) to know who was so observing, but I told him I should always wear it on that finger. (18.10.1829)*

The ring continued to cause some curiosity for several more weeks.

> *We had much sport again about the ring, which still remains on the <u>fourth</u> finger. Capt. W[hitehead] <u>thinks</u> there is <u>no</u> <u>hope</u>. (26.10.1829)*

The origin and the meaning of this ring are never revealed in the journal. However, it is certain that Harriett Low did not have a fiancé back home; otherwise she obviously would have corresponded with him or mentioned him in the journal. Besides, if she had had one, it would have been only natural to admit it. The most probable explanation for the ring story is that she wanted to portray herself as being engaged, either by her own will or following the advice of her parents or uncle, in order to avoid being immediately showered with attentions of all kind. This was inevitable anyway. The long list of presents received during her stay in Macau shows that the gentlemen stretched their imagination, in order to please her with gifts of varying sizes. They included everything imaginable (and at least one unimaginable present, as we shall see later), ranging from romantic to practical, such as self-composed poems, flowers, musical boxes, earrings, prints, books, gingerbread, leather for shoe soles, and many other things. After having received one more present by an admirer, she sighed:

> *I almost wish they would not give me so many things. I do not*
> *feel any happier for them, and it lays me under such a weight of*
> *obligations. (17.9.1832)*

At a much later stage, Harriett repeated the "mystery fiancé game", as we may call it, on receiving a miniature portrait of her sister, although motivated by different reasons, namely to have some fun.

> *Alexander & Blight in this morning. <u>Alex</u> is very anxious to see*
> *the miniature I have rec'd of late. I torment him and make him*
> *think it is some <u>lover</u> at home. Have excited his curiosity*
> *delightfully. (26.5.1832)*

This observation reveals another part of her personality that apparently does not correspond with many of her remarks of a more Puritan nature, but which was one of her characteristics, namely to tease others and to "love a good laugh". The "good laugh" referred both to laughing heartily as well as to a (morally) good laugh, as opposed to malicious joy.

> *We [Caroline and Harriett] have several capital subjects for a joke*
> *in Canton, and we expend all our <u>wit</u> upon them when we are so*
> *inclined. (22.3.1832)*

Social restrictions for young ladies

A young woman of the middle or upper classes, though materially cared for, used to live in a kind of golden cage with as little exposure to the real world as possible. A walk or drive to church on Sundays, a picnic in summertime, or holidays at a seaside resort, all of which were well chaperoned obviously, were among the few distractions of an otherwise home-based life, where she was prepared for her future life as wife and mother. As already mentioned, female education basically aimed at teaching young women to supervise a household, to speak a little French and to entertain guests on some musical instrument, preferably the piano.[1] Some of these girls and young women were even fluent in Latin and Greek, often as a "by-product" of their brothers' education, but they rarely had the chance to test their language skills abroad or to visit Europe's finest places as their brothers did, following the time-honoured route of the *Grand Tour*. No wonder that a sigh of envy often escaped their hearts, especially when listening to the travel experiences of their male counterparts:

> *Could not help audibly wishing that I was a man, that I could take*
> *up my bundle and go where I please. Felt half inclined to fall in*

*love with some Captain or Supercargo and make it in the agreement
that he shall let me go where I wish or wherever he does. I do hate
this dependent system. I do not like being in one place more than
a year. (8.4.1832)*

Therefore, one of the rules most detested by Harriett in Macau was that a young female could not walk alone, or in the company of only one man. The same was true indoors. Two unmarried people of the opposite sex could not be left alone, unless they were engaged, but even then they might be interrupted at any time. Shortly before Caroline's wedding with Thomas Colledge, Harriett described her invisible but omnipresent chaperone role, which she had already played back home in the United States with her sister Molly and fiancé.

*Now they [visitors] are gone and here I am writing, waiting for
Colly [one of Caroline's nicknames]. If I don't give her a scolding,
letting Tom stay so late — it is more than 5 minutes past 11 the
usual hour with you, you know when I made enquiries in old times.
The clock has begun to strike little ones, and it is time he was gone.
If I was as mischievous as I used to be, I should walk in and disturb
their tête-à-tête, but I believe I am a little more compassionate
than of yore. (21.2.1833)*

One may question her compassion, however, regarding the following wish, which probably was both true and false at the same time:

*"Colledge came in this evening to 'bebe[r] chá' [to have tea] as
the Portuguese say and Aunt Low & I very sagaciously left the
room — that is we had sagacity enough to suppose we should be
more agreeable in another room. Well I hope they will quarrel soon,
for I do not like this turning out business" (16.2.1833).*

Apart from the limitations in geographical and social terms, the female body was subject to constraints too, in the form of corsets, restricting the liberty of movement and increasing the likelihood to faint, if improperly or too tightly laced. In Chinese culture, women of well-to-do families were subject to an excruciating treatment, namely the binding of the feet. Only the big toe was allowed to stay in its normal position, while the other toes were broken and bent backwards, under the sole of the foot, and then everything was bandaged tightly to impede growth. They were called "lotus feet" and ideally should fit into a teacup.[2]

*As I was walking this morning I saw a poor creature toddling along
on her little feet. Oh the hours of torture she has suffered for this*

> *barbarous fashion — I am told that the agony they endure is beyond*
> *conception. They commence <u>swathing</u> the feet at the age of two*
> *and for years they suffer excessively. The poor child does nothing*
> *but scream from pain and all to gratify the pride of the mother who*
> *thinks her child will not be beautiful without. And yet I am told*
> *that the men do not like it, though they think it necessary to have*
> *their <u>first</u> wife with small feet. (17.2.1833)*

Interestingly, some Chinese drew a parallel between their own custom of binding the feet and the Western custom of contracting women's waists.

> *I was one day talking with a very intelligent compradore upon the*
> *subject, who seemed to think the custom of <u>nipping</u> in the waist*
> *was quite as barbarous and cruel as to pinch the feet — it seems*
> *to be a matter of astonishment with them "how we can <u>catchy</u> <u>chow</u>*
> *<u>chow</u>". That is how we can <u>eat</u>, which certainly would be a greater*
> *grievance to them than not being able to walk. (17.2.1833)*

After yet another reference to Chinese women and their feet, Harriett naturally defended her own culture's "achievements" with respect to beautifying female bodies:

> *Ought we not to be thankful that we are so much further advanced*
> *in civilisation? For although refinement and civilisation bring with*
> *them their evils, they are of a more <u>refined</u> and <u>civilized</u> kind —*
> *though I dare say, never having known better, the China woman*
> *is just as well contented with her situation as we are with ours.*
> *And indeed I am sometimes inclined to believe that she is to be*
> *envied when compared with a woman of <u>fashion</u>, who is "tortured*
> *with envy, malice, and all uncharitableness". (17.2.1833)*

Refined or not, the more important word is "evils" — instead of focusing on them, Harriett just defended her own culture's values and ideals, not seeing herself as a victim too.

Beaux and loves — flirting and being courted

Having been brought up at a time when young women were sheltered from men as much as possible, the sudden and direct contact with many of them in Macau was quite intimidating for Harriett, but only initially.

> *Do you recollect what a dreadful thing I used to think it to sit down*
> *to table with half a dozen gentlemen. Times have altered since that*
> *and I do not mind 30 or 40 or as many more as you choose. ...*
> *The critical moment is just when the ladies are about to go to*
> *dinner. The great point is to get between two pleasant people, but*
> *we poor dependent creatures have to put up with those who will*
> *put up with us. But I will not complain, I am generally very*
> *fortunate.* (13.5.1830)

Macau was indeed a good school for life, where she had to lose her shyness and insecurity and to learn how to make small talk. After a short period of acclimatisation, Harriett behaved as if she had grown up in this particular milieu. She even came to like and enjoy all the attention showered on her.

Gifted with a generally gay and easy-going disposition, quite a number of men became the object of her high spirits in the course of time. Some of them were only a mental prey.

> *O. H. Gordon made us a call of a few minutes this evening. Goes*
> *back [to Canton] tomorrow morning. As interesting as ever. If he*
> *was not so ugly, should certainly try to bewitch him. He has lots*
> *of cash.* (3.6.1832)[3]

Others were attacked directly.

> *Dressed and went to Mrs. Robinson. ... Had a very large party,*
> *danced all the evening. The chief of my amusement was in*
> *tormenting Mr. Huddleston, a demure, steady, serious-looking*
> *fellow, but handsome and very gentlemanly. Never was known*
> *to dance. At Mrs. Grant's I made a "dead set" at him and asked*
> *him to dance a quadrille with me, which he declined doing. For*
> *which he got well roasted. But he was incorrigible. So to night said*
> *I, "My beauty you shall not escape". So the first moment I got a*
> *chance I at him, and told him that I should not condescend to ask*
> *again, but I hoped to have the pleasure of seeing him dance. But*
> *all in vain. He said he was a wretch and never deserved to be*
> *forgiven, for which he said he would do any penance.* (13.3.1832)

Harriett's jokes became more daring as her familiarity with the new environment increased, but she never actually kicked the traces, because her conscience would not let her.

> *Well I confess I am a very naughty girl — is that any thing towards*
> *amendment. It ought to be, but I fear it is not. I soothe the*

> *clamorous appeals of my conscience by saying that it is only from*
> *the lips; I am sure in my heart I have not a spark of ill will. You*
> *know I always liked a good joke. (31.5.1832)*

This underlying goodness of heart was also recognised by others and contributed
to her popularity.

> *Says [Colledge] he has never heard anyone speak ill of me since I*
> *have been in the place. Do you not think that a compliment —*
> *but from him I believe it. I suppose they think I am a good natured*
> *<u>harmless</u> <u>crittur</u> [sic], but what matters it. I care not. (17.6.1832)*

It mattered, however, to her parents, who must have heard many stories about
Harriett's apparent popularity, but from which they were led to draw the wrong
conclusions about their daughter's firmness of character. The following passage
makes us understand how offended she was by her parents' misinterpretations.

> *I was not exactly pleased with my dear father's letter. It was short*
> *and appeared to me as though it was written in displeasure at me*
> *or my sentiments, which grieved me to the quick. Inasmuch as I*
> *am at such a distance I cannot explain. I should rather not have*
> *received it. A word or look of displeasure for him is quite enough*
> *to make me unhappy and always was and I do not find I feel any*
> *differently from what I did when I left in this respect. It seems he*
> *thinks I have caught the <u>immoral</u> <u>contagion</u> that prevails in China*
> *and mother thought my heart was gone and my <u>brain</u> turned. No*
> *wonder you feel anxious for me to return. (23.8.1833)*

Beaux

A word frequently used in the journal, especially after Caroline's arrival, is that
of "beau", referring to a pleasant member of the opposite sex, mainly regarding
his manners and company, and not so much his physical attributes, as the literal
meaning of the word would suggest. Therefore, only a very restricted number
of men reached this status. A beau was rarely the object of more profound
emotions. Yet those men who were, were not designated as beaux. A beau's
presence was somehow taken for granted and they were treated

> *as brothers. They [two beaux named Blight and Sturgis] say it*
> *seems so delightful to see two young ladies in China that they*
> *cannot help coming. Aunt Low gives the drawing room up to us*
> *and ensconces herself in her boudoir. (25.2.1832)*

Beaux were also the ideal partners for walking:

> *He [Sturgis] and Blight have gone to Canton. We shall be minus*
> *walking beaux. (1.3.1832)*

More serious subjects of reverie would be called "darling" or "love", and their
number was obviously more restricted than the one of beaux around. However,
one or the other beau might have been honoured with a promotion to "love",
without his knowledge obviously.

These affairs of the heart were usually discussed only under four eyes.

> *Caroline & I set over the coals chatting till ¹/₂ past 12, and it was*
> *long after 1 before we went to sleep. It seems as though our tongues*
> *were just unloosened as it is time to lay them by. (20.2.1832)*

> *We have these talking fits now and then, but I cannot tell you the*
> *subjects, for they are secret. (14.6.1832)*

Though "secret", once in a while some information escaped, as in the following
paragraph, where the "ideal husband" or the "ideal wife" were under discussion.

> *Have just had a <u>consu</u> in Caroline's room — I always go and sit*
> *down at her door to brush my hair and there we talk some times*
> *till 1 o'clock. We discussed beauty and accomplishments tonight,*
> *and concluded that <u>sensible</u> men looked for something more than*
> *beauty in their wives, and for our own comfort concluded that*
> *beauty gained a great deal of admiration but very little <u>sincere</u> <u>love</u>.*
> *Intellect is the thing nowadays, however. How different from the*
> *days of chivalry. I am sure we should feel no interest in a hero*
> *now, let him be ever so gallant, if he knew neither how to read or*
> *write. (14.8.1832)*

But Harriett did not have to worry about lacking the physical or mental attributes
of feminine beauty of her time, even if she might have felt so sometimes.

> *This morning was lying reading on my couch and the boy brought*
> *me something in the form of a note, which on examination proved*
> *an anonymous production addressed to Miss Low, which if you*
> *will not say is vanity I will copy for your perusal. I suspect who*
> *<u>may</u> be the <u>author</u> — he endeavoured to conceal the handwriting,*
> *but did <u>not</u> succeed.*
>
> > *There is a winning charm of gentle nature*
> > *On all thy being like a perfume thrown*
> > *Making each beauty both of mind and feature*

Inseparable — <u>not</u> to be <u>singly</u> known.
Something there is that as an unseen power
Subdues the wonted current of our thought
Leaving the heart all passive — But one hour
Of <u>thy</u> sweet converse, and the Soul is fraught
With feelings of a cast, oh! <u>too</u> deeply wrought. (22.8.1832)

These verses are written in the form of an acrostic, which is a composition where certain letters in each line taken together form a word. In this case, all the first letters of each line read "TOMISSLOW". However, what initially had pleased and flattered her, was discarded as *"foolish affair"* a few months later, after having found out the true author of these lines, namely a Mr. Ward, supercargo by profession, who by then had left Macau long since.

The house of the Lows was probably one of the most sought after places by the foreign bachelors in Macau and Canton. This was true, even more so, after Caroline Shillaber's arrival in December of 1831 — not because she would have been prettier or smarter than Harriett, but because it was double fun for all involved.

Verily think the spirit of mischief is fully developed in us two girls.
No stone remains unturned that will serve for our amusement.
(28.1.1833)

The address on a note to Harriett and Caroline illustrates very well how many men must have felt about the Low residence.

It was addressed to "Mesdames H. Low & Co., At the Palace of
'Sans Souci', Celestial Regions, Merchantesses". In reply to which
we wrote a long note — I do not think it worth copying.
(27.1.1833)

Together the two young women could also receive male visitors or go for a walk with them, something that would have been considered indecent for a single woman. After yet another "full house" until late at night on an ordinary day, Harriett was left to wonder, perhaps a bit naively, about their apparent popularity:

They all stayed till after 11, seem[ed] to hate to go then. The
mystery is what they want to stay for. They seem quite happy if
they are allowed to come and sit down in the house. <u>Strange</u>! but
true. They are all to come tomorrow evening. (3.7.1832)

Knowing about the shortage of young English-speaking women in Macau, we understand, of course, that most men visited just for the sake of the rare and pleasant female companionship. Others, however, had more serious intentions, and depending on the willingness of the girls to "play along", something like a courtship could develop. One interesting example in this respect is the case of James Perkins Sturgis (1791–1851), a Bostonian, who had came to China in 1809 and who, after having been successful in business, was living in a beautiful bungalow on Penha Hill. Another Sturgis, Sam Parkman Sturgis, was already one of the beaux of Harriett and Caroline. James P. Sturgis made his entrée as party interested in Harriett in the following way:

> After dinner walked <u>upon</u> the <u>Campo</u>. Only <u>think</u> <u>how</u> <u>strange</u> — but what makes it more wonderful is that <u>James</u> <u>P</u>. <u>Sturgis</u>, <u>Esq</u>. condescended to offer me his arm. Walked home, took tea with us, and made himself <u>extremely</u> <u>agreeable</u>. <u>Perhaps</u> it will be in the <u>Courier</u>!! ... He has been here 23 years, is to be sure an excuse for any enormity he might commit. Never been in ladies' society. Is of a most reserved and singular temper, but when in the humour can be quite delightful. He let me step into a heap of mud tonight, which I did not <u>much</u> <u>like</u>, because it was so heavy it took my shoe off and broke the string. However, he's near sighted, and then the <u>honour</u>. (30.6.1832).

James Sturgis was mostly called "Uncle Jem" by Harriett, due to the great difference in age between them. A few days later he visited again and

> I allowed him to make a cigar upon the terrace, a great favour. (2.7.1832)

And at his birthday a couple of days later, Harriett was seated at his side.

> This evening at 7 o'clock went to dine with <u>J</u>. <u>P</u>. <u>Sturgis</u>. His birth day. <u>Says</u> <u>40</u>, but — never mind. Has a magnificent house and every thing pleasant in it. Set between him & Colledge all the evening and at dinner, don't know when I have enjoyed an eve'g so much. Had about 12 at dinner. Wish I could tell you all the good fun. (9.7.1832)[4]

In the following days Uncle Jem continued to be "<u>very agreeable</u>," the two words always underlined. But soon the affair was over, terminated by Harriett.

> Wonder if he is as good as he <u>seems</u>. Oh, dear, I am dreadfully suspicious, unhappily so for my own comfort. But oh! This heartless deceitful world, or the people in it. People laugh and look quizzical at the <u>old</u> <u>man</u> — not that his <u>age</u> is at all objectionable to <u>me</u>. (12.7.1832)

In spite of her flirting and evident success, apparently she was not very secure about her feelings and let herself be influenced too much by the opinion of the "people". James P. Sturgis remained a bachelor for the rest of his life. He died in 1851 on board a ship at Anjier, on the way to London, after 42 years of residence in Canton and Macau.

A few months later, both Harriett and Caroline were raving about two new beaux, James Warner Seaver (1797–1871) and Philip Dumaresq (1804–1861), both North Americans.

> *We walked after dinner. Our two beaux joined us, and we had a delightful walk. They are both so respectful and gentlemanly, indeed all the gents here are. They never by look or word show any disrespect. They spent the evening with us. It is now about 12. Caro and I have been comparing notes and discussing the merits of the two, and wondering and wishing. Oh my dear sister that I could tell you all the "funny bits" and the strange manoeuvres of this place or rather the people. You do not know what it is to be one of two spinsters in a place. It is a distinction I would willingly give up and resign my post at any hour, but alas we cannot do as we would, here or there! (7.10.1832)*

Two weeks later, rumours started to spread, which quickly drew wider and wider circles.

> *It is currently reported in Lintin & Capsing moon,[5] that I am engaged to Dumaresq and Caroline to Seaver. And all for why, because they have been seen walking with us a few evenings. Poor creatures, I wonder any gentleman dares to walk with us for they engage us to every one, and if they happen to break off and not walk a day or two, why then they are juwaubed or in plain English refused.[6] We are quite independent of such reports now and only laugh at them. We warn new comers of their danger and find out if there is any one to be made jealous at home, for these reports do not rest here, but take wings to America, for they often rebound. (20.10.1832)*

As this was already the second engagement rumour in which Harriett was involved, it is not astonishing that her parents became worried about their daughter's reputation. After all, a girl's impeccable name was, apart from her dowry perhaps, the best guarantee to make a good party.

William W. Wood

Underlying the flirts described just now was a more serious love affair between Harriett Low and William W. Wood, amounting to a secret engagement. How and when exactly they got engaged is not revealed in the journal. Loines quotes extensively from a large fragment of a letter, directed to her sister and most intimate confident Molly. It was written in a moment of great despair, when Harriett knew that her relationship with Wood was definitively over. In a succinct and precise way it describes Wood's character, as well as the evolution of their relationship and her own feelings about it.[7]

> The youth [Wood] came out here two years this next February. He called upon us soon after his arrival.[8]

In Harriett's first description of Wood in her journal, his major traits are already revealed. It also alludes to some kind of tension — perhaps a first sparkle of mutual attraction — between them:

> I have been introduced to another American gentleman who came out in the Fanny of Philadelphia, a Mr. Wood, a very clever and pleasant young man. ... He is an immense talker. (1.3.1831).

> After dinner went to walk, got into a bit of a scrape, something about walking with Mr. Wood, however, not worth telling. (2.3.1831)

Remarks as the following are typical when referring to Wood:

> Mr. Wood made us a flying call after dinner, came down this morning. Did a week's talking in 10 minutes. (7.6.1831)

> Wood commenced talking at 7 o'clock and ceased at 10 without scarcely a response except a laugh from the rest of the party. (4.2.1832)

Whenever Wood was in Macau, he would call daily on the Low ladies, inviting them for a walk, and send poetry, books, drawing utensils and witty letters to Harriett. One of his attentions provoked a strange commentary:

> Found ... two annuals for me, a present from Mr. Wood with his compliments — so ceremonious it alarms me. Oh dear what animals men are. They are certainly incomprehensible. I do think I have had some odd specimens to deal with. (9.4.1832)

Drawing was Wood's hook, with which he thought to catch Harriett.

> *He draws very well; and he immediately took me under his protection and became my teacher. I received many little billet[s] doux upon the fine arts, but it never occurred to me that he cared at all about me till last winter. He was down several times, as soon as Mr. Vachell ceased his attentions. I always took great pleasure in his society and enjoyed it more than anyone I knew, but I treated him as a mere acquaintance, and if I ever did think that he cared about me I thought of it as an impossibility, and treated him with still more coolness. He wrote me several times upon the drawing, to which I of course replied, till Uncle requested me to stop the correspondence, which I immediately did. He then gave up all hopes. But in the summer there was another person who paid particular attentions [James P. Sturgis], which I have mentioned before. Mr. Wood came down about the same time, and he very soon found the other person had no encouragement. Mr. Wood made himself very agreeable. I found his conversation, tastes, sentiments and feelings all corresponded with mine.*[9]

His many talents, liveliness and spiritedness soon attracted her.

> *He is so <u>rich</u> in his <u>ideas</u>, and so keenly alive to the beauties of nature and all her works. ... <u>He</u> can amuse, instruct, and entertain; he is gay with the gay and grave with the grave. In a mixed company you would think him the greatest <u>rattle</u> that ever existed, but take him by himself, let him feel interested, then he shines. Will it ever be my lot to be <u>with</u> him? (29.11.1832)*

Twice she even referred to their conversations as *"most <u>extraordinary</u>"* and unforgettable for the rest of her life, but without explaining why.[10] Harriett, who had already resisted some suitors in Macau, could not resist Wood.

> *I did not wish him to propose for I knew how Uncle would feel. But it came and I could not say <u>No</u>, and I did as I have told you before, desired him to keep it secret till we went to America. But we afterwards thought it best to make it known to Uncle. The result you know already. Now I must live on. He says he cannot <u>change</u>, the spring which impelled him is now broken, and though he may perform his duties as before, he shall do it with an unwilling heart. He is too proud to go — but he will never be happy. I wrote him the other day as fully as I could — As yet I have had no reply.*

He is very busy assisting Uncle now. He gave up his own business
which perhaps was small and served instead [several words illegible]
and all for my sake.

Now for his personal appearance which is a small part, but
you may think he has a handsome face and that has won your
sister's heart — but it is not so. He is not handsome, though he
has a most intellectual face — high and noble forehead, blue eye[s]
and brown hair, a turn up nose and a sweet smile.[11]

It must have been in late October when Harriett's uncle told her to reconsider the engagement with Wood.

Got letters from Uncle this morning, which discomposed me for
the day. (22.10.1832)

Besides, Uncle also must have instructed his wife, in order to do what he could not do in person — talk her back to reason, as they must have considered their niece's relationship with Wood unsuitable.

Went into Aunt Low's room, had a long talk. Set there from 10
till 1 talking and settling the affairs of the nation. Don't know that
I ever felt more wretched. Had a letter while I set there from
Canton. What a world of trials and disappointments this is. Money
seems to be the one thing <u>needful</u>, the sine qua non of existence.
Oh <u>romance</u>, where dost thou dwell? Our dearest and fondest hopes
are often dashed for the want of the <u>filthy</u> <u>lucre</u>, our fairest schemes
defeated, our plans broken, and even our affections have some
times to be sacrificed for the want of it. (23.10.1832)

According to this commentary, the point of future financial security, typically overlooked by the young, seemed to have been one of the main arguments. As her uncle would bestow a small fortune on Harriett, as a reward for her companionship in Macau, he probably feared that Wood could waste the money. Harriett's daughter Katharine explains at this point in her edition of the journal:

The Mr. W[ood] so often referred as so clever and so charming
must be the person whose addresses were not received favorably
by the wise uncle, who knew him to be a man of irascible temper,
little steadiness of character, and with neither fortune nor prospects,
with nothing, in fact, but his brilliant talents to recommend him.
Miss L. fully acquiesced in the wisdom of her uncle's decision later
on, though it was hard to bear at the time.[12]

After the break-up of their engagement, Harriett still saw Wood several times in Macau, at the opera and while walking. But he never called on her, a behaviour that hurt her deeply, because for her the cancellation of the engagement did not mean the end of their friendship. For some time she still felt very attracted to him, although stating to the contrary.

> *This morning studied a little, then went to Chinnery's room. There is now a great attraction, a picture of my friend, which I was strongly tempted to* <u>*pocket*</u>*. It is a perfect likeness. I shall probably not see it again, as it is going to America — well I do not know why I should wish to; he is nothing to me. (8.1.1833)*

During one of their last encounters, Wood tried to speak to her. Harriett, though excited interiorly, was able to appear disinterested.

> *I was perfectly astonished at my own apparent coolness, while he was* <u>*choking*</u> *and* <u>*stuttering*</u>*, but it is astonishing what pride will do and for the* <u>*few*</u> <u>*moments*</u> *you would [have] thought me perfectly* <u>*indifferent*</u>*. Well I was satisfied with myself and came home feeling much better. (23.6.1833)*[13]

Wood left for Manila in mid-October of 1833. Indeed, he was never able to make a fortune as so many others did, which may be attributed not only to his lack of business skills, but partially to his abstention from trading opium. Although his future life seems to have confirmed the negative expectation of Harriett's caretakers, we do not know the turn that his life would have taken with the right woman at his side. For some time Wood worked on a coffee plantation at Jala-jala (Rizal, Philippines) and then as a clerk for Russell and Sturgis in Manila. He also continued to send animal specimen to the Academy of Natural Sciences of Philadelphia and to develop his skills with the *camara obscura*, which was already mentioned by Harriett as one of Wood's pastimes. Wood never married and the time of his death is not known. His last proof of existence dates from a scientific correspondence of 1874.[14]

Dr. Thomas Colledge and George H. Vachell

Apart from Wood, there were two other men, both of them English, to whom Harriett felt strongly attracted, namely Colledge and Vachell. They already lived in Macau when the Lows arrived. Right from the beginning and without exception, the entries in the journal about Colledge are in an admiring and sometimes almost enthusiastic tone.

> *Our good friend Dr. Colledge called. He is the best man I have seen yet, every body loves him and speak well of him. He has been truly kind to us. We are under great obligations to him. It is a shame that he is a Bachelor. (21.10.1829)*

After the arrival of Caroline, Colledge became a declared object for raving. The two girls seemed equally mad about him.

> *Dr. Colledge in this morning, a "darling", stayed two hours. The best Englishman I ever saw. He is truly good at heart, I believe. There is no nonsense about him. (13.3.1832)*

> *You may remember how I used to rave about a certain doctor at home. Well there is another Dr. here. Parfait amour. We met him on the Campo on horseback. By mutual consent we stopped, chatted, petted the horse (instead of his master) and made him promise to call tomorrow and see Aunt Low, as she is not very well. However, we will have the call. (30.3.1832)*

> *He is such a love. (15.4.1832)*

Colledge must have been flattered by the admiration and in the summer of 1832 his visits to the Low residence became more frequent. Once he even promised the girls wedding presents.

> *Promised Caroline and I a Cashmere Shawl when we were married and a lace veil. He is as good a man I believe as there is going. (15.6.1832)*

It is quite possible that Colledge was initially more interested in Harriett than Caroline, already before Caroline's arrival. However, it seems that he never made it clear enough for Harriett to understand. At the time when he apparently tried doing so, Harriett was already too involved with Wood to pay much attention to it.

> *[Colledge] made me a curious proposal which I do not intend to avail myself of. I do not mean he offered himself. He is a queer creature — everyone likes him. I hardly know his drift this morning. (14.7.1832)*

Harriett's friendship with the chaplain Vachell was a more gradual process. We already know that her first impression of him was that of a *"great buck"* (2.10.1829), although behaving *"very well"* (17.11.1829). In one book, he is described as *"gambler and the local flirt"*,[15] based upon which information I do not know. According to my understanding of Vachell's person, which derives mainly from the journal, this is not at all the case. I would characterise him as a person trying to live life to the fullest, with an interest in literature, music, nature and natural history.[16] Apart from this, his professional duties demanded a profound knowledge of both divine, and perhaps even more, human nature. He was a good listener and had wit.

> *Just 10 minutes past 10. Mr. Vachell has just sent his watch here for Aunt to set her's by. We were late at Church several times and he said he should <u>preach</u> <u>at</u> <u>us</u> if we did not come earlier. Every Sunday now, he very kindly sends us the right time. I should like to have you know him, he is one of the oddest mortals that ever inhabited this globe, I believe. (27.6.1830)*

Starting in around April of 1831, his name or the subjects of their conversation often appear underlined, for Molly to understand that something had changed in their relationship. In this respect, the sentence *"Mr. Vachell in this morning, <u>to</u> <u>bring</u> <u>me</u> <u>a</u> <u>book</u>"* (12.5.1831) is quite different from a simple *"Mr. Vachell in this morning, to bring me a book"*. On another day she received a letter from Vachell, *"written ¹/₂ way between here & Canton — not <u>very</u> <u>important</u>"* (6.10.1931). Once in a while he gave her small gifts, as did many other gents, one of which, however, of a *very* mysterious nature and probably alluding to matrimony.

> *After dinner Vachell came in and how you will laugh when I tell you what he brought me from Canton. You might guess till you were tired and would fail, I think. It is an article which is generally thought very important, when accompanied by something else, and which often make a great change in a person's life, but without the article that should accompany such a gift, I do not think it <u>very</u> <u>important</u>. It is however very pretty, and will serve as a remembrance, and will cause many a smile. I would not have it known here for any thing. Guess if you can, I will leave you in the dark at present. Mrs. Allport came in, she saw this article lying on the couch. She says, I think this should never be seen in the drawing room, nor should it be in the possession of a young lady. (23.4.1831)*

Harriett came to consider him as *"my best and indeed my only friend among the English"* (10.5.1831).

Over time Vachell really seemed to have fallen in love with Harriett, and very persistently so. But apparently his advances were not welcomed by her uncle, mainly after he had dared to offer his arm to Harriett in front of him and Talbot, the American consul in Canton. From then on she was forced to cut him.

> *Poor Vachell, I've had to <u>cut</u> him, not from any inclinations of*
> *<u>my</u> <u>own</u>, but to satisfy the <u>people</u>, they will talk so. (18.11.1831)*

But Vachell did not give up so easily. He would still have to hear more *"plain English"* from Harriett, until he understood that there could not be more than friendship between them.

> *After dinner we walked out to the barrier. Were joined by Mr.*
> *Vachell in spite of finesses and "ruses" of different kinds.[17] He is*
> *the most <u>wonderful</u> man; hints will not do for him. Before we got*
> *home I give him some more plain English. I do wish he would not*
> *torment me so. (4.4.1832)*

At that time Harriett had already become aware of Wood's interest in her, which must have facilitated the emotional separation from Vachell.

In June or July 1832 Vachell fell seriously ill, the news of which she commented on rather hard-heartedly and self-interestedly:

> *Very much alarmed but not without reason. I hear [he] makes a*
> *great many good resolves, which I hope he will keep, and that he*
> *may be able to say, "It is good for him that he has been afflicted".*
> *I fear there is great need for reformation in him as well as others.*
> *(5.7.1832)*

> *Believe his complaint is mostly nervous. Dreadful depression of*
> *spirits. (22.7.1832)*

For about six weeks Vachell was not able to preach and at the end of October of 1832 he sailed to England, after the arrival of his substitute, Rev. Charles Wimberley.

> *About 10 Vachell came in and bid us <u>good</u> <u>bye</u>. He leaves for*
> *England next month. 'Tis not pleasant to say farewell to anyone,*
> *particularly one whom you have been intimate with. He leaves*
> *Macao with the Factory tomorrow morning. (1.10.1832)[18]*

Vachell married in England and returned to Macau in 1834. At his death in 1839, he left a son and a daughter.[19] Vachell's name appears only very sporadically after his departure. Although there is no name mentioned in the following quotation, it clearly refers to him:

> *Mr. Wimberley is raised two or three pegs in my estimation by*
> *declining the Opera. They had tickets given them for the Season,*
> *but they do no go. It appears as though he took some interest in*

> *his profession and can make some sacrifices for it, which I fear*
> *would not have been the case with my friend. (8.5.1833)*

Harriett seemed to practise some kind of negative reinforcement, in order to convince herself that she was right rejecting him after all — however, her arguments, especially this one, are not very convincing ...

Married bliss versus unmarried solitude

The idea of ending up as a spinster or "old maid" lurked like a ghost over the women of that time. Marriage and motherhood were not only the propagated ideals for all female members of society, but also seemed to be a measuring rod for normality. A woman who did not marry had to shoulder all the blame for her disgraceful solitude alone.[20] In the Catholic world there was, however, one socially approved reason for female celibacy — the convent.[21] But again, a "normal" woman would not enter a convent. Clichés and romances about women who opted for a life as a nun abounded. As we already saw, in her description of the veil taking of a Catholic nun, Harriett invoked two such commonly assumed reasons: age and lack of physical attractiveness. Another, more romantic motif was that of unanswered or impossible love. Male celibacy, on the contrary, whether voluntary or not, has never been subject to the same denouncements and discrimination as the one of their female counterparts. This is already visible in the scarcity of vocabulary for a (male) bachelor, while there is a range of expressions like virgin, spinster, and old maid, to quote the more common ones, to designate female bachelorhood. Besides, the expressions referring to single women also imply an evaluation about their bodies, i.e. virginity, which the designations for males lack.

"Unhappy spinsters"

Considering the importance attributed to the married state, it is not astonishing that this topic appears regularly in the journal and that it was also, like religion, a rather common subject of conversation.

> *Another gloomy morning. Blight in and spent the morning. We*
> *had a long discussion on romance. Mr. Colledge was in, the most*
> *matter of fact person in the world. One observation of his*
> *introduced the subject. It's strange what ideas the English have of*
> *matrimony. He says every man ought to make it a business to get*
> *his daughters married and while they are in prosperity too. We told*

> *him he ought not to make such a speech before a party of*
> *Americans, for our motives for marrying are not so mercenary*
> *<u>generally</u> as theirs. Uncle & Blight were against Caroline as regards*
> *romance. Uncle is the <u>death</u> of every thing like it. If we admire*
> *the "dashing of the <u>billows</u>", he says "<u>it looks like soap suds</u>".*
> *(18.2.1832)*

There was still another fact that made the question of matrimony a worrisome one, namely the relative scarcity of men in certain parts of the world. Harriett mentioned that according to a recent census in her native state Massachusetts there were 14,000 more women than men (14.7.1831)! This figure must have troubled any woman who did not want to become an "old maid". During her long stay in Macau she also came to believe that *"there are as few men bachelors from <u>choice</u> as there are <u>old maids</u>"* (5.7.1833). Consequently, we can observe a certain exaltation of the married state:

> *Oh ye married ones! The privileges that are yours for having taken*
> *unto yourselves a helpmate! You may command, entreat, <u>obey</u> if*
> *<u>you please</u>. You can make a little world of your own and live within*
> *yourselves. Well, unhappy Spinsters! I say throw off all this*
> *<u>unfeeling</u>, <u>general attraction</u>, center it all in <u>one</u>, and then there is*
> *some chance for your happiness. (13.7.1832)*

 The anxiety about her own state as a spinster and the perspective of loneliness associated with it, caused her many a *"crying spell"* (13.7.1832) and the blues, amounting to a crisis of identity in the worst moments. But since unpleasant situations or tasks are more tolerable in company, Harriett and Caroline decided to stay together for the rest of their lives, sharing the burdens of spinsterhood, if there was no male willing to "rescue" them.

> *I have just left Carry's room. We have been anticipating the time*
> *when we shall be <u>ancient spinsters</u> having become almost disgusted*
> *with the <u>genus homo</u>, and almost determined to live a life of*
> *<u>celibacy</u>. We were thinking we would live together and do all the*
> *good we can. However I think if it is not Hobson's choice I shall*
> *yet espouse some poor unfortunate man, just to be the <u>torment</u> of*
> *some body's life. (25.12.1832)*

At other times, however, Harriett made up excuses for the case of not finding a spouse.

> *After all it makes very little difference whether one is married or*
> *not. If they are, ten to one they <u>repent</u> it and if not they are*

> *independent and can do pretty much as they please. After one's*
> *heart gets <u>callous</u> and our feelings too often thrown back upon*
> *ourselves, it matters little whether they are married or not. One*
> *should be very <u>unsophisticated</u> to get married I think. If they become*
> *old enough to look behind the scene, ten to one they never marry.*
> *(20.1.1833)*

Although this statement is quite exaggerated, Macau was an excellent showcase for unhappy, breaking and broken marriages, as we shall see later in "All kinds of marriages".

Thomas Colledge and Caroline Shillaber: a happy couple

After an intensive period of common flirting and raving about a series of young men, the happy time of mutual confidences was suddenly brought to an end by the one man who was most admired by both Harriett and Caroline:

> *Today my friend Mr. Colledge offered himself to my Caroline, and*
> *she has accepted him. I have given you his character before. She*
> *will make him an excellent wife. There is strong affection on both*
> *sides and will no doubt be happiness, at least it remains with*
> *themselves to be so or not. ... She has my best wishes and he too*
> *— for if I cannot be happy myself, I have no objection to seeing*
> *others so, indeed I am not so selfish as not to delight in the joy of*
> *my friends. But notwithstanding it does make me feel melancholy*
> *and more lonely than ever to see every one having some one worthy*
> *of loving, and poor I no one. I seem doomed to this and so I must*
> *bear it patiently, seem happy, lest those around should think me*
> *<u>envious</u>. ... I should like to shut myself in my own room and die*
> *a sort of temporary death till the time comes for us to leave this*
> *detested place. You can have no idea how tired how sick I am of*
> *it — time's wheels I once wished to <u>stop</u>, but now I say roll <u>swifter</u>*
> *on, for till I change the scene Life is almost insupportable. We dined*
> *at home and spent the evening in talking and thinking of the <u>electric</u>*
> *shock the people will have tomorrow. No one in the place out of*
> *our own family had any idea of such an event. (6.2.1833)*

In a marginal note we read:

> *You must not mind these <u>azure</u> <u>spots</u> in my books — they come*
> *and go.*

Indeed, as Harriett had predicted, the news about the engagement caused quite a sensation:

> *Latimer came in this morning and I had the pleasure of <u>electrifying</u> him. His astonishment was <u>great</u>. He could hardly realize it. I enjoyed it much. Colledge is beloved and respected by <u>all</u>, there is not a dissenting voice. All wish to see him happy. ... Latimer forthwith dispatched a boat to Canton to set the news afloat there, which will no doubt suspend all business for a time. The bachelors will feel they have lost one of their most worthy members, and the married men rejoice at such a <u>convert</u>. He had forsworn <u>matrimony</u>, but the charms of Miss S[hillaber] has overpowered his resolutions. It would have been a shame that such a man should not have been married, and happy <u>must</u> be the woman who marries him. ... Colledge came in while Latimer was here, and the congratulations were very <u>fine</u>. L[atimer] is one of his best friends. Colledge appeared "shut up in measureless content", looked perfectly complacent and happy and looked as though he would say "Let him laugh who wins". A <u>rival</u> was <u>thunderstruck</u> this morning at the announcement. It certainly could not have been very flattering or pleasing intelligence. (7.2.1833)*

In spite of all affirmations to the contrary, Harriett was deeply stirred by the engagement, implying the loss of her *"better half"* (19.3.1833) and intimate friend, the only one in Macau. From now on there would be some secrets that Caroline was not going to share with her anymore, shifting her priorities to her fiancé and husband. In the first days following the engagement, Harriett felt her own loneliness in a most desperate and exacerbated way.

> *Do you know, my dear Sis, what it is to feel alone? No, you do not. ... But let me tell you what it is — it is to be in a <u>far off land</u>, separated from your kin, in a place where the society is too small, the interests clashing, petty <u>feuds</u> existing, where the voice of friendship is seldom heard, where none feel interest in each other's happiness, in a word where all are strangers to each other; to be put into <u>such</u> a place, left there three years, and you will know what solitude is. (8.2.1833)*

Even her caring Uncle and Aunt could not help her in this situation.

> *They wish to see me happy and would do all in their power to make me so — but it is not in their power. They are happy in themselves,*

> *there is a sympathy of feeling between them which is worth all the*
> *world. They are all in all to each other. Their world lies within*
> *themselves. They cannot understand my feelings and therefore*
> *cannot fill the void.* (8.2.1833)

The only person of whom Harriett expected some understanding was Caroline, but when she "ventilated" her thoughts and feelings, Caroline felt guilty of her own happiness.

> *I have expressed it tonight, but dear girl it made her feel*
> *unpleasantly, so I will endeavour to say no more upon the subject.*
> (8.2.1833)

At an earlier occasion, also when feeling desperately lonely, she even compared her situation to one of the most famous biblical figures of suffering: "*I wonder how Job would have behaved had he been sent to China*" (14.12.1832).

But Harriett knew that she could not let herself down with this feeling, and soon afterwards her survival instinct got the upper hand again.

> *Caroline has promised to be married in 3 weeks from this time.*
> *Short work of it. I think my mind will not be regulated till she is*
> *"nuptified". So I shall be glad when it is over and I tell her [I] will*
> *do my best to get her out of the house. This morning I went to*
> *work and cut out a satin dress for her — consider myself No.1 at*
> *the trade.* (22.2.1833)

Caroline's blitz marriage called for speedy wedding preparations, in which Harriett participated energetically, especially because certain things were difficult to arrange and to get done in Macau.

> *This is a dreadful place to get married in — no shops to go to.*
> *Must pick up such things as you can catch, "asking no questions*
> *for conscience sake". You would laugh to hear us tell the*
> *Compradore send and "catch a Tailor" and then to see a great*
> *long tailed fellow trot in, impregnated with tobacco smoke, to take*
> *your work, which after much trouble you get stuck together, often*
> *in a manner that would little suit our particular ladies at home.*
> *But to get them done is the thing. If they have an exact muster*
> *they sometimes do pretty well, but the grievances are many, and*
> *one has to bear and forbear.* (26.2.1833)

> *One would imagine by my zeal that I was to be the happy bride.*
> *I am only too happy to be of any use.* (4.3.1833)

One of the last tasks was to write the invitations.

> *Have been writing cards all day. I shall send you a <u>muster</u> to show what the English custom is. If it comes in season [for your own wedding] you had better adopt it. I think it very pretty. (15.3.1833)*

> *Sent out about 65 invitations — something of a party. The Company's steward will arrange it. (16.3.1833)*

The bridesmaids were Harriett and one of the Misses Pereira. The latter, however, was second choice, because Rebecca Morrison, who had been invited to officiate, declined: "*She is very diffident and thinks she has no resolution*" (5.3.1833). Later Rebecca changed her mind, but by then it was too late.

> *Miss Morrison called to <u>retract</u> this morning, but we [had] invited Miss Pereira and she accepted. (6.3.1833)*

Caroline's evident happiness about the impending marriage even changed some of Harriett's ideas about this important event.

> *I have thrown aside my once cherished theories of long engagements and think it best they should be as short as possible. Don't ask me why? for I am sure I cannot say. (25.2.1833)*

This change of mind certainly contributed to the fact that within two years after her return to the United States, she was married too, while her sister Molly, for example, had been engaged for several years.

After frenetic wedding preparations, as we have seen, the great day was celebrated with all possible style and dignity.

> *This morning soon after breakfast I dressed the bride in white Satin with a lace handkerchief over her neck and veil on her head. She looked interesting of <u>course</u>. Dressed myself in white muslin and at 11 our party consisting of Mr. & Mrs. Low, Mr. Colledge, Miss <u>Shillaber</u> & brother, Mr. Plowden, Mr. Lindsay, Mr. Gover, Mr. Latimer, & Hudleston, groomsman, Miss Pereira & self bridesmaids, proceeded to the church or chapel, where the ceremony was read in a most solemn & impressive manner by Mr. Wimberley. There is much in the English service that I should think better omitted, but however we got through very well and returned to our house, where the tables were all elegantly laid for about 70 people. They all came in and were introduced to Mrs. Colledge as at our evening parties at home after a wedding. The Governor*

thought to make himself of consequence and kept us waiting an hour, so that we sat down to <u>breakfast</u> about 1. Latimer engaged a band of music to play to enliven the repast and play as we entered from Church. Every thing went off well. The Italian Singers volunteered to sing and they were a great acquisition. The party broke up about 4 and the bride & bridegroom went to their house at 6. We had the groomsman and bridesmaid to dinner at 7 with several other gentlemen. All together the day was passed in a very satisfactory manner. And feeling that the parties were well suited to each other and the proper affection existing we could but feel happy that they were thus united. I thought at the time that you my dear Sis might possibly be performing the same ceremony — if so may God bless you and make you as happy in your choice as I think Caroline is. There is no mistake in Colledge. Nor do I think there is in George [Mary Ann's fiancé]. Therefore I resign my <u>two sisters</u> with the greatest cheerfulness. (18.3.1833)

All kinds of marriages

As Harriett had observed earlier, only a few men were bachelors by their own will. Therefore it is not astonishing that the search for a bride was an important business. Since Macau did not offer a great range of potential spouses, they were usually sought in the countries of origin of the willing husbands-to-be. On knowing about the great surplus of women over men in Massachusetts, two of Harriett's countrymen, unlike her, seemed to be more than happy.

You would be amused to hear him [Talbot] and King rejoicing at the chance they shall have when they go home. ... They think they shall have their <u>pick</u>. It is rather desperate, I think. (14.7.1831)

In the case of the British and Portuguese, their colonies in India constituted an important resource in this respect, an option more or less halfway between Macau and Europe.

Dent called to say "good bye". Off for Calcutta, I hear, in search of a spouse, but <u>do no</u>. (19.3.1832)

Only one day later, she received news of a successful spouse hunt:

This evening a note from Ibar saying the Gen. Hamilton has arrived, having on board Capt. & Mrs. Macondre [Macondray]. Hyyah [Cantonese exclamation], it does not take long to "catch a

*wife". Only about a year since he left here, and here he is back
again with his Sposa [spouse]. Long to hear who he has married
and all the news, which I hope is good. Expect it will set some of
the other Bachelors on tip toe. (20.3.1832)*

Then as now, however, not all marriages were contracted out of mutual love.
Instead of being celebrated openly as it would be natural for a wealthy
Portuguese family, the following marriage was surrounded by strange
circumstances.

*[Colledge] tells me of a curious marriage there was at the Cathedral
this morning at 5 o'clock — a Miss Paiva, one of the most
respectable families here. He says he heard all the circumstances
from her brother so he can vouch for the truth of it. It seems this
young lady was several times in company with a gent (I forget his
name), but Capt. of the Camoens. She fancied him very much,
but he show[ed] no signs of partiality to her. But she was not to be
foiled by that. She told her brother, she liked him and if she was
married it must be him, and he must do all in his power to promote
the match. I believe she did not actually propose herself, but they
managed it so satisfactorily that the marriage was consummated.
But think you, it was love that bound him? Ah no, the 80,000
dol[lars] was the rivet, when, if they should be unfortunate, where
will they be — she is fat and ugly, and he worships the dollars.
He was worth nothing before, and I suppose considers himself
fortunate — but I should not think he would fancy the appendage
he must have with the money. (18.9.1832)[22]*

In the next example the villain is, for a change and perhaps more unusually, the
wife.

*You will notice in some of my books Mrs. Beaucaut's name. Now
I can give you the finale. She went home to England, and from
all I can learn from those who went in the ship with her, she was
there a disgrace to her sex, but let that pass. She went to England
and has eloped with a hatter — the whole to conclude, with Mr.
Beaucaut her husband and child, go into mourning for her. Yes
verily they put on black. What a farce. Did you ever hear any thing
so absurd? — but this is a finale no one expected, a high spirited,
proud woman to elope with a hatter. No one would have supposed
any thing less than a nobleman would have tempted her to such
an act, as I believe she was thought to act cooly and deliberately*

rather than from impulse. But there is no knowing what a wicked woman will not do. It will be a lesson for people here, not to <u>worship</u> every pretty face that comes along without any recommendation beside. (12.7.1833)

The marriage of one of Harriett's English acquaintances, Mrs. Davis, did not seem to have been very happy either. Her husband must have had a singularly difficult nature, as various other sources mention too, although they do not refer to John F. Davis's domestic behaviour but his public life.[23] There are however several passages in the journal which make reference to their marriage.

Spent the morning as usual, except a visit from Mrs. Davis. If there is a woman in the place to be pitied, it is her. (14.6.1832)

One month later, Harriett seemed to have witnessed her problems directly. Although the names of all the participants are not mentioned, the following episode quite likely refers to the Davis couple.

Spent the evening at Mrs. Davis's. At 9 we went out to sail in the Cutter with a full moon, a fine breeze — and a party of 9. Cannot say I enjoyed it much, for there was a scene that rather discomposed one, a <u>domestic quarrel</u>. At least a shameful affair on the part of the husband; the poor woman bore it quietly. Oh woman, how much you have to bear at times. I made some sage reflections upon the married life, what a lottery. I came home sick at heart I confess. (14.7.1832)

Illicit love affairs and love for money

Although Harriett Low reports a couple of cases of marital infidelity or of seduction with "visible consequences" as in the case of Nancy, her journal is not a reliable source regarding the true extent of illicit love affairs that were initiated by Western men for various reasons. First of all, she was only acquainted with a small and unrepresentative fraction of the men who made their appearance in Macau and Canton. Secondly, at that time it was unthinkable that men talked openly about their sexual adventures in the presence of ladies in the style of modern American soap operas or sitcoms, where nothing seems to be too delicate to be discussed and broadcast.

However, men did talk among themselves and write about their observations or conquests in this field.

Despite the unanimous protestations of virtue on the part of American traders, celibacy was by no means universal. A few personal letters, particularly by young bloods at Macao, show how varied were the opportunities for violating the seventh commandment.[24]

For their sexual escapades, men generally turned to females of a lower social rank than the wives, daughters and other female siblings of important traders or missionaries, who were more likely to be seen and assessed as potential spouses.[25] Therefore, they had to be more cautious when getting involved with a "respectable" girl, because the consequences for the seducer might be more severe, including the possibility of being challenged to a duel.

As Western women were barred from entering China, the men in Canton had to seek Chinese women. However, since the Westerners were living in seclusion on Shamian island in Canton, with little freedom of movement, or aboard the ships at the anchorages at Whampoa and Lintin island, this was no easy task. Therefore, the Chinese women had to seek the Westerners as much as vice versa. Since the language and cultural differences were very effective separation barriers, the majority of the Westerners who were looking for this kind of distraction, had to turn to prostitutes. In 1769, long before the heyday of the Canton trade, a British traveller to Canton reported that

near Whampoa, was a whole class of water-borne prostitutes, whose services presumably helped to calm restless sailors during their "lay-days" at the anchorage.[26]

The boats of the Chinese ladies of pleasure were known as "flower boats" and are depicted on many views of the factories among the myriad of boats on the river.

Downs mentions here that to his knowledge

sexual relations between Chinese and Americans were very rare until the Opium War.[27]

I wonder whether this was really the case or whether they are simply not well documented. History has recounted over and over again that prostitution flourishes where there is lots of money, present-day Macau is merely one example. The "Lisboa", five-star hotel and casino, illustrates this connection in its most blatant form: husbands or boyfriends, on the arms of their wives or girlfriends, are virtually assaulted by prostitutes, not to mention unaccompanied men! Therefore, it can be assumed that the sexual encounters between Western men and Chinese women in Canton grew side by side with the intensification of the trade in the decades to come.[28]

While it must have been virtually impossible to have a prolonged affair with a Chinese woman in Canton, things were different in Macau with its century-old tolerance of racial miscegenation. Here foreigners could have mistresses for shorter or longer periods. The temptation must have been great and money was a minor problem, as the following quotation from a letter by John Heard reveals:

> *The likeness of the Macao girl I sent you is a veritable portrait of one who is kept by an English gentleman there. She has a sister, also kept, who is nearly as good looking. And there is a little girl named "ayow" now about 15 years old who lives in a boat near our house, who is prettier than either of them. She is still virtuous & has refused an offer of $500, but I suspect will relent before long. These things are only looked upon here as amiable weaknesses, and there are a lot of bastard children kicking about Macao.*[29]

Considering that this amount corresponded more or less to the annual salary of a clerk in Canton, the offer was definitely not made by a poor man.

The indication that Ayow lived on a boat identifies her as Tanka girl. It was their profession to transport passengers from larger ships to the beach and to take people around on the water. They also had a reputation for providing more than this service.

> *Sampans or "wash boats" manned by three or four girls would pull alongside a newly-arrived ship. One girl would call out: "Ah you missee chiefee mate, how you dooa? I saavee him werry wen. You saavee my? I makee mendee, all same you shirtee last time." The sailors were delighted to see them and they were ready to be anyone's sweet-heart.*[30]

Downs mentions that

> *William C. Hunter kept a Tanka girl with whom he apparently maintained a very long and responsible relationship,*[31]

without explaining, however, how this relationship appeared in practice. But since Hunter was the only American who could speak Cantonese, at least they had something in common beyond the mere physical aspect of their relationship. Other Americans, apart from Hunter, who are known to have fathered children with their Macanese or Chinese mistresses are John Hart and Benjamin Wilcocks. The latter's daughter was later sent, without his knowledge, by another American trader to the USA to see her father, who at the time of her arrival happened to be looking for a wife in his hometown Philadelphia ...

New husband, new home: the challenges of housewifery

Once married, a girl's mind had to switch very fast from being taken care of to taking care of a husband and the common home. Daughters were socialised into their future role as housewives and mothers at an early age, thus constituting a valuable support to their mothers. Among the working class or peasantry they were even substituting for their mothers in cases where she worked outside the home or was dead. But not every daughter was happy with this arrangement and prospect for the future, especially if they had some kind of education. In the following passage Harriett wondered about her role at home after her return from Macau.

> *I suppose you are trusting that I shall come home a <u>venerable</u> <u>spinster</u> and be just fit <u>pour</u> <u>ménager</u>. The first is most probable, but the second not, for when I come home I suspect you will condemn me as a <u>drone</u> and turn me out of the hive. I must confess I never desire to see a kitchen, (you know I never had a <u>penchant</u> for the place) but in any other way that I can make myself useful I shall be most happy. (20.1.1833)*

Her few cooking experiences in Macau qualify Harriett as decidedly unfit for marriage, one of them having been an outright disaster.

> *This morning after breakfast having had a little molasses given me, I undertook to make some candy. A delightful employment for a hot day — but upon my word I felt no hotter for the fire. Indeed I have not been so <u>comfortable</u> for some time. I had a little Pogong or furnace put on the terrace which goes out from my room and had the apparatus brought up. And there I sat and stirred, reflecting on the many candy frolics I have had at home and the work we used to make for the servant alias "<u>help</u>". ... In spite of my reflections and my attention my candy all of a sudden <u>burned</u> — <u>because</u> the fire was too hot. A very good reason, sure. So I sung out to Achow that he must take it down and bring me another kettle or (what ever name it might be dignified with) and some more molasses and I would commence on the remains of the coals and be sure not to burn it this time. Sundry and divers regrets, but of no avail, so I laughed it off and was soon under way again — thinking as I had less fire I might take it more comfortably. So with my bamboo in one hand stirring with all my might and my book in another, and a fine breeze upon my back, I began to think I*

> *should make candy often, when suddenly I looked at my candy
> the fire was <u>defunct</u> and my <u>lasses</u> had stopped boiling. Thinks I
> to myself this won't do. So I <u>sung</u> <u>out</u> to Achow that the fire was
> <u>defunct</u> and the molasses would not <u>walky</u>. So up he came, the
> cooly with some coals, and the boy with some <u>fire</u>, for it takes three
> to do any thing here. And you would have laughed to see me sitting
> there in the midst of them with my bamboo and book and their
> operations are very amusing. Finally I was in order again and
> succeeded, à merveille. The Candy was delicious and the only
> difficulty was, <u>once</u> <u>in</u> the dish we could not get it out again —
> for it was not well buttered. Well I thought I must do my best to
> get some out for I had promised some of it to Mr. Wimberley and
> Caroline. After much trouble I succeeded in getting some out for
> Mr. Wimberley & Mr. Davis, which they thought very nice, and
> I had some very <u>facetious</u> <u>notes</u> in return. To Caroline I sent a
> dish as it was, and told her she would probably have to eat dish
> and all, for I despaired of getting it out. … But alas, alas, the last
> remains to be told. In the evening I wanted to taste my Candy
> and lo and behold it had returned to that from which it came and
> I saw nothing but a dish of <u>molasses</u>. (3.7.1833)*

Although well-off middle class households had a series of domestic helpers, and especially so in Macau where, as we saw, each task was carried out by a different servant or coolie, they had to be instructed and supervised. For Caroline, who like Harriett never had had to care about anything apart perhaps from sewing and needlework, the change into Mrs. Colledge seemed to have been quite a challenge in this respect.

> *About 2 I went to Caroline's and found her busy in <u>domestic</u> cares.
> I heard nothing but <u>Catties</u> of <u>Oil</u>, and <u>Taels</u> of <u>Fish</u>.[32] I laughed
> at her and rejoiced that I had nothing of the kind to bother my head
> and came home to dinner. I admire to plague her. I dare say she
> thinks it's all envy, but it is a fact that part of the business I should
> hate as much as she does. (13.8.1833)*

By now we understand perhaps why Harriett never married in Macau, or we understand enough to reject Teixeira's interpretation of this fact, who indicated two main reasons.

> *The first one is that a girl who goes out with everybody, ends up
> without anybody. The second explanation is the one that I once
> heard from a woman from Madrid … — the one whom I want*

> *does not want me and the one who wants me, I do not want him* ... .[33]

The reading of the full version of the journal does not admit the first reason indicated by Teixeira, who based his impression of Harriett on Hillard's edition of the journal. There is not even room left for the doubt that this Portuguese saying expresses. Although admittedly mischievous and ready for almost anything that could have provided her with a good laugh, Harriett was a young woman with a serious character and firm moral principles. There is more evidence in the journal regarding the second reason indicated by Teixeira, but it applies only partially. It is obvious that there were more false suitors than men to whose feelings she would have replied with the same intensity. But for a few happy weeks Harriett was the secret fiancée of William Wood and she did not end this engagement voluntarily,[34] for the better or worse of her future life, we will never know.

Joys and sorrows of motherhood

Marriage inaugurated a new life cycle in a woman's life, which, until the onset of menopause, was filled with an increasingly tiresome and exhausting activity: bearing children. No woman, Queen or commoner, could escape Nature's dictate in this respect.[35] At the beginning of her stay in Macau, Harriett missed the company of children, because at home there had been eight younger siblings. But since some of her new acquaintances in Macau had a whole bunch of them, a visit to or from them could easily satisfy her longings in this respect.

> *Has [Mary Turner] 4 pretty children, one about our little Ellen's age [then 2½ years old]. I was perfectly delighted to see something that looked like home. (5.10.1829)*

A few weeks later we read:

> *On our return Mrs. Turner called in and took tea with us sociably. ... She brought her little Richard with her, just the age of our Charley [then 5 years old]. I took him in my arms, and he went off to sleep. It really seemed like being at home to have a child in my arms. (14.11.1829)*

At a later stage, however, Harriett found the company of children rather strenuous, fearing that they upset the quietness of the Low household.

> *After dinner the little Daniells came to hear the organ. Fine children and very smart, but I should think troublesome, they are so full of life and roguery. ... They stayed an hour and I was really glad to have them go for I was not sure that any thing would be left in place. I am now so unused to children, and I am always afraid they will break some of their limbs. (13.4.1833)*

Motherhood also constituted a dividing line between married women and their unmarried counterparts. The fact of having neither husband nor children sometimes provoked a desire for isolation in Harriett.

> *About 6 I went out in my chair and sat alone upon [a] rock meditating and enjoying the fine breeze. A Little distance from me was a heap of married ladies, but as I have no feelings in common with them I would not join them and no doubt they thought me very unsociable. (28.6.1833)*

Harriett's aunt, though being childless herself, apparently engaged with interest in conversations about all kinds of topics about children.

> *Aunt Low & I went out this morning, called on Mrs. Clifton, Mrs. Wimberley, Mrs. Alexander, & Miss Barwell, Mrs. Rees, Whiteman, and Crocket — had sundry dissertations upon children, their rise & progress. All very entertaining to me, as you may suppose. Aunt L. seems to enter into the particulars with great pleasure and you would think she had $\frac{1}{2}$ a dozen herself. (10.10.1832)*

One of Harriett's favourite targets of criticism in this respect was the Morrison family.

> *I then went to see Mrs. Morrison whom I found very agreeable. She has just been confined and has another boy. A happy circumstance, the Missionary Society allow them something for every child they produce — why or wherefore I cannot say. Methinks it will cost them a pretty penny if they go on in this way one a year. (19.2.1833)*

Only when Mrs. Morrison was about to leave for England because of her health, which was worn out by too many births in Macau's tiring climate, Harriett showed some pity.

> *Called first on Mrs. Morrison. Found her comfortable, the old Dr.*
> *complaining — wants to get a sick certificate to go to England with*
> *his family. (10.9.1833)*

The latter comment is interesting, because it depicts a fatigued Morrison, who did not want to stay behind alone without his wife and the little ones. But apparently Morrison was indispensable for the British East India Company as translator. The family was not going to meet again. A casual remark of Harriett about the stout Morrison would become true even faster than she had thought: *"Think the old Dr. will die of apoplexy before many years"* (6.7.1833). She was right with her prophecy. The old doctor, who then was 51 years of age, died in the following year in Canton — whether of apoplexy or not, we do not know.

On hearing about Caroline's pregnancy, Harriett seemed rather relieved for having been spared that experience yet.

> *Went to see Caroline this morning. She is not very well and feels*
> *some of the troubles of matrimony. If you will believe me I came*
> *home quite satisfied with <u>single</u> <u>blessedness</u>. (7.8.1833)*[36]

Harriett had already left Macau when Caroline gave birth to their first son. However, the Colledges were not lucky with their children in Macau. In Macau's Protestant Cemetery we find three little tombs of sons of Caroline and Thomas Colledge, all having died in infancy.[37] Considering the love and energy that modern couples concentrate on their "only" one, or at best two children, we cannot but admire the physical and mental strength of those mothers who bore child after child, and had to see so many of them go at an age when they are most adorable. Harriett and her husband had to experience the same pain later. Of their eight children, only four daughters lived to full adulthood.

Another factor that caused lots of grief to the parents, but which was considered as a necessity, was the separation of some children from the family for the sake of education in Europe. Usually they were boys and they were sent at a young age. This tradition was prevalent among the power elite of the English colonists overseas. Harriett mentioned, for example, the case of Chay Beale, son of Thomas Beale, the owner of the aviary (27.3.1832). Wealthy Portuguese or Macanese families also seemed to have practised this custom.

> *Mrs. P[ereira]'s son has just returned from England. She did not*
> *know him, nor he any one of them, not even his mother. What a*

*sensation it must be not to be recognised even by a mother. It made
me shudder. (19.9.1831)*

Two years later, she wrote of the arrival of two more Pereira sons from England,
"where they have been many years" (29.10.1833).

Without the better half: widowhood

A walk through Macau's Old Protestant Cemetery will reveal that, compared
to nowadays, a disproportionately great number of people died in their 20s, 30s
and 40s. On some tombstones we also find an indication about the cause of death.
While complications at giving birth constituted an important factor for premature
death among women, many men suffered work-related accidents, such as
drowning in a typhoon, or they caught diseases from insalubrious working
conditions. Consequently there were a great number of both widows and
widowers. The English with their large colonial empire were particularly affected
by this phenomenon. Upon hearing about the arrival of two young English
widows in Macau, Harriett observed:

> *Poor things, they came out to India to meet their husbands and on
> their arrival found they were both widows — what a melancholy
> fate! How little the people in America know of these kind of
> sorrows. The English ladies have to wander over the oceans to meet
> their husbands, brothers, or fathers. Indeed how many of them live
> on the water except put on shore for a few days in a strange place
> while they have a fresh cargo. This [word illegible] colony in India
> separated thousands of families. (5.8.1831)*

Remarriage was considered with great pragmatism, as the women needed
somebody to provide a livelihood for them and their children, especially when
the latter were still young, while the men needed a caretaker for their children,
apart from the emotional companionship desired by both parties. Consequently,
this topic appears regularly in the journal.

> *Mr. Plowden has gone home and married a widow that <u>he</u> and
> several others were dreadfully in love with. (22.6.1831)*[38]

His return to Macau was commented by Harriett with little sympathy.

> *Two years ago this Mr. Plowden went home a widower with scarce
> a friend to see him off (but it might be a long story, so I shall not
> begin). Now he comes back with flying colours, a married man*

> *and now he will see smiles on every face. But alas it will be but*
> *outward show! I'd not be him for all India's wealth. (16.8.1832)*

There also existed a difference between the Americans and the English with regard to whom a widow/er should espouse, namely somebody from the family, ideally another widowed person such as a dead brother's/sister's wife/husband, or an outsider.

> *Mr. and Mrs. Daniell [English] have just been in. We happened*
> *to speak of Mrs. Cleveland [American] of her having married her*
> *sister's husband. It struck Mrs. Daniell with great horror, she says*
> *it is against the Ecclesiastical law to marry a sister in Law, and*
> *she thought it very dreadful. I told her it was very common with*
> *us, she was quite astonished. (6.3.1831)*

The advantages of such a union are evident: both partners already know each other fairly well, having had the occasion to observe each other's strengths and weaknesses over time; as regards the children, it may be easier for them to accept a relative as a step parent than a total stranger; and finally, in the case of a widowed sister-in-law, the money stays in the family. Later, there would be such a case among her own siblings, namely when her brother Abbot, who was the first one to follow Harriett to China, married his younger brother William's wife Anne Bedell, after both of them had been widowed. However, Harriett added the following observation to the above quoted entry: *"I must confess I should not like to marry a Brother in Law"* (6.3.1831). Harriett never remarried after having become a widow in 1859.

6
Macau, Canton and the China Trade

There are few places in the world that are self-sufficient. Thus, traders are among the oldest professions of mankind. But despite the many services rendered to their community often by risking their lives or fortune when travelling to purchase new products, or by financially supporting technological innovations and philanthropic deeds, the social status of this group varies greatly from culture to culture. Since the beginning of the Age of Discoveries, many Western governments had actively furthered maritime explorations and overseas trade to increase their power and competitiveness. Some countries even formed trading leagues for this purpose. The Church, hungry for new souls, also supported this endeavour.

Confucianism, however, had always been less benevolent towards traders and in particular towards those individuals who went to trade abroad or who traded with strangers. At various times in history, the Chinese had embarked on a self-isolation policy prohibiting foreign trade. Thus, the final encounter between the Western nations as advocates of free trade and China contained two very different mindsets. But united as the Westerners were in their rejection of the Chinese treatment of foreigners and the monopolistic trade structure practised at Canton, they were simultaneously fierce competitors on Chinese soil and for Chinese merchandise. As a result, conflict on all sides was inevitable.

The contribution of Harriett Low's journal to this topic lies in her lively portrayal of the personality of a great number of traders, including some of the principal Chinese *hong* merchants, and in her narrative of visits to Canton and to Lintin island, which at the time was the centre of the forbidden opium trade. She is also a kind of mouthpiece, or echo, of the generalised opinions of the American traders, who passed through the Low residence in Macau, on topics such as the US China trade policy and the Anglo-American relations.

* * * *

The American China trade and traders

The beginnings of the American China trade

During the Colonial Period of British North America, no direct contact between American traders and the Orient was allowed due to British mercantilist legislation. Instead, North Americans had to buy Chinese goods on the London market, which were supplied by the British East India Company. At this early stage, the items most in demand from China were tea,[1] nankeen,[2] and chinaware. Other items traded, though initially in minor quantities, consisted of silks,[3] Chinese-made clothing like jackets, vests, embroidered shawls, ladies' gloves or items in everyday use, such as umbrellas and paper fans.

Tea drinking had already become popular in North America in the 1720s. According to British customs records between 1750 and 1774, England exported about 200,000 tons of tea per year to all of continental North America. But more than likely a greater quantity of tea than that which was legally imported entered British North America through the backdoor, through smuggling from the Dutch West Indies, an activity dating back to the mid-eighteenth century. Smuggling was the major form of colonial resistance to British taxation.[4] It reached its climax with the Boston Tea Party in 1773, leading to the American War of Independence. In 1783, Great Britain had to concede defeat in the peace of Paris and definitively release its former colonies that in the meantime had constituted an independent, federal republic.

But already before the ratification of the first Anglo-American commercial treaty in 1795 (Jay's Treaty), Great Britain peacefully tolerated the presence of American ships in their most important ports on the way to China, namely St. Helena, South Africa, the Indian Ocean, India, and the British Straits settlements. This policy was advantageous for both parties. The Americans had safe havens on their long journey eastwards, and the British could levy tariffs, as well as restrict the American export of certain commodities that represented a threat to British interests, such as Indian saltpetre or opium. Later the British even used American ships as carriers for their own goods, for instance during the Opium War.[5]

The first American commercial voyage to China, or rather the first one that would reach China,[6] was a major joint venture between three businessmen, one Philadelphian and two New Yorkers, amounting to an investment of $120,000. A vessel of 360 tons was especially built for this purpose and christened *The Empress of China*. It left New York on Washington's Birthday, 22 February 1784, in the hands of two men recently relieved from the Revolutionary Army, namely captain John Green as her commander and Samuel Shaw, former aide-de-camp of General Knox, as supercargo (main commercial officer). According to historian John Kuo, this event

> *initiated the rise of New York City as the major port of the nation, and the rise of the nation as a global maritime power.*[7]

Its cargo consisted of 30 tons of Appalachian ginseng,[8] 2,600 furs, plus specie such as silver and gold coins, and woollen cloth. The huge amount of ginseng, more than all the British and Portuguese ships together had brought to China in 1784, guaranteed the Americans a friendly welcome by the Chinese in Canton. Their return cargo consisted of a variety of the most popular teas, such as souchong, bohea, hyson and gunpowder, as well as general sales items including fabrics, spices and porcelain. The general sales items alone brought a net profit of $30,000 to the three investors, who readied the vessel for another successful voyage to Canton.[9] Evidently, such profits encouraged traders in other cities along the East Coast, and it is estimated that until the end of the old China trade in 1842, there was a yearly average of 30 to 40 American vessels to China.[10] The craftsman community in Canton and China produced, according to H. A. Crosby Forbes,

> *more goods of consistently high quality and good taste, in greater variety over a longer period of time, than any other artisan community the world has ever known.*[11]

Nowadays, although mass production and imitation seem to dominate almost everything, it is still possible to find true masters of their craft in Guangdong province, who in poorly equipped workshops produce fine pieces in keeping with the old tradition.

Already in the early 19th century, an average Salem or Boston household had one-tenth to one-fifth of its possessions from China. This was true not only for the better-off households, but also for the homes of the common people, where cheaper Chinese products could be found, such as porcelain from misfires, nankeen (instead of silk products), or candied ginger.[12] Since products of a comparable standard would have been much more expensive if produced by American artisans, the merchants prospered greatly through the China trade.

A short profile of the successful American Canton resident

The young men that went out to Canton to acquire a "competency", or rather to make their fortune, share a number of characteristics that are more homogenous than those of traders from other nations. There was, above all, their purely economic orientation, which they maintained throughout, from the beginning of the American China trade until the Opium War inaugurated a new era of China trade. Unlike the case of the British, questions of political nature were absolutely secondary with them. This does not mean that the American Canton residents did not care about politics, but it was seen as important only in so far as political decision-making affected commercial relations.

Furthermore, most of the American China traders came from families of British origin that had lived in the USA for at least a generation, the Lows being no exception to this. In terms of geographical provenience, Northeasterners predominated — they were defined as embracing the area north of the Mason-Dixon line and east of the Alleghenies —, and included among them were the New Englanders. The second strongest party came from the Middle Atlantic states. Only one trader came from the South and the West. Another common factor shared by many Canton residents, which is linked to their geographical provenience, was their religious background. Members of Puritan persuasions were clearly over-represented, followed by Quakers as the second strongest religious party. There were only a few Jews and one Roman Catholic family.[13]

As regards their social background, middle-class prevailed. Thus, the great majority had had a good secondary school education or private tutoring. Some traders displayed scholarly, scientific or artistic interests, which occupied their free time in Canton and also beyond China. While few went on to college, the majority opted for an apprenticeship as clerks before leaving the United States. The latter was facilitated by the fact that many of the parents of successful China traders were engaged in commerce or seafaring. However, those men who became China trade nabobs were rarely sons in the direct line, but rather an impecunious nephew, cousin, good friend or promising apprentice, who felt pressure on them to succeed. There was the generalised belief in Canton that *"gentlemen's sons won't work"*, as William H. Low wrote to Samuel Russell about a well-connected "Boston aristocrat", who wanted to work for Russell and Company.[14]

> At Canton the firm still meant the family, or more precisely, the family was more important than the concern. The predominance of a few family names in almost any firm must strike the most casual observer. … Nepotism was obviously in the best interests of the family; even the admission of a nonrelative could be something of a family matter.[15]

Sometimes, economic interests were furthered by intermarriage between members of important trading families.

Once a fortune had been made, the profits of the China trade nabobs were reinvested in three main ways. First of all, they went into China-trade-related industries, such as shipbuilding or insurance companies; secondly, they were used for manufacturing, land speculation and new or improved forms of transportation such as railroads; and thirdly, they were invested in the betterment of society, through donations to colleges, hospitals, asylums, museums and charities of all kind.[16] Therefore, it can be said that the China trade led to a general stimulation of the North American economy, as well as to an improvement of social conditions.

The Canton system of trade: an insoluble *"conundrum"*[17]

The regrettable rich — the hong merchants

On arriving in Canton for the first time, the Americans were faced with a unique system of trade, the functioning of which they knew very little about. The Canton system of trade was a monopolistic trading system, according to which the foreigners could buy and sell products only through a reduced number of Chinese commercial firms, known as the *hong* merchants, who safeguarded their exclusive rights through the payment of an elevated annual sum to the Chinese court.[18] In 1720, they had founded a guild, called the *cohong,*[19] in order to strengthen their position against competitors. They also created a fund against cases of bankruptcy. Both the Chinese traders, who were not members of the *cohong*, and many foreigners were against this monopolistic trading structure at Canton, but if they wanted to do business, there was no way around it.

Although the *hong* merchants controlled the monopoly of trade and could fix the prices freely, they were exploited, or "squeezed" as it was called, by state officials, such as the governor of Guangdong province or the *hoppo*, the Chinese superintendent of maritime customs. Wood, for instance, mentioned that the *hoppo's* inspectors would wilfully destroy goods to be inspected, if a *hong* merchant refused to pay squeeze money.[20] Another contemporary American trader pointed out that they could not even retire when they wanted,

> the Mandarins well knowing that if the richer of them were allowed to leave the stage, a fertile source of revenue would be lost, and the trade would be in danger of falling into confusion.[21]

The only immediate and direct way out was bankruptcy, which however entailed exile to the "cold country" and therefore was not a very good solution. The *hong* merchants also had to contribute to military and river conservation works and it was expected that they gave presents on imperial birthdays and weddings. Furthermore, they collected foreign watches and clocks, commodities very much in demand at that time, to be passed on to the Court. As wealthy citizens they were also asked to donate to social institutions, such as schools or hospitals.

Travelling through China nowadays one will not get the impression that being engaged in commerce is a socially inferior activity. Indeed the opposite is true. However, when Confucian values dominated Chinese society, this was very much the case. In the Confucian value system traders figured behind scholars and landed gentry, peasants and artisans.

> *Hong merchants were distinctly subordinate to all imperial officials, even the district magistrates. Their chief source of influence was their wealth, the gentle background of some of their number, and their circumstances. ... Moreover they were very vulnerable, because wealth and expertise in China afforded very little personal power or financial safety. Only academic degrees and/or political office could give one substantial influence or security. Consequently hong merchants did whatever they could to elevate their families into the scholar-gentry class.*[22]

Sometimes they were even fined, in their capacity as security merchants, for crimes and other rude acts committed by the foreign traders.

> *They were men in a particularly sad state of responsibility to the local government for the conduct of foreigners. They were men of a superior class, whom we all respected and liked for their uniformly courteous manner.*[23]

Forbes even went as far as stating

> *we could wish no greater punishment to our worst enemy than that he might be made a "Hong merchant".*[24]

It is interesting to note that already more than half a century earlier, a similar positive judgement about *hong* merchants could be found in the journal of Major Samuel Shaw.[25] Their renown was such among the Westerners that it is difficult to find any negative word about them, even from authors who usually comment negatively about the Chinese in general, about their habits and the government. On the contrary, the *hong* merchants were seen as a class or caste apart and unlike the rest of the Chinese, the embodiment of virtues like honesty, generosity, and loyalty.

The lifestyle and fortune of the *hong* merchants can only be described as princely. The most famous of them were Houqua, Mowqua and Pwan-Kei-Qua.[26]

To give an idea of their wealth, Hunter estimated the value of the latter as *"over 20,000,000 dollars, within a third of the wealth of Howqua."*[27] Since Harriett Low never had had the chance to visit the estate of a *hong* merchant, the following short description is taken from Hunter, relating one of his visits to the dwellings of Pwan-Kei-Qua at Ho-Nam (Honam), on the opposite side of Shamian island, which was the place of residence of the foreign community in Canton.

> *The entire mansion — rather a series of villas — covers several acres of ground, and the whole is enclosed by a well-built brick wall, resting on granite foundations, about twelve feet high. Having been regaled with tea, fruits, &c., we walked over the grounds, getting good glimpses of Pwan's numerous wives. They were gorgeously dressed in violet, scarlet, plum-coloured, blue; many were quite handsome, with lustrous eyes and the prettiest hands and small feet of a <u>natural</u> size. They were quite as curious as we were, but walked about or sat in the open halls unconcernedly as we passed through.*[28]

Among some Western traders and individual *hong* merchants bonds of friendship existed, which could extend over several generations.

> *Jacob Waln [important Philadelphian merchant] wrote Houqua's nephew Lin Yan-ken that any package bearing Lin's seal was sufficient assurance of quality. He also hoped for personal visits between the Lin and Waln families, a wish which was subsequently realised in the visits of the heirs of these two merchants to each other's nations. One of Lin's descendants came to America in 1872 as a member of the first official group of Chinese students in the United States.*[29]

These close and well-known connections between the *hong* merchants and the foreign traders would be exploited later by the Chinese authorities to blackmail the foreigners into negotiations about their opium dealings in March 1839, by taking the *hong* merchants hostage. Harriett's brother Abiel Abbot Low, who worked for the house of Russell & Co. in Canton since 1833, reported this event in a letter to her, having assisted as an eyewitness.

> *On the 23rd of March a sudden & general meeting of the Chamber of Commerce was called at the request of the Hong merchants. Houqua and Mouqua were present with loose chains on their necks — and with these exceptions the other members of the Co-Hong — all deprived of their buttons. Gouqua and two others, they said,*

> had been imprisoned in the city. It was then explained by Houqua
> that the Gum-Chi had demanded to see Mr. Dent [important
> English opium dealer] for the purpose of making some enquiries of
> him; and had threatened to strangle two of them before night, if
> Dent did not go in.[30]

Although the Chinese authorities did not carry out their threat to kill some of
the *hong* merchants, it deeply upset the foreigners to see their friends in a
humiliating situation, making them turn even more against the Chinese
officialdom.

Harriett Low's encounters with hong merchants

Women were forbidden to visit Canton, but Harriett Low had the opportunity
to meet *hong* merchants in Macau on various occasions. Already on the first
such encounter, she came forth with a political question.

> Afterwards Mouquah, one of the Hong Merchants, called. He is
> a great character. He had on his winter dress. It is rather a singular
> dress. The cap is blue in front, the top scarlet with a blue glass
> button on the top; the whole dress was blue of different shades. I
> asked why they did not let ladies go to Canton. He says "too muchy
> man want to look". He says, "Canton too small no walky". He
> was very gallant I'll assure you. "It have China custom, no lady
> go Canton, and no can. Suppose Emperor say can, Can do".
> Houqua, Kinqua and Fenqua are down but they have not yet
> called. (1.11.1829)

The gallantry of the *hong* merchants is also evident in the following remark,
which pleased Harriett exceedingly:

> I recollect too hearing a Hong merchant say that "if he should live
> again, if he was to be a man he would be a Chinaman, but if a
> woman an English woman". This is in our (?) favour. (7.8.1833)

She must have interpreted the "our" as referring to the females of the English-
speaking community. The desire expressed by the *hong* merchant is also a good
indicator as regards the status of the Chinese female.

On the occasion of Chinese New Year, the *hong* merchants used to give
feasts for some of their important Western clients. When it was the Lows' turn
to be entertained, one of the *hong* merchants and Harriett both committed a faux
pas due to ignorance of each other's cultural "finesses".

*Old Tinqua had the audacity to ask me how old I was. He says
he has five wives, No.1 his father and mother chose for him. He
"no like No.1. Too much ugly". No.2 "he likey". He chose her.
He is sixty-two, but you would never think him more than thirty-
five. I thought I was paying a great compliment when I told him
so; but I hear that I could have said nothing more displeasing, they
like to be considered old.[31]*

Feast giving at Chinese New Year continues to be an important aspect of Chinese culture, but the weakening of the Confucian value system and the infiltration of Western values in modern China have lead, especially in urban communities, to a change in the respect for and pride in old age, thus assimilating it to the comparatively lower esteem in which it is held in Western cultures.

Pidgin English as language of communication between the Chinese and the Westerners

The few lines of conversation between Harriett Low and the *hong* merchants illustrate very well the common language used by Westerners and Chinese, called "Pidgin English" (spelled "Pigeon" by Harriett). It consisted basically of a mixture of English, Portuguese, Cantonese, and Indian words, with almost no grammatical construction. The word Pidgin is said to be a Chinese corruption of the word "business", attesting the importance to which Great Britain had risen in the trade with the Orient. Two hundred years back, a kind of Creole-Portuguese had been the language of commerce from India to Japan.

In his book *The Fan Kwae at Canton* Hunter dedicates several pages to the genesis, vocabulary, idiomatic expressions and use of Pidgin English.[32] For example, words of Portuguese origin in Pidgin English were *joss* from *Deus* (God), *pa-te-le* from *Padre* (religious: Father), *la-le-loon* from *ladrão* (thief), *grand* from *grande* (chief); words of Indian origin included *tiffin* (luncheon), *bazaar* (market), *chit* (note; letter), *kāārly* (curry), etc. Foreigners in general were designated as *fan kwae* (foreign devils). Once the Chinese had understood that they were not all the same, the foreign devils were assorted according to some conspicuous traits or other characteristics. As such, the Portuguese were known as *Se-yang kwae* (Western Ocean devils), and their descendents and the natives of Macau were designated as *Omun Kwae* (Macau devils). The Moors were the *Mo-lo* devils (*Mouro*, in Portuguese), the Americans the Flowery-flag devils and the Danish the Yellow-flag devils. The Dutch, who were the second European nation to appear in China after the Portuguese, were first known as Red-haired devils, but later changed to *Ho-lan* (Holland), and the English were known as

Red-haired devils of the new species, because of their later appearance in China than the Dutch. The Cantonese-speaking Chinese continue to use this flattering designation for Western foreigners, namely *kwae lo* ("white devils").

Hunter mentions that the Chinese who worked for the foreigners in Canton used to give nicknames to them, apparently inspired by their most conspicuous characteristics. Thus, the American missionaries Bridgman and Abeel were known as "old story-telling devils", Gover was "the fat devil", and Olyphant was "the idol devil" or devil who worshipped God, which sounds like an oxymoron to Western ears. Latimer was called "gong", from his habit to walk around in quest of news and to talk[33] and Robert B. Forbes was known as "old foxy", due to his shrewd business sense.[34]

The living conditions of the foreigners at Canton: "the golden ghetto"[35]

The reasons why Canton and not any other city on the China coast had been chosen for intercourse with the foreigners are manifold. They lie, on the one hand, in its century-old tradition as international trading city, dating back to the Tang dynasty, and on the other hand, in its geographical proximity to other South-east Asian countries. From the point of view of Peking, in Northern China, foreigners were thus kept at a reasonable distance, almost on the outskirts of the empirc. Furthermore, there was the proximity to Macau, the only European settlement in China, which had been in a profoundly symbiotic relationship with Canton for around 100 years, from the middle of the 16th century until 1640. According to Wood, the presence of the foreigners made this city particularly notorious all over China too.

> The dissolute character of Canton, is a proverb in China, and the cause is, with genuine Chinese duplicity and falsehood, attributed to the foreigners who reside there.[36]

Opposed to the "Thirteen *Hongs*" in Canton were thirteen foreign commercial agencies, called "factories".[37] They were all concentrated on a tiny reclaimed island called Shameen or Shamian. During their existence, the frontal view of the factories was portrayed over and over again both by Western and Chinese painters. The lower third of the paintings is generally dominated by river life with a wide variety of different types and sizes of boats together with their respective crews or owners, illustrating the business of the place. This is followed by an open square in front of the factories, with all kinds of activities going on, visibly in Chinese hands. At the centre, a row of colourful colonial-style houses catches the eye. A few tall flagpoles reach into the sky above, indicating which nations were represented by a consul.

Although seemingly small when seen from the front, the factories were about 150 meters long, constituted by a series of interconnected houses, referred to as "no.1 American *hong*", "no.2 American *hong*" and so on. The buildings were made of granite or brick and constructed on piles, which allowed the water from the river to flow up into the sewers that ran the length of the *hongs*. The tight row of houses was divided by a few very narrow streets, running into the Thirteen Factories Street on the back of the *hongs*. The factories of the *hong* merchants were adjacent to the block of those of the foreigners. Since no foreigner could own property in China, they had to pay rent to the owners of the buildings, most of whom were *hong* merchants.

Every kind of activity was carried out in the factories:

> While he was in Canton, a foreigner's factory was his home, place
> of business, recreation, storage, and even church.[38]

Such living conditions may elicit feelings of claustrophobia in modern readers, but excellent food and drink, as well as plenty of work and a reasonable amount of distractions, helped to overcome the great limitation of space. Furthermore, dedicated Chinese servants facilitated the lives of the foreigners in a way that they could not have previously imagined, as a quotation from a letter of Latimer to his sister in the United States reveals.

> I find the heavy complaints of all who go home are about the servants.
> This is an evil, thanks to our mother, I can remedy by waiting on
> myself. We have certainly the best servants in the world and any
> man who gives way to indulgence here much, afterwards becomes
> very helpless. I do not know if I ever told you of some of the minute
> attentions of Chinese servants. I will name a few: in the morning
> the first thing is to bring fresh water for washing — the clothes laid
> out on a couch, the heels of the stockings turned, shoes placed in front
> of the couch and a shoeing horn by their side — this before we rise.
> He then waits within call to remove the mosquito curtains, never
> leaves the house for a moment during the whole day, always within
> call and very attentive, serving with cheerful alacrity. These with
> many other little domestic comforts will be missed [at home].[39]

Outside China, only the aristocracy and perhaps slave owners could afford similar treatment. It was a "golden ghetto", as Downs has called it, in every sense of the word. Concomitantly, a "ghetto psychology" developed among the foreign residents,

> and vicious myths gradually became part of the common foreign
> perspective on China.[40]

These myths were at the basis of the contempt and superiority that many foreigners felt towards the Chinese and their culture and helped to justify evil deeds such as the opium dealings of people, who back home invested part of their profits into philanthropic works.

The spatially very limited living conditions of the foreigners in Canton were accompanied by a set of rules, which restricted their freedom much beyond the physical aspect, but to which they had to adhere, if they did not want to risk trouble with the Chinese authorities. For example, it was absolutely forbidden to bring women or firearms to Canton, to learn Chinese (this is one of the reasons why the need for an alternative language originated),[41] to stay in Canton once the trading season was over,[42] to deal with any Chinese traders other than the *hong* merchants, to come to Canton in the foreign boats (they had to be left behind at Whampoa), to employ only a certain number of Chinese male servants and no female maids, and others.[43] Another problem was caused by the sudden death of a foreign resident or sailor in Canton, because there was no cemetery for them. While the bodies of some illustrious individuals, such as Robert Morrison, were transferred to Macau, many others had to be buried somewhere ashore or at sea, quickly and anonymously, on the way to or from Canton. But there existed a foreign graveyard on an island in the Pearl River, which can be seen on old paintings. In 1984, it was rediscovered by Chinese historians, in desolate condition. They counted 237 American, European and Indian (Parsee) graves, among them the tomb of Alexander Hill Everett, First Resident Minister of the USA to China, who died in 1847.[44] Although the restoration of this cemetery seems unlikely, mainly because of financial constraints, it constitutes a missing piece in the "China trade puzzle".

According to Hunter, however, the rules existed in order to be permanently broken.

> *And so, in numerous other ways, everything worked smoothly and harmoniously by acting in direct opposition to what we were ordered to do. We pursued the evil tenor of our way with supreme indifference, took care of our business, pulled boats, walked, dined well, and so the years rolled by as happily as possible.*[45]

In spite of the frequent breaking of rules, the foreign traders and their Chinese counterparts, the *hong* merchants, got along very well with each other.

Although the factories have long since disappeared, the modern Shamian island still breathes Western air with its beautiful colonial-style houses along large tree-shaded alleys. It is also the location of the emblematic White Swan Hotel, one of China's best five-star hotels. Situated in the neighbourhood of the US Consulate in Canton, its lobby has for many years been the sight of moving scenes consisting mainly of American couples proudly promenading or giving bottle to their new Chinese adoptive baby daughter or son, and thus bringing a touch of humanity to its otherwise more businesslike routine.

An unlikely partnership: the interdependence of tea, silver and opium

The British in Canton: Company trade, country trade and independent trade

Among the many Western nations trading in Canton, the British were by far the most important. Until April 1834, British trade was characterised by the monopoly of the British East India Company. Although there were many private British traders too, their boats had to be licensed by the East India Company. The private trade was designated as "country trade", as opposed to the "company ships". But there was one group of private traders who escaped this rule, namely those who arranged to represent another country as its consul, which provided them with an independent status of the East India Company. For instance, Thomas Beale was Prussian consul, Thomas Dent was Sardinian consul, and James Matheson acted as Danish consul.

Great Britain was the leading industrial nation of the time and the most aggressive advocate of free trade. From their loud protests against the Chinese trade regulations at Canton, which culminated in the Opium War and the subsequent peace settlements, other nations would ultimately profit too. But the British superiority at Canton was not liked by many. Wood, for instance, who was no friend of the English, tried to downplay the ideas about the role and influence of the British East India Company existing in the West:

> *The misrepresentations with regard to China, and especially Canton, are incredible, particularly as that city is now more visited than ever, and by a great number of persons from whom accuracy and intelligence are expected. Among other erroneous impressions which have been made, is that of the consequence and importance of the English East India Company. Many suppose that the Company's factory is the only one, or, rather that all the factories are the Company's, and other nations visiting Canton are under the protection and control of this monopoly. ... The unity of the members as a body has enabled them to carry out measures which depended on the unqualified co-operation of the parties concerned. This has been impossible among Americans and others.*[46]

The Chinese mentality towards foreign trade

For all foreign nations involved in the China trade, one of the major problems was to find products that interested the Chinese. In order to know more about China, King George III of Great Britain, the technologically most advanced and economically most powerful nation of the late 18th century, decided to send a delegation, or embassy, to the Chinese emperor. It left London in September 1792, under the leadership of Lord Macartney. He had instructions to propose six major points to the emperor, mainly regarding the liberalisation of the trade at Canton and in China. However, the emperor simply ignored the petition, in the same fashion as he had disregarded all the petitions of previous European delegations to his court. Instead, he sent the following message back to Britain's King George III:

> We possess all things. I set no value on objects strange or ingenious, and have no use for your country's manufactures. ... It behoves you, O King, to respect my sentiments and to display even greater devotion and loyalty in future, so that, by perpetual submission to our Throne, you may secure peace and prosperity for your country thereafter.[47]

This blasé treatment of another country's sovereign corresponded to the century-old general Chinese belief that their country was the centre of the world, literally the Middle Kingdom (*Zhong Guo*), as the Chinese still call their country nowadays, with the emperor in Peking as highest ruler on earth. At the same time, he was seen as the connecting link with the heavens above, which is expressed in his title "Son of Heaven". All the other nations were considered barbarian tribes, while China alone was civilised. The impressions of China collected by Lord Macartney and his entourage, however, greatly diverged with the Chinese opinion of themselves and pointed in the opposite direction, prompting him to the following statement.

> She [China] may, perhaps, not sink outright; she may drift some time as a wreck, and will then be dashed to pieces on the shores; but she can never be rebuilt on the bottom.[48]

Considering China's encroachment by foreign nations in the 19th century and in the first half of the 20th century, Macartney was not so wrong with his prediction.

Fig. 1   Harriett Low, painted by George Chinnery (1833)
Courtesy of the Peabody Museum, Salem, Mass.

Fig. 2   William Henry Low, Harriett Low's uncle
Courtesy of the Peabody Museum, Salem, Mass.

Fig. 3 Mrs. William Henry Low, née Abigail Knapp, Harriett's aunt
Courtesy of the Peabody Museum, Salem, Mass.

Fig. 4 A page from the last (unbound) volume of Harriett Low's journal
Courtesy of the Library of Congress, Manuscript Section, Washington D.C.

19 Wind still light, but about sunset the Capt. called me to see the Island which he had just discovered, and none but the eyes of a mariner would have supposed it any thing but a small cloud — We all hailed it with joy and anticipate the pleasure of being near it tomorrow morning — Spent the evening in conversing with Madame Meuron, a lady of 70 years — What would grandmother say to that. this is her sixth voyage. she has seen great changes in her day. She is nobly related in France, has lived in great style and had a first rate education. she is now elegant in her manners full of life and very active. She was this evening giving me some account of her adventures, which interested me much and approaching the famous Isle of St. Helena, our thoughts were naturally turned to the fallen hero, who died there — she was in the same convent with Josephine at the time she was separated from her first husband Beauharnois, just before he was guillotined. She says She was loved by all and gives the same account of her character and manners that we get from books generally — but to bed hoping to find ourselves at St. Helena when we awake.

20th When we awoke found we were very near the Island and dropped the anchor about 8 oclock — dressed ourselves accordingly to go on shore. there is no bay here but good anchorage under the lee of the Island. I know not how to give you an idea of this place from the Ship. but I will do my best. the first appearance is like a huge rock rising perpendicularly out of the sea. after a while you discover a few houses and some trees at the entrance of a ravine between two mountains, which appear to have dissolved partnership (from time unknown) and retired from each other in mutual disgust or by mutual consent. since which time the town has grown up between them, which place,

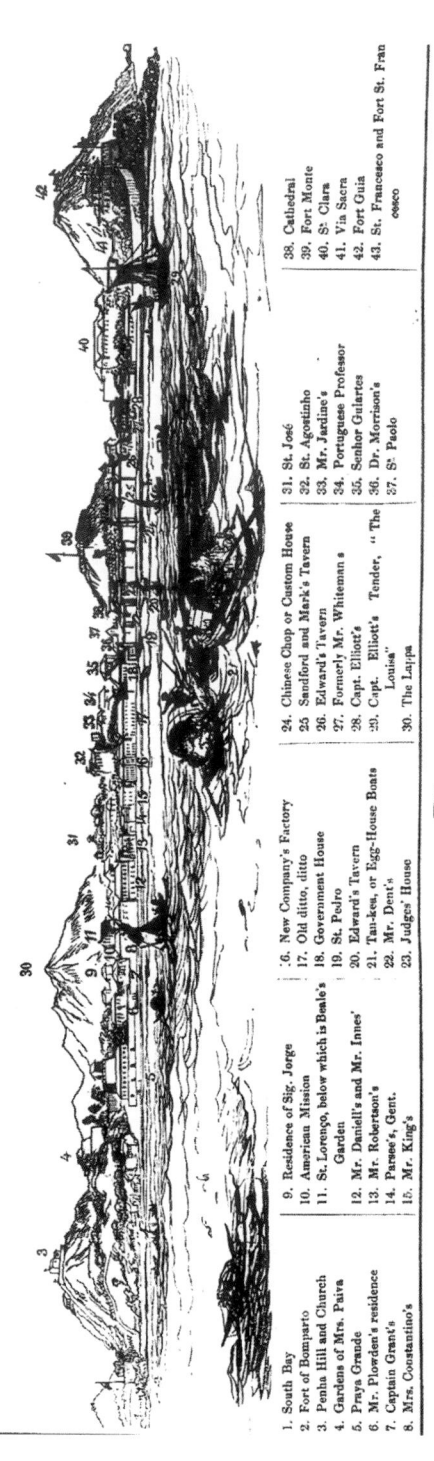
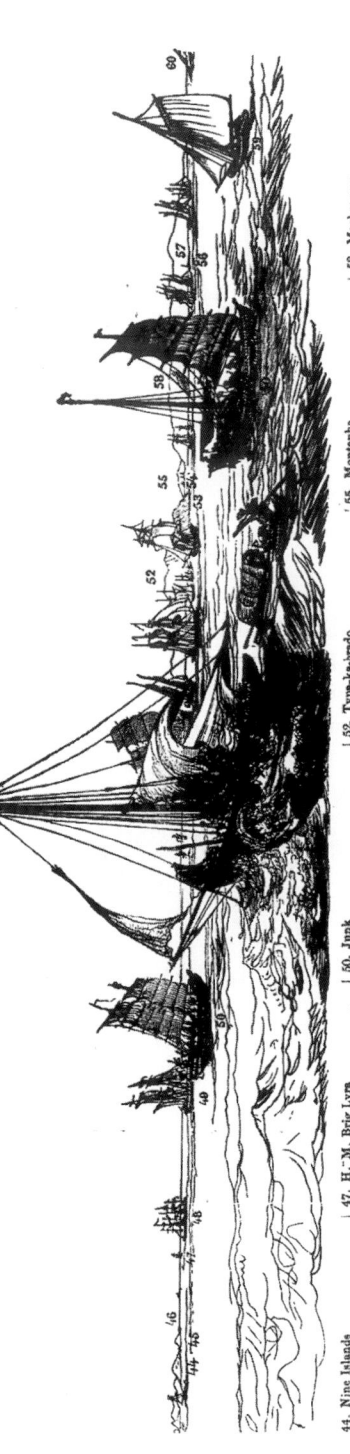

1. South Bay
2. Fort of Bomparto
3. Penha Hill and Church
4. Gardens of Mrs. Paiva
5. Praya Grande
6. Mr. Plowden's residence
7. Captain Grant's
8. Mrs. Constantino's

9. Residence of Sig. Jorge
10. American Mission
11. St. Lorenço, below which is Beale's Garden
12. Mr. Danieli's and Mr. Innes'
13. Mr. Robertson's
14. Parsee's, Gent.
15. Mr. King's

16. New Company's Factory
17. Old ditto, ditto
18. Government House
19. St. Pedro
20. Edward's Tavern
21. Tan-keu, or Egg-House Boats
22. Mr. Dent's
23. Judges' House

24. Chinese Chop or Custom House
25. Sandford and Mark's Tavern
26. Edward's Tavern
27. Formerly Mr. Whiteman's
28. Capt. Elliott's
29. Capt. Elliott's Tender, "The Louisa"
30. The Laïpa

31. St. José
32. St. Agostinho
33. Mr. Jardine's
34. Portuguese Professor
35. Senhor Gulartes
36. Dr. Morrison's
37. St. Paolo

38. Cathedral
39. Fort Monte
40. St. Clara
41. Via Sacra
42. Fort Guia
43. St. Francesco and Fort St. Francesco

44. Nine Islands
45. Canton Schooner
46. Peak Lintin

47. H.M. Brig Lyra
48. H.M. Ships, Volage and Hyacinth
49. H.M. Brig, Harrier

50. Junk
51. Cutter receiving Passengers and Goods

52. Type-ka-brado
53. Marria none
54. Bay of Typa

55. Montanha
56. Lorchas
57. Don Juan Point

58. Mackareera
59. Cutter
60. Entrance to the Inner Harbour

Fig. 5   Explanation of a View of Macao in China, by Robert Burford (1840)
Courtesy of Martyn Gregory Gallery, London

Fig. 6 The Praia Grande seen from Penha Hill (around 1900), with an indication of the house in which Harriett Low probably lived
Courtesy of João António Lamas

Fig. 7 European House at Macau, attributed to George Chinnery
Courtesy of HSBC Group Archives

Fig. 8   Sheet of study with Euphoria longon and a pair of exotic flying beetles with trunks, by a Chinese artist

Courtesy of Martyn Gregory Gallery, London

Fig. 9   The Ma Kok Temple of Macao, by William Prinsep
Courtesy of HSBC Group Archives

Fig. 10   Robert Morrison and his assistant in the translation of the Bible, engraved by W. Hall
from an original painting by George Chinnery
Courtesy of HSBC Group Archives

Fig. 11   Studies of figures in Macao, 1831, by George Chinnery
Courtesy of HSBC Group Archives

Fig. 12   A Tanka boatwoman with her child, in their craft off Macau, by George Chinnery
Courtesy of Martyn Gregory Gallery, London

Fig. 13   Silhouette portrait of Charles Guetzlaff, in left profile, by Pieter Barbiers the Younger
Courtesy of Martyn Gregory Gallery, London

Fig. 14   George Chinnery dancing, by Sir Charles D'Oyly
Courtesy of HSBC Group Archives

ITALIAN THEATRE

AT MACAO.

On ~~the 20th~~ the Musical Society will perform Rossini's celebrated Opera Semi-seria in two acts, entitled

LA GAZZA LADRA.

ACTORS.

FABRICIO VINGRADITO, rich farmer	Signor G. M. Mayorga.
LUCIA, his wife	Signor N. N.
GIANNETTO, Fabricio's son, Soldier	Signora M. Caravaglia.
NINETA, Fabricio's servant maid	Signora T. Schieroni.
FERNANDO VILLABELLA, Nineta's father, Soldier	Signor D. Pizzoni.
GOTARDO, Bailiff of the place	Signor J. Bellali.
PIPPO, Fabricio's Servant	Signor Garate.
ISAAC, jew retailer of hardware	Signor N. N.
ANTONY, jailor	Signor Garate.
JORGE, the president's Servant	Signor N. N.
President, of the tribunal	Signor N. N.

Chorus of Peasants and Judges. Attendants of Soldiers and Peasants.

THE SCENE REPRESENTS IN A VILLAGE IN THE NEIGHBOURHOOD OF PARIS.

Leader of the Orchestra—Monsieur THEOPHILE PLANEL.

ARGUMENT.

THE young, amiable and virtuous Nineta, daughter of an honest Soldier called Fernando Villabella, was servant maid in the house of Fabricio Vingradito, a rich farmer in the neighbourhood of Paris. One day that she expected to be the happiest of her life, having to reunite herself with her father, and her lover (the son of Fabricio,) whom returned from the war, was the most terrible, and failed very little that she would die on a shameful scaffold; * the whole owing to a combination of extraordinary circumstances, in which a Magpie had a great part. Fernando on his arrival in Paris asked leave to his Captain to go and see his daughter, and having refused it in a very bad manner, the former drew the sword and attacked him, for which he was taken, tried, and condemned to death. His companions made him escape, and he went desguised to the village where his daughter lived, delivering her a silver spoon in order to sell it, and to deposit the money in the hollowness of a chesnut-tree that there was at the entrance of the village. While Fernando was talking with Nineta, arrives the Bailiff of the place, and begins to tell her amorous expressions. A moment after arrives an ordinance, delivering to the Bailiff a letter, that contained the order to arrest Fernando, with the marks of his person. The Bailiff not being able to read the letter for want of his spectacles, gives it to Nineta, to read it for him. In order to save her father, instead of reading the true marks, she mentions others, and thus Fernando is saved, and goes

Fig. 15   Programme for the opera "La Gazza Ladra" addressed to "William Low, Esq." on the back, which was kept in the journal

Courtesy of the Library of Congress, Manuscript Section, Washington D.C.

Fig. 16 Thomas and Caroline Colledge, by George Chinnery
Courtesy of HSBC Group Archives

Fig. 17 Wu Bingjian —
Howqua, by George Chinnery
*Courtesy of HSBC Group
Archives*

Fig. 18 The Hong Merchant,
Mowqua, by Lamqua (Guan
Kiuchang)
*Courtesy of HSBC Group
Archives*

Fig. 19   Canton (Guangzhou): the Western 'Factories', by Sunqua, a Chinese painter
Courtesy of Martyn Gregory Gallery, London

Fig. 20   Opium Ships at Lintin, by William John Huggins
Courtesy of HSBC Group Archives

Fig. 21   Scene in a tea warehouse at Canton (Guangzhou), by a Chinese artist
Courtesy of Martyn Gregory Gallery, London

Fig. 22   An opium smoker
with his materials, by a
Chinese artist
*Courtesy of Martyn
Gregory Gallery, London*

Fig. 23   A Chinese lady [with lotus feet] seated in an interior playing the flute, by a Chinese artist
Courtesy of Martyn Gregory Gallery, London

Fig. 24   An East Indiaman off St. Helena, by William John Huggins

Courtesy of Martyn Gregory Gallery, London

The discovery of opium as substitute for silver and its nefarious consequences on the Chinese

Any commodity taken to Canton had to be well worth its weight and bulk; otherwise most of the sale price would have to make up for the transportation. But while the Chinese were not interested in a large variety of foreign products, as the emperor had stated, the Westerners registered an ever-growing demand of Chinese products in their countries, especially tea.[49] Thus, the balance of trade was strongly in favour of the Chinese until the 1820s with lots of silver entering the country. Frequently the cargo of a Western boat heading to Canton consisted of 90% of precious metals, or specie, and only of 10% of other commodities.[50] In the course of the 18th century, however, the British found one product with a constantly rising demand and a persistently high price in Canton — opium. Although the opium trade had been forbidden by a series of imperial decrees as early as 1729, it was very easy to bring opium to Canton and sell it to the Chinese, who were responsible for its distribution in China.

In the beginning of the opium trade, mainly young men from wealthy families consumed the drug, but its ready availability enticed people of all social classes and walks of life. From housewives to monks, merchants, soldiers and government officials of low and high rank, the craving for opium seemed universal. It is estimated that in the 1830s between 10% and 20% of the central government officials and up to 30% of the local officials smoked opium. At that time the total number of consumers of this drug was set at between two and ten million addicts. Opium had become a very serious social problem, ruining not only individual lives, but also the lives of entire families, and their property and businesses. Not even in India, the country of origin of opium, had it ever created so much human misery as in China.

> *The quantity of opium consumed in China, as an indulgence, (for it is little used in medicine) is startling to one who is unacquainted with the subject, and when the ravages it commits are presented to the eye, the regrets of the philanthropist are truly sincere. ... But to descend to plain English; those who habitually smoke opium, are in the intervals between the excitement of one dose and the period of its renewal, the most miserable and nerveless creatures, the artificial tone of their spirits being only purchased by their devotion to this destructive habit.[51]*

Opium traders, of course, saw the matter from a defensive point of view, by putting it at the same level with the widely accepted alcohol:

> As to the effect on the people, there can be no doubt that it was demoralizing to a certain extent; not more so, probably, than the use of ardent spirits; indeed, it has been asserted with truth that the twenty or thirty thousand chests, — say twelve to fifteen million pounds, — of opium, distributed among three hundred and fifty millions of people, had a much less deleterious effect on the whole country than the vile liquor made of rice, called "sam-shue".[52]

The English shipped by far the largest amount of opium to China.

> Dealing in opium was not looked upon by the British government, by the East India Company, or by the merchants, as a smuggling transaction; it was viewed as a legitimate business so long as the drug was sold on the coast, outside of the professed jurisdiction of China. It was certainly legitimate in India, where a large revenue was derived from it; it was certainly legitimate at Singapore, at Manila, at Macao, a Portuguese settlement; and it would have been very difficult to draw the line where it became smuggling.[53]

The Patna and Benares varieties exported by the British from India were the most highly rated because of their quality.[54] Since the opium trade was officially forbidden, the British East India Company devised an ingenious scheme to keep its name clean while at the same time being able to sell the drug. Officially it abstained from the opium trade, but the country traders were obliged to take the company's opium to China, if they wanted to have their license. There it was sold against silver. Since the export of silver was forbidden by the Chinese government, the company issued bills for the opium silver to the country traders, to be made payable in London. With the silver the company bought tea. Thus, country trade and company trade were mutually interdependent.

During the 1820s, however, more and more opium was shipped to China.

> It is only within a few years that the lucrative trade in opium has assumed so formidable an appearance. Notwithstanding the periodical fulminations against the importation and use of the pernicious drug, and the captures which are so repeatedly made, the trade instead of experiencing any depression or interruption, appears to flourish with tenfold vigour.[55]

Consequently, more and more silver flowed out of China. The figures indicated for the years 1831 to 1833 amount to almost 10 million taels of silver, with rising quantities as time went on. The drain of specie would become one of the major reasons for the outbreak of the Opium War, although some Westerners contested the severity of the outflow of silver.

> But, in fact, most of the cash received for it [opium] went to pay for tea and silk, and the remittances to India were made mostly in bills; so that there was no large drain of specie by reason of the opium traffic.[56]

Lintin island as centre of opium smuggling

The major British private firm was Jardine, Matheson & Company, selling about one third of all the opium in China in 1829–1830.[57] Harriett also knew Jardine, whom she called *"the great man of Canton, … 'case* [sic] *he's rich"* (2.5.1833). But according to Jardine,

> the father of all smuggling and smugglers is the East India Company.[58]

From 1800 to 1834, the company bought about three-quarters of all Chinese maritime exports, a large percentage of it with the silver from the opium trade.[59] When the East India Company lost its monopoly in 1834, the private dealers, namely the country traders, brought more and more opium to China. As long as the Chinese customs service and the public administration were corrupt, no effective control of the opium trade — and of the outflow of silver — was possible. While in the early days of the opium trade, the drug had been brought directly to Whampoa and sold there, at Harriett Low's time the whole business was concentrated on a small island in the Pearl River Delta, called Lintin, in order to be out of the immediate view of the authorities and also because the quantities of opium brought to China had become too large to conceal. But the financial part of the business continued to be done in Canton.

> The persons who purchase this drug from the foreign merchants there, are mostly brokers, and trade little on their own account, acting simply as agents between the buyer and seller, receiving their commission however from the former. On purchasing a lot of opium, the money is either paid previous to the delivery of the order, or the sale is made on credit. The orders, or "chits", as they are called, are mere notes to the captain or commanding officer, to deliver to the bearer a specified number of chests. When sales are made on credit, it is customary to pay a sum agreed upon as bargain-money, which is forfeited in case of non-compliance with

the terms of sale. A lot of opium passes through the hands of many persons, by means of these orders, without any of the parties ever seeing it. In so dangerous a trade, where the fluctuations of the market are at times of the most alarming kind, it may easily be supposed that great tact and finesse are requisite for conducting extensive operations successfully. Correct information, as to the probable importations, the stock on hand, and the price it is likely to fetch, is indispensably necessary ... and few men are better diplomatists than the merchants and Chinese brokers.[60]

However, according to Wood, very big transactions of opium were also done in Macau. The Portuguese, for example, dealt in Malwa opium from their Indian possessions, but it was considered inferior in comparison to the one traded by the British. Besides, large quantities of opium were imported on Chinese boats coming from Singapore or Batavia. These figures evidently did not appear in the estimates of the British traders.

Once the business was settled, the opium was then picked up at Lintin.

On the north-east end of Lin-tin there is a fleet of Chinese junks anchored for the ostensible purpose of putting a stop to the illicit trade in opium, but they lie there quite passive spectators of the hourly deliveries of opium from the ships, and the only effort made against the trade is an occasional chase of the Chinese smugglers. Periodical reports of their having destroyed and routed the "foreign barbarians", are sent regularly up to the authorities of Canton by the commander of these vessels, and they frequently get under way and sail by the fleet with colours and streamers flying, gongs beating, and a vast deal of ridiculous parade, and after a few equally vain manoeuvres return to their moorings, and despatch a most bombastic letter to Canton, announcing the annihilation of the "foreign thieves", who come to poison the subjects of his celestial majesty with this filthy drug. The anchorage in very heavy weather is not esteemed secure; and when strong gales commence, the vessels run into a passage to the eastward, called the Cap-sing-moon, where they are perfectly sheltered.[61] *Formerly some caution and secrecy were necessary in going on board of the ships at Lin-tin, but now the smugglers come down in the middle of the day, and sweeping alongside, go boldly on board, in the face of the revenue cruizers, most of whom are bribed, and all of whom are justly unwilling to risk a battle, except when they have considerable odds in their favour.*[62]

Harriett's observations during her stay at Lintin island confirm the practice of the open dealing and transfer of the drug. By the mid-1820s, Lintin's growing importance was not only due to the opium traffic, but also to the legal trade in other goods, such as rice, provisions, textiles and metals. In the 1830s, the island began to rival Canton in importance. It also served as a base for the trade up the China coast, which continued until after the Opium War.[63]

American opium dealers and abstainers

The example of earning a lot of money quickly, besides the profits made through the regular China trade, also attracted people from other nationalities than the British and Portuguese, who had easy access to the drug through their Indian possessions, to engage in this business. As regards the Americans, their major difficulty consisted in locating a good source of large quantities of opium. This is how they discovered Smyrna (modern Izmir) in Turkey as an alternative source of opium, at the beginning of the 19th century. Between 1805 and 1807, American traders from Philadelphia, Baltimore and Boston sold a yearly average of 100 to 200 chests of Smyrna opium, with a chest selling for about $1,000. This quantity quadrupled after 1815. At the same time the British sold about twenty times as much Indian opium as the Americans were ever able to bring to China.[64]

However, a few Americans were successful in the Indian opium trade, such as Wilcocks and Latimer, and also the members of Russell & Co., as a few rare entries on opium in Harriett's journal show.

> Heard Uncle reading letters in the drawing room. Went in, the table was filled with them, all from Bombay, from which the 4 Ships that come in last night have come — all about the drug, Opium. 2 more Ships in this morning — from Bombay, 2 of the Company's Ships. (26.7.1830)[65]

Furthermore, William Henry Low bestowed $60,000 on Harriett, which proves that in the four years of his stay in Canton he must have made quite a fortune there, because it certainly was only a fraction of his own profit. Harriett did not condemn the opium trade explicitly, instead she called this substance "that delightful drug, Opium" (22.6.1830) or simply "the Drug" (5.6.1832). And upon hearing about the return of an illegal British commercial expedition to northern parts of China, she almost lamented that there had not been any opium on board.

> Lindsay and my recherché admirer, Gutzlaff, returned today from the North. Hear their expedition is satisfactory. They met with a

> *warm reception wherever they went. Sold all their goods and could*
> *have sold lots of opium had they have had it. (5.9.1832)*[66]

All the references to opium quoted above are omitted in Hillard's edition of the journal. This has probably to do with the fact that at her time the moral condemnation of the opium trade had become much stronger and she wanted to keep the family name out of it. Only a small group of people, mainly those who were directly involved in it and their families, would be aware of this sordid means of making money in the heyday of the Canton trade. Other contemporaries who knew about it, such as academics, missionaries, and businessmen for instance, were not keen on denouncing the opium trade, because without being directly involved they profited from it through donations and also in other ways. Nowadays, the opium trade appears as just one more ugly stain among many others of our past. Modern historians do not feel obliged to protect names or institutions anymore.

> *By 1827 ... Russell & Co. was probably the most important*
> *American seller of the drug in Canton. ... Almost without*
> *exception Americans involved in opium during the last quarter of*
> *the old China trade went home with fortunes after only a few years*
> *in trade.*[67]

Russell & Co. stopped trafficking opium shortly before the outbreak of the Opium War, that is when Imperial Commissioner Lin Zexu had arrived in Canton, in order to carry out the total annihilation of the opium trade.[68] Harriett's brother Abiel Abbot, who was then a partner in the house, wrote to her in April 1839:

> *Shortly before the Commissioner arrived we sent a consul to our*
> *friend's declining to receive any further consignments; and for*
> *various reasons I am glad we are done irrevocably with a branch*
> *of business, that of late has seemed actually disreputable, a trade*
> *which has brought us into contact with the most degraded Chinese,*
> *and consequently served to sink us in the estimation of the better*
> *classes.*[69]

Yet the opium trade was too lucrative a business to be resisted for long. Russell & Co. recommenced trading the drug early in 1843. As there was a stigma attached to it, certain members, such as Paul Sieman Forbes and Robert Bennet Forbes, would not hesitate to lie about their involvement in public and even to perpetuate this lie in a book.[70]

Historians have tried to answer the question of how many Canton residents, who were known for philanthropic deeds back home in the USA, were not able to draw the line in the case of the opium trade. Downs brings it to the point when stating,

> *China traders were rational, profit-maximizing entrepreneurs in Canton, where few pressures from family, custom, religion, or law restrained them. They had come to seek a fortune; they would wrest it from China and go home to practice their ethics.[71]*

Goldstein broadens the spectrum of abuse and wrongdoing of early capitalists, for whom brutality was a normal part of everyday life and not an exception.

> *Those who denounced the traffic were noble voices, but voices crying far ahead of their time in a wilderness of eighteenth- and nineteenth-century entrepreneurship. The opium trade was, in many respects, a typical business form of that era, sharing a common quality of brutality with other enterprises in which many of the traders were simultaneously engaged: privateering; the purchase and sale of indentured servants and redemptioners; and the extraction of "sweatshop" labour from early Pennsylvanians in the mines, mills, and aboard the merchant ships.[72]*

Harriett Low seemed to have accepted the idea of the magnanimous opium dealer, as the following remark shows.

> *Then I was called out to see Mr. Gover, "known all the world over" that is the <u>Eastern</u> world. He is immensely rich, but as [Philip] Ammidon used to say of old <u>Crapo</u> [Gover], "he is too ugly to eat." The great danger one has to avoid in meeting him is to shun every topic that relates to <u>Opium</u>. He brings all his forces to bear upon that one topic and if by any chance you allude to it, you cannot or but rarely have the good fortune to escape an hour's dissertation upon its rise and fall, and the prophecies which he has made regarding it. His great pleasure appears to be in <u>amassing</u> wealth, but he does a great many benevolent deeds. On the whole he is a <u>bore</u>. (26.9.1833)*

Despite the easy money that could be made from opium, there were outspoken critics of it, based not so much on the fact that it was against Chinese law, but on ethical or religious grounds due to the misery and suffering it entailed. In this context, the statement of Montgomery Martin, a contemporary British observer of the opium trade, is particularly interesting:

> *What an abomination it must be in the sight of a great and good Deity to behold national prayers offered to Him to avert dispensation of calamity while the very nation that is offering them is daily inflicting destitution on more than three millions of our fellow-creatures!*[73]

Shortly before the outbreak of the Opium War in 1839, Imperial Commissioner Lin Zexu is said to have written the following impressive words to Queen Victoria:

> *The wealth of China is used to profit the barbarians ... By what right do they in return use the poisonous drug to injure the Chinese people? Let us ask, where is their conscience? I have heard that the smoking of opium is very strictly forbidden by your country. Why do you let it be passed on to the harm of other countries? Suppose there were people from another country who carried opium for sale to England and seduced your people into buying and smoking it; certainly your honourable ruler would deeply hate it and be bitterly aroused ... May you, O Queen, check your wicked and sift your vicious people before they come to China, in order to guarantee the peace of your nation, to show further the sincerity of your politeness and submissiveness.*[74]

However, according to Montalto de Jesus,[75] the letter actually never reached the Queen of England. And even if it had, it probably would not have changed much. The negative mind frame, or ghetto psychology of Canton, was later exported to the other treaty ports, adding a new dimension to the greed and egoism of many Canton residents. This new mentality is sometimes referred to as the "Shanghai mind", a term coined by Rhoads Murphey, implying a racist attitude paired with contempt for Chinese culture and civilisation.[76]

Opium consumption in the West

While the opium business was flourishing in the East, opium was also easily available in the West, where it was commonly used as a painkiller and obtainable without prescription at the chemist, at a very low price. The opium was not smoked as in China, but taken either in the form of pills or dissolved in alcohol known as laudanum. Harriett Low, too, was prescribed opium pills when her toothache, due to a failed extraction, had become unbearable.

> *The nerve was quite bare and he [doctor] gave me an opium and Camphor pill to kill it, which I kept in my mouth all the evening and all the night. (26.4.1834)*

It was also given to her uncle as a painkiller when terminally ill with tuberculosis. In England (and probably in other Western countries too) the abuse of opium existed among various social classes, such as intellectuals and workers, but not to the same extent as in China. While writers like Coleridge and De Quincey are said to have taken it for pleasure and in order to expand their faculty of imagination, for the working class opium was a cheap way to forget their miserable working and living conditions for a while. De Quincey, perhaps the most famous of all opium addicts, whose book *Confessions of an English Opium Eater* was reprinted constantly since its first appearance in 1822, observed on the widespread desire for opium in England:

> *Three respectable London druggists, in widely remote quarters of London, from whom I happened lately to be purchasing small quantities of opium, assured me, that the number of <u>amateur</u> opium-eaters (as I may term them) was, at this time, immense. … Some years ago, on passing through Manchester, I was informed by several cotton-manufacturers, that their work-people were rapidly getting into the practice of opium-eating; so much so, that on a Saturday afternoon the counters of the druggists were strewed with pills of one, two, or three grains, in preparation for the known demand of the evening. The immediate occasion of this practice was the lowness of wages, which, at that time, would not allow them to indulge in spirits: and, wages rising, it may be thought that this practice would cease: but, as I do not readily believe that any man, having once tasted the divine luxuries of opium, will afterwards descend to the gross and mortal enjoyments of alcohol, I take it for granted,*
>> *That those eat now, who never ate before;*
>> *And those who always ate, now eat the more.[77]*

Eating from the forbidden fruit: a secret visit to Canton

Among the many rules existing in Canton *"to be broken"*, as Hunter wrote, there was one rule, however, the adherence to which the Chinese insisted obstinately: the prohibition of foreign women coming to the Celestial City. Perhaps they feared that the example of a more liberal relationship between the sexes in the Western culture could influence the Chinese traditions negatively in this respect. Apart from this, once there were ladies in Canton, families would be founded, the offspring of whom needed schools, churches, hospitals, military protection and an increasing living space. Then they would claim to be governed by their own laws, all of which would cause trouble and therefore had to be avoided. But some Western ladies, who had followed their husbands around the globe defying storms and pirates, could not be intimidated by the existence of these rules, which separated them from their beloved ones for long periods of time. Therefore, a plan to go and visit their husbands, with the latter's approval of course, was hatched. The foreign community followed its preparation and execution with great interest. Almost naturally they were British ladies, who represented the strongest foreign community both in Macau and Canton. After about a fortnight of rumours about who would leave when, the first one to do so was the wife of the incumbent president of the Select Committee of the British East India Company, William Baynes.

> *Mrs. Baynes has this morning left Macao with all her children for Canton. She went in the Company's cutter. We shall now be all on tiptoe untill we hear. ... Varieties of opinion respecting the ladies residing in Canton, some for and some against. (16.2.1830)*

Initially, her presence did not cause great disturbance in Canton.

> *We heard of Mrs. Baynes safe arrival yesterday. The Hong Merchants, it is said, have called upon her, but they always call upon the Chief upon his arrival. They say "in one or two days more can see if that lady come up". It is not certain again whether there is a law against it. (21.2.1830)*

The peaceful tolerance of Mrs. Baynes and children in Canton encouraged other ladies to follow her. The next ones to do so were Mrs. Fearon and Mrs. Robinson. Harriett also planned to join them, but as they were moving to another house at that time, she had to postpone her plans. Two months later, the ladies and appendage returned to Macau, apparently without having been harassed too much by the Chinese.

> *Mrs. Fearon arrived this evening from Canton. I suspect [she] is glad to breathe Macao air again. They all say it seems delightful after coming from Canton, the air is so much purer. (14.4.1830)*

Harriett's and her aunt's turn to visit Canton came in November of the same year, when Mrs. Baynes was up again. This trip, however, is known only from fragmentary letters to Harriett's family, because one volume of the journal was lost, dating from 4 September 1830 to 1 March 1831. These letters are reproduced in the first edition of the journal in 1900.[78] Apparently this second visit of British women to Canton was not tolerated as well by the Chinese as the first one, probably fearing that it would become a habit. Therefore the departure of the Low ladies had to be postponed until things calmed down.

> *Oct. 27, 1830. — You will see that we are still in Macao, and, for all that we can see at present, here we are likely to be; for the Chinese are making a great fuss about us poor harmless Fanquis (foreign devils), and say, and persist in saying, that "that lady" (meaning Mrs. Baynes) "must go down", but "that lady" is very obstinate, and will not go. They have threatened to send soldiers to take her away, upon which Mr. B[aynes] has had up a hundred armed sailors from the ships, and cannon placed at the gate of the factory. For the last fortnight we have been in a great state of excitement, but it is thought generally that it will blow over, and, though the Chinese will never consent to ladies going to Canton, that they will wink at it, and, as Mouqua told Uncle, "they will shutty eye and shutty ear". I should be very glad to have the English carry the point if it can be done without bloodshed, but time will show.[79]*

The next entry in the journal was already written in Canton. The journey there was quite adventurous and the ladies had to wear large cloaks, in order not to be intercepted by the Chinese before their arrival at their final destination:

> *Canton, November 6. — Here we are in the Celestial city, in a fine house, with every comfort around us, but the Hong merchants are making a row, and it is doubtful whether we remain long. But I will go back to Macao, and begin my adventure from there, giving you the particulars of our passage up, the difficulties and troubles we had to reach the Celestial city, etc. It is a long story, so be patient.*
>
> *Well, Uncle arrived in Macao on Wednesday, November 3, in the little brig Terrier, belonging to Mr. Cushing, and which he had kindly offered for our accommodation, and on Friday morning we got into the Sumatra's pinnace at six o'clock, and went on board the Terrier, the Chinamen all refusing to give us the least assistance, except one boat-girl, more courageous than the rest, who lent us a board to step on as we got into the boat, for which she was liberally rewarded with a dollar. There is no doubt the mandarins got half, as the system of "squeezing" is carried on through all ranks. We got under way at seven, the wind cold and piercing, and blowing strong from the north (which was dead*

*ahead), and it was not long before both Aunt and myself began
to droop, and were pronounced to be quite "under the weather".
It would never do to say we were sea-sick. That would be too
vulgar. We went below into a neat little cabin, finished off in fine
style, where a nice breakfast had been prepared for us, but eating
was quite out of the question, and we were very glad to find
ourselves on deck again. We beat up to Lintin, arriving there about
two. It was thought best to send another boat with us, that we
might row up the river, should the wind fail us. We accordingly
took the* Sumatra's *boat in tow, with four of her men in it. Lintin
is a small island with a very high peak, and a fine anchorage for
ships, where all the outlaws (alias smugglers) lie, with their opium.
I counted about fifteen. The wind continued with the tide till about
four, when we were obliged to "take in the muslin" and anchor
just above Lintin, as the tides are so strong that it is impossible
to go against one without a strong breeze. ... About ten the tide
was again in our favor, and we made sail, and commenced beating
up the river. The continual noise on deck and the constant talking
were very disturbing, and just as wearied nature would begin to
forget herself, the vessel would have to tack, and, as I did not much
like sleeping head downwards, with the risk of a bump against the
other side of the cabin, I must needs tack, too. So you judge that
hard was my lot that night. You may suppose we did not feel much
the better for it in the morning. About daylight we again anchored,
a few miles below the Boca Tigre [Tigris], or the Tiger's Mouth,*[80]
as the Portuguese call it, where we found the Sylph, *a schooner
of about thirty tons, ready to take us the rest of the way. On each
point of land here there is a Chinese fort, and, while we were
waiting for the tide again, we might easily have been sent back from
here, had the mandarin suspected our presence. So we both wore
velvet caps and cloaks, to prevent their recognizing us as women.
At noon we went on board the* Sylph, *and passed the Boca in
safety, passed a man-of-war, too, but they did not molest us. We
were well armed. Had a delightful head wind till we reached
Whampoa, too late to see the beautiful scenery and the fleet of
ships now there. At eleven the moon rose in splendor, so that we
had a fine view of the pagodas as we neared Canton, and the
endless variety of boats. I forgot all my fatigue, and we stayed on
deck, admiring everything. Everything was still and quiet,
thousands and thousands at rest in a small space. It was more*

Chinese than anything we had seen before. The tea-boats are immense, and ranged along in such order that they form complete streets upon the water. There are also houses built upon boats, and forming streets. I have enjoyed it all very much, and have not yet repented that I came. We anchored about half-past twelve Saturday night, and came ashore without the least difficulty. Indeed, no one would have known that we were not "all samee boy" in our cloaks and caps, as we jumped out of the boat without waiting for arms. I said to Captain R., "Now I will walk directly to the factory"; and I did go straight to the door, I knew it so well by description. The porter opened the door, and for the first time we entered a Hong in the Celestial city of Canton. And now you will perhaps wish to know what a Hong, or factory, is. Perhaps you will fancy looms about; but it is nothing more nor less than a range of Houses built one back of the other, and entered by arches, with a passage under the houses to get to each. We have the advantage of being in front, where we can see everything that goes on. The rear houses are like prisons, as there is nothing to be seen from them but the walls of the houses in front. There are four houses in this Hong. Ours was empty, but … [Here the letter ends, the last sheet having been lost].[81]

The presence of the two American ladies soon caused quite a disturbance in the small milieu of Canton, much to Harriett's outrage. Her indignation did not only refer to the immutability of the Chinese position, but there is also some obvious disappointment regarding the weaker negotiating power of the Americans compared with that of the British.

November 15 — These despicable Chinese, who are not worth our notice, have the power to disturb us all. They yesterday issued a chop saying that trade would be stopped "if one Low did not immediately remove his family to Macao". Now it is so provoking that the Company ladies, because they are a body and can bully, are permitted to stay, and we, poor creatures, must go. You have no idea of the knavery of these fellows. As an instance, I will just tell you what old Mouqua told us a few days since. He said that, when Mrs. Baynes came up, he told the Viceroy that her husband was very sick (which was false), and that she had to come up and take care of him. When Mrs. Turner came, the Viceroy sent for him again, and he said that she was Mr. Baynes's cousin, "and he so sick he wanchy too much to see her". Now, he says, that

> we have come, "I no can talky sick any more. Now I know not
> what talky".
>
> We do not feel convinced that his chop is from the Viceroy,
> but suspect it is a forgery of the Hong merchants, and we shall have
> to go back to Macao, while the English ladies stay here and enjoy
> themselves. Mr. L[atimer] says it will be attended with great éclat
> if the trade of an empire is stopped on our account; but the upshot
> of the matter is, if the trade is stopped, we shall have to budge.[82]

During one of their last days in Canton, the two American women ventured
beyond the confines of the *hongs,* and a peaceful Chinese crowd were so
surprised at the sight of foreign devil women that their eyes nearly popped out
of their heads.

> November 27 — ... A walk was proposed, as it was a delightful
> moonshiny night. We walked in front of the factories without
> exciting much observation. We then went up Old China Street,
> through Bouquiqua Street, and down New China Street. We were
> discovered to be Fanquis there; and lights were called for, that the
> Chinamen might look at us. They kindled up fires in an instant to
> behold our fair faces, and we had quite a rabble round us before
> we reached the front of the factories again, though they were all
> perfectly civil, and made no noise, but only showed a little curiosity,
> of which they have a share in common with their fellow-creatures
> of more enlightened parts. But, when we reached the open square,
> the "gallant tars" that were promenading there espoused our cause,
> and scattered the mob in quick time. After they had dispersed, we
> sallied forth again, and went to Mr. L[atimer's] house. You have
> no idea how elegantly these bachelors live here. I don't wonder they
> like it.[83]

But due to the Chinese intransigency their days in Canton were numbered,
and grudgingly they prepared for their departure.

> It is now decided that we are to leave Canton on Tuesday or
> Wednesday next. They grant us a chop-boat to go down in, and
> in my next letter I shall be able to give you a description of a chop-
> boat, and of the inner passage to Macao, which is said to be very
> pleasant. We should have been very happy here for three months
> if they would have let us stay, but they will not. All the Chinese
> outside say that Chow Tuck (or Governor Le) has "lost face" very
> much by letting the English ladies remain and sending the

Americans down; but there is no reason in it, and I hope they will get paid for it one of these days. They say that a message has gone to the Emperor, and he will settle the business, but there is an insurrection in the upper provinces, and I doubt whether his Majesty ever hears of it.[84]

Judging from the feeling of relief about their return to Macau, Harriett apparently was not too sad about their premature departure from Canton, although she had expressed the contrary before.

The weather here is delightful, and since we returned from Canton we have enjoyed it highly, for, I assure you, we got completely tired of company while there. ...

Now for "the woman pigeon" [business]. The Chinese succeeded in getting us away, as they attacked us on a vulnerable point. Had they stopped the American trade in general, they would have had all the gallant youths fighting for us at the city gates, but they only stopped that of our house. I hear the last report was that the Emperor's answer had been received, forbidding <u>any</u> lady to visit Canton henceforth. Whether this is true or not we have our doubts. At any rate, the Viceroy has not seen fit to issue the mighty chop publicly, but will, it is thought, when the Company leave [for Macao after the shipping season at the end of March]. The Chinese are very cunning, and know very well what they are about. Uncle has not been down since the first of December, when he came with us; and we do not expect to see him till February or March. ...

Everyone advised Uncle to make the experiment of taking us up, and they were very shrewd, and knew just the tender point to touch, — the stopping of the trade of one house. So we were obliged to give in. Not that I wished to stay in Canton any longer. Three weeks answered my purpose very well, but I could not bear to let the Chinese know they could do anything with the Americans. For my own part, I was not well while there, and I am sure Aunt Low was not. It is very delightful to have our friends round us, and I would put up with many inconveniences to be with Uncle and a few others who live in Canton, but to be constantly subject, morning, noon, and night, to visits from people we care nothing about, but are obliged to treat civilly, I assure you, fond as I am of society and company, it was too much for me. On our return Macao it seemed more enchanting than ever. The lovely weather and the quiet were really delightful; and since my return I have employed my time much to my own satisfaction, which is very comforting.[85]

So much regarding the presence of the first Western females in the Canton factories. At least during the rest of Harriett's stay in Macau, there is no more mention of ladies venturing to the Celestial City. Considering the restricted, albeit comfortable, living conditions there, it is not surprising that the ladies should have preferred their larger and cooler houses in Macau, surrounded by gardens and the sea. But according to Hunter, not only the ladies were happy that everything returned to normal.

> *The [Low] ladies took their departure this evening. They went on board the boat that was to convey them, escorted by all the American gentlemen. While returning from Jackass Point an inveterate bachelor said, "I hope we shall never be bothered with ladies in Canton again!" but he was a notoriously crusty old fellow.*[86]

Surrounded by opium: a visit to Lintin island

During her stay in Macau, Harriett left the town only twice for a longer period of time, once to go to Canton, and the other time when she had the opportunity to stay at Lintin island, or rather on a ship in Lintin waters. This was shortly after the ordered break-up with Wood and a change of air was more than welcome.

> *Walked over to Mrs. Macondray's with Dumaresq. While there Mr. Macondray came from Lintin for his wife, and urged me to go up with them. I went home, asked Aunt Low, and she thought it a good opp'y, and as I longed to change the scene and get out of Macao for a while, I consented to go very gladly. Packed up my things accordingly, and was all ready to start the next morning. ... Wrote a long letter to Uncle on <u>special business</u> [Wood] which I shall probably write you in a letter. (27.10.1832)*

> *Got up at 5 o'clock this morning. The party for Lintin consisting of Mrs. Macondray, two Bradfords, Higginson, breakfasted with us at 6. We started in the Sylph at 7 and got aboard the Martha which anchored in the roads at 8 with a pleasant breeze. Our party on board was Mr. and Mrs. Macondray, Mr. Higginson, Dr. Bradford, and Dumaresq <u>Skipper</u>. The Martha is a fine little Ship, reminded me very much of the Sumatra and our departure from*

> *home, excepting the feelings. It was a beautiful Sunday morning*
> *just like the one [on which] we left our own dear shores. It was*
> *very still and very little motion, but notwithstanding I was so*
> *unromantic as to be <u>sea sick</u>. Was bright at intervals however and*
> *able to enjoy our pleasant sail. Our party was all very agreeable*
> *till toward night when Mrs. Macondray being delicate, was afraid*
> *to stay on deck and went below, leaving as triste a trio as you ever*
> *saw. My head ached most dreadfully, and there sit Bradford,*
> *Higginson, and my Ladyship all as deeply wrapped in our own*
> *meditations as we were in our cloaks, and not a word was spoken*
> *for some time. The moon was shedding her clear and beautiful light*
> *upon us and not a cloud was any where to be seen. The breeze*
> *had strengthened and we at 8 o'clock anchored at Lintin. Just at*
> *that moment I was again taken sick and I felt wretched enough,*
> *for there is nothing so depressing to the spirits and the strength as*
> *sea sickness — such a feeling of loneliness and utter hopelessness*
> *as you never feel in any other sickness.*
>
> *We were "<u>whipped</u>" into the Long Boat and were soon landed*
> *on boards the beautiful "barque Lintin".[87] I do not mean by*
> *whipping my dear Sis that they took a rope end to us, but we were*
> *put into a <u>chair</u> and <u>hoisted</u> over the side, the most <u>genteel</u> way of*
> *getting over the Ship's side. (28.10.1832)*

The days in Harriett's new floating habitation passed with basically the same
activities as in Macau, namely reading, walking and "having pulls" as a novelty,
waiting for and writing letters, listening to music, dancing, and socialising with
whoever dropped by. After a good night's sleep, though still with a weak
stomach, she approved of her new abode:

> *Went on deck, the Peak of Lintin close on our side, and about 23*
> *other ships around us. It is a very pretty sight I assure you. The*
> *Lintin has a fine round house on deck and fine accommodations.*
> *(28.10.1832).*
>
> *After dinner we went on board the Red Rover, expect to be quite*
> *a connoisseur in Ships before I leave. A lovely evening, a beautiful*
> *moon; were sitting on deck. Capt. Mackay and Capt. Lockwood*
> *came on board, spent the evening. Brought their little band of music*
> *which sounded very well. We danced a <u>quadrille</u> upon deck and*
> *the gents <u>waltzed</u>. Finished the evening with a game of Old Maids.*
> *(29.10.1832)*

As regards Harriett's remark about her knowledge of ships, the climax in this respect would be a visit to the British East India Company's ship *Orwell*.

> *The Ship is very near as large as the Frigate* Potomac, *her accommodations very fine, and they may well be called "floating Castles". There is a great deal of style and etiquette to be observed. They appeared to be bountifully supplied with every kind of stock for the passage, and must be as comfortable as it is possible to be at sea. ... We stayed on board an hour and a half, had a nice Tiffin and returned to our little Barque, which is very comfortable though a mite compared to this. (19.11.1832)*

Her first visit to Lintin island did not generate great enthusiasm, and the village generally reminded her of the ones in Macau.

> *The island of Lintin is rather barren, though there are some fertile spots, the rice plantations on the level ground look very pretty. Went through the village and saw women, pigs, and children all eating together, and inhabiting the same place. The great fat dirty pigs have the entree of all the houses, to say nothing of fowls, & etc. Perfect pictures of filth and all uncleanness.*
>
> *Saw the stuff they make the grass cloth of preparing; it is a large stock which they dry and beat till the fibers all separate. We had a delightful pull home to the Ship. Had the same band we had last night, and some fine singing from Mr. Gilman, mate of the Ship, who has a most delightful voice and sings with great taste. Capt. Lockwood also give us some amusing songs and we had one quadrille. Expect 'twill be reported all round the fleet that we are having Balls on board — every thing here is so exaggerated. (30.10.1832)*
>
> *Busied myself all the morning making myself useful to Capt. Macondray, writing and performing the office of Clerk. All around me gentlemen, chattering and talking with me. ... After dinner read aloud to Mrs. Macondray. Commenced* Waverley *and intend going through all Scott's novels (31.10.1832)*
>
> *Fine morning, got up at 7, had a fine bath, dressed, dispatched letters to Macao with dirty clothes, then sat down and brought up my journal which was a week behindhand. ... Capt. Howland of the* Florida *dined with us. Went on shore after dinner and walked half way up the peak with him — poor man, he was quite*

> *exhausted. Sailors are poor walkers on shore, they have so little*
> *practice. I am so used to it that I was not much fatigued. It was*
> *rather steep and the grass very slippery. ... About 10 rec'd letters*
> *from Macao, one from Aunt & Caroline and one from Canton,*
> *of which you will probably know the purport one of these days. It*
> *made me* <u>triste</u> *I assure you, and disturbed my night's repose. Some*
> *advice contained in Aunty's which is very hard to follow, for it*
> *goes much against my* <u>inclination</u>*, but I must follow it I believe*
> *and I hope it will prove for my good. But it is nevertheless very*
> *trying to the feelings. (1.11.1832)*

Since at that time the word Lintin was synonymous with opium, Harriett was confronted with the other, dark side of the China trade on a daily basis. Her description is very lively, but tainted with a clear feeling of superiority.

> *A lovely morning. Went on deck. A smuggling boat alongside.*
> *Such a sight you never saw. They contain generally about a 100*
> *men, when* <u>alongside</u> *they generally take this opportunity to eat or*
> *"*<u>catchy</u> <u>chow</u> <u>chow</u>*" and they form in little groups of 4 or 5 each*
> *round 5 or 6 little messes of fish and oysters cooked in divers ways.*
> *Each has his bowl of rice in his hand chop sticks in the other which*
> *each one dips into the* <u>public</u> *bowl and from these into their mouths.*
> *Having none of the delicate ideas of more refined people, they then*
> <u>shovel</u> *as much rice into their mouths as they can possible* <u>crowd</u>
> *in. They appear to eat with* <u>glorious</u> <u>appetites</u> *I assure you. They*
> *sit on their feet, and are* <u>dirty</u> *and* <u>ugly</u>*. They are generally the*
> *lowest class of people and as to morals, I will not say. If they have*
> *a moment's leisure, they commence* <u>gambling</u> *and I see them*
> *generally as soon as they have crammed down their food either have*
> *cards or dominos, each playing with all the interest possible. It is*
> *a curious sight to watch the expression of their faces and if by*
> *chance they have any expression at all, it is an expression of avarice*
> *and love of gain. You see one laying on the side of the boat smoking*
> *his long pipe with apparent indifference to every thing in this world*
> *and the next. I often wish to ask what they* <u>do</u> <u>think</u>*, or if they*
> *think at all. (13.11.1832)*

The days passed by, always in the same rhythm, without many novelties, except that Harriett stepped on a balance.

> *I was weighed and find this* <u>mortal</u> <u>body</u> *weighs 115 lbs., which is*
> *7 lbs. more than I ever knew myself to weigh before, but it is the*

> *first time I have been weighed for 5 years. I am now in very good*
> *care and look almost as fat as when I first arrived. (3.11.1832)*

By now she had become rather cautious about writing everything that passed
through her mind into the journal.

> *The incidents are fun, though there are many things happen that*
> *I do not put in my journal, partly from laziness and partly from*
> *prudence. Now I have just been interrupted by letters from Macao*
> *from my Aunt and Caroline. Poor girl she has heard the <u>awful</u>*
> *news of her mother's death.[88] She wrote me however and is*
> *composed. She says she is frightened at her own apathy and feels*
> *as if she should go mad. I expected she would be just so. She exerts*
> *herself too much to control her feelings. I have wept for her, yes*
> *bitter tears. Would I could alleviate her sorrows, but nothing but*
> *time can soften them. What can be said — words are a mockery.*
> *I wish I was there now, but I know not how to go. No <u>mail stage</u>,*
> *no <u>steamboat</u>. Aunt Low wishes me to come too. (9.11.1832)*

On one of the last days of her escape from Macau to Lintin, Harriett even
made mountaineering history.

> *This morning a Circular was issued for a party to Lintin Peak,*
> *from 15 to 1800 feet from the sea. At 1 o'clock we started from*
> *the Ship. Mr. Macondray, Dr. Ticknor of the Peacock, McKay,*
> *Crockett, Wilson, <u>Dailey</u>, Tish, & myself, with about 15*
> *attendants, carrying provisions, and a <u>band of music</u> and proceeded*
> *up the hill. The sun was rather hot and the roads rough and steep.*
> *We however reached the Peak at ¹/2 past 2. They give three cheers,*
> *I have the honour of being the <u>first lady</u> that has reached the*
> *summit. When I got up there I could have walked a great deal*
> *further; just began to get my limbs in walking trim. We had found*
> *a very good appetite on our way up and were very glad to shelter*
> *ourselves from the sun behind an immense mass of granite with*
> *which the summit is crowned, and finding a table formed by nature*
> *for the purpose, we assembled round it and drew forth the contents*
> *of each one's basket and had quite a <u>sumptuous repast</u> — the music*
> *playing at the same time, altogether would have made a most*
> *interesting group. I was the only lady of the party, and every thing*
> *was conducted with the most perfect decorum. Capt. Crockett*
> *arose and <u>palavered</u> a little about my <u>honoring</u> Lintin with my*

*presence and drank a toast which was, "May Miss Low attain her
wishes, how high ever they may be". I think that was it, upon which
I bowed and begged Mr. Macondray to make a* <u>*speech*</u> *for me upon
the occasion. He returned* <u>*many thanks*</u>*. We finished our meal and
made preparations for descending, after having admired the view
which is very extensive. This Island as well as all the Islands with
which these seas abound, are excessively barren, and capable of
very little cultivation; there are many wild monkeys upon the
Island, we saw one on our way up.*

*We descended on the opposite side, where the grass was very
long. Some of the gents sat down and slid from the top to the bottom
of the first ridge. I slipped down, supported by two gentlemen.*

*About ¹/₂ way down we came to a little cottage, just big
enough to hold the* <u>*ancient*</u> *Darby and Joan who were busying
themselves about the door, their* <u>*faithful*</u> *dog and some fowls seemed
to compose their worldly stock, with a chair or stool and mat. They
kindly invited us to enter their humble mansion and eat some* <u>*rice*</u>*,
which is the* <u>*one*</u> <u>*thing*</u> <u>*needful*</u> *with them, which we* <u>*politely*</u> *declined.
The old woman of about 70 handed me a stool and I sit down
under the shade of a tree to rest myself. The old woman seemed
much pleased with me. And my hands attracted her attention, she
saw my gloves were ripped and she looked upon them with an eye
of pity; as they were of a flesh colour I fancied she thought it was
my flesh. When I took it off the astonishment was very great, she
chattered something in Chinese and tried to put on my glove, but
she could not succeed. She then motioned to put her hand upon
my face to see if that was covered, but I did not like to have her
touch me, and made signs to that effect. She shew me her hands
to shew me they were clean. I gave her my gloves and bid her good
bye. I moralized upon her situation and concluded she was just as
happy there as one rolling in luxury and refinement — she looked
contented and happy, and having never known better, she appeared
satisfied with her lot.*

*We arrived safely at the Ship about 6, after having had a
delightful time and quite satisfied with having accomplished my visit
to the Peak. The gentlemen of the party took tea with us. Having
a band there, more from* <u>*Bravo*</u> *than anything, I stood up in a*
<u>*quadrille*</u>*, but for once my strength was gone. I sneaked away to
the Cabin below and reposed my weary limbs upon a couch. Soon
after went to bed. And Mr. Macondray thought then he should*

prefer going to Macao with me Thursday to tomorrow as I had expected. I agreed to wait. (20.11.1832)[89]

However, Capt. Macondray changed his mind and Harriett returned the following day to Macau.

I told him I was ready if it suited him, so I packed up my duds, eat my breakfast and bid Mrs. Macondray Adieu. In less than an hour was on board the Flora, a fine little schooner, and on my way to Macao. Being so long an inhabitant of the floating habitation, I was not at all sick and enjoyed our sail much. Set on deck all time, feel a little stiff from yesterday's walk. About 2 arrived in Macao, found Caroline and Aunt well, and delighted to see me. It is really worth while going away for a time for the pleasure of returning. I was chief speaker that day. Caroline seems in good spirits. I got dreadfully burnt coming down. ... Our house looks so magnificent after being cubbed in a cabin that I do nothing but look round in amazement at its vastness. (21.11.1832)

But there was one unpleasant remembrance of Lintin in her luggage:

Had a great deal to do this morning, putting my things to rights and talking too. Aunt Low says every thing smells of cockroaches and I should not wonder for there were many in my cabin. I never went into it without having to sing out to the Steward to come and kill two or three and sometimes more. So I tumble all into the wash. I have become quite accustomed to them now. (22.11.1832)

While Harriett was away at Lintin island for almost a month, to get over her relationship with Wood, Caroline and Colledge must have become better acquainted with each other and started their courtship, which would throw Harriett into another emotional turmoil only a few months later.

7
Intercultural Relations in Early 19th-Century Macau

When asking a group of people about the distinctive characteristics of any given nation, certain qualities will always stand out among the variety of answers. But what is commonly designated as stereotyping, in this case about national traits, is also a fertile ground for breeding prejudice. Macau and Canton, where so many different nationalities were thrown together on a very limited space, must have been an ideal location to examine one's preconceptions. The daily and rather intensive contact with people from other cultures was an unavoidable challenge.

Throughout Harriett Low's journal there are umpteen remarks on how "the others" contradict her expectations in what they say or do, thus confirming Mark Twain's proverbial statement that *travel is fatal to prejudice, bigotry and narrow-mindedness.* This would often lead to the dismantling of prejudices, at least between the Americans and the English, who probably interacted more intensively than the other nations present. Yet some prejudices continued to flourish or were even deepened, mainly between groups with a weaker common base in terms of language and culture than it was the case with those two nationalities. The regard for other cultures seems to depend proportionally on one's knowledge of the same. The cultures with the most negative interpretation were also the ones least understood, namely the Chinese and the Africans.

* * * *

Acclamations to the in-group: Americans among themselves

Anybody who has travelled and lived abroad for some time may have experienced a stronger feeling of solidarity and sympathy with other compatriots than would have been the case at home. For Harriett, too, there was nothing more pleasing than

> *a good American <u>dish</u> of conversation. … By the bye, friend Jenkins and myself eulogised on home sweet home and concluded the words of the song were strictly true, there is no place like home. (7.6.1830)*

They also used to have "all-American" gatherings and dinners, which apparently frightened off the more timid non-Americans:

> *We met Mr. Talbot [American] soon after we got out. He was proceeding to our hill and said he did not call for me because he took compassion on Vachell [English]. Now he [Vachell] will not come because he knows there are many Americans here and he feels that he is intruding, and so it goes. (5.7.1830)*

A similar episode happened a few weeks later, when Vachell was again intimidated by the presence of more Americans than he could seemingly tolerate (28.7.1830).

The awareness of being American was usually heightened on the Fourth of July, or Glorious Forth, the national day of the United States of America. As the years passed by in Macau, Harriett's praise of her country assumed a more and more enthusiastic tone.

> *Oh happy day! Hail to thee ever more! Liberty, how prized — our country, how happy. What changes in the aspect of things since the day on which that declaration was signed. Our happy country, growing in every sense of the word. How I long to be there once more, how I long to be able to ramble over fields or though cities, to have no barrier but my own will, which I hope will always <u>will</u> right and keep reason on its side. The Spirit of Independence, I am sure, is deeply implanted in the breast of every American, but how we are all controlled by circumstances! (4.7.1832)*

An almost religious feeling, or awe, towards George Washington, dominated her last Independence Day spent in Macau.

> *The glorious birth day of our Independence! How much I should like to know if <u>Union</u> and <u>peace</u> is still preserved. Mr. Beale, Mr. Chinnery, & Mr. Dent called this morning to congratulate us on another return of the day. … After dinner read Marshall's Washington and finished it before I went to bed. And then I retired*

> *envying Mrs. Washington. She was a widow when he married her. Am afraid she did not love him as he ought to have been loved, and yet how could she help loving such a man. Certainly he is the model for a good man. Fancy Napoleon's <u>genius</u> added to such a <u>heart</u>. Why he would have been more than mortal. Such patience, such perseverance, such energy, such firmness and decision of character are worthy of every praise and all the love that is bestowed upon him by his country and the <u>World</u>, for even his enemies must admire him. He appears to have been made for the circumstances. And his Army too, pity that every one who suffered and endured such hardships could not have his name set out in bold relief and enjoy the fame they richly deserve. And how many of the most deserving are never known or heard of! Well, now the name of Washington will never cease to be heard and loved. (4.7.1833)*

Modern political leaders can only dream of such eulogies, but then all their mistakes and secrets are in the media, even before they themselves are aware of them …

Harriett Low's opinion about the incumbent president of the United States, the Democrat Andrew Jackson (served 1829–1837), also known as "Old Hickory", was in direct opposition to the first one. While she depicted Washington as the noble hero, saviour of the American people and creator of the Union, she did not have any good word for President Jackson, although the North American economy fared extremely well during his two terms.

> *What a happy and prosperous state our country is in. We ought not to complain of <u>General</u> Jackson, for certainly his has been a good reign, although I do not think we owe it to him. His turn came in a happy time, like Napoleon's, only a different sort of <u>glory</u>. The domestic discords, however, do him no honor. (29.6.1832)*

Harriett also disliked Jackson's China policy, if it can be called "policy" at all. The views that she expressed quite certainly reflect the general opinion among the American traders at Canton. Had she been living in the USA, she probably would not have cared about it.

> *There has been some difficulty in Canton with the Consul. It is a great shame our rich "Uncle Sam" don't make the Consulate in Canton more respectable. There ought to be a salary and an establishment, instead of which there is neither honor or profit, not enough to <u>support</u> <u>the</u> <u>flag</u>. (31.5.1832)*

A few months later she complained about the same matter:

> *Here our president [consul] to begin with has not so much as the*
> *Chief of the British Factory, not half the sum. His generally*
> *amounts to 60,000 dol[lars], and our Chargés are not half paid.*
> *Then the Navy officers, poor creatures. How do they ever support*
> *a family — and if they die no provision for widows. It makes me*
> *cross, to think with such a revenue things should be conducted in*
> *such a miserly manner. I wish if you think <u>my</u> <u>opinion</u> will have*
> *any weight with <u>General</u> Jackson you would make it known to him,*
> *but alas pour moi. (28.11.1832)*

Consequently, Harriett painted a dark future for the United States on hearing of Jackson's re-election:

> *Uncle brings us dreadful news from America via S[outh] A[merica]*
> *& Sandwich Islands; that is the re-election of Jackson and the*
> *Declaration of Independence of the S. Carolinians. Well it is "truly*
> *awful" I think that the <u>people</u> should choose such a man. It is a*
> *disgrace to the country and I shall be prepared to hear any thing.*
> *The dissolution of the Union will follow I dare say. And the next*
> *thing Jackson will be declared King, Emperor or something the kind,*
> *and about the time we are ready to come home there will be civil*
> *war and all sorts of evils may be anticipated. Well I shall no longer*
> *fight for the happiness of our government when such a man as*
> *Jackson can fill the highest station, by consent of the <u>people</u>, too.*
> *I have been scolding furiously about it. (4.5.1833)[1]*

But somehow the "people" must have felt that Jackson was the right man for the troubled times ahead in the United States.

> *Was exceedingly pleased with the President's Proclamation with*
> *regard to Carolina and think with him that they ought to be <u>whipped</u>*
> *if they do not behave. I do not give the old gentleman the credit of*
> *writing this spirited and elegant production, but that he has had*
> *the good sense to subscribe to such sentiments has raised him some*
> *degrees in my estimation. I do not feel very anxious now about*
> *the division as I think the Carolinians will certainly yield. There*
> *seems to be terrible times in Europe too, rebellion here and rebellion*
> *there, and all about this said <u>independence</u>, a spirit which is placed*
> *in every human breast. (7.6.1833)[2]*

Despite American claims of being the only democratic country among all nations present in Macau and Canton, a fact that often caused feelings of moral superiority towards non-Americans, there were clear divisions of social class among the Americans too. Lacking an "official" aristocracy as the British had and still have, aristocratic feelings and behaviour existed nevertheless among certain Americans, mainly among the wealthy elite of Anglo-Saxon origin. The following comment shows that in reality life in the USA was not so egalitarian after all:

> Mr. Sullivan called this morning ... He is one of the Boston aristocrats and perhaps would not <u>speak</u> <u>to</u> <u>us</u> at home. However, they are very gracious here and very polite. (19.7.1831)

A year later she wrote about the same young Sullivan:

> Has lots of aristocratic feeling, his father being an Hon[ourable] I believe. I told him he was [a] very <u>proud</u> <u>young</u> <u>man</u>, which he granted, but he says he has improved. So we may hope when he has seen a little more of the world and become a little older he will have corrected that feeling. (3.7.1832)

Another observation regarding Chay Beale, son of Thomas Beale, the owner of the famous garden and aviary, also illustrates that the Low family in the USA would not have social intercourse with certain individuals, even if their situation was not their fault at all:

> This youth perhaps (with your scrupulous ideas of what is good and proper) might not make one of your circle, as he is an illegitimate, but he has been educated in England and visits in the best society here. Alas these misdeeds are too common in the eastern world to be looked upon with the shame they should be. (27.3.1832)[3]

Some of Harriett's mocking commentaries about newly arrived countrymen also display a certain snobbishness.

> Lieut. Pinkham, Mr. Berry and Mr. Warriner dined with us. ... He [Warriner] is a genuine Yankee, <u>caught</u> in the country most probably. He wandered through Mr. Blight's house, returning ever and anon and expressing his delight at every thing. He says "he has often heard of eastern magnificence, but he had no idea of it before". You must know Mr. Blight's house is one of the plainest in the place, very comfortable, but no elegance about it. He is a very

> *pious young man it is said, but knows little of the wickedness of the*
> *world. We have several good jokes at his expense, but I shall not*
> *note them, for my sister would say I was getting scandalous. ...*
>
> *Well,* <u>Mr</u>. <u>Berry</u> *was mate of the* Friendship *... He is a*
> *Salemite, as I have said before — as* <u>vulgar</u>, *fat, and greasy a*
> *muster as I should wish to see. I was as polite as possible to him*
> *for* <u>friends</u>' *sake. (31.5.1832)*

Each American firm in Canton had its own subculture, based on a set of common factors, such as the origin of the partners, their business specialization and ethical values. Despite many common traits shared by the American residents in Canton, tensions within the community were provoked by the incompatible nature of some of its members. While Harriett Low never mentions anything negative about her uncle, even when he ordered her to break up the engagement with Wood, William H. Low's difficult personality made him an unpopular figure in Canton.

> *Although apparently a good businessman, he was nervous, touchy,*
> *and bearish. He held grudges, saw subversion of the concern's*
> *interests (with some justification, it must be admitted) in every*
> *negative comment made by tired fellow merchants, and he sent*
> *Russell reams of worried letters after the latter's departure in 1831.*[4]

His unpopularity also reverberated on his family in Macau, apparent in the venomous leaflet, which circulated after the hanging of two brothers of Abigail Knapp Low. The real purpose of it was to take revenge on her husband, because of a private business conflict.[5] Excessive labour at the desk and sickness forced William H. Low to leave Canton before the completion of his time. He was replaced by John C. Green, who accomplished a profound reform through the rationalisation of many procedures, thus helping Russell & Co. regain its competitiveness and reputation.[6]

Almost like kin: Americans and the English

The great point of reference and comparison during Harriett Low's stay in Macau was the English, due to many similarities and influences existing between them and the North Americans, mainly regarding language and culture, and also because they were the ones with whom the Lows had more contact. Therefore, the customs and habits of the English are a frequent topic in the journal. Usually Harriett considered them old-fashioned and boring.

> *The English resemble the Chinese in this respect; even though their reason tells them they are wrong, they stick to old habits. (1.2.1833)*

The preoccupation with the English is still apparent in the preface to the first edition of the journal, written by her daughter Katharine Hillard. In it, she does not even mention the word "Portuguese", or that Macau was under Portuguese administration, but states that her mother went

> *to live in China under the auspices of the East India Company, and in all the luxury and formality of the English society of that time.*[7]

The English and their fame

The haughtiness and stiffness of the English must have been quite proverbial, and therefore any experience to the contrary was all the more surprising and pleasing.

> *Dr. Colledge and Dr. Pearson called, Sir John and Lady Claridge with Capt. Whitehead. Lady Claridge is about my age. Had a very social call, although a titled person. I have altered my opinion of the English entirely. We have found none stiff, as we anticipated. On the contrary, affable, polite, and pleasant. (15.10.1829)*

Naturally, as Harriett got acquainted with more English, her opinion changed again or rather oscillated constantly between pro-English and anti-English sentiments, depending on the individuals presented to her. Besides, India seemed to have been a far worse place than Macau as regards English aristocracy and etiquette.

> *Mr. Chinnery has been giving us some accounts of the state of society in Bengal, Calcutta and Madras. I would not live in either place it appears to me upon any account. I never [heard] of so much aristocracy as in these places. It I should think would destroy all pleasure and every thing else. I cannot endure it, for my part — it does not suit our republican ideas at all. (7.4.1830)*

According to Hunter, one of the reasons why Chinnery fled Calcutta, apart from his wife and debts, was precisely because of too much aristocracy there.[8] Chinnery is said to have feared a permanent curvature of the spine from too much bowing and bending. One of Harriett's later remarks shows that she had come to share Chinnery's opinion about the English from this latitude.

> *The* Sylph *in 17 days from Calcutta, shortest passage ever known.*
> *Brings accounts of lots of people coming here from Calcutta. So*
> *our gay season will soon commence; fashionables too! I don't like*
> *Calcutta people though, they only abuse the place and make every*
> *one dissatisfied. (1.9.1832)*

The long-term Macau residents considered people who stayed only for one season or less, like these Calcutta people, outsiders and "birds of passage".

Worse than real nobility though, were pretentious people, as Harriett found after a dinner at the Fearon's, who were then occupying Macau's most beautiful mansion, the Casa Garden.

> *We returned at 12, not much delighted with our host. He seemed*
> *inclined to tell every one that his wife was the daughter of a baronet*
> *and a general officer. She was well born and bred. Which made*
> *him quite ridiculous, but we excused him by thinking that he had*
> *had a dinner party. (22.10.1829)*

Therefore, she registered their social "fall" not without a little gloating over Mr. Fearon:

> *Called on Mrs. Fearon. She has removed out of the beautiful house*
> *into a smaller one where she seems much more comfortable because*
> *it is snug, and where I dare say she will be quite as happy. She*
> *has one of the sweetest dispositions possible. In order [to] gratify*
> *the foolish & ostentatious disposition of her little husband they have*
> *lived here far beyond their means, and now having completely run*
> *through their little stock, they have been obliged to haul in their*
> *horns. (21.3.1832)*

Yet in this general climate of "to be" and "to have", there also were people who seemingly did not have social ambitions.

> *Went from here to Mrs. Robinson's. We found them walking in*
> *their garden arm in arm with their children digging in the ground.*
> *These two people are happier I should think than any in Macao.*
> *They are perfectly satisfied with each other. They are both six feet*
> *tall and no beauty to boast of; very well matched as regards*
> *intellect, and not at all troubled about the fashions of this world.*
> *(5.4.1832)*

Interestingly, a few months later they might have become the target of much envy, not because of their happiness, but because of a title:

> Henry Robinson called, a queer muster. His brother has lately received the title of a Baronet without <u>estate</u> or <u>fortune</u>. Now we have a <u>Sir</u> George & <u>Lady</u> Robinson. (9.8.1832)

Furthermore, throughout her stay in Macau Harriett continued to be suspicious of the male representatives of the British nation. Upon returning from a day at the horse races, she concludes her journal entry with the following words about English men:

> [They] are a <u>good</u> <u>for</u> <u>nothing</u> <u>set</u> <u>of</u> <u>rascals</u>. <u>Do</u> <u>not</u> <u>tell</u> <u>anybody</u>. But all they are about is eating, drinking, and frolicking. (5.11.1829)

Three years later, a similar judgment, though in an attenuated way, found its way into the journal:

> English people are different from what we know of Americans; they don't seem to think it any harm to have a <u>small</u> <u>flirtation</u> with married ladies. Never mind — no treason here. (16.8.1832)

This may explain why Harriett never really dared to lose her heart to an Englishman.

English ideas of the United States and its people

One subject that often provoked tensions and disagreements between both parties was the English view of America and American politics.

> One youth looked so astonished when I told him I was from America. He seemed to wonder I was not a savage — at least I thought so. I was quite amused with this person. (27.10.1831)

Since news travelled very slowly at that time, people lived in a permanent state of anxiety about the well-being of their country, particularly the Americans whose country was still in the making.

> Mr. Daniell told me he had just had a letter from Canton which said the Roman brought accounts "not only of a dreadful insurrection among the slaves in the Southern States, but of a great disturbance in New England", that the lower class of people had risen upon the higher and that many lives had been lost. The former

no doubt may be true, but I told him it must be a mistake for I
had letters to the 23d of October which did not mention it and I
did not believe it. The English admire to catch at anything against
our free government, and often make a "mountain out of a
molehill". Mr. Daniell is a true Englishman and I believe <u>hates</u>
Americans and admires to ridicule them. I often have to <u>squabble</u>
with them both, for the wife imbibes the feelings of her husband I
find. (5.4.1832)

The Americans were very proud of the achievements of their country and saw
themselves akin to torchbearers in matters of independence and liberty, setting
standards for other nations to follow. Thus it was not astonishing that any move
backward, like the installation of a monarchy on North American soil, was
considered unimaginable and its proponents would be booed out of the room.

He [Colledge] prophecies we shall before many years have to <u>indent</u>
for a <u>king</u> for America, which we all opposed with a true republican
Spirit. (1.2.1833)

But in general Harriett would genially include anybody with a favourable
disposition towards the United States as one of their own:

We had a dinner party consisting of Mr. & Mrs. Colledge, Mr.
Inglis, Bradford & Blight. All Americans but <u>two</u>, and as Colledge
has married an American lady we take him on our side, and Inglis
has been there considerable and is a great <u>lover</u> of it, to say nothing
of having lost his heart to one of our Boston belles, which is said
to be the cause of his being still a bachelor. <u>She</u> is now married.
(11.5.1833)

A bomb in the disguise of a book

There was however one topic that kept the spirit of discussion between
Americans and English alive for months and years, namely the publication, in
1832, of Fanny Trollope's (née Frances Milton, of Bristol) *Domestic Manners
of the Americans*. After the financial ruin of her husband, then 48-year old Fanny
tried to escape their bad luck with three of their six children by joining a utopian
community across the Atlantic, in Tennessee. This was a rather fashionable thing
to do in certain European intellectual circles. After the experiment had proven
an outright failure, they lived for two years in Cincinnati, Ohio, then a frontier
town. Yet they were not blessed with luck or fortune there either, having to fight
for their mere survival. On their return to Europe, however, Fanny capitalised

on the experiences gained in the United States in a way that was completely unexpected and overwhelming even for her. In a letter to her son Anthony, Fanny Trollope described the reception of her book, which was an immediate success, among the English:

> The Countess of Morley told me she was certain that if I drove through London proclaiming who I was, I should have the horses taken off and be drawn in triumph from one end of town to the other! The Honourable Mr. Somebody declared that my thunder storm was the finest thing in prose or verse. Lady Charlotte Lindsay <u>implored</u> me to go on writing — never was anything so delightful.[9]

Apart from their personal odyssey in the United States, in her book Trollope described many of the specimens of American people she came across during their stay of three years, and she also denounced the major inconsistencies observed in the behaviour of the Americans. One of the most obvious contradictions in this respect was the statement in the American constitution *"all men are born free and equal,"* which amounted to pure hypocrisy considering the flagrant deviation from this principle in practice, namely the existence and tolerance of slavery and the genocide of the native Indians. She also denounced religious hypocrisy and fanaticism. Still nowadays, her descriptions may sound very familiar to anybody who has ever watched religious shows on American television or who has had contact with their radically proselytising Protestant sects. American politics, the inexistence of manners as well as false delicacy, and many other topics, were all reviewed in Trollope's book. Besides, she also explained many words and idiomatic expressions of Yankee English, which sounded hilarious to the ears of the English. A member of the aristocracy even told her that her book

> had quite put English out of the fashion, and that everyone was talking Yankee talk.[10]

Trollope's final verdict on the Americans, after having seen and suffered so much and been exhilarated at the same time, could only be one:

> I do not like them. I do not like their principles, I do not like their manners, I do not like their opinions.[11]

Evidently, the reaction to Trollope's book in the United States was of the same intensity, but all sentiments towards the authoress were exactly the opposite to those manifested in England. For years and decades to come, generations of North-American writers and journalists would satirise her and draw all kinds of conclusions from her unfortunate name, homophonic with "trollop".

The book had a similar impact in Macau, where it still arrived in the year of its publication.

> I hear a Mrs. Trollop[e] has been ridiculing the manners and customs of our good country tremendously. (18.8.1832)

> Chief subjects of conversation, Mrs. Trollope's book on America and other travellers in that happy country, which they <u>abuse</u> delightfully. (29.8.1832)

For a while Harriett even believed that Trollope was a member of the opposite sex.

> I should like much to know who this Trollope is, for she is a trollope in every sense of the word, except in name and I think it is a man.[12]

As the book made its rounds, more and more people started discussing it.

> Mrs. Davis came in and we had a long talk about that Mrs. Trollope's book, which the English are all <u>crowing</u> over. It is as much as we can do to fight for our country and our <u>refinement</u>. I believe the sole motive of publishing this book is to put down the spirit of emigration to the United States and to drive them to Canada [which was still an English colony at that time]. Mrs. Davis thinks to suppress the spirit of égalité that prevails in England now. She certainly writes with great spirit, but the idea of her going over with Fanny Wright[13] is enough to tell what class of society she visited in. She tells many truths but much that is false; or at least facts so embellished or <u>discoloured</u> that there is no such thing as weighing the facts. I will not pretend to say that there is that degree of <u>refinement</u> in America that there is in England, nor do I believe there is, but I know there is decency and civility, elegance and luxury — but not to the extent there is in England. But they will laugh, and they may if they will believe every word that is written, by every person who chooses to wield the pen. (2.9.1832)

A few months later, an antidote to Trollope's attacks on America fell into Harriett's hands, in the form of another book with the title *Tour in England, Ireland, and France in the Years 1828 and 1829*, written by Hermann Pueckler-Muskau, a travelling German aristocrat. Harriett decided that in the case of future assaults founded on Trollope's book, she would base her defence on Pueckler-Muskau's arguments and descriptions, of whom she wrote with great satisfaction:

> He seems to be an inveterate hater of English people and manners.
> ... I think many traits of English character must be true as it suits

very well most of our friends here and the idea I had formed of
them from other books. I must confess I am not an admirer of
them. He is very sarcastic, and whips them well in some parts.
(13.5.1833)

However, Fanny Trollope was not the first or the last English person to write
about America. Before her, there was Captain Basil Hall's book about his *Travels
in North America in the years 1827 and 1828* (2 vols., 1829), and after her,
Harriet Martineau published *Society in America* (1837) and Charles Dickens his
American Notes (1842). Like Trollope, Dickens for instance had left with high
expectations about the young democracy, and like her he was deeply disappointed
in the end, though both were moving in different social circles while in the United
States. Although it was easy for the Americans to ridicule Trollope and her book
and call her a crazy old lady, Dickens' impressions could not be discarded in
the same way. Regarding the situation in Macau, we can say that any opportune
news about America or England, whether in the form of a book or even a casual
remark in a letter, served to confirm the prejudices of the respective communities
about their countries and, of course, to have some fun. The teaser of today would
be the teased of tomorrow and vice-versa. Sometimes there were even "traitors"
in one's own rows, which made the matter still more hilarious.

> *Reeves [British] says his father had a letter from Mr. Dunn*
> *[American] in America who says he does not like the manner of*
> *living, that he is <u>freezing</u> to <u>death</u> and the <u>help</u> is no <u>help</u> at all. A*
> *capital story for the English. (18.8.1832)*

British English versus American English

One of the most visible, or rather audible, differences between the two parties
— considering that it must have been very difficult to distinguish a North
American from an English just by looking at them — was their language and
their use of certain words. What was current, everyday language for one group,
frequently caused admiration, laughter and also mockery in the other group, as
the following example of the American "slapjacks" illustrates. For the latter,
"slapjacks" are a sort of pancakes, while the English looked at the literal meaning
of the word, to "slap Jack". Harriett wrote:

> *Mr. Lindsay says I hope you do not eat "slap Jacks". I assured*
> *him I eat two every morning. To tell the truth I eat 4 but I thought*
> *I would not <u>shock</u> him too much. He begged me to get a more*
> *Euphonic name for them, begged me not to say I eat "slap Jacks".*
> *"<u>Oh horrid</u>," he <u>says</u>. (13.3.1831)*

The slapjacks acquired a certain fame in Macau and the Lows even invited an English couple, the Davis, to their house to try them.

> We told him he must come the morning next at ¹/₂ past 8. They said they would. Says Mr. Wilcox [Wilcocks] used to give them something very nice he used to call "hominy": Says he himself used to call it the "ablative case of Homo" [homine, in Latin]. He is a droll creature. In the evening he says "Miss Low I shan't sleep tonight, visions of 'slap jacks' will be before me all night." They laugh at the name. (27.9.1831)

But in the end the British surrendered to the slapjacks. "They came this morning punctually. Liked the cakes much" (28.9.1831).

The Americans, on the other hand, were amazed at the broader use of certain words by the English, in a wider sense than they themselves would have used them, such as "clever" for instance.

> Mrs. White arrived yesterday, came on Shore today. Also Mrs. Crocket who is said to be a very nice person or rather a "clever" which expresses every thing good with the English. (2.6.1830)

But Harriett's favourite in this respect was the little word "nasty".

> No walk and every thing so damp and nasty as the English say. You would be astonished to hear how common this word is. It is applied to every thing, both people and things. It sounded very odd at first for I remember it is never used with us except in nasty cases. I think they cannot laugh at the Americans for odd expressions. (11.3.1833)

The differences and nuances between British and American English in the use of vocabulary and idiomatic expressions seemed so numerous that they could provide entertainment for a whole evening.

> Spent a very pleasant eve amusing Mr. Vachell with some American sayings, and some of the food things they have, those such as slapjacks, dough nuts, etc. (16.6.1830)

But Harriett also had to admit that

> one gets to be rather particular, living so much with [the] English for they are always ready to call you to an account for such and such words — & though unwillingly, I must allow that generally they speak most correctly. (1.7.1833)

Backstage figures: the local Portuguese, Macanese and other nationalities

In some of the previous chapters we already saw that Harriett Low and other Western foreigners did not think very highly of the Portuguese, mainly regarding their skills at governing Macau. Besides, their religion, Catholicism, constituted an aggravating factor of dislike for Harriett. Once, when their maid Nancy was severely ill, the Lows had to arrange a temporary substitute, and in her usual biased way against members of this creed Harriett commented:

> We have been obliged to get a Portuguese woman to come for a few days till she gets better. ... But it is a great nuisance having these people in the house, none of them are to be depended upon. They think it is no sin to steal from heretics, and we shall be obliged to look about us. Moreover they are the greatest tattlers that ever lived. I believe all the little domestic anecdotes come from these people.[14]

Another aspect that might have lowered the Portuguese in the eyes of other Western nations was their darker skin colour and their relatively low threshold regarding racial miscegenation, mainly if compared with the strict British policy of racial separation in their colonies.

> Mr. Mendez who we should call black, ... is pure blooded Portuguese, and if ever so black is considered above a half caste. (25.5.1831)

Apart from this, they were also seen as rather passive and reactive.

> The guns have been firing all day, and the bells ringing, flags $^1/_2$ mast, mourning for the old queen who died 2 years ago. They never move till they receive official accounts. (8.8.1831)[15]

The image of inertia which seemed to have been associated with the Portuguese is underlined by the following observation, which had occurred to Harriett while musing on Penha hill and watching Portuguese and Chinese scrape small oysters from the rocks below:

> Portuguese & Chinese ... I suppose never sit down to think except upon what they shall have for dinner. (17.6.1832)

In general the Portuguese are mentioned quite sporadically throughout the journal. Apart from questions of religion, they appear at celebrations of public events such as the arrival of a new governor, or the coronation of a new Portuguese king.

> *The whole town in commotion to day to celebrate the coronation
> of Don Miguel. For 3 successive evenings the town is to be
> illuminated. The churches and forts from the top of the hill are very
> pretty objects. The whole town looked quite brilliant. A temporary
> fort was erected on the green where they had a masquerade Ball.
> I mean the Portuguese. (28.1.1830)*

Social contact with representatives of the Portuguese or Macanese[16]
community was very limited. The two families with whom the Lows seemed to
have had more contact were the Pereiras and the Paivas, but social intercourse
existed mainly with the Pereiras. Both families had established themselves in
Macau in the second half of the 18th century. Although they were Portuguese,
many members may have spoken Cantonese, due to the existence of Chinese
wet-nurses and servants who took care of the children. At this stage, however,
there was no mixture with Chinese (Asian) blood.

> *Mrs. Pereira called to see us to day. She was most splendidly
> dressed in a rich crimson velvet pelisse neatly trimmed, with a
> handsome white hat. She is a very pleasant woman. (20.11.1829)*

Harriett visited their mansion various times, describing it as

> *a perfect palace. She has 18 Caffres live with her and is obliged to
> keep 12 sepoys to take care of them beside China servants,
> Bengalies and every thing else. She has an immense household.
> (5.12.1829)[17]*

The Misses Pereira also had a governess.

> *She is about 20. Poor creature, I pity her. A Governess in this
> place is not an enviable situation. (22.5.1831)*

It is not clear, however, whether Harriett pitied the governess for having come
to Macau, or for having to work for the Pereira, who had numerous children. The
atmosphere at the Pereira was one of wealth and elegance with an Eastern touch,
which was so typical for the social elite in Macau until well into the 20th century.

> *Went to Mrs. Pereira's in the eve — found quite a party there.
> They have a splendid hall; it must be a hundred feet long. Mr.
> Beale and Mr. Pereira sat smoking their Hookahs. It makes me
> feel that I am in the eastern world. (20.6.1831)*

Shortly before her departure from Macau, Harriett still mentioned the wedding
of a Pereira daughter with a member of the Paiva clan.

> *Hear Amelia Pereira is to be married on Tuesday next, a sudden*
> *thing at last. Mamma has been trying for this <u>consummation</u> a long*
> *time, but Papa was not <u>agreeable</u>. But he has at last consented.*
> *(20.10.1833)[18]*

When both mother and daughter pull at the same string, fathers, it seems, have very little influence.

As regards other Western nationalities apart from the English, Portuguese, and Macanese, Harriett knew Scottish, Irish, French, Spanish, Dutch, German, Norwegian and Swedish "specimens" in Macau, as well as half-castes of various races. In general, she did not display any special preferences or dislikes towards them in particular. Once in a while, however, a hidden prejudice surfaced, such as in the following remark.

> *This morning Mr. and Mrs. Thornhill arrived — came to*
> *congratulate Caroline [for her engagement] and settle <u>accounts</u> with*
> *me. She is real Irish inasmuch as she cannot live without*
> *quarrelling. (19.2.1833)*

The impression of the Irish as argumentative may have been intensified by the fact that Wood's challenger for the duel, Keating, was also Irish.

There remains, however, one unidentified species — the *"Noñes"*:

> *On Sunday evenings the Noñes all turn out, and such a display*
> *of <u>figures</u> you never saw. It is really very amusing, they <u>smoke</u> as*
> *they go and generally walk in groups of 10 or 20, and it is quite*
> *dreadful to get in the rear of one of these groups with a head wind*
> *for you are in danger of being suffocated with smoke and fumes of*
> *garlic. (28.4.1833)*

Hillard's translation or description as *"idlers"*[19] for this particular group does not sound very convincing. Who were they, why did they gather and why should they come out on Sunday evenings? I believe that Harriett intended to refer to the *nhonhonha* (*nhonha*, singular), or Macanese ladies,[20] who assembled for a relaxing Sunday evening walk. Since she had a basic knowledge of Spanish, her way of spelling this word, which looks like a perfect tongue twister, seems reasonable. As regards the *"fumes of garlic"*, Harriett's remark is typical for non-garlic eaters and certainly exaggerated, while smoking seemed to have been a tolerated and widespread habit, even among adolescents. When describing how local boys make their kites and fly them, Harriett observed:

> *Their sisters and little brothers sit down on the hills with their cigars*
> *or cheroots in their mouth, which, I suppose, would look very funny*
> *to you, but most of them use them.[21]*

Worlds apart: Americans and the Chinese

Chinese servants

As we already know, books about China and the Chinese were conspicuously absent from Harriett's extensive reading list (except the one written by William Wood). Contrary to many Western traders in Canton, who had come to appreciate some of the qualities of the Chinese, such as honesty or generosity, through their dealings with the *hong* merchants, Harriett did not find much about them to recommend. The Chinese mentioned in her journal were almost invariably either at the service of the Low household, or what is called the "common people", namely the tailors, Tanka women, hawkers and whatever professions and functions they may have exercised. As such they did not interest her much and with a few exceptions they were generally looked on as strange and incomprehensible beings. When talking about them, Harriett displayed a typical ethnocentric attitude, considering everything different from European or American standards as inferior, such as the language, which was designated as "jabbering" and "jargon", the religion, which was discarded as superstition and "heathen worship", or the music, which was considered "noise". Towards the end of her stay, however, Harriett seemed to have become intrigued with Chinese in its written form, which to foreigners is perhaps even more fascinating than the spoken language.

> *Brought some translations of Chinese Letters which I intend to copy. Commenced one tonight but the mosquitoes were so busy that I was obliged to quit. (30.10.1833).*

By *"Chinese Letters"* she obviously means Chinese characters.

Harriett was known as "Miss Haya" among the Chinese. For them her name must have been quite a tongue twister, because Chinese does not "foresee" the pronunciation of an "r" and much less of a double "r". As in all well-to-do households in Macau, the Chinese servants slept on the ground floor, where the storerooms were also located.

> *The China men are jabbering below. I should admire to have you hear their jargon. There is no words to be made of it to my ears, it seems to consist of low guttural sounds. They are a stupid set of people. They spend most of their time in sleeping. That is the servants. They will do only just such work as belongs to each one, and when that is done, you hear them snoring. (2.11.1829)*

Although it was certainly practical to have so many helpers at hand, their proximity could sometimes be disturbing.

> *The coolies are "sleeping audibly" enough under my room — I never knew people snore so loud as they do. Aunt L. has frequently sent down to them to turn them over of an evening. (2.4.1830)*

Apart from this, if the servants did not get along well with each other, the master or mistress of the house had to restore domestic peace. Considering the difficulty in communication between both parties, it was not an easy task for sure.

> *This morning the Servants raised a rebellion. One complained of the other. There was three of them uttering bitter complaints but it is now hanging by the lids waiting proof, as the word of neither is to be depended on. (5.4.1830)*

The Westerners also had to teach their servants many things, if they wanted to feel at home.

> *The coolies and Nancy are dancing about our rooms now cleaning up. I dare say it would seem very odd to you to see two men coming to clean up and sweep your room — and such sweeping, "a lick and a promise". They cannot fancy the use of doing the same thing every day. They say, "Suppose make clean to day, all same dirty tomorrow. What for so fashion clean". They think it a great waste of labour. However they are pretty well drilled now, and know what they must do — it has become a custom. (20.9.1831)*

But there were things that the servants could not be trusted with.

> *I was working hard all the morning. Cannot remember when I have perspired so much with working, and what do you think I did. Why, put all the books in order into the book case. The servants know nothing about books. And it is such a job, having to stoop to the floor to pick them all up. (22.4.1831)[22]*

Once in a while, the servants proved to be insurmountable barriers:

> *Went to Mrs. Cartwright's but her man [guard] would not let me in. I knew he was telling me a fib, and I told him so. I told him to go up and tell his mistress that Miss Low had come. He says "No Sir, no occasion, I talky true Mrs. no have at home" — all this with a long face and I was obliged to go away. Went to Mrs.*

> *Whiteman's. Met Mr. Cartwright there. Said his wife was at home. (15.11.1831)*

The servants at the Low household apparently liked to play the same game too.

> *Aunt went to make some calls about 5. I heard Vachell come to the door, but the servant told him all Mrs. had gone out, so he started off. Suppose they think no gentleman should be allowed to come when "ole Mrs." (as they call Aunt) is out. (2.5.1831)*[23]

Such capricious behaviour by the servants could make the foreigners feel totally at their mercy and the ignorance of each other's language may sometimes have been exploited by the Chinese to their own advantage, for whatever reason, like for example having some fun, getting their revenge, laziness, and others. Certain offences could lead to temporary removal from the staff or even to dismissal.

> *As we found one of our coolies had been sitting in the [sedan] chair smoking all the evening for which offense I entered a complaint & he is to be dismissed tomorrow. (28.3.1832)*

In the absence of the men during large periods of the year, the women depended on the servants for their protection. The following incident illustrates how easily the feeling of safety in one's own house could be upset, if something was wrong with the servants.

> *About 6 o'clock this morning Aunt Low got out of bed to go to her dressing room and found to her great surprise (by being called to a side window by some noise) the boy in her room hiding himself behind a screen. She awoke me by angrily asking him why he was there, to which he made no reply. Told him to go out, but he moved not. She went into her room to take off her night cap, came back to see if he was gone, but there he stood and stared at her as though he was stupefied. She at last succeeded in getting him out. We strongly suspect he smokes opium as we have noticed several times lately symptoms of <u>aberration</u> from some cause or other. We cannot fancy what sent him there or how long he had been there. He must have gone through my room to have got there, and he had a door to open which opens so hard that Josepha never can open it without awaking us, although she always tries. I cannot fancy what possessed him unless he was under the influence of that horrid opium. He is a youth of 18 or 19. Our headman is gone and we feel anxious to have him return.*

> *Was delighted after breakfast to see our headman Achow walk in. He never met with so kind a reception from me before for he is not a favourite, but we feel so undecided regarding the conduct of the boy or rather the <u>cause</u> that we are very happy to be no longer under his <u>guidance</u> and <u>protection</u>. Aunty immediately related her grievances which Achow seemed to think a very great offense. Said it was bad "pigeon". He forthwith went to examining the offender, but he could not extract a word from him. Says "sorry, no <u>savy</u> what he have got <u>inside</u>". However before night they had called a <u>jury</u> of Uncles and China doctors and pronounced the boy <u>delirious</u>, having a violent fever, or as he expresses it "too muchy <u>fire</u> inside". The verdict having been given <u>non</u> <u>compus</u> [non mentis compos — not in possession of sanity] by these said <u>savants</u> our anger changes at once into <u>pity</u> and a good dose of the <u>all</u> <u>powerful</u> <u>epsom</u> <u>salts</u> was at once dispatched, and if this is true he may be better in a few days. At any rate it would be hard to turn him out of the house. I should like to have Colledge see him, for it may be a <u>hoax</u> after all. (19.8.1833)*

One day later, after Colledge's confirmation of the boy's sickness, they decided to send him away.

Once being accustomed to the comfort offered by an army of well-trained servants, it is not astonishing that many Westerners wanted to take a Chinese servant with them when they returned to Europe or America for good, the Lows being no exception.

> *Had a number of China servants offering today to go with us. I should like to shew you some of the long tailed <u>species</u>. (30.10.1833)*

The person finally chosen was Ayok, son of Dr. Colledge's helper Afun. Although this fact is revealed in the journal only about half a year later, Ayok seemed to have satisfied their requirements. As regards his fate in the United States, nothing is known. He probably continued to work for Harriett's aunt. Apart from personal servants, the China trade nabobs also used to take Chinese cooks with them, which testifies to the excellence of Cantonese cuisine.

Some general impressions of the Chinese and their habits

Like every newcomer to Macau or China, Harriett was most astonished by the many differences between Western and Chinese culture, and initially their aspect and habits were described as a novelty. Later, the Chinese were mentioned only if they were thought to behave strangely, usually in a negative way, such as was the case with the servants in the Low household. There were first of all the physical differences between the Westerners and the Chinese. Harriett never mentioned their dark almond eyes or the jet-black hair of the Chinese, because even at that time people were supposed to know what a Chinese looked like.[24] But she was impressed with the haircut imposed by the Manchus on the Chinese males.

> *The men here dress their hair most singularly, having the front of their head shaved close to the skin. The hair they let grow long on the back of the head and braid it from the top, and you almost always see them with a cue of hair hanging to the bottom of their trousers. They take great pride in their long hair. In our walk we saw a little child about the size of Ellen. Its Mother had commenced braiding its hair and shaving it. The braid was then about as long as your finger. It looked very funny. (19.10.1829)[25]*

The most impressive feature of the Chinese female evidently was the bound feet of the upper classes and the peculiar walk associated with it. To a person outside China, the "golden lilies" must have been unimaginable and even Harriett always appeared to be newly impressed when confronted with this subject:

> *Abbot sent me a pair of Chinawomen's shoes, which I shall bring or send for your first girl. They will fit it when she is about a <u>week</u> old. It seems incredible that they can wear such things, but I have seen them as small upon the Campo. The foot is above it, or as you may say out of the shoe. So dreadfully distorted that it is quite painful to look at it, when they become a little advanced, the limb is completely withered and nothing but the skin and bone remains. What astonished me more than any thing is that they live to arrive at old age. (2.11.1833)*

Wood also commented on this particular custom, which continued to exist into the 20th century, for the very same reasons indicated by him.

> *Those who are blessed with the celebrated small feet, invariably outrank the other females of the family, who are unhappy enough to have their extremities flourishing in a state of nature. ... We have heard Chinese fathers speak of this custom in terms of reprehension, but urged the prevalence of the custom, and the ridicule to which those who neglect it are exposed, as an excuse for its continuance.[26]*

As regards the attractiveness of Chinese women for Western men, according to William Wood, they did not seem to be very much enticed by the charms of the Chinese upper class ladies. However, they were virtually inaccessible to them, living secluded lives and under the strict supervision of other family members and servants. As well as this, their bound feet did not allow for freedom of movement.

> *The Chinese women are generally very ignorant, their instructions being principally in domestic affairs. A learned lady is so uncommon, that her attainments are a theme of admiration, she is immortalized in odes, and her fair resemblance magnificently illuminated on fans, screens, &c. for the admiration of posterity. The poorer classes are engaged in various menial offices, while those of rank employ their time in music, smoking, and other accomplishments. A lady of fashion is of course guiltless of any manual labour, and consequently, the nails are permitted to acquire an enormous length, particularly that of the little finger. ... No female whose means permit it, ever goes abroad except in a palankeen or sedan chair, most of which are furnished with curtains, which effectually conceal the occupant. In fact, so few of the Chinese women have any pretensions to personal beauty, according to our idea of it, and those who have, are so covered with paint, that further than as objects of curiosity, they have few attractions for a foreign eye.*[27]

Wood showed a good deal more respect and admiration for the Chinese women of the working classes.

> *They perform not only all those offices which are assigned to them in other countries, but on them and their children principally, devolves the task of navigating the multitudes of small boats which cover the Chinese rivers. They are the moving power of these floating houses, for such in fact they are, born and dying in them, never living on shore, and possessing nothing but their boats and the contents. The women, from the continual exposure to sun and wind, become very dark, lose all that soft listlessness of expression, and delicacy of form, for which the higher classes are distinguished, and resemble in their exterior another people. ... Women of the poorer classes, show themselves without the least reserve in all public places.*[28]

Another novelty for Harriett Low in Macau was the Cantonese dialect spoken by the Chinese, which had nothing to do with any other foreign language ever heard before. Even after several years of residence in Macau, she still seemed truly astonished that the "sounds" produced by the Chinese had any meaning at all, as the next example of a casual meeting with a little Chinese boy of about 8 years shows. Caroline and Harriett had met him on one of their walks and as he was on his way home from school, they asked him to read something for them.

> He selected a _poem_ and to our great surprise we heard in such an audible _singing_ tone _something_, I cannot say _what_. Caroline thought he was suddenly seized with _convulsions_. He however totally disregarded our _shouts_ and went on quite self satisfied till he came to the end, quite to our amusement and he concluded no doubt much to our gratification. (30.4.1832)[29]

Then there was the great difference in living standards between the Westerners in Macau and the Chinese. Apart from Macau's large floating population, there were also several small Chinese villages scattered in the northern half and in the extreme south of the peninsula, which they used to cross on their walks.

> After dinner Mr. Higginson and Seaver called for us to walk. I undertook to pilot them though the village, but I found I had entered crowds of huts with legions of squalling children who greeted us with a shrill shout at the tops of their voices, dogs barking, and altogether a perfect Babel. Our imaginations stretched to the utmost could not convert the scenes into any thing like romance or even neatness and simplicity. And although we were let into the secrets of family arrangements as we passed their open doors and saw mothers performing the most maternal offices on every side, yet we could not compare them with the meanest villagers at home. Dirty, filthy creatures I saw no escape from it either, but after some time we made our exit and got on to the open hills, rejoiced to breathe the fresh air. (11.10.1832)

Harriett was also impressed by the apparent ease and pragmatism with which the Chinese seemed to face their poverty. But in general she displayed a strong tendency to romanticise poverty.

> You would be amused I think to take one walk with us, to see the China men. To day as we went along there were 8 or 10 of them

ranged along sitting as comfortably, one knee over the other —
some in Turkish style, some smoking their pipes, and all with fans
in their hands. Indeed you never scarcely see a China man, or
woman, without a fan, even the chairbearers for themselves as they
carry their burden. They sometimes perch themselves on the highest
hill, and there sit gossiping. We see them after dark lying about in
every direction, take their mats out, and through [throw] them down
in the best place they can find and make a rock their pillow, they
are not at all particular about their pillows. Indeed they never use
any but a bamboo. Some of them arrive at this luxury. It may be
truly said here that "nature's wants are few". Give a China man
plenty of rice and fish, a bamboo mat and a small piece of cloth
for their waist and he can live, that is in the summer. In the winter
they suffer much from the cold and require a great many clothes.
... And they seem quite happy as the richest people. Oh I never
did, and never will believe that riches add to happiness — or rather
that it constitutes happiness. What would appear to us here the
most miserable of beings, I dare say if questioned, it would be found
that he had as much real happiness I must say as any of us —
that is, he is careless and free and cares for nothing. (31.8.1830)

But Harriett also had some positive things to say about the Chinese. An aspect mentioned several times is what she called their "civility". For example, on their excursions to Lappa or to Lintin, whenever they met Chinese on their rambles, they were offered tea and some pie-like food or fruits, although the people seemed extremely poor. These were other occasions for her to idealistically muse on the happiness of the poor. And once, when facing a "gang of Chinamen and boys" on a lonely walk, she concluded:

I did not know but they might give my earrings a twitch which
would not be agreeable, but a Chinaman is a great deal more civil
than I fear the same class of my own countrymen would be. I am
sure had these been English or Americans I should not have dared
sit there. (23.6.1833)

Sometimes there was a paternalistic attitude obvious in the treatment of the Chinese.

It began to rain and we had to put in at the gardeners. It was quite
dark. ... We succeeded in getting from the gardener two umbrellas
full of holes to cover our bonnets, which were all we cared for.
We got home very well; fortunately did not rain much. Mr. Millet

> *returned two new umbrellas with the old ones, to encourage their*
> *kindness and reward them for it. (30.4.1832)*

As regards the Chinese customs, soon after their arrival the Lows could witness the most important Chinese festivity, (Chinese) New Year. It is a mobile holiday, starting with the new moon on the first day of the new Lunar Year and ending on the full moon 15 days later. A family feast par excellence, it was the only time of the year when the incessant activity of the Chinese, whose week consisted of seven working days, came to a halt. Harriett's description may still sound very familiar to anybody who has ever spent this time of the year among Chinese, be it in China or in any China town overseas.

> *The Compradore Chin Chin'ed us not to ring the bell on the next*
> *day, being New Year day. They have an idea it will call [yin] or*
> *the devil. They fire crackers all day for the purpose of keeping off*
> *the evil spirit for the coming year. (24.1.1830)*

> *A great day with the Chinese. They all have a new suit of clothes,*
> *and keep a sort of holiday, go home to their families, Chin Chin*
> *Joss, etc. They are all obliged to pay their debts at this time.*
> *(25.1.1830)*

Similar to present times, the latter fact usually leads to an increase in criminal activity before Chinese New Year.

> *Some person or persons attempted to get into our house and took*
> *a very unpleasant method too for they burned the door ¹/2 <u>way</u>*
> *up. They must have got over an immensely high wall. Fortunately*
> *the smoke was smelt, but the thieves were not caught. They are*
> *very busy now, stealing all they can get hold of. We were very*
> *glad they did not <u>burn</u> us up. As all the gentlemen are in Canton,*
> *they would not have had an opp'y to show their gallantry.*
> *(7.12.1832)*

Another important holiday in the Chinese calendar is Ch'ing (Cheng) Ming, usually held at the beginning of April, the main purpose of which is to pay respect to the ancestors. Since there were many graves on the Campo, one of their most common walking grounds, they could observe the rituals very well.

> *Walked after dinner. On our return met the Colledges and Blight,*
> *we sit upon a China <u>tombstone</u> for sometime chatting and laughing.*
> *I could not help thinking with what different feelings to what we*
> *should have set upon the graves of an unknown countryman. It is*

strange, but I suppose it is because we have no sympathy, no feeling in Common with the Chinese. As I passed along I noticed some Chinamen about <u>Chin</u> <u>Chinning</u> *their fathers as they term it. I walked up to the grave to see what they had prepared. They had an immense quantity of gilded papers which they were about to* <u>burn</u>. *Then I counted 15 different messes of "<u>chow</u> <u>chow</u>" or food which they were to place there I believe with the idea that they come forth or the spirit and eat it and find they are still remembered. I noticed in the Evangelist (a paper just published) a prayer offered at these times which I will copy thinking you may not see the paper. At these times you see all the graves with a piece of red and white paper put upon the top of the mound and two fresh pieces of turf dug from another place to keep it down. There is something written upon these papers which of course I cannot read. (30.4.1833)[30]*

A very important aspect in Chinese burials was and is the location of the grave, because not only the dwellings of the living, but also of the dead are influenced by *feng shui* (literally "wind-water"), an ancient Chinese belief and science. Originally discarded as superstition, *feng shui* is becoming increasingly popular in Western cultures, as shown by the growing number of publications on this subject. Thus, a grave with a good *feng shui* guarantees the happiness of the dead members of the family, which means that they will not disturb the living ones.

They are very superstitious respecting the place in which they bury their dead. "Cumwa" a merchant in Canton whose mother died two years ago has just found a satisfactory place to bury her in, having kept her above ground during that time. And it seems he was not very successful after all, for the late inundation of the rivers came up within two feet of her grave, so that he was in great trouble and obliged to have her taken up again. They endeavour to get the driest place possible and have samples of the earth brought to them that they may judge of it. The rich about Macao bury them on the tops of the highest hills, and around them an immense deal of stone work. (7.8.1833)[31]

Many modern Macau Chinese opt to be buried in China, where space for graves is more abundant and cheaper and where it is easier to find a place with a good *feng shui* than in Macau. Traditional Chinese graves can still be found on the hills of Coloane island, hidden in its dense vegetation. During her stay, Harriett was also confronted with the mourning rituals for a leading member of the Chinese court, on which she commented rather sarcastically.

> *The Empress of China is dead, and the people will all have to*
> <u>*mourn*</u> *for 100 days. The men are not allowed to shave for that*
> *space of time so we shall have* <u>*beautiful*</u> *looking servants.*
> *(19.7.1833)*[32]

Another incomprehensible facet of Chinese culture was their concept of justice, mainly when the death of a person was involved. According to Chinese custom, the loss of a life had to be compensated with the loss of another life, independently of whether it was the result of intentional murder or accidental killing.

> *I understand the Chinese wish one man to be given up for the*
> *China man that was killed. They do not care* <u>*who*</u> *so that they have*
> *blood for blood. (16.11.1833)*

Already the first Americans who came to China witnessed the truth of this observation. In the journals of Major Samuel Shaw we can find a description of the famous *Lady Hughes* incident, which happened in 1784. A British boat, *Lady Hughes*, fired a salute on entering Canton, which accidentally killed a Chinese and wounded two others. The Chinese immediately demanded the surrender of the gunner, which the British refused. Then the Chinese captured a British supercargo, threw him into prison, cut off the water and food supplies of all Western factories and recalled the Chinese servants. The outcome of the story was that the weakest and oldest sailor of the boat that had fired the fatal salute, in exchange for the supercargo, was surrendered to the Chinese and executed.[33] The case Harriett referred to involved a violent argument between the stranded sailors of a British opium ship and the inhabitants of a Chinese village, in which both sides lost a life.[34] The final consequences of this quarrel are not explained further in the journal. The Chinese concept of justice and the great variety of cruel punishments, which reminded the Westerners of times long gone by in their own countries, were the main reason why they did not want to submit to it.

Harriett's most vivid description regarding the Chinese habits is dedicated to a procession. Due to the variety of audio-visual stimulations, they were always impressive events.

> *I wish I could give you the least idea of a Chinese procession that*
> *passed here this afternoon. It seems they are dedicating a new*
> *church or Joss house, and it makes a great fuss in town, but were*
> *I to fill page after page and give you my best description I fear I*
> *should fail in giving you an idea of it. In the first place, the length*
> *of it, the variety of objects, dresses, the music, etc. is beyond every*

thing. The dresses many of them were very splendid, or rather made of the most splendid colours and material you can imagine, but loaded on in such style that it can not please the eye of any person possessed of any taste. There were females splendidly attired on horseback seated astride on the animal, little boys rigged up with the most grotesque looking hats and dresses, carrying most splendidly wrought banners of the richest colours. Then there were children suspended in air, so that they appeared to be standing on nothing. They were very ingeniously contrived. There was also a little Venus coming out of her shell — and millions of other things that I am sure I cannot remember. And then for the music. Music did I say? Oh heavens. If such discordant sounds can be called music, it must have been the height of perfection, for never was there such a noise. Their whole wish, and aim, seemed to be to make as much noise as possible — the horrid gongs beating, some sort of a kettle I thought that they beat on for a bell. We could not hear a person's voice though ever so near to us. But you should see and hear to imagine it. Oh not to forget the interesting pigs. Poor piggy was murdered, roasted and lacquered for the occasion, and carried along on cars. There was one lamb, poor little thing killed and the hair taken off, and set up on a car as though it was alive. Then followed a pig all ready for cutting up. On another, there was one roasted and another lacquered — you must know at all the marriage processions, funerals, or what not, these poor innocent pigs must sacrifice their lives — then cars of fruit, as presents to Joss I presume. (6.8.1830)

How Harriett would have marvelled at the spectacle opening modern Chinese banquets, where a procession of waiters, each one shouldering on a large tray one of the poor piggies with flashing red light bulbs for eyes and as flat as a flounder, is heralded by a group of musicians producing trumpet-like sounds! In order to heighten the ghostly effect, the lights may be temporarily turned down, until each piglet has found its table, where its eyes continue to flash even when, after a delicious repast, there is nothing left but the carcass.

In general and in conclusion, we can say that Harriett's knowledge about China and the Chinese was very restricted and characterised by the stereotypes of her time. The Chinese were seen as slaves of their traditions:

But I assure you there is no comparison to be drawn between the Chinese and any other nation in the world. They will not allow any innovation upon "old custom", and will ding these words into your ears forever if it is not for their interest to violate it, when it is quite a different thing. Another thing they acknowledge is that they "cannot talky reason", and must be "bullied".[35]

Although Harriett's general opinion of the Chinese was quite low, openly racist observations towards them are quite rare in the journal. When they occur, however, they are generally accompanied by some kind of excuse. The most direct and offensive statement in this context, which was written after reading about the drowning of five Chinese during a rainstorm, is the following:

I can hardly account for the indifference we feel regarding these creatures. We hear of their being killed and drowned and misfortunes of divers kinds occurring but not with the feelings that we should have in parallel cases in our own country or Europe. It must be that we have no sympathy with them, they appear to me to be a connecting link between man and beast, but certainly not equal with civilized man. And [as] you see the different grade and links in all the rest of nature's works is it not reasonable to suppose there are higher and lower orders of men? They certainly do not possess the sensibility and feelings of other nations. And when we hear of these accidents, our imaginations never picture distressed and bereaved families, and happy families destroyed — for knowing their brutal customs we cannot think such distresses exist. (23.2.1833)

But as a firm believer in the progress of the human race, Harriett hoped that the day of liberation would come to the Chinese too:

We shall, or others will see these Chinese *exalted in the scale, their turn must come, I think — the barriers must be broken down, ignorance must give place to knowledge, and slavery to freedom. Females will then be exalted. (17.2.1833)*

The question of slavery

At the bottom of society were the slaves, for whom Harriett did not show much sympathy.

My chair was stopped on its way home with old Golatti beating his slaves. They misbehaved and he took his stick to them and gave

> *them some <u>awful</u> thwacks, and I was made an unwilling witness*
> *of it, for my bearers would not go on, thinking I suppose they might*
> *come in for a <u>share</u> in passing. These streets are so narrow.*
> *(13.8.1833)*[36]

Slavery in Macau dated back to the city's earliest days. Although this social group is commonly neglected in historiography, evidence of their presence was given at particular events. In June of 1622, for example, a fleet of Dutchmen launched a large-scale attack on Macau, in the defence of which the slaves played an important role. It is said that afterwards their masters freed many as a reward for their courage in fighting, and that even Chinese officials sent a gift of rice to the slaves, so impressed were they by their bravery. At Harriett Low's time, New Year's Day seemed to have been one of the few occasions when the slaves were given a certain degree of liberty.

> *The Caffres were all dressed in most fantastic dresses parading the*
> *streets, singing and enjoying themselves — seem the happiest*
> *creatures in existence. Animal pleasures alone constitute their*
> *happiness, however. (1.1.1833)*

While the Chinese had long since imposed on the Portuguese not to enslave Chinese, slavery as such was abolished in Macau only later in the century.

Harriett Low's positive attitude towards slavery was even more obvious during their stay in South Africa, on the way home to the United States. The topic of slavery appears several times in the journal, always with the same tenor.

> *People talk of slavery and consider that their emancipation will*
> *make them happier, but it is far otherwise in my opinion. [Slaves*
> *were emancipated December 1, 1834.] If there is any advantage,*
> *it will be for their masters, for they are great torments. Now they*
> *are well fed, clothed and taken good care of. Then they must look*
> *out for themselves and I suspect they will not be able to say then,*
> *as now, that we have no beggars, no town paupers. (2.2.1834)*

Though being considered as "torments" by Harriett, the slave owners certainly preferred being "tormented" than having to pay them or work harder themselves.

> *Several Dutch gentlemen here to tea complaining sadly of the*
> *English government and ridiculing their customs. It seems they do*
> *not like to loose their <u>slaves</u> as some of them have half their property*
> *invested in them and they will not be $1/2$ paid for them. (5.2.1834)*

8
Homeward Bound

Man proposes and God disposes could be the leitmotif for the journey homewards. If Harriett Low had known how arduous it would be and how different from the outbound voyage, especially in emotional terms, she certainly would not have been so eager to leave Macau. Religion and resignation to her fate, but also thankfulness for the many graces received, are the dominating themes in the last few months of her journal. Yet despite — or because of — tragedy, the narrative continues to be captivating and lively. Two longer stopovers in South Africa and England present a welcome contrast to the limited life on board and to the years of physical restraint in Macau. A short stopover on St. Helena serves as an opportunity to indulge in one of her passions, history. The entries in her journal finish a few hours, or days, before the arrival in New York.

While the publication of the journal could have established her fame as authoress, as half-jokingly dreamt of in Macau, Harriett Low preferred to realise another one of her aspirations, namely to become a wife and mother. This period, which presents a contrast to the carefree and gay time spent in Macau, is documented by letters that do not compare, however, with the wealth of information of a journal, nor has her entire correspondence survived. There are recurring references to Macau and China, because of the Low family's growing involvement in the China trade and also as a source of bittersweet memories that like good wine improve with age.

*   *   *   *

Farewell to Macau

After the break-up of Harriett's secret engagement with Wood and the wedding of her best friend Caroline, life in Macau became increasingly tedious for her. The boredom and dullness felt are clearly reflected in her writings.

> *I verily think if I was condemned to live here for 10 years I should go crazy. Oh dear, oh dear. I hope I shall never be put into such another place. (23.8.1833)*

The same tenor prevails in a letter to her parents dating from summer 1833, where she complained:

> *That I am heartily sick of Macao I have long since told you. I am now generally at home and Aunty and I are together most of the time, that is, we are generally about our own business. We have our studies regularly and, I think, have a very good knowledge of the French. Practice only is necessary.*[1]

Therefore, when a reason was found to leave before the initially planned stay of five years in Macau, Harriett's happiness was great. However, it was a mixed joy, because the motive for their premature departure was the rapidly deteriorating health of her uncle, William Henry Low. In the same letter to her parents she described his fragile condition, without suspecting yet that it would lead to an earlier return home.

> *Uncle has been in Macao and made us a visit of six weeks, which is wonderful for him. He came down very thin but we fatted him finally so that when he left he was quite a different looking person. He had been troubled with a little hacking cough which worried me very much, but he has nearly got over it. I dread another winter's work for him, though; their constant confinement to a desk is very trying.*[2]

Seemingly her uncle tried to hang on as long as possible, both out of financial reasons and a sense of duty. But in such situations, outsiders often see the situation clearer than the ones affected, as Harriett's argument shows.

> *What is money without health though it is not that that would trouble him, but not fulfilling his duty to others that he thinks of. But if he can do nothing what is the use of his staying. (21.9.1833)*

Even repeated sojourns in Macau, the application of leeches and all the care and fattening could not do away with the cough. In October 1833, William H. Low's physician insisted on their immediate going away, which accelerated plans made earlier about an eventual departure in January 1834.

> *Colledge told Aunt Low this morning that she could not get her husband away too soon, that he never will be any better here, and*

> *that it is necessary he should go at once. So we may be sent off in*
> *a month. (9.10.1833)*

Harriett added still another reason why their exit from Macau should be a fast
one.

> *I have more than Uncle's health which makes me wish to leave —*
> *there is a <u>demon</u> here in the shape of a man who for revenge has*
> *undertaken to abuse my dear Aunt. Fortunately his character is*
> *so well known, all he can say makes no impressions upon any one.*
> *(1.10.1833).*

Although she did not specify the circumstances or the name of the "demon",
the remark refers to the murder of Joseph White by Abigail Low's brothers and
the person in question is thought to have been James P. Sturgis, who only a
year before had counted among her beaux and suitors.[3]

Once the Lows had decided on a rapid departure, all their attention was
focused on the necessary preparations for the long voyage home. Arranging the
required clothes, from larger items such as flannel waistcoats for the cooler
regions to be crossed, to smaller ones such as pocket handkerchiefs, involved
great effort:

> *Busy all the morning cutting work again, but the thought of the*
> *end in view softens all my labours and I would willingly wear the*
> *skin off my fingers were it necessary for the sake of leaving this*
> *place. We are thinking now of the middle of November.*
> *(11.10.1833)*

> *Uncle expresses great astonishment at my <u>industry</u> and hopes it*
> *will <u>continue</u>. I only want a motive to exertion and no one is more*
> *active. (12.10.1833)*

Another tiresome task was the sorting out of things to be left behind or to
be dispatched.

> *This morning went to work about packing directly after breakfast,*
> *and was on my feet till 3. ... We have enough to do I assure you*
> *to pack things to send home, things for the voyage, things to make*
> *ready for Auction and for England, beside Uncle to attend to and*
> *to write for him. (28.10.1833)*

Some possessions were subject to destruction, as a matter of precaution, such
as the majority of the letters received. This surely must have been very depressing
for somebody whose existence almost depended on them.

> *Tore up 2 large baskets full. It made me sad for I have a great
> veneration for these little testimonies of affection, but it is impossible
> to keep them for I should not like to have them exposed. Have not
> torn one third and not one of my <u>real</u> valuable ones. (3.11.1833)*

Having accompanied Harriett's life in Macau so far, we may correctly guess
which letters were her "real valuable ones". She also prepared a separate box
with items much treasured by her, to be dispatched in another ship.

> *I should like to have a green tin box that I shall send kept as it is
> till my return, if I should be preserved. If not, take what you please
> yourself, my dear and distribute them as you like among those I
> ought to remember. (29.10.1833)*

The last task in Macau consisted of bidding farewell to everybody, which
is always a fatiguing exercise, mainly in emotional terms.

> *This morning we sallied forth to see the world and falter out <u>Adieu</u>.
> Saying <u>Adieu</u> in this place is not like saying it in most others, it is
> true people do not care much about each other and do not pretend
> to and in saying good bye there is more of a feeling of envy than
> any thing else and they all congratulate you on your escape and
> hope their turn will come next. We called on all the Ladies almost.
> Say what you will of it though, it is not <u>pleasant</u> to leave the most
> <u>indifferent</u> with the thought it is the <u>last</u> time we may ever meet.
> Got home quite exhausted in <u>spirits</u>. (12.11.1833)*

The Lows aim high in China

The exit of the first batch of Lows from China, however, was not the end of
their presence in this corner of the world, but rather the beginning. Three brothers
followed Harriett Low's footsteps and took up residency in China, or rather
Canton.[4] A fourth brother became a clipper captain, cruising regularly between
New York and Hong Kong. The first of them arrived in September 1833. It was
Abiel Abbot Low (1811–1893), nicknamed Botus, the oldest male among
Harriett's brothers. Ardently and anxiously awaited by her, his arrival was a
dream come true.

> *I have never passed so happy a day in China with such <u>genuine
> home feelings</u>. If Uncle was only well! After breakfast I skimmed
> over my many letters [brought by Abbot] and feel glad that I am
> still remembered. I had thought otherwise. (12.9.1833)*

The home feelings were heightened by the appearance of an uncle (shortly before Abbot) and a cousin (shortly afterwards). Probably never after this moment, were there so many Lows in China, which caused her to remark:

> The Lows swarm at this season. I never knew any thing like it.
> (27.9.1833)

Naturally Harriett was eager to show the newcomers some interesting corners of Macau.

> After dinner Abbot and I went to walk. We went to the Joss House. Could not start Uncle James, he will not condescend to admire any thing in Macao. He immediately compares with Europe, and "comparisons are odious" you know. He is a very different person from what I thought him. (20.9.1833)

But neither the city nor Harriett could convince Abbot to stay longer in Macau, for whom business was his *"ruling passion"* (17.9.1833).

> Abbot and Uncle James left us at 10 o'clock this morning. I was busy all the morning helping him take an account of his clothes and books, and now he is gone and I am all alone. Oh dear. He was quite impatient to be employed and I could not keep him any longer. Beside I thought if he could be of any assistance to Mr. Heard he ought to go. But it is hard to have him go again. Perhaps I may not see him again for 5 or 6 years. (23.9.1833)

Abbot's first news from Canton told her about a malaise with which Harriett was all too well acquainted.

> Rec'd two letters from Abbot this morning. Don't tell me how he likes Canton — but says he had had the "blues" which does not say much for first impressions. However when he comes to be employed he will be contented I dare say. (29.9.1833)

Abbot, who had started as a clerk with Russell & Co., became a partner in 1837 and retired to New York in 1840, when trading had become difficult due to the Opium War. After he had spent a few weeks in Canton, Harriett quite correctly judged his aptness for the particular milieu reigning there.

> Had a letter from Abbot this afternoon and wrote him another in return. We keep up the fire pretty constantly. I admire his stability of character and <u>prudence</u>. He is just suited for Canton and will I think get on very well. I think he bids fair to make a sterling man. (7.10.1833)

Abbot would also be something like an anchor in Harriett's later life, supporting her materially, when she had serious problems with her husband's unemployment and love for alcohol.

Ploughing the waves again

Once more upon the Waters, yet once more

— with this melancholic quotation of Byron's *Childe Harold* (Canto 3) Harriett Low begins her journal of their homeward journey, written aboard the "Hon[orable] E[ast] I[ndia] Comp[an]y's Ship 'Waterloo'." Although she was happy that this period of her life was coming to an end, her departing thoughts were not very cheerful.

> *Left Macao this morning at 9 o'clock, embarked at Mr. Pereira's Wharf. Went on board a "<u>Lorcha</u>"⁵ accompanied by Uncle James Low and my brother Abbot, Dr. Bradford, Capts. Roundy, Macondray, Dumaresq, and our Capt. Blakely and after a little <u>squeeze</u> by the Mandarins and satisfying the Boat girls, bidding adieu to Mr. Colledge, we made sail, and left Macao I trust <u>forever</u>. Four years residence there, cools one's love for it and I for one give up all its comforts and everything pleasant it <u>does</u> possess, without a sigh; that is, all its <u>fixtures</u>, such as pleasant walks, pleasant views, etc. There are some <u>few</u>, aye very few, that I regret leaving, but most probably our parting will be likewise forever; for when different countries claim us, and those so far separated as Europe and America there is little chance of meeting. But now, I have left the place, I will <u>in</u> <u>shades</u> let it rest; I shall often think of it, and with much pleasure. Time like the grave, will bury many of the thousand annoyances, I then had and I shall wonder, perhaps, at some future time, why I was not perfectly happy there; well let it pass; I trust it has not been time spent in vain. I have learned many useful lessons and if they have not as yet made me happier, they will no doubt stand as shields in my future life; I shall at least be guarded from the <u>like</u>. (19.11.1833)*

Two more passengers from Macau, the Dutch Consul Van Basel and Dr. Rutherford, joined their party.

> We made sail with a fair wind, cool and delightful and were
> alongside our Castle which sat like a <u>rock</u> in the water, at 11
> o'clock. Our party was all cheerful and none of us were at all sick,
> we were <u>whipped</u> on board, our friends saw us safe in our Cabins,
> in the midst of tons of baggage, and had only time to say a few
> words as the Boatman hurried them and our Ship was under weigh.
> So we were soon obliged to say <u>good bye</u> again, to my dear brother
> and all, who it seems but a few days since, I had the pleasure of
> welcoming. Well we have to make the best of all these things, and
> with a few tears and a wave of my handkerchief as they passed
> our Stern, lost sight of them all in a few minutes. God bless them!
> (19.11.1833)

But there was little time for musing:

> The Boat and all gone, we were soon obliged to give orders about
> our Cabin arrangements. Every thing must be "<u>Cleeted</u>" and
> "Lashed" to keep them from "fetching away" and the <u>most</u> must
> be made of room. (19.11.1833)

Soon afterwards, Harriett and her aunt Abigail were in the claws of seasickness
once more.

> At dark, the wind increased and we both began to give up what
> we thought belonged to us. But there was no doubting the <u>appeal</u>
> and we <u>surrendered</u> and were very glad, as soon as possible to resign
> <u>ourselves</u> to our Couches. Poor Uncle, sick as he was, was the
> only one not quite helpless and instead of our nursing him, he was
> obliged to turn nurse himself. (19.11.1833)

   The journey homewards resembled their journey to Macau in many ways,
especially the on board entertainment, which basically consisted of reading,
eating, working (that is sewing or writing letters for her uncle), playing games
and admiring nature. Therefore Harriett found it necessary, once more, to warn
her sister of a boring journal.

> One day is a facsimile of another my dear sister and the ocean has
> become so familiar to me that I fear this journal will be far less
> interesting than the first. For how often we find that it is only the
> gilded charm of novelty that excites our admiration. (13.12.1833)

Again, the Lows were very lucky with the crew of their floating home. Unlike a German ship they came across, where *"the Capt. and all hands get drunk together" (6.12.1833)*, on the *Waterloo* such irresponsible behaviour seemed unthinkable. Everything and everybody functioned like clockwork.

> *A clear sky above us and the clear blue waters all around us, with about 8000 yds. of Canvass to waft us along assisted by a good breeze was no mean sight. I enjoyed it awhile, and also the perfect order of the Ship. Everything goes on so regularly and with so little noise that it is really surprising when you consider that there is 150 men on board. The Boatswain's Whistle was heard while we sat there, and the deck was instantly covered with men, each one bearing off on his shoulder his own hammock, which are neatly rolled up and numbered and piled upon the railing of the Ship. It was a pretty sight and looked a busy scene for the moment and all was still again. (22.11.1833)*

Even the Sundays were very similar to those on the *Sumatra*.

> *Every thing calm, still and quiet. Everybody dressed clean which reminds me of Sunday at home in Salem, where you know people only had a clean shirt once a week. The wind and weather being favourable, we all assembled at 5 bells on the Quarter deck to hear prayers read. (22.12.1833)*

The sailors also kept animals for their amusement. Having passed through the warmer regions of the globe, it was only natural that these animals were more exotic than the pigs (the final destination of which was the cooking pot anyway) on the *Sumatra*.

> *Speaking of Monkeys, the sailors have 50 or 60 on board and it is very amusing to see them frisking about and carrying their young so carefully with them. They never come aft. (30.12.1833)*

And another animal, believed to be equipped with special magical powers, was also brought along.

> *The "Black Cats" are <u>petted</u> but all to no effect. Our Capt. pretends to have great faith in these creatures, but he is far too sensible a man to credit such <u>superstitions</u>. However they are always treated with <u>great respect</u>, while the poor <u>tortoise shell cat</u> is sadly abused if she goes further aft than the main mast. (7.1.1834)*

Even the gales had the flavour of *déjà vu*.

> The breeze strengthened this morning, and was blowing a 10 knot
> breeze before sunset, but as clear a sky as possible. The
> "Barometer" was falling however and the Capt. very <u>reluctantly</u>
> obeyed its warning, but as he goes altogether upon the Barometer,
> he dared not disobey. And just before I came down the men were
> ordered to take two reefs in the top sails. (2.1.1834)

Throughout the following day the barometer maintained low pressure, making
everybody wonder about its seemingly capricious behaviour. But the captain's
precaution finally paid off.

> Before morning we were fully convinced of the fidelity of our
> "Barometer" and see the advantage of listening to its warnings and
> were awoke various times by the "<u>fetching</u> away" of some of our
> traps that had hitherto escaped our attention. I was awoke by the
> pelting of <u>books</u> which came into my couch by dozens from a book
> shelf over my head. Thanks to my good condition I had no <u>bones</u>
> broken. I have already been so knocked and bruised with my
> awkwardness in running against trunks etc., that were any one to
> <u>pick</u> up one of my legs below the knee they would find some
> difficulty in deciding its complexion. ... a violent gale commenced
> about 4 o'clock in the morning of this day and continued to blow
> with great violence till 12 and gradually grew lighter through the
> day. I will not pretend to say that I saw much of the sublime
> outside, but I can vouch for the <u>ridiculous</u> inside. Had I not have
> been violently <u>sick</u> I might have enjoyed the <u>sport</u> but I defy any
> one to be amused with any thing in such a situation. I succeeded
> in dressing myself after having risked my bones in many perils, but
> got through without serious injury. But every thing was in a state
> of confusion it is in vain to describe, for you cannot imagine how
> dreadful it is, and the decks so slippery that one slides from one
> end to the other. I did manage to look out my windows, the sea
> was an entire sheet of foam. And our great Ship seemed <u>trembling</u>
> for its safety, it seemed neither to advance nor recede. The wind
> was dead ahead and we had only 3 <u>storm</u> <u>sails</u> set. All our usual
> sails were furled. (4.1.1834)

In other aspects, however, the journey home was very different. For instance,
Harriett was deeply impressed with the quality of some of the ship's
accommodations.

> *The officers' Cabins are all neat and well fitted up, so different from our Ships. Of course the size makes a vast difference, but I doubt whether the American officers would take the trouble and go to the expense of making themselves so comfortable even if they had the room. But an Englishman must have his comforts. (12.12.1833)*

Another side of British navigation which Harriett could highly recommend to her countrymen, was the elaborate signalling system in use for ship-to-ship communication. The speechlessness and deafness of American boats was blamed on her favourite scapegoat, Old Hickory alias General Jackson.

> *This morning went on deck to look at a Ship which was approaching us. It proved to be an American, but we were braced sharp in the wind and could not go near her, and as our Capt. fights shy of these Ships there was no prospect of speaking her as it was for her to make the advances. I could not help thinking she might have letters for me on board. Wish you would make my compliments to General Jackson and request him to order our American Ships to learn to talk. We yesterday endeavoured to make the other Ship converse, but she had no bunting and was dumb. The English Ships all have "Mariot's [Marryat's] Signals" which enable them to converse on any subject (even "Metaphysics"), but our Ships have not yet arrived at that pitch of perfection. (5.12.1833)[6]*

Although a much larger ship than the *Sumatra*, Harriett's freedom of movement on the *Waterloo* was not greater, as could be expected, but more restricted, thus confining her to the cabin much more than desired.

> *On deck after dinner enjoying the breeze and the delightful evening till half past 7 when we retired to our Cabins, rather reluctantly, for after being in them all day long it is a relief to get out. But it would not be decorous to stay on deck without Aunty and she is obliged to go [to take care of Uncle]. So I make the best of it. (28.11.1833)*

As their first few weeks on board were passed in the tropical and subtropical zones, confinement to the hot and sticky cabin was real torture, for the sick Uncle and also for his two assistants, who, according to the fashion dictates of their time, wore a corset like a second skin. But Harriett had already learned to relieve herself of this problem in Macau, evidently at the risk of not being presentable to anybody but a familiar or intimate friend.

> *I stripped myself all but my <u>chemise</u> and perched like a cat in my cabin window where I was sure no earthly being could see me, and as the angels do not wear "<u>Corsets</u>" I thought it was no matter if they did see me; and as for the spirits of the "vasty deep" I did not much care. But more than that, every thing appeared to be asleep in the Heavens above and the waters below. ... Here I sat musing till about 10, then turned in, and slept all night at the rate of 10 knot. (3.12.1833)*

Sleeping, of course, was a kind of pastime too, in which Harriett apparently excelled:

> *The Capt. says they cannot know all my <u>qualifications</u> in America. He laughs a great deal about my being able to sleep 16 hours on one tack. (1.12.1833)*

But their major concern on the way towards the Cape of Good Hope was naturally the health of William H. Low. Shortly before their departure, Harriett had had a lesson in anatomy with Colledge, which helped her understand the basic problem of her uncle's condition.

> *I think I should like the study of anatomy very much. If I was a man I would be a <u>Dr</u>., an M.D. most certainly. I asked "Colledge" to shew me some plates of the lungs, and he did and proved that a "little learning is a dangerous thing", for I saw enough to see just where Uncle is affected. I know the whys of Colledge's questions and know where his complaints are and <u>tremble</u>. It made me feel uncomfortable and my dreams were <u>anatomical</u>. I should like to have asked a great many more questions, but I felt delicate about it. (6.11.1833)*

At that time there was no absolute certainty about the nature of many diseases and both the sick people themselves and their relatives were only too eager to believe that a slight improvement indicated the onset of cure or merely some minor ill. Sureness about the cause of a disease could only be obtained through a post-mortem examination, a thought that both the afflicted person and the relatives naturally abhorred.

Harriett also explained to Molly, why she tried not to mention their Uncle too often:

> *I do not mention him daily, for I do not know that it can be of any use to note the changes, which are perhaps too gradual to be noticed, but you may judge how many of our thoughts are given to his situation. (19.12.1833)*

Evidently, the suffering of William Henry Low was a big worry to his wife and Harriett.

> We catch hold of the slightest clue to strengthen our hopes, but as yet I consider it doubtful whether he recovers. His feet swell and he has new complaints; his blood is so very low that he is liable to almost any thing. (16.12.1833)

When leaving Macau, the Lows were still hopeful of reaching England without having to interrupt their journey on the way.

> Have felt quite in spirits today for Uncle has seemed a little better. His pulse has been better than any day before. But the Dr. thinks if he gets a great deal better he ought not to go further than St. Helena, that is, he ought not to go to England at that Season. (13.12.1833)

Yet this prospect was reduced by the deterioration of William Low's general condition.

> Uncle proposed to the Capt. today to leave us there (at the Cape) as it will be much better than at St. Helena as regards climate and accommodations. The Capt. has been wishing for an excuse to stop there and thinks it will do, but has not said decidedly. The Dr. thinks it the best place. (14.12.1833)

Knowing about Harriett's impatience to reach her beloved home country, her uncle even suggested that she travel ahead of them, because he foresaw, or rather hoped for, a slow recovery period for himself.

> He proposed this morning my leaving them at the Cape and going on either to St. Helena to wait for Uncle James[7] or going on to England. But I should be unwilling to leave him in the state he now is, although I would jump at the proposal if he were better or I could see him in a fair way of recovering. But then again I should not like to go without a female servant unless there was some other lady in the Ship. I could not bear the thought of going with all these Bachelors, for there is not a married man among them, not but that I should feel perfect confidence in the Capt. and not doubt the <u>politeness</u> of any, still it would not be pleasant. However I shall say no more of it at present. It would seem like leaving my parents again, and that I dread. (16.12.1833)

South Africa, the first stopover: a matter of life or death

Seven weeks after having left Macau, they finally reached the *"land of the Caffre and the Hottentot"* (6.1.1834), as Harriett called South Africa. For a few more days, however, all they could do was wait patiently and hope to reach terra firma soon. Strong breezes,

> *which would have carried us straight to the South Pole if we had been disposed to go,* (8.1.1834)

prevented their advance.

> *We were obliged to keep in our couches till dinner time as much as possible as there was no such thing as sitting or standing. The Capt. Says he hardly ever saw such a sea, so irregular and confused. Poor Uncle has hung in his Cot all day, for his poor bones would suffer from the bruises mine get.* (9.1.1834)

Three days later, the *Waterloo* finally entered Table Bay.

> *Looked out after breakfast and found we had the Cape of Good Hope nearly <u>abeam</u>. … We have been sailing past it rapidly and I have been watching its changes from our port. Table Mountain was covered, as the Capt. says, with a cloth which looked light and airy, but which Capt. Blakely says is a sure sign of a S.E. gale. This Mt. is 3582 ft. high. I wonder if I shall ever attempt its summit. Our abode will be at the <u>foot</u> of it. … The Purser will go on shore tonight and get some accommodation for us, and we shall go tomorrow morning. I almost dread it for Uncle, he is so weak, but we must trust to Providence.* (12.1.1834)

Cape Town received the Lows with beautiful weather.

> *This morning feels sharp and cool and reminds me of our delightful summer mornings or May mornings in America; it brought the colour into my cheeks at once and it actually seemed as though I was breathing my own native air. … We were landed at the jetty about 9 and a <u>Coachman</u> walked up and said the <u>Carriage was ready</u> — a novel sound to our ears, who have not seen a Carriage for nearly 5 years. Nevertheless we jumped into it and we went to our boarding House. Every thing looks strange of course though many look homish, and though I do no feel at <u>Home</u> yet I feel as though I was nearer it. … Every one seemed so <u>busy</u> and so many*

> *running about and what astonished us most was to see ladies so*
> *plenty walking about so briskly in the middle of the day. Our*
> *officers were in and out all the morning, but at 2 went on board*
> *after having bid us Adieu.*
>
>> *Had a delightful dinner, and <u>such</u> an appetite. After dinner*
> *as we had the carriage at our disposal for the day, and Uncle feeling*
> *too tired to go out, the two ladies and myself jumped in and we*
> *had a delightful ride. Went to Green Pt. and saw the Waterloo*
> *some way out with a fine breeze and all sails set. God bless them*
> *all. (13.1.1834)*[8]

Harriett's uncle went into the care of a local doctor immediately.

> *Dr. Murray called this morning to see Uncle. Says he must go*
> *directly into the country where he will have finer air and that he*
> *does not intend to give him any medicine, but to eat every thing*
> *good — in fact, to live on the fat of the land, which is rich enough*
> *I assure you. Every thing is so abundant particularly compared to*
> *Macao that we are quite ravenous. You would think I had been*
> *starved to see me eat, but coming from sea every thing tastes so*
> *fresh. (14.1.1834)*

The latter fact prompted Harriett's fear that she would soon turn into a *"Dicker fatty"* *(21.1.1834)*, a Dutch expression for corpulent people.

Although her aunt rarely left the side of her husband, Harriett enjoyed everything that Cape Town had to offer in terms of beautiful gardens, sights, walks and promenades, shops and a museum.

> *Miss Cruywagen and myself dressed and went <u>shopping</u> this*
> *morning — what I have not done for 5 years. (16.1.1834)*

Before leaving for the countryside, the Lows became acquainted with two particular winds haunting the residents of Cape Town, the so-called South Westerners and South Easters.

> *The clouds of sand were rolling in the air so thick that we could*
> *not see across the street. We were obliged to close every window*
> *and even then the sand came in. The S.E. they say are much*
> *worse. I have often heard of them. Every <u>place</u> as well as every*
> *<u>body</u> must have its "something". (17.1.1834)*

> *I tell the young ladies [Cruywagen] I shall write you word the young*
> *ladies at the Cape all have dirty faces. For my own part, I cannot*

keep my face clean. This red sand keeps one dirty the whole time.
I can't bear it, every thing you touch is covered with it.
(27.1.1834)

Waiting and hoping at Kirstenbosch

The place chosen for Uncle's convalescence was Kirstenbosch, an hour's drive
from Cape Town. Harriett's description of the journey there sounds like a road
to paradise.

> *With Dr. Murray to accompany us, we had a most delightful ride*
> *through one of the most charming countries I ever saw. Nature*
> *seems to have done her best to bring every thing to perfection and*
> *to have concentrated them all here. The tall pines and magnificent*
> *oaks that line the roads are superior in size to those of our own*
> *forests, the "Silver tree" grows in great abundance and looks very*
> *beautifully, a great variety of Heath too in full flower to delight the*
> *eye, and "any <u>quantity</u>" of Blackberries would have delighted the*
> *taste could we but have got them but we could not stop. (29.1.1834)*

The new domicile of the Lows was in a lovely location and run by the
Eksteens, a sympathetic Dutch couple with four nice children.

> *We arrived at Kirstenbosch about half past 4, at a most delightful*
> *little thatched Cottage situated directly under the mountain, not*
> *at the foot of it but some way up. We see it towering directly above*
> *us, and being high we have a fine view of the Country around us.*
> *We were kindly received by our host, hostess, and daughter who*
> *all speak English, and a very genteel and respectable family. The*
> *air is very different here from what it is in town, cool and bracing*
> *and we hope it may be beneficial to Uncle. He bore the ride well*
> *and was quite comfortable after it.*
>
> *We are now upon the other side of the mountain, the side*
> *which is most productive. Being the[re], we [are] not exposed to*
> *the S.Easters and not so much exposed to the scorching sun. There*
> *is a vast difference in the appearance I assure you. ... My room*
> *would look quite English had it not Dutch <u>tiles</u> for the floor. It opens*
> *on to the "Stoop" in front of which the roses are blooming in great*
> *abundance. (29.1.1834)*

Surrounded by a forest, vineyards and an abundant orchard, the place seemed to be perfect, except for the presence of tiny, but mortifying insects.

> To support my assertion a few pages back, that every place has its
> "sussin" [something] as the old woman said, I must tell you what
> this has, for it is not without millions of _fleas_, as large (Aunt Low
> says) as _coach_ _horses_. Now no doubt this is exaggerated, but I
> assure you they have power enough, whatever may be their size,
> to make me exceedingly uncomfortable and disturb my repose.
> Uncle says he should have no amusement if it was not for them,
> but I must confess I am too much fretted with them to be pleased.
> (30.1.1834)

Except for her uncle's illness, their stay in South Africa would have been perfect bliss for Harriett.

> I have not felt so free and happy for a long time. It is what I have
> long been wishing for, to feel that I can move my _length_ without
> constraint. (1.2.1834)

And moving she did a lot, on her own two legs, by carriage, on horseback, and even for the first time in her life on a donkey. Together with the Eksteen children and some neighbours, she explored the surroundings of Kirstenbosch both near and far. One excursion on horseback, which took the pleasure of riding from her for some time, is particularly descriptive.

> In the first place, my horse was lazy and if perchance by whipping
> I urged him into a canter it was almost at the expense of my poor
> bones, for I had not yet recovered from yesterday's [mounting]
> frolic. To add to my miseries, the breeze was strong and got the
> pins out of my dress, and I had great difficulty in keeping it in
> _decent_ order. Then my bonnet kept blowing off and what with my
> lazy horse, my sore bones, my whip, the reins, my bonnet and
> my dress, I had more than I could manage. I could have cried
> almost with vexation. Whether Mr. Jones saw my _knees_ or not I
> do not know, but he was kind enough to keep in front a little.
> Before we got to our destined end, my comb had contrived to make
> its escape and my hair was hanging over my back, so you may
> judge how I looked, but I cannot tell you the agony I was suffering.
> (12.2.1834)

On another occasion, Harriett got an opportunity to sample Dutch family life in Africa.

> Went to "Stellenberg", a very pleasant place, to a sister of Mrs. Eksteen. The Dutch are so kind, friendly, and hospitable, I like them much. There is no formality, they are a great contrast to the English in this particular. They like good frolics. I was introduced to about 20, I should think in all. There was grandpapas and grandmamas, Uncles and Aunts, <u>lovers</u>, governess, etc., all in one house. It is a novel and a pleasant sight to me, to be once more where the bonds of family affection are so visible. (7.2.1834)

Harriett also visited Constantia, then as nowadays renowned for its wine, where she was introduced to the secrets of its production:

> After dinner we went to the famous "Constantia". I had an idea it was a village, but it seems it is the residence of Mr. Jacob Cloete, Mrs. Eksteen's brother. Here is where all the celebrated Constantia wine is made. It is a most delightful place, a fine house and from the Stoop we have a fine view of the country round & of False Bay in the distance, also "Hanglip", one of the Southern Capes. Mrs. Cloete has a large family and an interesting daughter grown up. I am astonished to find what polished and elegant manners all the young ladies have here. You would suppose they had been brought up in a great deal of society. I was much pleased with Miss Maria. ... This place was built many years ago by one of the old Dutch governors and named for his wife (in English Constance). The wine made here and which is so famous is very rich. She tells me of the real Constantia there is only 30 leaguers (150 gals.) made a year. They leave the grape till it is so ripe that it begins to look wilted like a raisin, so that there is very little juice to express. It is consequently very sweet and rich and I am told that if the seed of this grape is sown elsewhere, the flavour of the wine is different from "Constantia" wine. It may not be correct, but it may [be] the peculiar situation. There is no doubt an immense deal of spurious wine is exported & no doubt much of the common sweet Cape wine is drank for Constantia. They say to witness the making of the wine is quite enough to sicken you. And from all accounts I should think would be as good as a <u>temperate</u> society — the little <u>sweaty</u>, <u>dirty</u> negroes are sent into the tub to express the juice with their feet, they cannot do it by machinery lest they should break

the stones. After they have got the juice out, then the skins are pressed to give the wine a colour.

There are five different kinds of Constantia wine, the White Muscatel and the red, the Frontignan made of a light coloured grape, and the Pontac which is the most expensive, and the most rare. There are now several other places built near Mr. Cloete to which they have given the name of Constantia, but this is [the] <u>real</u> one. Before coming to the house we ride through long avenues of old majestic oaks while the milk white house in the distance has a very pretty appearance. And oh if you could see the beautiful myrtle hedges. They grow above my head and so luxuriantly that they look splendidly. We took a walk in the gardens, and after talking awhile we bid them good night and had a delightful moonlight ride home. These people all live very genteely, very different from our Country people; more like the Virginia farmers, from descriptions I have had of them. They have a great many slaves who do the work of the farms. (16.2.1834)

As regards Harriett Low's uncle, the "great waiting" had begun for him in Kirstenbosch. Either he would recover enough to leave this place, or die there. On the doctor's advice he started to take *"Asses Milk" (31.1.1834)* and *"Caffre medicine made of Herbs from the Caffre country" (2.2.1834)*. As on the *Waterloo*, their hopes and fears alternated almost daily.

Dr. Murray was out, says he finds we all look better when he is better, and indeed it makes a vast difference in our spirits. I have nothing to say, do, or think of at present but him. (22.2.1834)

Unlike Harriett, however, her Aunt rarely left the room of her invalid husband.

Poor Aunt is never of our party, Uncle does not like to have her leave him. (10.2.1834)

Only six weeks after their arrival at the Cape, her Aunt *"took a walk for the first time" (9.3.1834)*, an event worthy of being noted. Therefore, it was a most welcome distraction to receive visitors at Kirstenbosch. Apart from their new South-African acquaintances, the Lows were even visited by some of their friends from China, when their ships made a short stop in Cape Town, on their way to England. First came Mr. Plowden and Capt. Locke and a week later it was the turn of Capt. Whitehead,[9] although they did not bring any particular news. At that time the Lows had regained hope from a new diagnosis.

Uncle still continues better and the Drs. now think his disease
proceeds from the Liver, which encourages us that he will yet
recover. (5.3.1834)

But it would be for the last time, because less than two weeks later, Harriett
wrote:

Saw Dr. Murray, he tells me he has no doubt now that Uncle's
lungs are the seat of his disorder. That being the case we have little
hope of his recovery. His perspirations have returned and he feels
himself growing weaker instead of stronger. He told Aunt Low this
morning he thought he never should be any better. (15.3.1834)

Preparing for a life's last journey

This was also Harriett's last entry in her journal for a fortnight. The next one,
written on 30 of March, describes the last day and hours of William Henry
Low, on the 22 of the same month, as well as his burial the following day.

He asked Aunt L[ow] to lie down early that she might relieve me
in the morning and about ¹/₂ past 8 p.m. she did and went to sleep.
I sat by him and wiped the cold perspiration from his forehead.
He asked me once for a little tea which I gave him. He coughed
once soon after and said "that is the <u>last</u> of it". Soon after I noticed
a strange appearance in his eyes, and got up to give him something
but I could not make him speak. I took hold of his hand and it
appeared stiff. I awoke Aunt Low with the dreadful sound of "my
dear Aunt I believe he is dying, I cannot make him speak". We
found it but too true. He was quite speechless and hardly appeared
to know us, though he once turned his eyes upon her as though he
knew her voice. My poor Aunt took his hand, prayed that Jesus
might receive his Spirit and at about 11 he yielded up his Spirit to
the God who gave it I trust. Such an hour I never passed before,
my dear Sister. His two sole relatives in this part of the world sitting
by him as he requested. We called no one till all was over. It was
¹/₂ past 9 when I awoke Aunt and 10 minutes past 11 when he
breathed his last. He died quite easy, no convulsions, not the least;
the spark of life went out like an expiring lamp. ...

And now one word for my dear Aunt, who is one thus
afflicted. It is truly the last link, it is <u>all</u> she has loved on earth,
the idol of her heart, and the sharer of every joy and every sorrow.

254 EVERYTHING IN STYLE

He is now gone, taken from her, and she is to live on solitary and as it were alone. She has for the last six months devoted her whole time and strength to him, and at the last has not only ministered to his bodily wants, but has assisted in preparing him for to meet his God. Truly she has been a ministering angel to him. I never saw her equal for devotion, for firmness & fortitude; for tenderness, kindness, and deep enduring affection she is unsurpassed. She would not let him concern himself about her, but bid him give his whole thought to his Maker, telling him his time was short, praying for him, with him, and that she herself might be strengthened till the last, receiving all his last requests, and disguising the agony of her own feelings that she might not give him pain. ... After we had done all in our power we called the family and they kindly performed all the last sad affairs for our dear departed one. Need I, can I tell you the dreadful feelings when all is over and we see our dear friend a cold and lifeless corpse? No, I cannot. Although strangers and in a strange land, we have been thrown among the best and kindest people. They have done every thing for us and they will have their reward. (30.3.1834)

An autopsy was performed before the funeral, which brought them the final, sad certainty about the cause of William H. Low's death.

The body was examined (by Uncle's request) by Dr. Murray and Bailey, and we have the satisfaction of knowing, that every thing has been done for him possible. His disorder was wholly in the lungs. The right one <u>entirely</u> gone, the left nearly so. But we shall bring the statement with us. (30.3.1834)

The burial took place the next day.

The remains of my dear Uncle were consigned to the grave on the following Monday, the 24th. He was buried in the Episcopal Burying ground, Cape Town. And the first that lies there, it is a new one and lately consecrated by the bishop on his way to Calcutta. (30.3.1834)[10]

It is a quiet spot looking upon the sea, towards Green Pt. There is an iron railing 5 ft. high all round it, and we are going to have the cypress & myrtle all about it. (1.5.1834)

A plain inscription stone bearing his name, place of birth, and age will mark the spot where he lies, and if any who ever <u>knew</u> him in

*his life should chance to read it, I am sure a tear and a sigh will be
their legacy at his grave, but none, none can know but us who
witnessed his death, how calmly, how willingly, how cheerfully he
resigned his breath in submission to the will of his heavenly father.
(3.5.1834)*

In all this time, Harriett had never mentioned the Chinese servant who
accompanied them on their homeward journey. He appeared for the first time
in the journal after the death of her uncle, seemingly after having performed
Chinese mourning rituals at his grave.

*Ayok came to me at noon and told me he had been to Chin Chin
at his Master's Grave. He asked me if it was not our custom to
do so too? I told him No. He said with great feeling that he thought
it a very good custom, and with them they go twice a year. I was
pleased with his attention and apparent good feeling, indeed I have
never met a Chinaman who has manifested such good feelings as
he has ever since he has been with us, at Kirstenbosch particularly.
We have become quite attached to him, he has been so faithful. If
he only continues so we must consider ourselves very fortunate.
(13.4.1834)*

Life and the journey must go on

After her Uncle's death there was no further reason for Harriett and her Aunt
to stay in Kirstenbosch. They returned to Cape Town to search for a suitable
ship to take them to England, which proved no easy task. After ten days, they
got notice of a vacancy on the *Royal George* bound for London, and "The
Captain is exorbitant in his demands" (23.4.1834). Checking out the conditions
aboard would normally have been the task of Harriett's Uncle, but now the two
women had to deal with all these duties.

*Ah this makes one feel what is lost. So helpless is a poor female!
particularly when abroad in the world. (24.4.1834)*

Since neither her Aunt nor any other female felt like accompanying her to see
the *Royal George*, Harriett had to go in the company of gentlemen only.

*Not very pleasant, but I started off and said nothing. We were
three quarters of an hour beating off. A fine breeze but dead ahead.
Found the Capt. a pleasing person, and the Ship very neat and
very small compared to the Waterloo, but I smelt no Cockroaches*

> *and think the accommodations are as good as we can expect. There is but one small cabin for us and we shall be well squeezed. There are many passengers mostly French, so we may learn to <u>speak</u> French. Stopped about a quarter of an hour. Was introduced to the Surgeon and made sail for the Shore. ... Came home, reported favourable to Aunt Low, and she has made up her mind to take it. I am sorry to say she will not sail till a week from tomorrow. (25.4.1834)*

Before embarking, Harriett still had to suffer a great deal. Plagued with a painful "face ache", since the time when her Uncle was still alive, any remedy — even the most disgusting one — had only brought her temporary relief. An examination of her mouth cavity by the equally desperate doctor finally revealed the real cause of the face ache.

> *Dr. Murray thinks I had better have a tooth out which he thinks may be the cause of all my pain. I think I had better before I go to sea. (25.4.1834)*

The first operation was not successful and its description illustrates well how rough medicine used to be then.

> *Dr. Murray came afterwards and brought his cold iron in his pocket, so without any further demur I summoned all my resolution, raised my courage to the striking point and sat myself down to the dreadful operation. Unfortunately instead of coming out, it broke <u>short</u> off. It gave me great pain for an hour or two. (26.4.1834)*

The days and nights ahead were spent fearing the continuation of the operation and more than once Harriett ran away from Dr. Murray.

> *I am out of tune. I am kept awake at night by the tooth ache and my days are spent in dreading its being extracted. It must come I fear, and I am a coward that is certain. (29.4.1834)*

A few days later, Harriett had to concede defeat.

> *Dr. Murray came today and would not let me escape, took out the <u>torment</u> and I <u>behaved</u> <u>very</u> <u>well</u>. (2.5.1834)*

One day before the departure Harriett and her Aunt went to church for the last time in Cape Town, listening to a sermon *"on the benefit of afflictions, very appropriate to our situation"* (4.5.1834). After the last farewell of the faithful Dr. Murray, the two Low ladies embarked on the *Royal George*, on May 5th.

the springs. On the summits of these mountains and on other high places are fortifications for the defense of the Island. And on the sides of these mountains you discover the roads which give you an idea of the winding paths of the Alps, but more of this anon. Then there is the vast ocean around us, and one wonders in vain what could have produced this enormous excrescence in the midst of it.
...

After having had our breakfast and having gone through the customary visits from health boats, etc., with our best bibs and tuckers on we were whipped into the boat, in company with Madame Grant, her three children and two sisters, and several gentlemen of our party, and in a few moments were again on terra firma, which is always pleasant, be it what land it may. ... There are very good steps for landing and all convenient, but such a queer place I never saw before. Our eyes had not deceived us, we were actually walking on the quay with the rock rising a thousand or more feet perpendicular and in some places jutting over our heads, and not a trace of vegetation to be seen. Some miserable little houses were built at the foot of the rock, the sides and roofs of some being formed by it, and making one tremble lest some convulsion should bury them all. We marched on a little further and the next [thing] that struck our eyes was a <u>ladder</u> from the foot of the hill or mountain reaching to the fortification on the top. This is also nearly perpendicular, or at this slope. The idea of going up made one dizzy. I have been told it is 3000 ft, it certainly looks 2500.[11] I shall endeavour to find out. It was built by the E[ast] I[ndia] Company and cost 200,000$. We walked on a little further and entered a gate which locks up the <u>city</u> at night. Passed through a very clean street, the principal, saw some pretty looking houses and <u>one</u> <u>pretty</u> girl and arrived at the Hotel of Mr. Solomon, a <u>Jew</u> — a very neat and commodious house and well furnished. Made inquiries at once for American papers and letters, but the only one for us had been sent to the Cape (very gratifying). No papers of late date could be obtained. (Well one must pocket one's disappointments and see others reading theirs with <u>patience</u>).

The Capt. immediately ordered carriages to take us to the tomb of Napoleon, as we had no time to lose. The sight of the roads we were to mount were rather awful in appearance. However, we soon saw our <u>voitures</u> at the doors. I hardly know what to call them; I should say they resembled mostly double *buggies with four wheels very small, which brought us very near the ground. A driver sits upon the horse and leads them part of the way. There were no tops so that we were exposed to the sun which was not very agreeable. ... Our course was a zigzag path up the side of the mountain, the valley below us at the distance of many hundred of feet, the mountains towering above us. There is a little wall to guard us from the precipice on one side.*

Being above the valley we had a fine view of the town, which runs up some distance between the mountains till it finally tapers off <u>and</u> <u>is</u> <u>no</u> <u>more</u>. It is not a quarter of a mile wide, the streets very narrow but looked clean, the houses mostly small and built of mud and stone. We saw some pretty gardens and a variety of most beautiful green <u>trees</u> — the banana and other tropical fruits. They have one church, plenty of fortifications, mountains on three sides of them and the beautiful blue waters in the distance, or on the fourth side, visible. ...

I was enchanted with the scenery and as we gained the <u>summits</u> felt <u>much</u> <u>nearer</u> <u>heaven</u>, for some how or other it always seems to exalt the feelings to be towering so high. ... When we had nearly gained the summit we were obliged to get out of our carriages and descend a little way into the valley to visit the tomb. Our companions were all violent Bonapartists and looked sad and sentimental as we approached. It was indeed a time for réflexion. It recal[l]s so many facts and leads to so many conclusions that one is almost égaré and again I could not but in the midst of all, rejoice that my dear Uncle was not brought here. I am sure he would not have been half so comfortable. The valley must be dreadfully hot and the ride up the mountain would have been far too fatiguing for him to have bourne. Then again I could not help thinking how much he would have enjoyed it, had he been here with us in good health. <u>Allons</u>, a truce to reflections.

The tomb of the great man, of whose fame the world knows enough, is situated on the side of the mountain in a most quiet and delightful spot. There is not a letter upon the stone, to say <u>who</u> or <u>what</u> lies there, owing to the foolish jealousy of the English government. The tomb is enclosed by a great iron railing, a sort of lily growing at the two head corners and the four sticks remaining which supported the "Forget me nots" planted by Madame Bertrand after his decease, but which has since died. Within the outer enclosure there are two large willow trees which <u>waved</u> over the grave, but they too must die and they are nearly _dead_.[12] A few green leaves upon the branches show they once had life, but the trunks are quite white. The present Gov[ernor] Dallas has planted some cypress trees which are growing well. An old Sergeant lives near by and will give you [a] slip or two which was there during Napoleon's residence and looks like a piece of antiquity. His little cottage is just above, surrounded with geranium, growing wild and luxuriantly. It is a most enchanting spot, but far to quiet for the spirit of such a man as rests here. As Byron says, "Quiet, to 'quick' spirits, is a hell", and it must have been so to him, for how could he reflect upon his career, in this lone and desolate place with any _peace of mind_? What a change to be sure! from the courts and palaces of kings in the midst of courtiers and dependants, to this isle in the ocean, and the cottage in comparison, on St. Helena heights!! Whew!! A prisoner! And alone!

Finding a book at the entrance for the travellers' name to be inserted, I took it up and how quick it recalled the favourite saying of Napoleon himself, "There is but one step from the sublime to the ridiculous",[13] for one glance at this said receptacle for names and remarks, was quite sufficient to excite one's risibles. Here were huddled together eulogy and invectives, sentiments of all kinds, of friend and foe, poetry and prose, good and bad, of the literate and the illiterate, of all nations, tongue and kindred. One bit I was particularly struck with but unfortunately I remember only part of it, but enough to give you some idea of its merits: "Here lies Bony part ... He rests in peas", written in a very bad hand; and much more of the same kind. Such a book of trash I never saw before but no doubt is like many others adapted to such occasions or places.

I merely wrote the names of our party and we bid adieu to the tomb and returned to our carriages and proceeded to Longwood where Napoleon lived and died. But there is hardly a trace of what it then was. It is in a most shocking state of filth and delapidation and converted into stables, etc. It is a pity I think that they did not let it fall honourably to decay, but his bed room is now turned into a stable, his sitting room where he died is a room for machinery in a wretched state, his flower garden into a pig stye. Pity, pity, I think. They shewed us the grounds etc., but there was no trace of anything that belonged to him. The house stands on one of the highest points and has a most commanding view of the sea etc. They shewed us the rooms of Las Cases and Montholon, and we also passed the house of General Bertrand. I was amused to see our friends carrying away large pieces of the <u>wall</u> and the <u>floor</u> where he died and saying how happy they should make their friends in France and at the Mauritius by dividing the <u>Spoil</u>. ...

So we left Longwood, saw the new house built by Napoleon containing 52 rooms, but as the Gov[ernor] is residing there at present we could not go to it.

We went down the same way we came up and were almost suffocated with dust, and the sun was very hot. Thus finished our excursion. Our next demand was for a <u>bath</u> (I told you, keep in mind, Mr. S. <u>was</u> <u>a</u> <u>Jew</u>) which we had and felt exceedingly refreshed and comforted by it, for we were quite fatigued. This done and dressed again, we sallied forth into the streets, bought a spool or two of cotton, and enquired the prices of some things; all and every thing here are the most <u>awful</u> prices. ...

We dined at 5 o'clock, had a good dinner, which cost <u>15 shillings</u> <u>sterling</u> <u>a</u> <u>piece</u>. It was a very nice dinner to be sure, and relished well, consisting of Turkey, Goose, partridges, Fowls, pies, pastry, etc., fish & soup of course, and fruits, figs, delicious plantains, Pears, Guavas, fruits of the Islands and dried imported fruits. But we should have said nothing of this but when we were demanded 7 shillings sterling for each Bath we exclaimed in perfect astonishment and I said N.B. never say any more of <u>Chinese imposition</u>, they are excelled by Europeans'. But there was no disputing this charge and we found every thing else was charged accordingly, and we were not [at] all sorry to bid adieu to St. Helena, or to think our stay was limited to one day. But I hope you will remember Mr. S. is a Jew, though he is not alone in these charges. There may be reasons for all this, that is living may be very dear, but I cannot forget the hot water. It is true they are very nice rooms well fitted up, and then I suppose they do not get customers very often. But hope I shall remember to warn my friends when they may go to St. Helena to ask the price of a bath before they call for it.

At 8 o'clock our party mustered. A most beautiful moonlight night, and we walked to the Quay and went once more on board our ship and were quite tired enough with our day's exertion to go to bed. (20.5.1834)

From St. Helena to London

From St. Helena it would take them almost two months before setting foot on land again, in London, their last stopover on the voyage home. This particular period is perhaps the most arid part of the journal in terms of descriptions and reflections, as Harriett admitted herself.

> I find a sea life has become so familiar to me that my journal is neglected for many days together and I sometimes think it best to spare my paper all together and reserve it for something more interesting on my approach to land. There my poor brain will be overrun and I shall be glad to relieve it of its burden. (26.5.1834)

As regards their fellow passengers, both Harriett and her Aunt never became very friendly with them, largely due to their relative ignorance of each other's language.

> Could I have the privilege of conversing with them, I should hear some sage remarks and perhaps be regaled with a "feast of reason and a flow of soul", but unfortunately it is otherwise. For their rapidity of utterance debars me from any intercourse in the general conversation and in my private chats I never venture to express my sentiments. This being the state of the case we keep out of the way, and either sit upon the poop or read in the eve'g and in the day are in our own cabins. The manners of the party are not very elegant, and judging from the very frequent utterance of Mon dieu I should not say much for their reverence of one whose name is so irreverently spoken but on this subject I dare not judge. To our ears it is very unpleasant. (15.6.1834)

Eventually on 30 May they crossed the equator, and suddenly she felt much closer to home.

> Awoke this morning with the Sun and saw him rise from his watery bed in great splendour. I fancied the sky looked more homish than usual. (31.5.1834)[14]

Three weeks later, however, she did not have to evoke her imagination anymore, in order to feel more "homish".

> Now we are just getting into the Lat. of the U[nited] States and our time begins to accord so well with yours that I can actually fancy what you are about. In China I was always obliged to

> *suppose you <u>snoring</u> while I was employed and vice versa.*
> *(21.6.1834)*

The temperature also told them that they had left the warm and hot zones definitively behind them.

> *Still growing cold and being all summer <u>birds</u> on board, there is*
> *great shivering among us. (27.6.1834)*

> *All we want is plenty of exercise to make us feel delightfully, for*
> *I really recognize my native air in these breezes, though I do not*
> *know you will account for it when I declare they are from the S.E.*
> *Never mind, they are just like them at any rate. Today we are in*
> *the Lat[itude] of New York. Even that is pleasant to us. I only*
> *wish I could turn our Ships head and bring her up in New York*
> *Bay or harbour. (28.6.1834)*

But since this was obviously not possible, Harriett Low had to spend one more Day of Independence abroad. The feelings about this day, however, were as fervent as ever.

> *The "peace and prosperity of our country" with a pretty little speech*
> *from Captain Embleton, was proposed as a toast and drank in good*
> *fellowship by all after dinner. (4.7.1834)*

In the journal this entry is followed by a patriotic poem addressed to the American Eagle.

As they were coming closer to their destination, the number of ships encountered increased almost daily.

> *4 Ships in sight before breakfast, but soon shot by us. About 11*
> *we spoke an English Ship bound to Quebec and soon after another*
> *Dutch vessel passed within hail, perhaps bound to New York, but*
> *she was not inclined to speak. We have had a dozen ships about*
> *us today, and have been quite amused by beating several of them.*
> *It is very cheerful after a monotonous voyage of six weeks.*
> *(3.7.1834)*

The monotony was definitively over, once they were within sight of the British coast, which quite charmed Harriett.

> *The land on this coast appears well cultivated, and I observe all*
> *the divisions of land are made by beautiful hedges, which have a*
> *far better appearance than our dreary <u>stone walls</u>. On enquiring I*

find it is the case <u>generally</u> throughout the Island. This coast it is said is rather barren, though a few miles inland it is the richest county in England and celebrated for pretty girls, the "<u>Devonshire lasses</u>". (8.7.1834)

On the following day, all the French passengers disembarked.

Was awoke this morning at 3 o'clock by the Capt. rousing his French passengers. I got up at 4 to see them off. We then had the coast of France in sight, and the Pilot boats all in readiness. The immense quantity of baggage delayed them a long time as there were 20 people in all to leave. They did not get away till half past 6. When we bid them all adieu, which is always painful, I felt it particularly in parting with the three sweet children. They made themselves beloved by all on board. (9.7.1834)

Reading about her astonishment regarding the French way of greeting, one is left to wonder what their French instructor in Macau had taught them, if not one of the essentials of French etiquette?

We were saluted in French style by a kiss on each cheek. I was amused yesterday to see the young ladies and all offer their cheeks, with the most perfect nonchalance to a French gentleman who left. It is true he was a married man and an elderly one. I do not know whether it would have been the same with a <u>young</u> one or not, but however <u>custom</u> <u>sanctions</u> every thing. At eight o'clock we lost sight of the boat and our friends probably <u>forever</u>. I should like much to hear from some of them. We parted good friends with all, and could we have had a little more communion with them, think I should have become much attached to the young ladies. <u>Fortunately</u>, perhaps! We have now our head again turned towards England and shall tonight make the land again. Most lovely weather, we are particularly favoured. I <u>am</u> thankful I am sure. (9.7.1834)

As they passed along the English coast, Harriett's previous mental image of England was confirmed by reality.

Think I had formed a very good idea of the appearance of England. I am not disappointed, nor had I exaggerated. (10.7.1834)

Besides, being an avid reader of history and historical novels, she started to feel the weight of history of the old continent Europe, something that her young country lacked.

> Dressed and went on deck, realized the sight of "Dover's chalky cliffs" I have so often heard of … I like the looks of Dover very well, an ancient castle crowns the summit of the cliffs at the right of the town (entering). It is said it was built by the Romans. … On the beach were many bathing <u>carriages</u> which are run into the sea. … Passed many splendid looking palaces along the coast of "Kent" and I have made the most of it. Passed "Margate" & "Ramsgate". All appear to be built of free stone, castles, fortresses, and lighthouses in their respective places, and bring all sorts of things to one's mind, of the bloody battles & etc., but in a word the scenery here is beautiful. (10.7.1834)

Harriett was also pleased with a technological novelty of her time.

> As we got abreast of "Dover" this morning the "Steam boat" had just started for Calais. It is really beautiful to see them, they truly go "like a thing of life". Ayok was highly delighted and says, they say, "Suppose have go foul wind can walky". I replied yes, "suppose no got wind at all can walky" which seemed to heighten the pleasure & surprise. (10.7.1834)

One thing, however, about which Harriett had read in her books or heard when conversing about England, seemed to be missing.

> All <u>looks</u> peaceful and happy, but we cannot always judge from <u>appearances</u>. Though I certainly have seen no appearance of starvation in any of the boats, every one looks well and worthy the title of John Bull. (11.7.1834)

If she had moved further north to the industrial cities, she certainly would have been confronted with more poverty than in the more agricultural, southern regions of England. At a later stage, however, when going to church in London, Harriett mentioned that the "charity children" (27.7.1834) of the parish sang and said the responses during mass, indicating their number as about 600. The figure appears to be very high, considering that she referred to one parish only, but may be seen as a mirror of inner-urban poverty. This observation is followed by a thoughtless commentary, which was in a way typical for her when faced with poverty.

> *When we went in, there were about 6 couples at the Altar being married. I thought from that and the number of publishments that there is not much regard paid to either Malthus or Chalmer's Political Economy. (27.7.1834)*

In the heart of the British Empire: beautiful, buzzing, busy London

On 12 July 1834, they finally moved out of their floating habitation.

> *We were in a perfect Babel till about two o'clock nothing but tacking Ship, & etc. till we arrived at Gravesend where confusion was made still worse by the landing of <u>live stock</u>. The pigs were <u>rebellious</u> and the geese d[itt]o. Then all our steerage passengers went, and soon after a steamer took us in tow and we went on smoothly defying the wind. At about 5 we were at Blackwall and our trunks were looked into on board, but passed without trouble, and we congratulated ourselves, but when going on shore at Blackwall in full view of all the houses on shore our boat was stopped and another "Philistine" boarded us, demanded our keys and overhauled them; my blood boiled but we were obliged to submit, and bear it patiently, but I never felt so much annoyed. (12.7.1834)*

On shore they became acquainted with a new means of transportation, or rather a new word for it, an omnibus. Although initially hated by Harriett, probably because of the rough coachmen, after a few weeks in London she loved them, because *"one is privileged to be sulky in them, which is agreeable" (28.7.1834)*. During the first few days they stayed at the house of Captain Embleton, who had brought them safely from Cape Town to London and who was living at a place that certainly sounded familiar to their ears, namely *"No. 5 Canton Place, East India Road" (12.7.1834)*. While staying there they received their first visitor from China days, Harriett's Spanish teacher Ybar.

> *He told much news, of marrying and giving in marriage. My <u>friend</u> Vachell is married and gone to China. (13.7.1834)*

Other friends from China, such as Rebecca Morrison and her stepmother, and the missionary Abeel, would call later at their lodgings in London,

> *at Wright's Hotel, No. 2 Adams St. where our dear Uncle wished us to go, and where he put up before. (14.7.1834)*

They even came across many more of their acquaintances and friends from Macau, but only in effigy.

> *About 2 we started in a one horse "<u>fly</u>" for Bedford Square to Mr. Daniell's,[15] the Artist, where we saw the pictures of Mrs. and Mr. Colledge and were very much pleased. It seemed like bringing them before us. Ayok burst into quite a hysterical laugh when he saw his father's face in the picture. ... We saw Mrs. Davis' picture too. They were all too late for the exhibition, unfortunately. Chinnery's paintings are liked much here, but they say his greatest fault is <u>deadness</u> of colouring. I noticed this myself the other day at "Somerset House". (19.7.1834)[16]*

"The other day" referred to a visit to the same place which had occurred a few days earlier, when Harriett's attention apparently was taken not so much by Chinnery's paintings, but by something else ...

> *We walked to "Somerset House" where we saw a vast collection of paintings and were very much delighted. The house is immense. There was one room filled with statuary, looked very old and extremely dirty. I could not prevent a blush when I entered the room. For it seemed indelicate and hardly fit for a lady, however I thought it would never do to be so <u>unfashionably</u> delicate and I walked through with apparently great nonchalance, but I was very glad to make my exit. I am a novice at these things as yet, indeed I would not be quite dead to these feelings, but I saw some ladies sitting down and enjoying it. I must confess I <u>directed</u> my attention to the models of <u>buildings</u>, with a <u>sly</u> look at figures, but this was nothing to some of the public exhibitions. (16.7.1834)[17]*

The scene is reminiscent of Harriett's reaction at the sight of "unclad" Malays during her voyage to Macau, showing that she continued to be prudish.

Until their departure for New York at the beginning of August, Harriett and her Aunt took pleasure in the historical and modern London as much as they could, although their enjoyment was intermingled with bouts of the blues from time to time.

> *Walked as far as Waterloo Bridge then having bought some books returned to those dear companions which cheer us in every situation. They are indeed the only antidote to the <u>blues</u>. (15.7.1834)*

Harriett loved London's parks full of people, and the "Bazaars", or shopping malls as they are known nowadays.

> Really one might spend a fortune in a few minutes. A dangerous place for ladies who cannot resist temptation, but I flatter myself I can. (14.7.1834)

But above all Harriett adored London's famous historical buildings, such as St. Paul's Cathedral, Westminster Abbey and the Houses of Parliament, which even then seemed to have generated a lot of tourism, with their guided visits. Finding her own descriptions insufficient, on several occasions she recommended her sister to read Washington Irving's *Sketchbook* about England, for example in the following scene in Westminster Abbey.

> Be assured my dear, it is impossible to enter such without moralizing on the mutability of all things. It would take volumes to tell you the heaps of reflections that rush upon one in such an ancient and venerable building. We went to the Chapel of "Edward the Confessor" who built this place. See Sketchbook. ... In another chapel there are wax figures of Elizabeth, William & Mary, Queen Anne, & many others, all in their own robes, in the fashion of the day the ornaments were imitations. They were all quite dusty and defaced by time. ... We wandered about a long time and could have spent much more. Oh we went to the Chapel where the Kings and Queens are crowned and had the pleasure or <u>honor</u> of sitting in the Coronation Chairs, — old fashioned things and under the seat of the King's chair is an immense rock of granite brought from <u>Scone</u> where the Kings of Scotland used to be crowned.[18] Our guide amused me very much, reciting what he had to say. I suppose he has said it so many times that he has it all at his finger's end, he went through it so rapidly that it was difficult to follow him. (24.7.1834)

The only "problem" in their outings was their faithful servant Ayok, who was a real eye-catcher, thus invariably drawing the attention to the Low ladies. Ayok too was not happy with the enquiring glances of everybody whose path they crossed.

> Poor Ayok excites so much attention that I believe he will be very willing to doff his China Costume. Being rainy today he had on his great umbrella hat, and cut a curious figure to be sure to those who are not in the habit of seeing them. (19.7.1834)

On 22 July aunt and niece finally solved their major problem in London.

> At 12 we took a carriage and first drove to St. Katherine's Dock
> to look at the Montreal and were very much pleased with her
> accommodations, and finding it will be an immense deal of trouble
> and expense to transport ourselves and luggage to Liverpool we at
> last determined to take a Cabin in this Ship the first of August.
> Once decided we all felt relieved of a heavy load, for it had caused
> us great anxiety before. The Ship is splendid in her
> accommodations, and having no "Cockroaches" we shall feel quite
> happy. (22.7.1834).

The remaining days were spent much the same way, mainly sight-seeing and
shopping, as well as parting calls and packing.

> Got up early and packed up our duds to send on board with Ayok,
> at 10 they started. And we go tomorrow to Portsmouth and that
> is all for the present my dear. Think I shall not edify you with any
> more of my long stories, my next will be viva voce I hope. Adieu.
> (1.8.1834).

But of course Harriett would not stop writing, just because another volume of
her journal had come to an end. The remainder, however, is all written in pencil,
probably for the same reason already indicated at an earlier stage during the
passage St. Helena — London.

> I have been obliged to make these observations with a pencil for
> the ship is in such commotion I can have no safe place for ink.
> (15.6.1834).

Crossing the North Atlantic towards New York

On their way to Portsmouth they had one last chance to admire the lovely English
countryside, which never ceased to charm Harriett.

> Left London August 2d for Portsmouth in a very nice Coach which
> holds four persons inside and loaded outside with all sorts of
> etceteras. We had two very pleasant ladies who were on their way
> to the Isle of Wight to rusticate for a time during the warm weather.
> ... We travelled through the most delightful country imaginable,
> and passed through the town of Guildford the only large town on
> our way. The scenery after passing that from the hill is very

> *beautiful, you have every thing to make a perfect landscape. There*
> *was a romantic old ruin, a castle in the distance, a highly cultivated*
> *country, and in short was delighted and want to bring it all to*
> *America. I am charmed with England, but do not be jealous, I*
> *am ready to leave it, for the heart the heart is [word effaced —*
> *possibly American] still. … We left our lodgings at 9 in the morning*
> *and arrived at the Fountain Hotel, Portsmouth about 6 in the*
> *evening, not having left the* <u>Coach</u>*. We changed horses 7 or 8 times*
> *with the greatest despatch and were never detained many minutes.*
> *For the noble horses were all harnessed and waiting for us, splendid*
> *animals; think we do not have such in America. (2.8.1834)*

However, Harriett and her Aunt had to be patient for several more days, because their ship did not arrive due to head winds. Once on board the *Montreal* Harriett was astonished not to feel seasick, but most of the other passengers were not so lucky.

> *Some are very, very ill and suffer much, others doubtful and all*
> *envious of me and two other young ladies who went on board at*
> *London. … Our cabin and indeed the whole Ship is a perfect*
> *hospital. The first thing we heard this morning was that a man in*
> *the steerage had cut his throat and thrown himself overboard in*
> *the night, judge of the feelings of all if you can, particularly those*
> *in the steerage. The weather is dark, rainy and dismal and all*
> *together we have an odd mixture of the comic & tragic. Some of*
> *the ladies are much alarmed tonight with the sea. We do not get*
> *on at all. (6.8.1834)*

The *Montreal* was able to accommodate many more passengers than any of the ships they had been on previously, and therefore there was a greater variety of people from all walks of life aboard. That is why Harriett used to refer to her fellow-passengers as *"strange medley"*, *"mélange"* or even *"menagerie"*. Once she visited the steerage, where the low-fare passengers were jam-packed.

> *Enquired for their health and condition. Poor creatures we*
> *complain, but we might not when we consider how comfortable*
> *we are in comparison. There are 120 people huddled together,*
> *getting short of provisions, and quite comfortless. (18.9.1834)*

The two great topics that characterised and dominated the last leg of their voyage back home were head winds and gales, making it a very exciting, morose and above all long journey.

> *Have now been out 24 days and we had only 30 hours of fair wind in the whole <u>time</u>. We are quite discouraged for we have all the disagreeables combined. Then the anxiety of getting home and not getting there quite unfits me for any thing. I certainly never read so little on board before. I cannot compose my mind to anything. The weather is very pleasant, but we are not yet half way and although we have been going at 8 & 10 knots the best 3 days we have not made more than 1 degree. (28.8.1834).*

This is also the part of the journal with the biggest lacunae in terms of keeping track of daily events. Several times we can find gaps of a week between the entries, and where more than two weeks fit on less than a page. This was very untypical of Harriett Low, but it can be understood as a clear expression of her impatience and irritation.

However, even the longest journey comes to an end one day, and although we don't know exactly which day this was, Harriett's last entry in her journal is full of hopes and expectations and, after such a long time away from home, doubts too.

> *Think you will begin to look anxiously for us now for we are a week or two over our time. The first questions this morning was, any land in sight, and how's the wind. The responses were any thing but agreeable. No land, wind ahead and but just moving. Can't possibly get there today.*
>
> *Get up and eat my breakfast as usual, not so usual either for I breakfasted in the ladies' Cabin. Stoned some raisins with several other ladies, for plum pudding. Next time hope it will be for Thanksgiving <u>at</u> <u>home</u>. It reminded me of old times.*
>
> *Went on deck, walked awhile. A Ship and Brig in sight. A most lovely morning it would have been to have gone in to the Bay. So bright and clear. Went on to the round house, wind light and ahead. Have no work to do, cannot read, and the day has seemed as long as <u>six</u> when employed. I sit and muse and cannot fancy at all how I shall find you, but I endeavour to keep myself quiet trusting to that being who has been so merciful to us in all the perils by which we have been surrounded and not doubting that whatever he sees fit to do will be for our good, and feeling too that sufficient*

unto the day is the evil thereof. I cannot explain how I feel. It is a sort of all <u>overness</u> and yet it appears to me that I am going to a strange place as I have been to so many before —. (21.9.1834)

At home: nothing but an intermezzo

Thus finished the journal of Harriett Low and her life as authoress. If it were not for a short postscript added by her daughter Katharine Hillard to the first edition of the journal, nothing would be known about her reception and feelings at home, during the two years preceding her marriage. This postscript illustrates very clearly that Harriett Low must have fought with great problems of readjustment at her new home in Brooklyn.

> *That Miss Low's apprehensions as to the strangeness she was to encounter were not wholly unrealized, we may judge from the fragment of a letter written to her by an old friend, in the most gushing and sentimental style of the day. The change from the comparatively brilliant society life of Macao to the deadly dullness of Brooklyn in 1834 must have been overpowering, and even in the home circle there were changes. The elder sister, for whom the journals were written, was married, the oldest brother was in China, and the next sister (born after a succession of seven boys) was then a child, about nine. Old friends had been left behind in Salem, everything was to be begun again, including the finding of a place in the family circle, so long left vacant, and probably now filled up. As all such gaps are filled in time. There must have been some complaint of loneliness and lack of sympathy to have drawn forth the epistle just mentioned, which sounds as if it might have been written by Amanda Malvina FitzAllan; but it is unsigned, being but a fragment.*
>
> *"Would that I could open the windows of my soul, dearest H. ... and enable you to see how fully, how entirely, the spirit understands and sympathizes in all the emotions which dictated your two last precious letters! the sense of loneliness, the incipient discontent of unappropriated affections, longing to rest on some kindred bosom! But, my dear, you would be more than human, could you utterly annihilate such seasons of weakness. If after bright years of youth passed in the hot-bed of adulation, — after living almost exclusively in the softened and tender atmosphere of flattery,*

admiration, and affluence, where so many studied your happiness, and so many sought but to share it and be blest, — could you return to the still, monotonous course of duty which you now pursue, with only the quiet though inestimable domestic affections living in your bosom, — without experiencing moments like those you have so touchingly described, — of sickening, heartless, uncheered existence? Condemn not too severely the momentary intrustion of such natural emotions, my dear girl, but be comforted, sweetest; moments there are in store, which, if not wholly unspotted, are still bright and glowing, and vivid enough to repay long years of negative existence, here below; and there is, you know, a hope that beyond this terrestrial scene all the most ardent boundings of the heart, if pure, shall be satisfied, — filled to overflowing!"[19]

The letter had been written on 15 September 1835, that is a year after Harriett Low's return to the United States, and according to Hillard at around the time of Harriett's engagement to John Hillard,

a man of cultivated tastes and charming manners. They were married on the 3d of November, 1836; and their wedding-cards, which still survive, are quaint and curious. There are two cards, both small and very highly glazed. The smaller of the two bears my father's name in his own handsome handwriting, the larger simply says: "Miss Low, At Home, Thursday evening, November 3, at 9 o'clock", with residence, but says nothing about marriage! The two cards are put up in a small envelope, fastened with a transparent wafer, and that is enclosed in a piece of white paper folded in an oblong shape, and tied up with a piece of narrow white satin ribbon.[20]

John Hillard was four years her junior. The young couple went to England right after their wedding. From this new period in Harriett's life, which we may call her "second exile", considering that her major aspiration in Macau had been to live among her own people, a series of letters exist, many of which are quoted in Loines's book, besides others that are kept in the Library of Congress. Together with family letters, both those directed to her or others in which she is mentioned, her footsteps can be followed for some time more.

Once more in foreign lands, yet once more

Harriett Hillard, née Low, and her husband went to live in London at first, where he was partner in the bank Coates & Co. Already during the first year there, the couple passed through exciting times when many banks around them failed and Coates and Co. was threatened by failure, too.

> *Hillard and Coates have both said so confident all along that they should not fail, that the chance of it was a severe shock to me, and we were all happy enough on Saturday night to hear the word* <u>safe</u>.[21]

Knowing Harriett's addiction to writing and receiving letters, it is to be presumed that she continued a lively correspondence with her family scattered over three continents, at least initially. However, as her own small family was growing, Harriett felt the obligations of a housewife and mother for the first time.

> *Tell Grandmother that I have so much to do with my house, my husband & two babies that I have not so much time as I used to have, and only* <u>answer</u> *letters, one of hers never lies long unanswered.*[22]

Sometimes, lack of time even compelled her to kill two birds with one stone:

> *Tell my good brother Abbot that if I had had time I would have written him to have thanked him again for the beautiful dress he sent me.*[23]

Her letters also manifest a continuing interest in the events happening in Macau and Canton.

> *I have not yet received Abbot's letter which you said you should send per London packet. wish you would bear it in mind to send me the "Canton Press" and Repository which he has sent, after you have read it. And also a book of paintings, which he mentions. … I feel anxious to hear that the Canton houses will suffer. I hope not. I have written Abbot several times via Calcutta and direct.*[24]

From 1833, the year of Abbot's arrival, until the end of 1849 at least, there was always a Low brother in Canton, which allowed Harriett to receive eyewitness accounts of the most important events in those agitated years, including the Opium War and the collapse of the Canton system of trade.

Her family continued to increase in England at an almost yearly rhythm. Their first child, a son, was still-born in October 1837. Only four girls would live to maturity, among them her eldest daughter Katharine, who prepared the first edition of the journal and Mary, the mother of Elma Loines, who compiled and edited *The China Trade Post-Bag*.[25] Twin boys died within three months of birth and another daughter, Sarah, at age 6, from scarlet fever. Harriett was a proud mother and liked to praise the virtues of her children in her correspondence. Perhaps she then remembered her own rather unkind observations about mothers in Macau who liked to talk about their little darlings, and in a letter to one of her sisters she asked a bit naively:

> *I wish you could tell whether my children are* <u>*really*</u> *more interesting than other people's or whether every body thinks their own so? Can you answer this question? Perhaps* <u>*mother*</u> *could.*[26]

By then she also must have understood that inevitable natural law of procreation that left her an eightfold mother, an attribute which when observed in some other couples in Macau, had earlier attracted her opprobrium, for example the Morrisons.

In the winter of 1844/45, the family moved to Manchester, where Hillard should find more business for Coates & Co.

> *I do not know that I ever had a greater trial of my patience, than having to pack up again and in the very midst of all the coldest & dreariest winter that I have ever felt in England.*[27]

Harriett never came to like Manchester, which she described as bleak, dark and filthy, and she was increasingly tired of living abroad.

> *I long to be among you again. I am weary of making new acquaintance and living among strangers.*[28]

Her solitude in England would be mitigated by prolonged visits of her two youngest sisters, Sarah Elizabeth and Ellen Porter, and by a short stopover of at least one brother, Josiah Orne. In any case, there was only one ocean between the Low siblings, and progress in ship construction led to faster and more comfortable passages. Together with Sarah, Harriett fulfilled a dream several times mentioned in Macau, namely a visit to Paris, which was carried out in spring 1844.[29] Sarah's stay in London was also successful on another plane, because she came to know her future husband, Edward H. R. Lyman, in Harriett's home. They married in summer 1846. The Hillards, apparently very satisfied with their matchmaking, attended the wedding ceremony in the United States, and considered it as a *"capital match"*.[30] We also know of at least one encounter between Harriett and her best Macau friend Caroline Colledge, née Shillaber. The meeting took place in Edinburgh, in spring 1840.

> As soon as Mr. Colledge has finished his course of Lectures we are going to Abbots Pond & it is possible to Stirling, though Kate [her daughter Katharine] is an objection, I must take her whenever I go to stay all night, I shall probably return to London about the first or second week in May. I wish it was to meet Hillard, but I fear he will not be there before June — I suppose you will see Abbot in July or June, he thought of taking passage with "Kinsman". I shall expect him to come & see me before he settling himself any where, I shall invite him to that effect.[31]

Eleven years after the arrival of the Hillards in England, during another series of bank failures, Coates and Co. was not so lucky as before. Consequently, Harriett's letters written between February and May 1848 are quite gloomy and full of uncertainty about the future.

> No idea when we shall be able to leave England. Unless I go and leave him with the children, which I do not much like to do — though sometimes think it would be best. He says, there is no knowing when he shall be free — and then he does not seem to want to go to America on account of proceedings there — the settlement then is postponed for 9 months and goodness knows, I do not, when it will end — I always thought it was easier to fail in America than elsewhere … from all I can learn, it will be doomsday to us, before it is settled, but I think Hillard always looks on the dark side and I make some allowances — our quarter here will be up now, in about a month and "To Let" is all over our windows — then there must be a sale previously, and Hillard is again going to London, and all the packing & preparation will come upon me.[32]

The change from Manchester was not only a geographical one, but also a social one, because they moved into an apartment with furnished rooms, in a less central area of London:

> I can hardly realize that I am in London. We are so remote from the parts in which we have formerly lived and I know and are known so little here, that makes me feel as though I had never been here before. And I am in all respects so differently situated that I am sometimes tempted to ask "if I, be I?".[33]

The death of the bank seemed to have been a slow one, because in another letter one month later she thought that it was safe after all. But it was a false hope. In June 1848, after all the sad formalities that accompany an event of this kind had been dealt with, the Hillards were finally free to sail back home.

The family, who could have lived quite comfortably from the money that William H. Low had bestowed on her as a reward for keeping company to his wife Abigail in Macau, was faced with another financial calamity.

> When an uncle in America lost through poor judgment a part of Harriet's small fortune left her by her Uncle William H. Low, Abbot counsels his sister to remember the many good turns that same uncle had done to people in financial distress and recommends her to balance them in her mind.[34]

Probably only a person with a deep faith comparable to Harriett's can make sense of this kind of advice. John Hillard was never able to overcome the blow caused by the failure of Coates & Co. He became increasingly unstable and fond of alcohol. A sea voyage, then considered as a cure for many evils, on one of Abbot's clippers to Shanghai, did not improve his condition. He died in July 1859, aged 44. In 1862, Harriett lost another daughter, Fanny (aged 19), who had suffered from tuberculosis, a disease she was very well acquainted with.

For the rest of her life Harriett Low lived below the level she certainly had dreamed of as a gay young woman in Macau. At the same time, however, she had two motives of pride — her daughters, who turned out strong and independent women, and the rise of the name and fame of the Low house. Between 1844 and 1873, a fleet of more than a dozen ships roamed the oceans, displaying the Low house flag with five red and yellow stripes and an L in the centre.[35] Harriett's brother Abbot seemed to have become something like an anchor in her life. He gave her a house in Brooklyn to live with her daughters and where she died on 27 December 1877.[36]

Coming back to Virginia Woolf's quotation that inaugurates Hummel's transcription of the journal (quoted in the Preface to this book), the question about the ongoing appeal of a journal as simple and complex as the one of Harriett Low, does not seem difficult to answer. Although only two centuries, so far, separate us from Harriett's birthday, the journal is keeping her "genius" very much alive and with it the spirit of a bygone era. Technology and progress have changed our world beyond recognition, but they have not visibly interfered with the central human themes that float above cultural representations and are universally understandable: Love and unfulfilled love, greed and generosity, sadness and joy, courage and fear, rebellion and conformity, prejudice and openness, hope and resignation, loyalty and betrayal, faith and faithlessness. It is their incarnation in different persons at different times and places, a young American lady in early 19th-century Macau in this particular case, which makes each story unique, but at the same time understandable to readers who are generations and continents apart from the protagonists on the stage of life.

Annex

Biographical data on some of Harriett Low's contemporaries

The subsequent selection is restricted to a few basic data on those people, with whom Harriett Low had a more regular contact or who are noteworthy otherwise. Once more, a special acknowledgement must be made to Nan Hodges and the late Arthur W. Hummel, on whose work the Annex particularly relies. More information on certain individuals can be found in the footnotes to the text.

Abeel, David (1804–1846). He was among the first American missionaries to China and a member of the Dutch Reformed Church. Abeel contributed regularly to the *Chinese Repository* and was author of *A Narrative of Residence in China*, 1834 (See Nan P. Hodges and Arthur W. Hummel (eds.): *Lights and Shadows of a Macao Life. The Journal of Harriett Low, Travelling Spinster*. 2 parts, Woodinville (WA), The History Bank, 2002; footnote 24, pp.389, 390).

Ammidon, Philip Jr. (1804–?). He was the son of Philip Ammidon Sr., co-founder of the trading house of Russell & Co. in Canton. Ammidon Jr. went to Macau on the *Sumatra*, together with the Lows, and visited the Low ladies occasionally in Macau (*Ibidem*, footnote 3, p.368 and footnote 71, pp.394, 395).

Alexander, Henry Robert. Son of a formerly wealthy but failed Calcutta merchant. He worked for the British East India Company (*Ibidem*, footnote 101, p.380).

Allport, Thomas and wife. He was a consignee of British country ships and associated with the firm of Thomas Dent & Co. The couple was shuttling between India and China. Whenever in Macau, Mrs. Allport used to see the Low ladies (*Ibidem*, footnote 74, p.376).

Baynes, William (1789–1866) and wife Julia Smith (1793–1881). He was a member of the Select Committee of the British East India Company at Canton and its President in 1830. His wife is said to have been the first European lady to venture openly to Canton. They had three sons and four daughters (*Ibidem*, footnote 113, p.381; see also footnote 104, p.400).

Beale, Thomas (d. 1841) and son Chay. Thomas Beale, an English merchant, was a member of the opium firm Magniac & Co. For some time he acted as Prussian consul. His magnificent garden and aviary are described in many accounts of the time, including Harriett's journal. He died in poverty, under mysterious circumstances. His son Chay was born out of wedlock and therefore not considered as "good company" by conservative minds (*Ibidem*, footnote 66, pp.374, 375 and footnote 6, p.414).

Blight, James Henry (1797–1880). He was one of several brothers from Philadelphia, who traded at Canton at one time or another (*Ibidem*, footnote 107, p.380).

Bradford, James Hewlings, Dr. (1802–1859). He was resident physician to the independent traders at Canton, who subscribed his salary. In 1835, he returned to his hometown Philadelphia (*Ibidem*, footnote 134, p.384).

Bridgman, Elijah Coleman (1801–1861). He was the first American Protestant missionary to spend his life in China. Bridgman was sent out by the American Board of Commissioners for Foreign Missions. He founded the *Chinese Repository*. His wife Eliza Gillett Bridgman edited a book on her husband with the title *The Life and Labors of E. C. Bridgman*, 1864 (*Ibidem*, footnote 25, p.390).

Calvo brothers. They were from France. For a certain time, one of them taught French to the Low ladies (*Ibidem,* footnote 30, p.416).

Chinnery, George (1774–1852). He was the premier English painter and portraitist of his time in the East, known for his wit and eccentric lifestyle in India (1802–1825) and Macau/Canton (1825–1852). Chinnery portrayed Harriett, her uncle and aunt, among many others. Her portrait sessions are described in detail in the journal. For some time, Harriett had drawing lessons with him (*Ibidem*, footnote 93, p.378).

Cleveland, William, Capt. (1777–1842) and Lucy Hiller Cleveland (1780– 1866). He was a native from Harriett's hometown Salem. His wife, who accompanied him on his journeys, liked to draw and sketch. In the Hodges/ Hummel edition of the journal, there are several drawings of Macau characters from her sketchbook, including one of Apun, the Low house-boy in Macau (*Ibidem*, footnote 84, p.377).

Colledge, Thomas Richardson, Dr. (1796–1879). He was Assistant Surgeon to the East India Company's establishment at Canton and founder of the Ophthalmic Hospital for the Poor in Macau. Colledge was also one of the founders, in 1838, of the Medical Missionary Society in China and remained its President until his death. He married Harriett's friend Caroline M. Shillaber in March 1833. They returned to Great Britain (to Edinburgh first and later to Cheltenham) at the time of the Opium War. Their last residence of many years, Lauriston House in Cheltenham, is still standing (*Ibidem*, footnote 65, p.374).

Daniell, James Frederick N. and wife, Jane. He was a member of the Select Committee of the East India Company. For Harriett, the Daniell couple was an example of happiness and style and she was very fond of their children (*Ibidem*, footnote 145, p.386).

Davis, John Francis, Sir (1795–1890) and wife Emily Humfrays. He was the last Chief of the Company's establishment at Canton and governor of Hong Kong from 1844–1848. Davis was one of the first serious scholars of Chinese and China in the English-speaking world (*Ibidem*, footnote 4, p.401).

Dent, Thomas and Lancelot. Both brothers were active in the opium trade and members of the firm of Thomas Dent & Co. Thomas Dent returned to England in 1830, while Lancelot stayed on in Canton until 1842 (*Ibidem*, footnote 121, p.382).

Dumaresq, Philip (1804–1861). Harriett was very positively impressed by the looks and manners of this American captain. In Forbes's book *Personal Reminiscences* (1876) Dumaresq is described as *"that prince of captains"* (*Ibidem*, footnote 1, p.791).

Dunn, Nathan (1782–1844). Dunn, a Quaker, returned to Philadelpha in 1831, after a residence in China of 12 years. He opened the first Chinese Museum in the USA, with life-size clay figures, referring to all aspects of Chinese life. The exhibit was shown in London in 1842, with Dunn escorting Queen Victoria and Prince Albert through it (*Ibidem*, footnote 81, p.396).

Fearon, Christopher and wife Elizabeth Noad. He was Hanoverian Consul and member of the firm of Ilbery, Fearon & Co. The Fearons lived for some time in one of Macau's most beautiful mansions, the Casa Garden (*Ibidem,* footnote 63, p.374).

Forbes, John Murray (1813–1898). He was one of the three Forbes brothers and member of the firm Russell & Co. from 1834–1838 (*Ibidem,* footnote 44, p.405).

Forbes, Robert Bennet (1804–1889). He was another one of the three Forbes brothers and head of the firm Russell & Co. from 1839–1844. Robert B. left many writings, among which are his *Personal Reminiscences* (1876) and *Remarks on China and the China Trade* (1844) (*Ibidem,* footnote 13, p.402).

Forbes, Thomas T. (d.1829). This Forbes brother was head of the house of Perkins & Co. He drowned, together with a Mr. Monson, head clerk of Russell & Co., in August 1829, when his schooner upset on the way to Macau harbour. The circumstances of his death are related in Robert B. Forbes's *Personal Reminiscences* (1876, pp.128–130) (*Ibidem,* footnote 50, p.372).

Gordon, Oliver H. He was an American trader at Canton, who was connected with several American firms during his time in China. Harriett also refers to him as "Duke of Gordon" or "Gaffer" (*Ibidem,* footnote 72, p.395).

Gover, John. He was a private British trader who dealt heavily in opium, which explains his nickname "Old Patna". Patna is a region in North India, where high-quality opium was grown (*Ibidem,* footnote 133, p.384).

Goyena, Gabriel de Yureta. Usually referred to as "Don Gabriel", he was one of Harriett's Spanish teachers. His presence at the Spanish Factory in Canton can be traced back to 1826 (*Ibidem,* footnote 56, p.393).

Green, John Cleve (1800–1875). After a time as supercargo of the New York-based ship *Panama*, he succeeded William Henry Low as head of Russell & Co. in 1834 (*Ibidem,* footnote 99, p.379).

Guetzlaff, Karl (1803–1851). A native of Prussian Pomerania, this Protestant missionary was a man of many talents and interests, which not necessarily were always related to religion. He wrote many tracts and articles in Chinese, English and German. Guetzlaff also acted as interpreter for the English on various (illegal) expeditions along the Chinese coast and served as government interpreter at Hong Kong (*Ibidem*, footnote 16, pp.792, 793 and footnote 19, p.801).

Heard, Augustine (1785–1868). A former supercargo and captain, Heard was admitted as partner at the firm of Russell & Co. in January 1831 (until 1836) (*Ibidem*, footnote 85, p.410).

Hillard, John (d. 1859). A banker from Boston, he became Harriett's husband in November 1836. They spent the first half of their married life in England, where eight children were born to them. After the failure of Coates and Company, the banking firm of which Hillard was partner, they returned to the to the USA in 1848. He was unable to arrange work again, becoming unstable and sick (*Ibidem*, Introduction, pp.14, 15).

Houqua (1769–1843), or **Wu Ping-chien** by his real name. Houqua was the most well known of all Chinese *hong* merchants, respected for his honesty and magnanimity. His portrait, painted by Chinnery, is reproduced in many books on the old China trade (*Ibidem*, footnote 125, p.383).

Hu(d)dleston, Robert Burland (1801–1877). He was a writer and superintendent of office at the East India Company at Canton (*Ibidem*, footnote 96, p.379).

Hunter, William C. (ca. 1812–1891). He first arrived at Canton as a boy of 13. Hunter entered Russell & Co. as a bookkeeper in 1829 and was a partner of the firm from 1837 until 1842. He left two interesting books, *The "Fan Kwae" at Canton before Treaty Days 1825–1844 by an Old Resident* (1882) and *Bits of Old China* (1885) (*Ibidem*, footnote 27, p.390 and footnote 91, p.411).

Jardine, William (1784–1843). Before his career as opium dealer, Jardine was a surgeon on ships of the East India Company. In 1832, Jardine and James Matheson, both Scotsmen, founded the firm of Jardine, Matheson & Co. (*Ibidem*, footnote 20, p.802).

Keating, Arthur Saunders (d.1837). He was a hot-blooded Irishman, who challenged William W. Wood, Harriett's secret fiancé, to a duel that never took place, however (*Ibidem*, footnote 28, p.416).

King, Charles William, (ca.1809–1845). He was a partner, since 1832, of the American firm of Olyphant & Co., known for its refusal to deal in opium. King contributed to the *Chinese Repository* and is author of *The Claim of Japan and Malaysia upon Christendom,* 1839 (*Ibidem,* footnote 56, p.373).

Kinqua (d.1837, at age 37), or **Liang Ch'eng-hsi** by his real name. He was one of the Chinese hong merchants (*Ibidem,* footnote 126, p.383).

Latimer, John Richardson (1793–1865). The business of this independent American trader was mainly opium. Latimer returned to the USA in 1834. His correspondence is kept in the Manuscript Section of the Library of Congress (*Ibidem,* footnote 11, p.388).

Lindsay, Hugh Hamilton (1802–1881). He was a British aristocrat, who temporarily worked as a writer for the East India Company and later had his own firm of Lindsay & Co. in Canton. Lindsay was the leader of a trading expedition to Northern China in the *Lord Amherst* in 1832, with Guetzlaff as translator (*Ibidem,* footnote 95, p.379).

Little, William Coffin (1796–1839). He was an American captain, sailing between Canton and Mexico via the Sandwich Islands (Hawaii) (*Ibidem,* footnote 54, p.393).

Ljungstedt, Anders, Sir (1759–1835). He was the last chief of the old Swedish Company's Factory at Canton. Ljungstedt is the author of the first book on the history of Macau, with the title *An Historical Sketch of the Portuguese Settlements in China and of the Roman Catholic Church and Mission in China & Description of the City of Canton* (1836) (*Ibidem,* footnote 72, p.375).

Low, Abiel Abbot (1811–1893). He was Harriett's eldest brother, whom she used to call Abbot or Botus. Abbot became a clerk in the house of Russell & Co. in 1833, and a full member in 1837. On his return from China he established A. A. Low & Bros. in New York, becoming a very successful businessman. His son Seth Low later became the first mayor of Greater New York. Following the death of his first wife, Ellen Dow, Abbot married Anne Bedell, the widow of his brother William Henry Low (II) (*Ibidem,* footnote 24, p.370).

Low, Abigail (née Knapp), (1800–?). She was the wife of William Henry Low (I), a younger brother of Harriett's father Seth Low, and the main reason for Harriett's voyage to China. Although quite close in age, she is treated as "Aunt" throughout the journal. Widowed in 1834, Abigail married a Mr. Carter in June 1839 (*Ibidem,* footnote 31, p.371).

Low, Charles Porter (1824–1913). A younger brother of Harriett, he was a clipper ship captain and author of *Some Recollections, 1847–1873*, 1905 (*Ibidem*, footnote 43, p.372).

Low, Daniel (b.1792). He was a younger brother of Seth Low, who worked in Paris as commission trader (*Ibidem*, footnote 96, p.411).

Low, David. There were two of them. One was the eldest brother of Seth Low, the other David being his nephew and son of Daniel Low (*Ibidem*, footnote 39, p.391).

Low, Edward Allen (1817–1898). A younger brother of Harriett, he was connected with the Low-Moore Iron Co. of Virginia (*Ibidem*, footnote 61, p.373).

Low, Ellen (1827–1898). She was Harriett's youngest sister and the twelfth and last child of Seth Low and Mary Porter Low. In 1849, she married Ethelbert Smith Mills (1815–1873) (*Ibidem*, footnote 25, p.370).

Low, Josiah Orne (1821–1895). He was a younger brother of Harriett (*Ibidem*, footnote 3, p.791).

Low, Mary Ann (1808–1851). She was Harriett's eldest sister, nicknamed Molly, and the eldest of the twelve Low brothers and sisters. Mary Ann was the main reason for the existence of Harriett's journal and its addressee. In March 1833, while Harriett was in Macau, Mary Ann married George Beckford Archer (1803–1881) of Salem, who went into business with their father in Brooklyn (*Ibidem*, Notes to Volume I, footnote 2, p.367).

Low, Mary Porter (1786–1872). Harriett's mother was born at Topsfield (Mass.), near Salem. She was married to Seth Low at the age of 21 and had 12 children with him, Harriett being the second eldest. Mary Porter Low is said to have found great strength in her religion. She also knew how to manage a large household in economically difficult times (*Ibidem*, Notes to Introduction, footnotes 2–4, p.367, and footnote 42, p.372).

Low, Sarah Elizabeth (1822–1863). A younger sister of Harriett, she spent the winter of 1844 in Paris with her. In 1846, she married Edward H. R. Lyman of Northhampton, whom she had known in Harriett's home in England. Sarah kept a diary from April 1843 to March 1844, while visiting Harriett, which is now in the Library of Congress, among the Low-Mills family papers (*Ibidem*, footnote 15, p.369).

Low, Seth (1782–1853). Harriett's father was a native of Gloucester, Mass. He began his mercantile career in Salem, importing drugs and other products from overseas. In 1807, he married Mary Porter (1786–1872). In 1829, the Lows moved to Brooklyn. He also helped found the first Unitarian Congregational Society in that city (*Ibidem*, footnote 12, p.368).

Low, Seth Haskell (1812–1857). He was a younger brother of Harriett (*Ibidem*, footnote 32, p.371).

Low, William Henry I (1795–1834). He was a younger brother of Harriett's father, who had invited her to accompany him and his wife Abigail Knapp to China. He is treated as "Uncle" throughout the journal. William Henry Low was admitted as partner in the firm of Russell & Co. as of October 1, 1829 (*Ibidem*, footnote 16, p.369).

Low, William Henry II (1816–1845). He was a younger brother of Harriett, who worked in Canton from 1839 to 1841 (Opium War) and for a short period afterwards. He and his wife, Ann Davidson Bedell, were also painted by Chinnery. After his tragic death on returning from a voyage to China, his wife married her brother-in-law Abiel Abbot, who had been widowed earlier. Some of William Henry's letters from Canton are among the Low-Mills family papers in the Manuscript Section of the Library of Congress (*Ibidem*, footnote 68, p.408).

Macondray, Frederick William (1803–1883), Capt., and wife. He was in charge of R. B. Forbes' opium receiving ship *Lintin*, at Lintin island. His wife lived with him at Lintin, but made frequent visits to Macau (*Ibidem*, footnote 226, p.397).

Marjoribanks, Charles. He replaced William Baynes as President of the Company's Select Committee in November 1830, but returned home to Scotland in 1832, due to ill health (*Ibidem*, footnote 103, p.399).

Matheson, James (1796–1878). Acting as Danish consul, Matheson could trade independently of the East India Company in Canton. In 1832, he founded the firm of Jardine, Matheson & Co., together with William Jardine. He is said to have been one of the founders of the *Canton Register* in 1827 (*Ibidem*, footnote 122, p.382).

Morrison, John Robert (1814–1843). He was the eldest son of the missionary Robert Morrison and appointed Chinese Translator to the British merchants in Canton at only 16 years of age. At the time of his death, he was acting colonial secretary at Hong Kong (*Ibidem*, footnote 80, p.396).

Morrison, Robert (1782–1834). He was the first Protestant missionary to China, sent out by the London Missionary Society. Morrison is famous for his translation of the Holy Scriptures into Chinese and for the compilation of a Chinese-English dictionary, apart from many other writings. He also worked as translator for the East India Company at Canton. Morrison had two children, John and Rebecca, from his first marriage with Mary Morton (1791–1821), and five children with his second wife, Eliza Armstrong (d.1873), who is the Mrs. Morrison referred to in Harriett's journal (*Ibidem*, footnote 64, p.374).

Morrison, Mary Rebecca (1812–1903). She was the eldest child of the missionary Robert Morrison and his first wife, Mary Morton Morrison (1791–1821). Rebecca was one of the few single, English-speaking ladies in Macau. At the age of 35, she married the medical missionary Benjamin Hobson (1816–1873) (*Ibidem*, footnote 29, p.390).

Mouqua, or **Lu Wen-chin (d.1835, age 49)** by his real name. He was one of the Chinese *hong* merchants (*Ibidem*, footnote 124, p.382).

Otaduy (Otadui), Eugénio de. He was one of Harriett's Spanish teachers, who returned to Manila in August 1832 (*Ibidem*, footnote 22, p.389).

Pearson, Alexander, Dr. (d.1837). A surgeon to the English factory, Dr. Pearson is famous for having introduced vaccination against smallpox to China in 1805 (*Ibidem*, footnote 86, p.377).

Pereira, António and wife. The Pereiras were one of the few Portuguese families with whom the Lows socialized throughout their stay in Macau. He was a heavy dealer in opium and consignee of British and Portuguese country ships from Calcutta and Bombay. Pereira was the owner of the beautiful Casa Garden that he rented to the English. He was also a judge in the local court (*Ibidem*, footnote 70, p.375).

Plowden, William Henry Chichely (1788–1880). He joined the East India Company in 1805 and during much of Harriett's time in Macau he was President of its Select Committee (*Ibidem*, footnote 77, p.376).

Robinson, George Best, Sir (1797–1855), and wife Louisa Douglas. He worked for the East India Company, but seems to have dedicated substantially more time to his family than to work, according to Harriett's journal (*Ibidem*, footnote 38, p.391).

Roundy, Charles, Capt., (1794–1886). He began life at sea at the age of 15 and made six voyages in the *Sumatra*, retiring from the sea in 1836. In Caroline Howard King's *When I Lived in Salem, 1822–1866*, there are long quotations from two letters which Captain Roundy wrote to a nephew describing events on board the *Sumatra* during the voyage with the Lows to Macau (*Ibidem*, footnote 7, p.368).

Russell, George Robert (1800–1866). He was a nephew of Philip Ammidon Sr. After graduating from Brown University (1821), he engaged in trade in South America and then in Manila, where in 1828 he formed the house of Russell, Sturgis & Co., together with Henry Parkman Sturgis (*Ibidem*, footnote 52, p.373).

Russell, Samuel (1789–1862). In 1824, he established the house of Russell & Co. at Canton, together with Philip Ammidon Sr. He left China in March 1831. His mansion in Middletown (Conn.), which was given to Weslyan University for its Honor's College in 1936, is said to resemble the front view of the Thirteen Factories at Canton (*Ibidem*, footnote 62, p.372).

Se(a)ver, James Warner (1797–1871). A graduate from Harvard, he dedicated his later professional life to seafaring. He and his ship *Alert* were immortalized in R. H. Dana's *Two Years Before the Mast* (1840), when rounding Cape Horn (*Ibidem*, footnote 21, p.793).

Shillaber, Caroline Matilda (1812–1880). An acquaintance of Harriett's from Salem, she became her friend and confidant in Macau. Caroline arrived in December 1831 and stayed at the Low residence until her marriage to Dr. Thomas Colledge in March 1833. Three of their sons are buried at the Protestant Cemetery in Macau, but three other children lived to maturity. In the 1840s, when both Caroline and Harriett were living in England, they met occasionally (*Ibidem*, footnote 77, p.409).

Shillaber, John (b.1791). He was U.S. consul in Batavia since 1825. After having failed in business, Shillaber left for Macau in September 1831, together with his sister Caroline. In Canton, he entered into business with Jardine,

Matheson & Co. He resigned as consul in 1835, but maintained his dealings with Jardine, Matheson & Co (*Ibidem*, footnote 77, p.409; footnote 61, p.797 and footnote 28, pp.802, 803).

Sturgis, George (1817–1857). This Bostonian was connected with his brother's firm in Manila, Russell, Sturgis & Co. After his death, his wife Josefina Borras (1828–1912) married Don Agustin Ruis de Santayana. They are the parents of the famous philosopher and Harvard teacher George Santayana, who described many interesting personalities of his American family in his autobiographical writings *Persons and Places* (*Ibidem*, footnote 44, p.795).

Sturgis, Henry Parkman (1806–1869). He joined in partnership with George R. Russell in July 1828, to form the house of Russell, Sturgis & Co. in Manila. The house failed in 1875 (*Ibidem*, footnote 51, p.372).

Sturgis, James Perkins (1791–1851). He was an uncle of the four Sturgis brothers mentioned here. For a short while, he was also one of Harriett's suitors. Harriett sometimes refers to him as "Uncle Jem". His life is described in greater detail in William C. Hunter's *Bits of Old China* (*Ibidem*, footnote 146, p.386).

Sturgis, Russell (1805–1887). At first he was with Russell, Sturgis & Co. at Manila and Canton, and later joined Russell & Co. After 1849 he was with Baring Brothers in London, becoming senior partner (*Ibidem*, footnote 100, p.399).

Sturgis, Samuel Parkman (1808–1877). He was another member of the Sturgis clan in Manila and Canton and brother of George, Henry Parkman and Russell (*Ibidem*, footnote 101, p.399).

Sullivan, William A. Harriett refers to him once as one of the "Boston aristocrats". His grandfather James Sullivan was governor of Massachusetts, his father a lawyer and writer and his mother the daughter of James Swan, a financier and friend of Lafayette (*Ibidem*, footnote 60, p.407).

Talbot, Charles Nicoll. He was U.S. Consul at Canton for some time and member of the firm Olyphant & Co. Several members of the Talbot family were active in Canton (*Ibidem*, footnote 26, p.390).

Thornhill, John B. He was a clerk at the British East India Company and had an Irish wife (*Ibidem*, footnote 111, p.381).

Turner, Richard and wife Mary. He was a British agent in Canton and his wife became one of Harriett's best friends in Macau (*Ibidem*, footnote 71, p.375).

Vachell, George Harvey, Rev. (1798–1839). He was the British East India Company's Chaplain at an annual salary of £800. Vachell was one of Harriett's friends and most persistent suitors and appears often in the journal (*Ibidem*, footnote 67, p.375).

Wilcocks, Benjamin Chew (1776–1845). This Philadelphian was noted for his epicurean lifestyle and tastes. He was a pioneer in both the Turkish and Indian opium trades. Wilcocks was also U.S. Consul at Canton for some time. He returned to the USA in 1827 (*Ibidem*, footnote 94, p.411).

Wimberley, Charles, Rev. Wimberley substituted Vachell for two years as the Company's Chaplain during the latter's absence in England (*Ibidem*, footnote 23, p.793).

Whitehead, Capt. He was Captain of *H.C.S. Duke of Sussex* and loved to give parties whenever in Macau (*Ibidem*, footnote 69, p.375).

Wood, William Wightman (b. ca.1804/05). He was engaged to Harriett for a few months and therefore appears very often in the journal. His parents, William Burke Wood and Juliana Westray Wood, were celebrated actors in Philadelphia. A portrait of his mother, painted by Rembrandt Peale, is at the Smithsonian Institution. His own portrait, painted by Chinnery, seems not to be known now (*Ibidem*, footnote 3, p.400; see also footnote 52, p.406).

Ybar, Joaquin. Harriett sometimes misspelled his name as Ibar in her journal. He was the last agent of the Spanish Factory at Canton, which ceased activity in 1832. Harriett read Spanish with him (*Ibidem*, footnote 73, p.395).

Notes

Preface

1. Nan P. Hodges and Arthur W. Hummel (eds.), *Lights and Shadows of a Macao Life. The Journal of Harriett Low, Travelling Spinster*. 2 parts, Woodinville (WA), The History Bank, 2002.
2. These two abbreviated, very similar editions were prepared by close relatives of Harriett Low, namely her daughter Katharine and her granddaughter Elma. See Katharine Hillard (ed.), *My Mother's Journal. A Young Lady's Diary of Five Years Spent in Manila, Macao, and the Cape of Good Hope from 1829–1834*, Boston, George H. Ellis, 1900, and Elma Loines (ed.), *The China Trade Post-Bag of the Seth Low Family of Salem and New York*, Manchester (Maine), Falmouth Publishing House, 1953. Regarding the differences between the two editions, see footnote 3 of chapter 1.
3. Another journal and letters written by an American lady in Macau between 1843 and 1847, Rebecca Chase Kinsman, have not been studied yet to the extent they deserve. Being a married woman and mother, her life, interests and responsibilities were obviously different from those of the single Harriett Low. But many impressions about daily activities and the life and society in Macau are very similar to the ones depicted in this book, considering that only 10 years had passed since Harriett Low's departure from Macau in 1833. However, many situations described in this book could not be experienced by Rebecca Kinsman anymore, because of the dramatic changes in the Sino-foreign relations following the Opium War. For a short selection of excerpts from Kinsman's letters and diary see Cecília Jorge, "Rebecca Chase: an American in Macau", in *MACAU*, no.11/2002, pp.38–53.
4. Hodges relates the following about the circumstances of their acquaintance: *"A letter of introduction from George Stillman Hillard, a brother-in-law in Boston, had enabled the young attractive couple of Harriett and John Hillard to be introduced to Martineau, her mother, and the tight circle of friends around the outspoken writer"*. In Nan P. Hodges and Arthur W. Hummel (eds.), *op. cit.*, p.1.
5. The letter was written in London on 5 June 1837. See Harriett Low, *Letters*, Washington D.C., Library of Congress, Manuscript Section, Low-Mills Family Papers, Box no.2, Folder "General Correspondence, 1836 to 1870".
6. Nan P. Hodges and Arthur W. Hummel (eds.), *op. cit.*, p.17.

Chapter 1   A Passage to China

1.   In those times, travelling was still closer to its etymological meaning of "work" or even "torture"! The English noun "travel" has its origin in the French word *travail*, meaning "work", "hardship", and also "being in labour". This French word in turn derives from the Latin word *trepalium*, referring to an instrument used in torture.

2.   See Mary Susan Schriber, *Writing Home. American Women Abroad, 1830–1920*, Charlottesville and London, University Press of Virginia, 1997, p.13.

3.   See Elma Loines (ed.), *The China Trade Post-Bag of the Seth Low Family of Salem and New York*, Manchester (Maine), Falmouth Publishing House, 1953, p.16 and pp.315, 316. This book is a tribute to the descendants of Seth Low and to their achievements in the China trade throughout much of the 19th century, namely from the 1830s to the 1870s. It also contains an almost untouched copy of Hillard's edition of Harriett Low's journal. The major difference and improvement in Loines's edition consists in spelling out fully the names of the individuals mentioned in the journal, which in Hillard's edition often appear abbreviated to the first letter of their name or surname. Obviously, this complicates their identification, as there were several Mr./Mrs. B. (Baynes, Beale, Blight, Bradford, Bridgman) and so on. Most other documents in Loines's book are commented transcriptions of letters belonging to the Lows who had spent some time in Macau and Canton, together with a series of photographs and maps. Of the descendants of Seth Low, Harriett was merely the first to go to Macau, accompanying her uncle and aunt. Four brothers would follow later.

     It must also be mentioned that Hillard, apart from abbreviating the journal substantially, is not always loyal to the original in her quotations. As a rule, she never indicated any omissions or leaps in the original text. At other times she changed the sequence of words in a sentence, made two sentences out of one and vice versa, or substituted certain words with synonyms without any apparent necessity. Apart from these stylistic changes, she also introduced passages, probably from letters, and sometimes forgot to indicate this.

4.   In Nan P. Hodges and Arthur W. Hummel (eds.), *Lights and Shadows of a Macao Life. The Journal of Harriett Low, Travelling Spinster.* 2 parts, Woodinville (WA), The History Bank, 2002; see p.3.

5.   For an exhaustive history of the house Russell & Co. see Jacques M. Downs, *The Golden Ghetto. The American Commercial Community at Canton and the Shaping of American China Policy, 1784–1844*, Bethlehem, Lehigh University Press, 1997, pp.162–189. The book also contains portraits of its most important members. Downs's book continues to be the most complete work on the individual members and companies of the American community in Canton from its beginning until the signature of the Treaty of Wanghsia (Mong-Há) between China and the USA in Macau, in July 1844. Shorter descriptions of the house Russell & Co. can be found in Elma Loines (ed.), *op. cit.,* pp.301, 302, and in William C. Hunter, *The Fan Kwae at Canton before Treaty Days 1825–1844 by an Old Resident*, Shanghai and others, Kelly and Walsh, Limited, 1911 (b), pp.156, 157.

6.   See Elma Loines (ed.), *op. cit.,* p.17.

7. Regarding the motivations for diary writing among nineteenth-century American women, see Catherine Petroski, *A Bride's Passage. Susan Hathorn's Year under Sail,* Boston, Northeastern University Press, 1997, footnote 14, p.240. But not only American women were keeping diaries. For a European perspective on diarists, both male and female, see Alain Corbin's *"The Secret of the Individual"*, in Michelle Perrot (ed.), *A History of Private Life. Vol. IV. From the Fires of Revolution to the Great War*, Cambridge (Mass.) and London (UK), The Belknap Press of Harvard University Press, 1990, pp.497–508.

8. In Mary Susan Schriber, *op. cit.,* 1997, p.13.

9. Rear Admiral Samuel Eliot Morison in the Introduction to Elma Loines's book, *op. cit.,* p.viii.

10. Katharine Hillard (ed.), *My Mother's Journal. A Young Lady's Diary of Five Years Spent in Manila, Macao, and the Cape of Good Hope from 1829–1834*, Boston, George H. Ellis, 1900, p.v.

11. Ammidon Jr. would only stay for a short while in Canton. Early in 1831, William H. Low was trying to get rid of him as clerk, describing Ammidon Jr. as *"useless lumber"* and even as *"fillup"* (in Nan P. Hodges and Arthur W. Hummel (eds.), *op. cit.,* footnote 71, pp.394, 395). His example thus confirmed the negative opinion reigning in Canton about the male offspring of successful former residents, who aspired to follow in their father's footsteps, but frequently proved to be wastrels. See Jacques M. Downs, *op. cit.,* p.225.

12. Katharine Hillard (ed.), *op. cit.,* p.v.

13. *Ibidem*, p.v.

14. The quotation is from *The Fireside* by Nathaniel Cotton, Stanza 3. In Nan P. Hodges and Arthur W. Hummel (eds.), *op. cit.,* p.22.

15. Before publishing Harriett Low's journal, Hodges edited the journal of a naval surgeon, Benajah Ticknor. He had met Harriett Low at Lintin Island near Macau. It was through him that Hodges became interested in Harriett Low. See Nan P. Hodges (ed.), *The Voyage of the Peacock: A Journal by Benajah Ticknor, Naval Surgeon,* Ann Arbor, University of Michigan Press, 1991.

16. William C. Hunter, *op. cit.,* 1911 (b), p.7.

17. Arthur W. Hummel, "The Journal of Harriet Low", *The Library of Congress* **Quarterly Journal** *of Current Acquisitions*, vol.2, nos.3 and 4, 1945, pp.972–989. Quotation on p.977. This article is Hummel's only publication on the journal.

18. The governments of several sea-faring nations had offered high rewards to the person/s who could solve the longitude problem. It took British clockmaker John Harrison (1693–1776) 40 years to come up with the perfect timekeeper, which nowadays is known as the chronometer. For a more technical description of the calculation of the longitude see Manuel Bairrão Oleiro and Rui Brito Peixoto, *Museu Marítimo de Macau*, Macau, Museu Marítimo de Macau, s.d., pp.122–125.

19. See Nan P. Hodges and Arthur W. Hummel (eds.), *op. cit.,* footnotes 51 and 52, pp.372, 373. More on the different members of Russell, Sturgis & Co. in Manila and the complicated relations with Russell & Co. in Canton can be found in Jacques M. Downs, *op. cit.,* pp.190, 191. In 1840, Russell & Co. absorbed Russell, Sturgis

& Co., resulting in the strongest American company in the East and second in business after the British company of Jardine, Matheson & Co.

20. *Bancos* and *Cascos* are types of native Philippine boats.

21. *Calzada* is Spanish and means paved road or highway.

22. Harriett must have known the designation only from hearsay, because this is the way an English-speaker would spell the Portuguese word *Guia* (guide, lead). *Guia* is the highest elevation in Macau (90 metres).

23. Josiah Quincy (ed.), *The Journals of Major Samuel Shaw, the First American Consul at Canton*, Boston, Wm. Crosby and H. P. Nichols, 1847, pp.239, 240.

24. William W. Wood, *Sketches of China; with Illustrations from Original Drawings*, Philadelphia, Carey & Lea, 1830, pp.23, 24.

Chapter 2   Macau — Then and Now, Old and Modern

1. There are a variety of books on the history of Macau in English. In terms of general readability and interest, Jonathan Porter's *Macau: The Imaginary City. Culture and Society, 1557 to present,* Boulder (Col.), Westview Press, 1996, is highly recommendable. Other titles, in alphabetical order, are Austin Coates, *A Macao Narrative*, Hong Kong, Oxford University Press, 3rd ed., 1993; Ralph D. Cremer (ed.), *Macau — City of Commerce and Culture*, Hong Kong, API Press, 2nd ed., 1991; Geoffrey Gunn, *Encountering Macau: A Portuguese City-State on the Periphery of China, 1557–1999*, Boulder (Col.), Westview Press, 1996. An interesting approach to Macau's history through the presentation of short texts from a variety of literary sources is Donald Pittis and Susan J. Henders's *Macao. Mysterious Decay and Romance*, Hong Kong, Oxford University Press, 1997. More references can be found in the bibliography, see for instance Christina Miu Bing Cheng, Anders Ljungstedt and C. A. Montalto de Jesus.

2. Charles R. Boxer, *The Great Ship from Amacon*, Macau, Instituto Cultural de Macau, 1988, p.7. Boxer is the great historian of Macau's first Golden Era, the period of the Japan trade (1557–1639). In this book he describes the yearly Portuguese voyages to Japan, which were undertaken in the so-called Great Ship or Black Ship (*nau do trato*, in Portuguese).

3. In Charles R. Boxer (ed.), *Seventeenth Century Macau in Contemporary Documents and Illustrations*, Hong Kong, Heinemann (Asia), 1984, p.80.

4. This letter is part of the documents inserted by Hillard in her edition of Harriett's journal, in order to bridge the gap of a volume lost at sea. It is dated 3 March 1831. See Katharine Hillard (ed.), *My Mother's Journal: A Young Lady's Diary of Five Years Spent in Manila, Macao, and the Cape of Good Hope from 1829–1834*, Boston, George H. Ellis, 1900, p.86.

5. William W. Wood, *Sketches of China; with Illustrations from Original Drawings*, Philadelphia, Carey & Lea, 1830, p.20.

6. Father Manuel Teixeira (1912–2003), an eminent local historian and priest who came to Macau as a boy and retired to Portugal in 2001, distances himself from these

two authors in his foreword to a complete reprint of Ljungstedt's work in 1992. In Anders Ljungstedt, *An Historical Sketch of the Portuguese Settlements in China and of the Roman Catholic Church and Mission in China & Description of the City of Canton*, Hong Kong, Viking Hong Kong Publications, 1992, pp.xi, xii.

7. William W. Wood, *op. cit.,* pp.20, 21.
8. Anders Ljungstedt, *op. cit.,* p.30.
9. This quotation is from a letter home, dated 3 March 1831. In Katharine Hillard (ed.), *op. cit.,* p.86.
10. This topic will be dealt with extensively in chapter 6.
11. As regards the genesis of the name of Macau and other designations referring to the peninsula, see for example Manuel Teixeira, *Toponímia de Macau*, 2 vols., Macau, Instituto Cultural de Macau, 2nd ed., 1997, vol.I, Ruas com Nomes Genéricos (Streets with Generic Names), pp.38–41 and 162–165, and Jonathan Porter, *op. cit.,* pp.36–42.
12. Anders Ljungstedt, *op. cit.,* p.22.
13. William W. Wood, *op. cit.,* p.23. Batalha mentions that in Portuguese India a distinction was made between *cafre* and *Negro*, or *preto* (black), until the 18th century at least. *Cafre* referred to Blacks from the eastern shoreline of Africa, while the other two expressions were applied to Blacks from the western shoreline. In Graciete Nogueira Batalha, *Glossário do Dialecto Macaense. Notas Linguísticas, Etnográficas e Folclóricas*, Coimbra, Faculdade de Letras, Instituto de Estudos Românicos, 1977, p.100.
14. Hillard introduced this description from a letter, which is more detailed than Harriett's reference to the new house in the journal. The letter is dated 3 March 1830. See Katharine Hillard (ed.), *op. cit.,* p.60.
15. The fortress refers to the Fortress of St. Francis (Fortaleza de São Francisco), next to which existed a convent with the same name. Both were demolished in 1864, to make way for the Barracks of St. Francis, which today are used as headquarters of the security forces.
16. Teixeira was the first to edit a small booklet about Harriett Low's journal in Portuguese, based on Katharine Hillard's book, with the title *Macau no Século XIX Visto por uma Jovem Americana* [Macau in the 19th century as seen by a young American lady], Macau, Direcção dos Serviços de Educação e Cultura, 1981; see the Foreword, *Duas palavras* ("A few words"), no page number.
17. Both Loines in her book *The China Trade Post-Bag* (p.125) and Teixeira in his *Toponímia de Macau* (vol.I, ch. XXIV, no page number) include a photograph of the house, in which Harriett Low is said to have lived. However, the two buildings are clearly different. The picture in Loines's book, taken by Hummel in 1953, does not seem to be the correct house. On the photograph in Teixeira's book, showing a lateral view of the house, a small part of the cathedral is visible, thus making it a more likely hypothesis.
18. Anders Ljungstedt, *op. cit.,* p.25.
19. When Morrison's first wife Mary died in 1821, there was no place within the city walls where the Protestants could have buried their dead, because the Catholics

would not allow them to be interred on their cemetery or territory. Therefore, they were buried near the northern extremity of the peninsula, on Meesenberg Hill (which has disappeared long since to serve as fill-in for land reclamation). However, since this was near Chinese villages, it was feared that the graves might become subject to vandalism and desecration. Seeing Morrison's despair about a safe burial place for his wife, the British East India Company managed, with the help of a Portuguese, to establish a small cemetery. Mary Morrison was the first person to be buried there. The history of the cemetery and its "inhabitants" was carefully traced and written down by Sir Lindsay Ride and his wife May in their beautiful book *An East India Company Cemetery: Protestant burials in Macao*, Hong Kong, Hong Kong University Press, 2nd ed., 1998 (edited by Bernard Mellor).

20. *Ibidem*, p.67.

21. This is the location indicated on a panoramic view of Macau from 1840 (see plate 5). Teixeira mentions that Beale lived in Rua do Hospital (Hospital Street), which was in quite a different corner of Macau, namely in the road of the former St. Raphael's Hospital, which now houses the Portuguese Consulate (in Manuel Teixeira, *op. cit.,* vol.I, p.284). Interestingly, on plate 7 we can see a *volière* next to a luxurious mansion, with the St. Lawrence's church and the St. Joseph's church (Igreja de São José) in the background, which seems to confirm the indication on the panoramic view. However, it is possible that Beale's house was not located next to the garden, but elsewhere.

22. For more details regarding Thomas Beale's life and earthly possessions, his debts and mysterious suicide, see Teixeira, *Ibidem*, pp.284–295. William Hunter also dedicated a few pages to this dazzling figure in his *Bits of Old China*, Shanghai and others, Kelly and Walsh, Limited, 1911a, pp.73–77.

23. See Martyn Gregory Gallery, *Artists of the China Coast*, Catalogue no.57, Summer 1991, p.31.

24. Teixeira mentions the names of influential Portuguese and Macanese contemporaries of Harriett Low, who possessed properties alongside the Praia Grande, such as members of the Pereira and Paiva families. See *Toponímia de Macau*, vol.I, p.68.

25. *Ibidem*, p.74.

26. Anders Ljungstedt, *op. cit.,* p.19.

27. See Manuel Bairrão Oleiro and Rui Brito Peixoto, *Museu Marítimo de Macau*, Macau, Museu Marítimo de Macau, s.d., pp.100, 101.

28. See Robin Hutcheon, *Chinnery, the Man and the Legend*, Hong Kong, 1975, p.74. A sampan boat is a very simple embarkation with a stern-oar. The literal translation from Chinese means "three boards" (*sam-pan*).

29. *Tiffin* is a word of Anglo-Indian origin referring to a light meal, especially lunch (see Graciete Nogueira Batalha, *op. cit.,* p.281). The *Josh* (or rather *Joss*) house mentioned must be the Lin Fong temple, which nowadays is far away from the shore. *Joss* is Pidgin English for "God", a word derived from the Portuguese *Deus* ("God").

30. Anders Ljungstedt, *op. cit.,* p.20.

31. *Lascars* were people from India, usually seamen.

32. *Cavaleiro* means "horseman" in Portuguese. *Rua*, *Beco* and *Rampa* refer to the type of street.

33. Manuel Teixeira, *Toponímia de Macau*, vol I, pp.284–286.
34. William W. Wood, *op. cit.*, p.157.
35. Anders Ljungstedt, *op. cit.*, p.19.
36. The church is dedicated to the mother of God, as the inscription "Mater Dei" can be clearly seen written in stone above the main entrance. Therefore, the correct designation for it would be Church of the Mother of God (Igreja da Madre de Deus). According to Pereira, the first designation for the Monte Fort also carried the name of "Mother of God". But since the Jesuits were commonly called "Paulists" by the local population, because many of them had studied at the College of St. Paul's in Goa, the structures erected and operated by them were called "St. Paul" too. For further details see Fernando A. Baptista Pereira, "A 'Acrópole' de Macau. O Complexo Religioso, Cultural e Militar da Companhia de Jesus", in *Um Museu em Espaço Histórico. A Fortaleza de S. Paulo do Monte*, Macau, Edição Museu de Macau, 1998, pp.14–58.
37. "Catty" is a weight unit used in China and southeast Asia corresponding, with local variations, to about 500 to 600 grams. In China a catty corresponds to 500 grams.
38. A few days before this entry, Harriett had decided to get up at 6 o'clock, in order to make better use of the day.

Chapter 3   The Power of Religion

1. The classic to quote here would be Émile Durkheim's *The Elementary Forms of Religious Life (1917)*. A more recent reference, on how religion influences our behaviour, life and society, both positively and negatively, is Michael Argyle's *Psychology and Religion. An Introduction*, London and New York, Routledge, 2000.
2. The supporters of Monarchianism, a Christian school flourishing between 150 and 300, insisted on the unique and indivisible divinity of God. It was intended to strengthen monotheism within Christianity. The followers of the orthodox doctrine of Trinitarianism defended the equality of the three divine persons, God the Father, the Son and the Holy Spirit. The Trinitarian version of God's nature was adopted as official Christian doctrine in the 4th century, but the controversy was revived again during Reformation, on which modern Unitarianism is based.
3. Quoted in Elma Loines (ed.), *The China Trade Post-Bag of the Seth Low Family of Salem and New York*, Manchester (Maine), Falmouth Publishing House, 1953, p.20.
4. Samuel Couling, *The Encyclopaedia Sinica*, Hong Kong and others, Oxford University Press, 2nd impression, 1991, p.382.
5. Quoted from a letter to her sister Mary Ann, written in December 1829, in Elma Loines (ed.), *op. cit.*, p.34.
6. Arthur W. Hummel, for example, quotes Samuel Wells Williams, who knew Morrison personally and who wrote of him: *"He was not by nature calculated to win and interest the sceptical or the fastidious, for he had no sprightliness or pleasantry, no versatility or wide acquaintance with letters, and was respected rather than loved by those who cared little for the things nearest his heart"*. In Arthur W.

Hummel (ed.), *The Journal of Harriet Low. Annotated Transcription*. Washington D.C., Library of Congress, Manuscript Section, Low-Mills Family Papers, boxes 22 and 23, footnote 62, p.964.

7. See Jacques M. Downs, *The Golden Ghetto, The American Commercial Community at Canton and the Shaping of American China Policy, 1784–1844*, Bethlehem, Lehigh University Press, 1997, pp.229–231. Excerpts from the works of other Western missionaries, who lived in China in the 19th century, can be found in Colin Mackerras' *Sinophiles and Sinophobes. Western Views of China*, Oxford (and others), Oxford University Press, 2000. Far from focusing on religious questions only, the missionaries also discussed social problems such as female infanticide, official corruption, opium consumption, and others.

8. Two months later, this event was mentioned again and explained more in detail:

> *Capt. Little says just before he left the Presbyterians there <u>compelled</u> by the point of the bayonet a little band of Catholics to leave the Island, and treated them in the most unchristian manner, and for some time past had had a guard of soldiers stationed at the Catholic Church door to prevent any native from entering, and if they attempted it to take them from it by force. (11.6.1832)*

9. Ideas of "happy, unspoilt primitives" or of the sagacity of non-European rulers as compared to absolute European monarchs were very popular during the Enlightenment, mainly among the French encyclopaedists. However, Harriett does not seem to have known, for instance, Voltaire's *L'ingénu*.

10. Jacques M. Downs, *op. cit.,* p.93.

11. Guetzlaff used to dress like the Chinese. Chinnery once made a full-figure drawing, showing him in Chinese outfit from top to toe. Because of his perfect understanding of Chinese, Guetzlaff was sometimes even mistaken for a Chinese. His Chinese name was Kuo Shih-li.

12. This is an extract from a letter to her brother Abbot, written in December 1831. It is quoted in Elma Loines (ed.), *op. cit.,* p.48.

13. *Ibidem*, p.48.

14. Nan P. Hodges and Arthur W. Hummel (eds.), *Lights and Shadows of a Macao Life. The Journal of Harriett Low, Travelling Spinster*, 2 parts, Woodinville (WA), The History Bank, 2002; see footnote 16, p.793.

15. Samuel Couling, *op. cit.,* p.345.

16. See Arthur Waley, *The Opium War through Chinese Eyes*, Stanford (California), Stanford University Press, 1968, pp. 222–244. The quotation is on p.233.

17. Trinity Sunday is the Sunday after Whit Sunday. Athanasius was an ardent opponent of the doctrine of Arianism, a movement in early Christianity, which also contested equality between Father and Son. He defended what later would become official orthodox doctrine through the Council at Nicaea in 325, that God was three persons in one, being the Son consubstantial with the Father.

18. This is particularly visible in the case of the wives of Protestant ministers and missionaries. While he is in charge of the spiritual well-being of his flock, the wives are involved in fulfilling the more physical — or lower-order — needs of

the community. In the case of the Catholic Church, the nuns are comparable, in terms of free labour, to the wives of the missionaries, although their greater number and organisation seems to make them more efficient. Another example of a social institution that gets two (or more) people for the "price" of one is the government, which often advises against or even forbids diplomats' wives to pursue their own career for the sake of serving their country in a variety of unpaid jobs and functions.

19. Jacques M. Downs, *op. cit.,* p.57.

20. In her defense of Unitarianism, Harriett Low may have inspired herself in publications such as *One Hundred Scriptural Arguments for the Unitarian Faith,* published by the American Unitarian Association, which tried to impress its readers with numbers. *"Of 1300 passages in the N.T., wherein the word <u>God</u> is mentioned, not one necessarily implies the existence of more than <u>one person</u> in the Godhead, or that this one is any other than the <u>Father</u>".* In American Unitarian Association, *One Hundred Scriptural Arguments for the Unitarian Faith,* Boston, Bowles and Dearborn, 4th ed., 1827, p.16.

21. Harriett in a letter to her *"beloved parents",* dated 20 April 1832. In Elma Loines (ed.), *op. cit.,* p.50.

22. *Compradore* is the designation used for the Chinese agents employed by the Westerners in Canton, in order to buy and sell their goods. The term derives from the Portuguese word for "to buy" (*comprar*). A detailed description of the tasks and duties of a *compradore* is given by William C. Hunter in his book *Bits of Old China, Shanghai and others,* Kelly and Walsh, Limited, 1911 (a), p. 53 and pp.55, 56.

23. *Walky* was supposed to refer to a procession. In chapter six of this book, a few lines are dedicated to the special language in use among foreigners and Chinese, known as Pidgin English.

24. Mr. Otaduy was one of Harriett's Spanish teachers and Mr. Pereira was a very wealthy Portuguese. *Misericórdia* literally means "mercy". The full designation for this institution is Santa Casa da Misericórdia (Holy House of Mercy). It is one of the oldest institutions in Macau, dating back to 1569. Then as now, its main task is to take care of the needy, without distinction of race or religion. See Manuel Teixeira, *Toponímia de Macau,* vol.I, Macau, Instituto Cultural de Macau, 2nd ed., 1997, pp.103–105.

25. Nowadays, the procession of Our Lord of the Passion (Nosso Senhor dos Passos) is the most important Catholic procession in Macau. It is held on the first Sunday of Lent. The statue of Christ carrying the Cross is taken for one night from the St. Augustine's church to the Cathedral. On the following day it is carried through the streets and restored to St. Augustine's.

26. This is an extremely sentimental romance by the French author Sophie Cottin (1770–1807). The full title of the book is *Mathilde, ou Mémoires Tirés de l'Histoire des Croisades* (1805).

27. Manuel Teixeira, *Macau no Século XIX Visto por uma Jovem Americana,* Macau, Direcção dos Serviços de Educação e Cultura, 1981, p.36.

28. The idea of American exceptionalism can traced back to John Winthrop, who was

fleeing England in 1630 with his Puritan brethren. Aboard the *Arbella* he delivered his famous sermon "A Model of Christian Charity", in which he compares America to a "city on a hill", in direct relation to Jesus' Sermon on the Mount. The quote not only reflects the idea that America is special in the world, but also a responsibility to do good. The concept became known to a wider audience through Alexis de Tocqueville's book *Democracy in America* (vol. I, 1835; vol. II, 1840).

Recently, Staci Hosford formulated a variant of American exceptionalism, in her study of "gendered exceptionalisms". She examined Harriett Low and other American women in the light of her concept of "maternal exceptionalism", being defined as "*a gendered form of American exceptionalism. It is the ideology that expatriate women preached — intentionally or unintentionally — to fellow Americans ... and occasionally to non-Americans — that the United States and U.S. culture is special, unique, or "chosen" in particular ways. This exceptionalism is linked to American expatriate women's sense of themselves as particularly unique because of their opportunity to live outside the U.S. ... As such, their narratives reflect the way American women used their national identity and their gender identity to 'teach' or 'preach' in 'motherly', 'helpful', or 'nurturing' ways*" (in Staci Ford Hosford, *Gendered Exceptionalisms: American Women in Hong Kong and Macao, 1830–2000*, The University of Hong Kong, PhD Dissertation, Feb. 2002, p.6). Hosford describes the factors that lead to Harriett's feelings of exceptionalism and specialness and the impact on and changes in her identity as an American woman resulting from the cross-cultural encounter (see *Ibidem*, pp.11–57).

29. William W. Wood, *Sketches of China; with Illustrations from Original Drawings*, Philadelphia, Carey & Lea, 1830, pp.28, 29. Elsewhere in his book (pp.178–181), Wood describes the two major religions in China, Buddhism and Taoism, mostly based on Morrison's writings.

Chapter 4   The Daily Life of Foreign Women on the China Coast

1. Katharine Hillard (ed.), *My Mother's Journal. A Young Lady's Diary of Five Years Spent in Manila, Macao, and the Cape of Good Hope from 1829–1834*, Boston, George H. Ellis, 1900, p.vi.

2. The best source for Harriett Low's letters from Macau days is Elma Loines's *The China Trade Post-Bag of the Seth Low Family of Salem and New York*, Manchester (Maine), Falmouth Publishing House, 1953. Loines mentions in the Foreword that she had already given most of the original letters in her possession to the Library of Congress and intended "*to give the rest*", but I have not found any of Harriett's letters quoted by her, which seem to be the most interesting ones, among the Low-Mills papers.

3. Quoted by P. D. James in the Foreword to Olga Kenyon's book *800 Years of Women's Letters*, Harmondsworth, Penguin, 1994, p.viii.

4. Sometimes the letters and other written elements, such as newspapers or maps, were

detained by the captain, if he thought that business rivals might gain an advantage by their release. For an example of this practice see Nan P. Hodges and Arthur W. Hummel (eds.), *Lights and Shadows of a Macao Life. The Journal of Harriett Low, Travelling Spinster*, 2 parts, Woodinville (WA), The History Bank, 2002; see footnote 90, pp.397,398.

5. Jacques M. Downs, *The Golden Ghetto, The American Commercial Community at Canton and the Shaping of American China Policy, 1784–1844*, Bethlehem, Lehigh University Press, 1997, p.47.

6. In his annotated transcription of the journal, Hummel tried to trace the names of the authors, the exact title and the publishers of the books read by Harriett. Hodges completed all missing details in Hummel's bibliography, such as place or year of publishing, and often adding a few lines on the main characters and the plot of the books.

7. This is the ground that brought forth the influential American movement of Transcendentalism during the late 1820s and 1830s. It is intrinsically linked to Unitarianism, counterbalancing its rationality with the introduction of a certain sentimentalism.

8. Admirers of Jane Austen will be astonished not to find any reference to her among Harriett's extensive bibliography, leaving them to wonder when Austen's fame reached the USA. Her *Northanger's Abbey*, for instance, provides some interesting thoughts on writing letters and journals and on reading novels that certainly would have pleased Harriett Low, apart from the plot obviously. Another possibility is that she had read Austen back home already.

9. The word "poetess" is written in enormous letters. The *Canton Register* was a weekly English-language newspaper.

10. Arthur W. Hummel (ed.), *The Journal of Harriet Low. Annotated Transcription*, Washington, D.C., Library of Congress, Manuscript Section, Low-Mills Family Papers, Boxes 22 and 23, footnote 85, p.974.

11. See Roswell S. Britton, *The Chinese Periodical Press, 1800–1912* (Shanghai, Kelly and Walsh, 1933), in Nan P. Hodges and Arthur W. Hummel (eds.), *op. cit.,* footnote 30, p.403.

12. Charles Marjoribanks was then President of the British East India Company's Select Committee (*ibidem*, footnote 103, p.399). More examples of Wood's aggressive style can be found in footnotes 63, 64 and 78 of the joint Hodges/Hummel edition (*ibidem*, pp.407–409).

13. Paul Pickowicz analysed in detail Wood's editorial activities in Canton, as well as his political intentions and the economic goals that he wanted to achieve through them. See his article "William Wood in Canton: A Critique of the China Trade Before the Opium War". In: *Essex Institute Historical Collections*, no.107, January 1971, pp.3–24. Wood was even challenged to a duel once by the editor of the *Canton Register*, Arthur Saunders Keating, because of a disagreement, which was battled out publicly via the *Register* and the *Courier*. However, Keating withdrew in the last minute and Wood could consider himself as *"honourably exonerated from the duel" (30.4.1832)*, according to Harriett, who relates the whole story of the duel-

to-be. Jacques M. Downs also refers to this case, with particular emphasis on Wood's and Keating's seconds, Augustine Heard and James Innes respectively (*op. cit.,* pp.55, 56).

14. Samuel Couling, *The Encyclopaedia Sinica*, Hong Kong and others, Oxford University Press, 2nd impression, 1991; p.105. The *Canton Register* and *The Chinese Repository* constitute important documents for the study of this particular time period. Hummel, for instance, is constantly referring to the *Canton Register* in his (unpublished) edition of the journal.

15. Jacques M. Downs, *op. cit.,* p. 92. Regarding the products that came out of the commercial and the religious (or missionary) printing presses in Macau and Canton, see Jacques M. Downs, *op. cit.,* pp.91–93.

16. William C. Hunter, *Bits of old China*, Shanghai and others, Kelly and Walsh, Limited, 1911 (a), p.156.

17. Harriett Low, *Letters*, Washington, D.C., Library of Congress, Manuscript Section, Low-Mills family papers, box 11, folder 21, "Material Concerning the Far East", 1829–1831.

18. Otherwise the expression "made in Macau" is nowadays representing quality clothes that can be found on many designer labels in both Europe and North America. Textiles are among Macau's most important export items.

19. Harriett in a letter to her parents, written in April 1832. In Elma Loines (ed.), *op. cit.,* p.50.

20. As regards Chinnery's life and work, see the informative and beautifully illustrated books of Patrick Conner, *George Chinnery, 1774–1852. Artist of India and the China Coast*, Woodbridge, Antique Collectors' Club, 1993, and of G. H. R. Tillotson, *Fan Kwae Pictures. Paintings and Drawings by George Chinnery and Other Artists in the Collection of The Hongkong and Shanghai Banking Corporation*, London, Spink and Son Ltd., 1987. Conner's book also contains interesting information on other Macau residents.

21. For the joint edition of the journal, Hodges chose several drawings of Chinese and Portuguese from Lucy Cleveland's sketchbook as illustrations.

22. Hodges reports that Wood had learnt to sketch, among other useful accomplishments such as operating a printing press and preparing natural specimens, at the Charles Wilson Peale's Museum in Philadelphia. He was also a member of the Academy of Sciences of his hometown and collected natural specimens for it even after his time in Macau. His talent with the pencil had made him one of the main illustrators of the second volume of the book *American Entomology* by Thomas Say. In Nan P. Hodges and Arthur W. Hummel (eds.), *op. cit.,* footnote 3, pp.400, 401.

23. Harriett copied her last sketch from Chinnery, a representation of Camoens's cave, on 15 November 1833, a few days before their departure from Macau.

24. Conner mentions that this seemed to have been common practice, mainly when Chinnery's clients found that he had exaggerated in the use of vermilion around their noses or eyes. See Patrick Conner, *op. cit.,* pp.121, 122.

25. William C. Hunter, *op. cit.,* 1911 (a), pp.273, 274.

26. Harriett in a letter to her sister Mary Ann, written in December 1829, in Elma Loines

(ed.), *op. cit.,* p.35. At this point a reference has to be made to the work of Susanna Hoe, and in particular to her book the *The Private Life of Old Hong Kong. Western Women in the British Colony, 1841–1941*, Hong Kong and others, Oxford University Press, 1991. Her book actually begins with accounts of (mainly) British women in Macau, be it the wives of Company traders or of independent country traders, who had accompanied their husbands to China, and many of whom would later continue in Hong Kong. Hoe also includes several quotations from the Hillard edition of Harriett Low's journal.

27. Knowing about the intense social life that would await them in Macau, Harriett's uncle had paid for dancing lessons for her before their departure to China, which was not common in Unitarian circles. See Nan P. Hodges and Arthur W. Hummel (eds.), *op. cit.*, p.3.

28. The day before Harriett had been to a party at the Davises', characterising Mrs. Kierulf: "*There is a Danish lady here or rather Norwegian, her husband is a Dane. Her Norwegian airs are very pretty and her execution fine, the airs are quite wild and different from what we are accustomed to, and peculiarly suited to her voice.*" *(6.5.1831)*

29. Harriett, Caroline, Aunt Abigail, and Mrs. Macondray, the wife of an American captain who had arrived on the day of the party from Lintin island.

30. A *punkah* is a large wooden frame covered with cloth and suspended over a table or a bed, kept in motion by a servant pulling a rope, sometimes from an adjoining room. It is therefore something like a man-powered fan.

31. In a marginal note to this entry written on 17 August Harriett remarked: "*That was by partial eyes. You will observe what follows regarding them.*"

32. The play was *The Poor Gentleman* (1801) by George Coleman.

33. Jacques M. Downs, *op. cit.,* pp.47, 48.

34. Aunt Cleveland was the wife of a captain, and met the Lows in Macau. They were all from Salem.

35. Jacques M. Downs, *op. cit.,* p.54.

36. The murder case or references to it are omitted in Hillard's edition of the journal. Loines quotes one of Harriett's letters to her parents, written in summer of 1830. "*We are of course horrified at the account of old Mr. White's murder. Old Salem, who would have looked for so shocking an event in peaceful old Salem! It is to be hoped for the sake of the innocent suspected, that the guilty ones may soon be discovered*". In Elma Loines (ed.), *op. cit.,* p.37.

37. Nan P. Hodges and Arthur W. Hummel (eds.), *op. cit.,* footnote 18, p.810. Other references to the murder case can be found in footnote 92, p.398 (the murder story); footnotes 32 and 35, p.404 (on Nathaniel Knapp, a third brother of Abigail Knapp, who was a Harvard-educated lawyer); footnote 53, p.406 (on the efforts of Nathaniel to get his brothers out of prison), and footnote 13, p.415 (W. H. Low paying for the debts that the hanging of his wife's brothers caused her family). The author of the "Air" turned out to be James P. Sturgis, who "*did not deny authorship of a scurrilous song referring to Mrs. Low's family*" (in Jacques M. Downs, *op. cit.,* p.55).

38. This explanation about the spread of cholera by the atmosphere was the standard medical view at that time, also designated as miasmatic theory. See Nan P. Hodges and Arthur W. Hummel (eds.), *op. cit.,* footnote 49, p.796.

39. The painting is reproduced in Patrick Conner's book on Chinnery (*op. cit.,* p.232).

40. One of Harriett's brothers, William Henry, who was in Canton at that time, described Colledge's loss to Harriett in a letter dated 1 August 1841. "*Mr. Colledge lost his books and papers and a large quantity of clothing, of Chinese and European manufacture. These things are very valuable as they are not easily replaced. When Mrs. Colledge left China for home in the* Akbar *(April 12) with your old friend Capt. Dumaresq, Mr. C. very foolishly removed everything from his house in Macao to Canton. He received but very little sympathy from his countrymen, as he of all others should have left Canton in time, having nothing to detain him*". In Elma Loines (ed.), *op. cit.,* p.92.

41. The letter, written in September 1829, is quoted in Elma Loines (ed.), *op. cit.,* p.28.

42. In her introduction, Hodges insinuates that Colledge may have fathered the child, stating "*Dr. Colledge's concern for Nancy may have been more personal than Harriett wanted to admit*". (See Nan P. Hodges and Arthur W. Hummel (eds.), *op. cit.,* p.9). A passage in the journal seems to confirm that Harriett had heard a rumour about Colledge's possible fatherhood of Nancy's child, although the subject is never mentioned directly (*"The man whom above all others I thought perfect, or the one who for the last three years I have thought not capable of a dishonorable act, has sunk in my mind to the level with the rest of his sex"[22.12.1832]*). However, she rejected this idea immediately in a strong and incredulous manner. Already on the following day, according to my interpretation, Colledge's innocence was proven. (*"When the sun [Colledge] appeared behind the clouds, all was cleared up and we find it untarnished by the clouds which have dimmed it. I thought so, I knew it would prove so. Yes! ... It should teach us to be slow in condemning" (23.12.1832)*). As there are no more doubts raised about Colledge's moral integrity further in the journal, the suspicion seems unsubstantiated to me.

43. Traditionally, the orphanage of the Holy House of Mercy has accepted Chinese orphan girls or any abandoned girls, such as the child of Nancy, and raised them in the Catholic faith. There they also received basic instruction in what a future (house)wife should know, like cleaning, cooking and needlework. As such they became eligible for marriage by Portuguese men at a time, when Portuguese women were scarce in Asia. Many girls, however, were not thus fortunate and had to earn their living as maids or even prostitutes. See Ian E. Watts, "Bi-racial identity, bi-racial status: Two Chinese orphans raised by the Canossian sisters in Macao", in *Review of Culture,* ser.2, no.31, April to June 1997, pp.77–88.

Chapter 5   Matters of the Heart and of the Home

1. There is an interesting analysis of the social role of the piano in post-revolutionary France by Alain Corbin in Michelle Perrot's *The History of Private Life. Vol.IV.*

From the Fires of Revolution to the Great War, Cambridge, Mass. and London, UK, The Belknap Press of Harvard University Press, 1990, pp.531–533. Although referring to the French cultural domain, some of Corbin's main findings are also true for neighbouring European countries. *"The great vogue for the instrument began in 1815. Prudery helped, because the harp, the cello, and the violin all came to be seen as indecent. ... The ability to play the piano well established a child's reputation and gave public proof of a good education. Virtuosity figured, along with the rest of the 'aesthetic dowry', in marriage strategies. ... Finally, the piano helped women idle away the hours while awaiting the arrival of a man. According to Hippolyte Taine, playing the piano helped women resign themselves to the 'nullity of the feminine condition'"(Ibidem*, pp.531 and 533).

2. Sandra Adams has published a well-illustrated article about the two major deformities that tradition and fashion dictated on women in the East and West, foot binding and lacing. See "A Woman's Place in the West and East: Corset versus Bound Feet", in *Review of Culture*, ser.2, no.24, July to September 1995, pp.62–83. Since the 1990s the body of literature on foot binding has been increasing rapidly, there is also a wealth of information on foot binding and corsets on the Internet, but because of the volatility of many sites I refrain from quoting any. In China, foot binding is not a closed chapter yet. According to a study carried out by researchers from the University of California San Francisco in 1997, based on a randomly drawn sample of 193 women in Beijing aged above 70, 38 percent of women in the 80s age group and 18 percent of women in their 70s displayed bound foot deformities. The last factory in China to supply special shoes for women with lotus feet ceased production in 1998.

3. Gordon's nickname was Old Patna (see 28.6.1830), which reveals the cause of his wealth: opium.

4. According to Hunter, who described the bungalow of James P. Sturgis on Penha hill in detail, as well as the view from there, it *"was the most beautifully situated of all others"*. See William C. Hunter, *Bits of Old China*, Shanghai and others, Kelly and Walsh, Limited, 1911 (a), p.159.

5. Cap-sing-moon was an anchorage to the east of Lintin island, the centre of opium smuggling, where boats would seek shelter in the case of a typhoon.

6. *"Jawaub is said to be ... a Hindi word meaning dismissal, 'also used in Anglo-Indian for a lady's refusal of a marriage offer, whence the passive verb "to be jawaub'd" ' "* (in Nan P. Hodges and Arthur W. Hummel (eds.), *Lights and Shadows of a Macao Life. The Journal of Harriett Low, Travelling Spinster*, 2 parts, Woodinville (WA), The History Bank, 2002; footnote 59, p.805).

7. The letter was written on 16 December 1832. See Elma Loines (ed.), *The China Trade Post-Bag of the Seth Low Family of Salem and New York*, Manchester (Maine), Falmouth Publishing House, 1953, pp.308, 309.

8. *Ibidem*, p.308. This was Wood's second visit to China. He had come for the first time in 1825, when he shared an office with Hunter at Russell & Co.. See William C. Hunter, *op. cit.*, 1911 (a), p.271. During his second term in Canton, Wood worked temporarily for Harriett's uncle.

9. In Elma Loines (ed.), *op. cit.,* p.308.

10. This was on 18 March 1832, and on 31 July 1832. The latter date was possibly decisive for Wood's proposal to Harriett.

11. In Elma Loines (ed.), *op. cit.,* pp. 308, 309. Hunter's description of Wood corresponds to the one given by Harriett Low regarding Wood's main characteristics and talents, and it also adds some new piece of information on Wood's looks. *"The poor fellow was awfully pock-marked; his face resembled a pine cone, but his expression was one of very good humour and full of intelligence. He was besides well educated and a most gentlemanly young fellow. He was the son of the famous tragedian of Philadelphia. ... Wood was clever at drafting and sketching; thus on his visits to Macao, as well as in Canton, he met Chinnery constantly, and being brother chips with the pencil, of similar tastes, besides being a most amusing fellow, and a toss-up in respect to looks, they became fast friends. Wood was quite equal to Chinnery in wit and metaphor, while over their mutual disfigurement each one insisted that he was the most marked of the two. Meeting one day at Macao, Chinnery assumed an air of displeasure, held up his clenched hand, and shaking it at him, exclaimed, 'Oh, you wicked man! I was some one until you came. You are marked, it's true, but I was remarked. Passers-by would say, 'There goes old Chinnery, what an ugly fellow.' Poco poco [Macao-Portuguese, 'poco-poco', little by little], my title became undisputed. What a triumph! Now you would carry off the palm. Oh, you ugly piece of wood.' There followed, of course, a deal of fun"*. In William C. Hunter, *op. cit.,* 1911 (a), pp.270, 271.

12. Also quoted in Nan P. Hodges and Arthur W. Hummel (eds.), *op. cit.,* footnote 36, pp.794, 795.

13. Hodges quotes from an article written by Wood in the *Chinese Courier* (24.11.1831) under the pseudonym Hesperus, with the title "A Defense of Bachelors". In this "manifesto", Wood blames the existence of misogynists on the practice of *"jilting, ... which is no doubt very agreeable to the fair renegade, but has the same effect upon a lover's temper as thunder upon small beer"* (*ibidem*, part 2, footnote 73, p.799). If he had but seen into Harriett's heart, he would have known better ...

14. *Ibidem*, part 1, p.16.

15. Lindsay and May Ride, *An East India Company Cemetery. Protestant Burials in Macao*, Hong Kong, Hong Kong University Press, 2nd ed., 1998, edited by Bernard Mellor, p.44.

16. Vachell was corresponding with the famous English naturalist and friend of Charles Darwin, Rev. Leonard Jenyns (1800–1893). He also prepared a *hortus siccus* (literally "dry garden"), including a variety of Chinese flower and fruit seeds, and a Herbarium for Jenyns, both for him and for the Botanical Garden in Cambridge. Besides, he sent various specimens preserved in spirit to England, for a museum in Cambridge, such as all kinds of sea animals, land animals and insects. Interestingly, on the list accompanying the boxes is also *"a model in plaster of the foot of a young Chinese Female of Rank, with the bandages by which the growth of the foot is impeded in infancy, the 4 toes will be seen are turned under the sole of the foot"*. Quoted from Roger Vaughan's Homepage (www.rogerco.freeserve.co.uk/), *The Events in the Life of the Rev. Leonard Jenyns in the Year 1830 and 1831*.

17. … to avoid meeting him. At an earlier occasion, when Vachell had incidentally joined their party at a walk, Harriett remarked: *"Am sorry because it will make a fuss in Canton"* (18.11.1831).

18. The designation "the Factory" refers to the members of the British East India Company, which is sometimes also called "John Company".

19. See Nan P. Hodges and Arthur W. Hummel (eds.), *op. cit.*, footnote 67, p.375.

20. The attitude of society towards "old maids" is very well documented in Cécile Dauphin's article "Single Women", in Geneviève Fraisse and Michelle Perrot (eds.), *A History of Women in the West. Vol. IV. Emerging Feminism from Revolution to World War*. Cambridge, Mass., and London, UK, The Belknap Press of Harvard University Press, 1995, pp.427–442.

21. The Immaculate Conception, for example, became dogma in 1854. At around that time, the cult of the Virgin reached its climax, too. See Michelle Perrot and Anne Martin-Fugier: "The Actors". In Michelle Perrot (ed.), *op. cit.,* p.150.

22. The marriage took place at the St. Lawrence's Church and the name of the lucky husband of Ana Rita de Paiva was Portugal-born Bernardino da Costa Martins (see Nan P. Hodges and Arthur W. Hummel [eds.], *op. cit.,* footnote 25, p.794). In Jorge Forjaz's *Famílias Macaenses*, the date of the wedding is indicated as 10 September 1831, i.e. one week earlier (see vol.III, Macau, Fundação Oriente, Instituto Cultural de Macau, Instituto Português do Oriente, 1996, p.962).

23. *"He was a scholar and a philanthropist, but he does not seem to have given much satisfaction to Hongkong as a diplomatist and governor, and when he left Hongkong in March, 1848 there was no public farewell or banquet; the leading paper of the Colony stated that the was 'unpopular from his official acts and unfit for a Colonial Government by his personal demeanour and disposition'"*. In Samuel Couling, *The Encyclopedia Sinica*, Hong Kong and others, Oxford University Press, 2nd impression, 1991 p.140.

24. Jacques M. Downs, *The Golden Ghetto, The American Commercial Community at Canton and the Shaping of American China Policy, 1784–1844*, Bethlehem, Lehigh University Press, 1997; p.49.

25. Right after the arrival of Caroline Shillaber, for example, her physical and mental attributes were discussed in various letters by John Murray Forbes to Augustine Heard (and probably in letters of other writers that did not survive to our times), William H. Low's partner. After an initially positive impression, which apparently was gained at night time, Forbes wrote: *"By day she looks <u>haggard</u> and old — her Hair and eyes are very beautifull and her figure is good — but she has not been enough in Ladies society to be exactly 'the thing'"* (quoted in Nan P. Hodges and Arthur W. Hummel [eds.], *op. cit.,* footnote 12, p.792). In Caroline's defence it must be mentioned that just before arriving at Macau she had recovered from a severe illness in the Indonesian archipelago. Forbes admitted in the same correspondence that he would prefer Harriett Low for a *"rib"* (wife), although he was not tempted.

26. Jacques M. Downs, *op. cit.,* footnote 112, p.389.

27. *Ibidem*, footnote 112, p.389.

28. Austin Coates wrote a captivating historical novel, based on true characters, which focuses on this particular topic, around the turn from the 18th to 19th century in Macau. His book with the telling title *City of Broken Promises* describes the rise of Martha Merop from abandoned Chinese orphan girl to *"pensioner"*, a euphemism for a slave-like prostitute, to powerful trading tycoon. Her full body portrait is in the Holy House of Mercy (Santa Casa da Misericórdia) in Macau.

29. Quoted in Jacques M. Downs, *op. cit.,* p.50.

30. In Robin Hutcheon, *Chinnery, the Man and the Legend*, Hong Kong, *South China Morning Post*, 1975, p.74.

31. Jacques M. Downs, *op. cit.,* p.49.

32. "Catty" and "tael" are weight units used in China and other southeast Asian countries. The words are of Malay origin (*kati* and *tahil*). The weight of a catty in China corresponds to 500 grams. One tael is 1/16 of a catty.

33. In Manuel Teixeira, *Macau no Séc. XIX Visto por uma Jovem Americana*, Macau, Direcção dos Serviços de Educação e Cultura, 1981 p.27.

34. *"I know Uncle and Aunt are very glad it is all off — But I had no wish to change. I feel that I have done <u>right</u> — and that is a* [the rest of the letter is missing]*"*, quoted from a letter to her sister dated 16 December 1832, in Elma Loines (ed.), *op. cit.,* p.309.

35. Queen Victoria (1819–1901), for example, had nine children herself and probably would have had more, if her husband Albert had not died relatively young, at the age of 42.

36. According to Dauphin, "single blessedness" was an expression frequently used in early 19th century American writing. See Cécile Dauphin, "Single Women", in Geneviève Fraisse and Michelle Perrot (eds.), *op. cit.,* p.440.

37. See Lindsay and May Ride, *op. cit.,* pp.175–178.

38. William Henry Chichely Plowden (1788–1880) was President of the Select Committee of the British East India Company for quite some time during Harriett Low's stay in Macau. The name of his second wife, by whom he had two sons and a daughter, was Annette Campbell.

Chapter 6   Macau, Canton and the China Trade

1. Many books dealing with the China trade contain a description of tea culture in China and of the various kinds of tea and their quality. See for example in Elma Loines (ed.), *The China Trade Post-Bag of the Seth Low Family of Salem and New York*, Manchester (Maine), Falmouth Publishing House, 1953, pp.311–315, and in Robert B. Forbes, *Remarks on China and the China Trade*, Boston, Samuel N. Dickinson, 1844, pp.69–75. Downs includes statistics on the American tea and opium trade with China, as well as the destinations of American exports from Canton. See Jacques M. Downs, *The Golden Ghetto, The American Commercial Community at Canton and the Shaping of American China Policy, 1784–1844*, Bethlehem, Lehigh University Press, 1997, appendix 2, pp.348–357.

2. This was a very durable and coarse cotton cloth in various colours, such as brownish, yellow and blue, and *"served, along with native American homespun, as the workaday fabric of early America"*, in Jonathan Goldstein, *Philadelphia and the China Trade, 1682–1846, Commercial, Cultural, and Attitudinal Effects*, University Park and London: The Pennsylvania State University Press, 1978, p.3. In later decades, however, it was the turn of the Americans to export cotton goods of native production to China. The figure indicated for 1842 and early 1843 is 500,000 pieces American cotton goods (in Robert B. Forbes, *op. cit.,* 1844, pp.27–29).

3. Like tea, the production of silk was another Chinese millenary art, or science. Many of the names commonly used in the 19th century to designate various types of silk and their use, such as pongee or sarsenett, cannot be found in the average English dictionary anymore. The export of Chinese silk in American vessels grew steadily, due to the rapidly increasing demand for this fabric. From 25,000 pieces silk in 1805/06, the quantity gradually rose to a high of 421,000 pieces in 1827/28, and fell to around 260,000 pieces in 1830/31 (in Robert B. Forbes, *op. cit.,* 1844, p.26).

4. See Jonathan Goldstein, *op. cit.,* pp.17, 18.

5. *Ibidem*, pp.24, 25.

6. The first ship venturing east was the Boston sloop *Harriet*, in December 1783. However, she never reached China because she was able to sell her cargo, consisting mainly of ginseng, to a captain of a British East India vessel at the Cape of Good Hope. The exchange rate of two pounds of tea for one pound of ginseng was considered very good (*Ibidem*, pp.26, 27).

7. John Kuo quoted in Staci Ford Hosford, *Gendered Exceptionalisms: American Women in Hong Kong and Macao, 1830–2000*, The University of Hong Kong, PhD dissertation, Feb. 2002, p.14.

8. The Chinese still use ginseng as a cure-all and aphrodisiac. In North America it was found in the Appalachians from Quebec to Georgia, and along the valleys of the Mississippi and Ohio rivers. Until recent times ginseng could not be cultivated artificially. According to Goldstein, one particular variety *"was selling in China as late as 1911 for 250 times its weight in silver"* (*op. cit.,* p.21).

9. *Ibidem*, pp.26–30.

10. *Ibidem*, p.34.

11. Quoted in Jonathan Goldstein, *op. cit.,* p.3. Excellent illustrations and authoritative information about the large variety of products fabricated in Canton and other parts of China, from painters to weavers to cabinet makers and many others, can be found in Carl L. Crossman's book *The Decorative Arts of the China Trade, Paintings, Furnishings, and Exotic Curiosities*, Woodbridge, Antique Collectors' Club, 2nd impression, 1997.

12. See Jonathan Goldstein, *op. cit.,* pp.2, 3.

13. Jacques M. Downs, *op. cit.,* p.236.

14. See Nan P. Hodges and Arthur W. Hummel (eds.), *Lights and Shadows of a Macao Life. The Journal of Harriett Low, Travelling Spinster.* 2 parts, Woodinville (WA), The History Bank, 2002; quoted from footnote 60, p.407.

15. Jacques M. Downs, *op. cit.*, p.227. See also pp.223–229. In the appendices 4 and 5, Downs lists the *"Known Partners of American Firms at Canton, 1803–1844"* and describes *"Commercial Family Alliances"*, pp.364–366 and pp.367–370 respectively.

16. See Jonathan Goldstein, *op. cit.*, pp.40–45. Downs (*op. cit.*, pp.237–245) divides the returned Canton residents into *"second careerists"* and *"retirees"*. While members of the first group continued to work actively in commerce, industry or management as a way of investing their wealth gained in Canton, individuals from the second group bought estates and property to enjoy for the rest of their lives. Former Canton residents of both groups, however, served in honorary positions in a wide variety of institutions, from the government to boards of trade, museums, universities and all kinds of social organisations.

    Downs also includes a section on *"The Good Life"* (pp.245–255) of China trade nabobs, in terms of material well being, after their return to the US, showing photographs of their magnificent stately residences and countryseats, some of which still exist.

17. Only an insider could describe the general situation at Canton in such a succinct and appropriate way as Hunter did: *"Life and business at Canton before Treaty days was in fact a conundrum as insoluble as the Sphinx"* (in William C. Hunter, *Bits of Old China*, Shanghai and others, Kelly and Walsh, Limited, 1911 (a), p.3).

18. The origin of the *hong* merchants dates back to the late Ming period, when thirty-six *hongs* were trading with foreign countries. The number of *hongs* dropped to thirteen at the end of the Ming period, when the designation "The Thirteen Hongs" originated. It continued to be used during the Ch'ing period, although the number of *hongs* oscillated quite a lot. Only twice, in 1813 and in 1837, their number was thirteen (in Immanuel C. Y. Hsü, *The Rise of Modern China*, New York and others, Oxford University Press, 5th ed., 1995, p.142).

19. *Cohong* is the corrupted version of the Chinese designation *kung-hang* (officially authorised guild), which was used by the Westerners in order to refer to his organisation (Jonathan Goldstein, *op. cit.*, p.27).

20. William W. Wood, *Sketches of China; with Illustrations from Original Drawings*, Philadelphia, Carey & Lea, 1830, p.222.

21. Robert B. Forbes, *op. cit.*, 1844, p.12.

22. Jacques M. Downs, *op. cit.*, 1997, p.76.

23. William C. Hunter, *op. cit.*, 1911a, p.278. See also Immanuel C. Y. Hsü, *op. cit.*, p.142–146 and Robert B. Forbes, *op. cit.*, 1844, pp.10–17.

24. Robert B. Forbes, *op. cit.*, 1844, p.14.

25. See Josiah Quincy (ed.), *The Journals of Major Samuel Shaw, the First American Consul at Canton*, Boston, Wm. Crosby and H. P. Nichols, 1847, p.183.

26. The names of the *hong* merchants are written differently in various publications and languages. I follow the spelling of the respective authors. The suffix *qua* in their names is an honorific designation deriving from the Chinese word *kuan*, meaning official. It was attributed for important contributions to the imperial court.

27. William C. Hunter, *op. cit.*, 1911a, pp.80, 81.

28. *Ibidem*, pp.31, 32. A more detailed description of the splendid gardens and dwellings can be found on pp.79–80 of the same book.
29. Jonathan Goldstein, *op. cit.,* p.69.
30. Abiel Abbot Low, quoted in Elma Loines (ed.), *op. cit.,* pp.68, 69.
31. This passage, most probably quoted from one of Harriett's letters home, was introduced by Hillard on 3 February 1830. In Katharine Hillard (ed.), *My Mother's Journal. A Young Lady's Diary of Five Years Spent in Manila, Macao, and the Cape of Good Hope from 1829–1834*, Boston, George H. Ellis, 1900, p.51.
32. William C. Hunter, *The "Fan Kwae" at Canton before Treaty Days 1825–1844 by an Old Resident*, Shanghai and others, Kelly and Walsh, Limited, 1911b, pp.60–64.
33. William C. Hunter, *op. cit.,* 1911a, p.269.
34. In Lindsay and May Ride, *An East India Company Cemetery. Protestant Burials in Macao*, Hong Kong, Hong Kong University Press, 2nd ed., 1998, edited by Bernard Mellor, p.258.
35. This is the title of Downs's book, much referred to in this work. It is the most complete and exhaustive book on the individual members and companies of the American community in Canton from its beginning until the signature of the Treaty of Wanghsia (Mong-há) between China and the USA, in July 1844.
36. William W. Wood, *op. cit.,* p.140.
37. Hunter (*op. cit.,* 1911b, p.20) explains that *"the word 'factory' was an importation from India, where the commercial establishments of the 'East India Company' were so designated, and synonymous with 'agency'"*. The word actually derives from the Portuguese word *feitoria*, meaning exactly "commercial agency". When the English arrived in India, where the Portuguese had had trading posts or colonies since the early 16th century, they incorporated the word *feitoria* into their language, adapting it to "factory".
38. Jacques M. Downs, *op. cit.,* p. 27. On page 26, Downs reproduces a map-like sketch of the Canton factories and their immediate surroundings, with an indication of the respective nation occupying them. On page 28 follows a diagram of a factory, subdivided into ground floor and second story, and its functional division into go downs (storage rooms), offices, kitchens, servants and coolies rooms, counting rooms, parlours, dining hall, chambers, and so on.
39. In Nan P. Hodges and Arthur W. Hummel (eds.), *op. cit.,* footnote 105, p.400.
40. In Jacques M. Downs, *op. cit.,* p.73.
41. Quite a few members of the British East India Company studied Chinese, such as John Francis Davis, who was also one of the first British sinologists, James F. Daniell, and others. William C. Hunter, as already mentioned, was the only American trader fluent in this language. The missionaries must have acquired the basics of the language, too, at least in its spoken form.
42. The trading season lasted from October to March, when the ships sailed home. During the following "dead season" the men could spend more time in Macau, except for the opium traders, whose business thrived all year long.
43. For a full set of the rules existing in Canton, see for example Immanuel C. Y. Hsü, *op. cit.,* pp.150, 151.

44. See Tom Mitchell's article "A Foreign Affair", in *South China Morning Post* Features, 15 April 2002.
45. William Hunter, *op. cit.*, 1911a, p.3.
46. William W. Wood, *op. cit.*, pp.64, 65.
47. Immanuel C. Y. Hsü, *op. cit.*, p.161.
48. *Ibidem*, p.162.
49. Between 1700 and 1725, the British East India Company bought around 400,000 pounds of tea per year from China, this amount rose to 23.3 million pounds in 1800, and to 26 million pounds after 1808. These quantities are twice as much as those shipped by other countries (in Immanuel C. Y. Hsü, *op. cit.*, p.149).
50. *Ibidem*, p.168.
51. William W. Wood, *op. cit.*, pp.206, 207.
52. Robert B. Forbes, *Personal Reminiscences*, Cambridge (Mass.), John Wilson and Son, 1876, p.144. For a more interesting and less apologetic comparison between the effects of alcohol and opium, see W. A. P. Martin's article on "The scourge of opium" (in Colin Mackerras (ed.), *Sinophiles and Sinophobes. Western Views of China*, Oxford (and others), Oxford University Press, 2000, pp.83, 84). Many missionaries like Martin were outspoken critics of the opium trade.
53. Robert B. Forbes, *op. cit.*, 1876, pp.144, 145.
54. William W. Wood (*op. cit.*, p.210) provides some interesting details about the varieties of opium on the market, as well as about the shipment, packaging and storage of opium. See also Immanuel C. Y. Hsü, *op. cit.*, pp.168, 169, and Austin Coates, *Macao and the British; 1637 to 1842. Prelude to Hongkong*, Hong Kong and others, Oxford University Press, 2nd impression, 1989, pp.65–67.
55. William W. Wood, *op. cit.*, p.206.
56. Robert B. Forbes, *op. cit.*, 1876, p.144. See also the statistics on *"Specie and Bills Imported by American Ships"* in Jacques M. Downs, *op. cit.*, pp.361–363.
57. For a short description of the major foreign opium dealers and companies see Austin Coates, *op. cit.*, 1989, pp.139–143.
58. In Immanuel C. Y. Hsü, *op. cit.*, p.171.
59. Jonathan Goldstein, *op. cit.*, p.49.
60. William W. Wood, *op. cit.*, p.209.
61. *Ibidem*, pp.35, 36.
62. *Ibidem*, p.211.
63. See Jacques M. Downs, *op. cit.*, pp.128–131.
64 . See Jonathan Goldstein, *op. cit.*, pp.53, 54, and Jacques M. Downs, *op. cit.*, pp.112–128.
65. In Jacques M. Downs, *op. cit.*, pp.124–128, *"Americans and the Indian Opium trade"*.
66. It is said that the *Lord Amherst* expedition actually incurred a loss of more than £5600 (see Nan P. Hodges and Arthur W. Hummel (eds.), *op. cit.*, footnote 10, p.414).
67. Jacques M. Downs, *op. cit.*, p.127.
68. There is a six-foot granite statue and a museum in Macau's Lin Fung Temple (Lotus Temple), commemorating the incorruptible commissioner and this particularly

agitated period in Sino-foreign relations. The temple itself is among the oldest in Macau, dating back to the late Ming dynasty. For centuries it accommodated Chinese mandarins from Guangdong province on visit in Macau, and Lin himself visited it on the occasion of his call at Macau in September 1839.

69. Abiel Abbot Low, quoted in Elma Loines (ed.), *op. cit.,* p.72.

70. See Jacques M. Downs, *op. cit.,* pp.331, 332.

71. *Ibidem*, p.335.

72. Jonathan Goldstein, *op. cit.,* p.51.

73. Quoted in C. A. Montalto de Jesus, *Historic Macao*, Hong Kong, Oxford University Press, 1984, p.296.

74. In Immanuel C. Y. Hsü, *op. cit.,* p.180.

75. C. A. Montalto de Jesus, *op. cit.,* p.295.

76. See Jacques M. Downs, *op. cit.,* pp.334–336 and 337–340.

77. Thomas De Quincey, *Confessions of an English Opium-Eater*, Harmondsworth, Penguin Books, 1986 (edited with an introduction by Alethea Hayter), pp.31, 32.

78. In Katharine Hillard (ed.), *op. cit.,* pp.75–86. The visit to Canton is also copied, from the same source, in Nan P. Hodges and Arthur W. Hummel (eds.), *op. cit.,* pp.190–196.

79. Katharine Hillard (ed.), *op. cit.,* p.75.

80. The designation for this passage derives from the special formation of rocks, which are said to resemble a tiger's open jaws.

81. In Katharine Hillard (ed.), *op. cit.,* pp.76–79.

82. *Ibidem*, pp.79, 80.

83. *Ibidem*, pp.81, 82.

84. *Ibidem*, p.82.

85. *Ibidem*, pp.83–85.

86. William C. Hunter, *op. cit.,* 1911b, p.121.

87. The *Lintin* (390 tons), which originally had been built for R. B. Forbes, was later co-owned by Russell and Company, with F. W. Macondray as commander (in Nan P. Hodges and Arthur W. Hummel (eds.), *op. cit.,* footnote 40, p.795).

88. In the Hodges/Hummel edition of the Harriett's journal, the lifetime of Sarah Procter Shillaber is indicated as 1758–1832 (footnote 18, p.793). Since Caroline was born in 1812, which would make her mother over 50 years old when giving birth, I suspect that Caroline was raised as Sarah Shillaber's daughter and that the real mother had died untimely or abandoned her.

89. The Dr. Ticknor mentioned here as member of the excursion is the one whose journal was edited by Nan P. Hodges with the title *The Voyage of the Peacock: A Journal by Benajah Ticknor, Naval Surgeon*, 1991.

Chapter 7   Intercultural Relations in Early 19th-Century Macau

1. The South Carolinians tried to nullify the Federal tariffs of 1828 and 1832. Jackson answered with a Nullification Proclamation and threatened with military suppression in the case of any defiance to Federal Law. The conflict was solved in 1833 through a compromise tariff, which prevented a final confrontation. See also Nan P. Hodges and Arthur W. Hummel (eds.), *Lights and Shadows of a Macao Life. The Journal of Harriett Low, Travelling Spinster.* 2 parts, Woodinville (WA), The History Bank, 2002, footnote 25, p.802.

2. Harriett was right with her guess about the Proclamation, which was written by Edward Livingston, Jackson's Secretary of State. (*Ibidem*, footnote 35, p.803).

3. *"Consul for Portugal in Shanghai in 1851 and awarded the French Legion of Honor in 1856, Chay Beale achieved a position in society that Harriett may not have foreseen"*, in Nan P. Hodges and Arthur W. Hummel (eds.), *op. cit.,* footnote 6, p.414.

4. Jacques M. Downs, *The Golden Ghetto, The American Commercial Community at Canton and the Shaping of American China Policy, 1784–1844*, Bethlehem, Lehigh University Press, 1997, p.55. Hodges confirms this characterisation of William H. Low, most clearly in part 2 of the Hodges/Hummel edition of the journal: *"He [Coolidge] admired Heard and Low as business men, and found Heard kind and friendly, but felt that Russell and Company labored 'under one serious disadvantage; which cannot but be, in time, an injury to their business: this is the unpopularity of Mr. Low'"* (in footnote 66 on p.806).

5. See Nan P. Hodges and Arthur W. Hummel (eds.), *op. cit.,* footnote 18, pp.809, 810.

6. See Jacques M. Downs, *op. cit.,* pp.166–168.

7. Katharine Hillard (ed.), *My Mother's Journal. A Young Lady's Diary of Five Years Spent in Manila, Macao, and the Cape of Good Hope from 1829–1834,* Boston, George H. Ellis, 1900, p.VI.

8. William C. Hunter, *Bits of Old China,* Shanghai and others, Kelly and Walsh, Limited, 1911 (a), pp.265–267.

9. Pamela Neville-Sington (ed.), in Frances Trollope, *Domestic Manners of the Americans,* Harmondsworth, Penguin Books Ltd., 1997, p.XXIX.

10. Pamela Neville-Sington (ed.), *Ibidem,* p.VII.

11. Frances Trollope, *op. cit.,* p.314.

12. Harriett in a letter to her sister Mary Ann, dated 29 July 1833. Quoted in Elma Loines (ed.), *The China Trade Post-Bag of the Seth Low Family of Salem and New York,* Manchester (Maine), Falmouth Publishing House, 1953, p.53.

13. Fanny Wright was an early advocate and activist of women's rights.

14. Harriett in a letter to her family, dated 20 July 1830. In Elma Loines (ed.), *op. cit.,* p.38.

15. It was not the queen, but the Queen-Mother, Carlota Joaquina, who had died in

January 1830. See Nan P. Hodges and Arthur W. Hummel (eds.), *op. cit.,* footnote 74, p.409.

16. The Macanese have been defined traditionally by three vectors: mixed blood (usually Chinese or other Asian from the female side and Portuguese from the male side), bilingual fluency (Portuguese, written and spoken, and Cantonese, spoken only) and Catholic religion. Nowadays the increasing sinification of the Macanese can be observed. See João de Pina Cabral and Nelson Lourenço, *Em Terra de Tufões. Dinâmicas da Etnicidade Macaense,* Macau, Instituto Cultural de Macau, 1993, pp.20–23. See also Jorge Forjaz, *Famílias Macaenses,* vol. II., Macau, Fundação Oriente, Instituto Cultural de Macau, Instituto Português do Oriente, 1996, pp.988–991.

17. *Caffres* was the designation for black Africans from the eastern shoreline, while the word *negro* or *preto da Guiné* was used to refer to blacks from West Africa. Slaves from Timor were also grouped with *cafres* and *pretos*, because of their dark skin colour (see Graciete Nogueira Batalha, *Glossário do Dialecto Macaense. Notas Linguísticas, Etnográficas e Folclóricas*, Coimbra, Faculdade de Letras, Instituto de Estudos Românicos, 1977, p.338). The word *sepoy* is of Hindi origin and was employed for natives of India who worked as soldiers or guards for Europeans.

18. In Jorge Forjaz's *Famílias Macaenses* (vol. II, p.989) the date of the wedding is indicated as 29 October 1833. The wedding took place at the private chapel in the mansion of the Pereira. The Paiva family history is described in Jorge Forjaz, *op. cit.,* vol. II, pp.961–964.

19. Katharine Hillard (ed.), *op. cit.,* p.198.

20. For more information on the Macanese ladies and their peculiar dress see Ana Maria Amaro, *O Traje da Mulher Macaense. Da Saraça ao Dó das Nhonhonha de Macau*, Macau, Instituto Cultural de Macau, 1989. An interesting photograph, showing a group of Macanese ladies from the back at the Praia Grande (p.134), seems to be well fit to illustrate the scene described by Harriett Low. There is no way, however, to exemplify her olfactory impression in this book. Graciete Batalha also traces the controversial etymology of *nhonha* (*op. cit.,* p.230).

21. Harriett in a letter to her brothers William, Edward, Francis and Josiah Low, written on 18 July 1831. Quoted in Elma Loines (ed.), *op. cit.,* p.41.

22. Harriett had to remove all her books temporarily, when her room was painted new.

23. "Ole Mrs." is Pidgin English for *Lao T'ai-t'ai*, the Chinese term of respect for the older married women of a household. See Nan P. Hodges and Arthur W. Hummel (eds.), *op. cit.,* footnote 29, p.403.

24. Several of the former Canton residents contributed significantly to the introduction and divulgation of knowledge about China and the Chinese on their return to the United States. One of the most important initiatives in this respect was Nathan Dunn's "Chinese Museum", which contained life-size clay figurines made in China and dressed in full costume, such as mandarins, scholars, ladies, actors, and others. There was even a farmer with a water buffalo pulling a plough. More than 100,000 Americans visited the "Chinese Museum" between 1839 and 1842. See Jonathan Goldstein, *Philadelphia and the China Trade, 1682–1846, Commercial, Cultural,*

and Attitudinal Effects, University Park and London, The Pennsylvania State University Press, 1978, pp.73–79. A medley of impressions about China and the Chinese throughout the centuries is gathered in Colin Mackerras's book with the telling title *"Sinophiles and Sinophobes. Western Views of China"*, Oxford (and others), Oxford University Press, 2000.

25. Ellen was Harriett's youngest sister, then aged 2.

26. William Wood, *Sketches of China, with Illustrations from Original Drawings,* Philadelphia, Carey & Lea, 1830, pp.135 and 137. As to the whys of foot binding, which dates back to the Southern Tang dynasty (907–923), the habit is said to have begun at the Court, from whence it spread gradually to the lower classes. There were seven exigencies for the perfect feet, they had to be thin, small, pointed, crooked, perfumed, soft and symmetrical. Obviously, this refers to golden lilies in shoes, because the sight of a bound foot *in natura* was certainly not pleasurable at all. Besides, they were considered a most intimate part of a woman's body and never openly displayed. The peculiar walk of a woman with bound feet was supposed to have an erotic effect on men. It is also said that the muscles in the female abdomen changed through foot binding, tightening the muscles of the vagina and thus making sexual intercourse more pleasurable for men. Later, during the Qing dynasty, bound feet served to distinguish Han Chinese women from the women of the Manchu invaders, who did not practise this custom. Considering the importance of the feet in Chinese traditional medicine, as mirroring the body as a whole, foot binding assumes a dimension of cruelty far beyond the physical pain endured by the girls and women, who were forced into it. Therefore, the current fashion — mainly among Western residents in China or travellers to China — of having shoes for bound feet as decorative items in their homes, comes close to the exhibition of medieval instruments of torture for instance, which thankfully have not reached decoration status yet.

27. *Ibidem*, pp.133–135.

28. *Ibidem*, pp.134, 135.

29. In the Hodges/Hummel edition of the journal it is explained that *"the 'singing tone' of the school boy was the monotone in which he repeated the classics by heart as he stood, with his back to the teacher. The Chinese called it* pei-shu, *'backing the book'"*. See footnote 29, p.416.

30. There is another, earlier description of the "sweeping of the tombs", as this ritual is called, which is not so detailed however (see 1.5.1830).

31. Near Canton there was a place known as City of the Dead, where rich people kept their deceased family members, until a *feng shui* master had found an auspicious place for a grave, which however could take months or even years. A Portuguese traveller, who visited the City of the Dead at the turn of the 19th to the 20th century, wrote: "*In this* city, *which houses more than a hundred or two hundred coffins, … there is no bad smell or anything offensive to the viewer, everything is nicely whitewashed and gilded, painted, swept, tidy, in short spotlessly clean, which makes the contrast with the city of the living, where there are dirt, negligence, bad smells and ugliness, all the more striking. … Some of the deceased are waiting there for*

their burial places in China since more than three years". In Filipe Emílio de Paiva, *Um Marinheiro em Macau — 1903. Album de Viagem,* Macau, Museu Marítimo de Macau, 1997, p.21.

32. Crespo confirms this rule and added another one, which however applied only to the male members of the Imperial Family, namely that during the mourning period they were forbidden to have sexual relations. According to him, when the wife of a prince gave birth shortly after the mourning period, her husband was punished with some rod blows, for (supposedly) having violated this rule, although the poor prince was probably innocent … See Joaquim H. Callado Crespo, *Cousas da China. Costumes e Crenças,* Lisboa, Imprensa Nacional, 1898, pp.152, 153. More detailed information on the prohibitions and ceremonies connected with this kind of events can be found in the *Chinese Repository* for July 1833, in Nan P. Hodges and Arthur W. Hummel (eds.), *op. cit.,* footnote 71, p.806.

33. See Josiah Quincey (ed.), *The Journals of Major Samuel Shaw, the First American Consul at Canton,* Boston, Wm. Crosby and H. P. Nichols, 1847, pp.339, 340, and Austin Coates, *Macao and the British; 1637 to 1842. Prelude to Hongkong,* Hong Kong and others, Oxford University Press, 2nd impression, 1989, pp.79, 80.

34. See Nan P. Hodges and Arthur W. Hummel (eds.), *op. cit.,* footnote 34, pp.811, 812.

35. This quotation is an extract from fragmentary letters to her family, introduced by Hillard in her edition of the Journal, in order to fill in the gap created by the loss of a volume of the journal at sea. See Katharine Hillard, *op. cit.,* p.84.

36. In 1830, the total number of slaves amounted to about 1150 in Macau, according to estimates by Ljungstedt (see Nan P. Hodges and Arthur W. Hummel (eds.), *op. cit.,* footnote 83, p.807).

Chapter 8   Homeward Bound

1. Quoted in Elma Loines (ed.), *The China Trade Post-Bag of the Seth Low Family of Salem and New York*, Manchester (Maine), Falmouth Publishing House, 1953, p.52.
2. *Ibidem*, p.52.
3. See Nan P. Hodges and Arthur W. Hummel (eds.), *Lights and Shadows of a Macao Life. The Journal of Harriett Low, Travelling Spinster.* 2 parts, Woodinville (WA), The History Bank, 2002; see footnote 18, pp.809, 810.
4. According to the letters transcribed in Loines, Harriett's brother Edward Allen was in Canton still by the end of 1849. His last letter quoted dates December 1849. See Elma Loines (ed.), *op. cit.,* p.284.
5. According to Batalha, in Macau the word *lorcha* was used only to refer to big fishing boats. Other ships of a similar design, but used for cargo, were called *junco* or *tous*. In English, there is only one word for them, namely "junk". This type of boats could be seen in the harbours of the Pearl River Delta until far into the 20th century. Nowadays, some of them have been converted for tourism (See Graciete Nogueira Batalha, *Glossário do Dialecto Macaense. Notas Linguísticas, Etnográficas e*

Folclóricas, Coimbra, Faculdade de Letras, Instituto de Estudos Românicos, 1977, pp.471, 472).

6. On another occasion (7.7.1834), Harriett Low mentioned the distance, namely 5 miles or more, at which people could hold conversations by means of these signals.

7. James Low, a brother of Seth and William Henry Low, was master of the ship *Cabot*. He had arrived in Macau on 2 September 1833 (in Nan P. Hodges and Arthur W. Hummel (eds.), *op. cit.,* footnote 7, p.809).

8. The *"two ladies"* were the daughters of the owner of the Boarding House, a Mrs. Cruywagen.

9. The gentlemen visited on 3 and 9 March 1834.

10. Hodges informs that the cemetery was considered as unsanitary by the city authorities of Cape Town in 1870. The remains and stones were later transferred to another site, but no trace of William Low's gravestone survived. See Nan P. Hodges and Arthur W. Hummel (eds.), *op. cit.,* footnote 47, p.815.

11. Jacob's ladder, as it is known, was built in 1829 and rebuilt in 1871. It has a length of 924 feet and ascends over a vertical height of 602 feet. In certain places the ladder is as steep as 45 degrees.

12. In 1840, exactly 25 years after his arrival on St. Helena, Napoleon's remains were transferred to Les Invalides in Paris. On old engravings of this spot one can see the tomb as described by Harriett Low, including the mourning willow trees.

13. Hodges located the quotation: *"To the Abbé du Pradt, on the return from Russia (1812), referring to the retreat from Moscow"*. In Nan P. Hodges and Arthur W. Hummel (eds.), *op. cit.,* p.749

14. Marginal note: *"How much fancy will do"*.

15. Thomas Daniell (1749–1840) and his nephew William Daniell (1769–1837) were both painters. In 1810, they published *A Picturesque Voyage to India; by the Way of China by Thomas Daniell and William Daniell*. See Nan P. Hodges and Arthur W. Hummel (eds.), *op. cit.,* footnote 65, p.817.

16. As already mentioned earlier, Ayok's father worked for Colledge and was depicted together with him and three other Chinese showing Colledge in the exercise of his profession as an eye surgeon.

    Somerset House was the venue of the yearly Summer Exhibition of the Royal Academy of Arts, for which Chinnery had sent some paintings. It still is a thriving centre for the arts in the heart of London. Since 1869, the Summer Exhibition is held in Burlington House.

17. Hodges contrasts Harriett's reaction with that of Fanny Trollope, who at the Philadelphian Academy of Fine Arts had been asked by an attendant to speed up her view of the sculptures while there were no men in the gallery, which she considered an affront. See Nan P. Hodges and Arthur W. Hummel (eds.), *op. cit.,* footnote 63, pp.816, 817.

18. The famous Rock of Scone, also known as the Stone of Destiny, was returned to Scotland on 15 November 1996, 700 years after the army of King Edward I of England had dragged it away to Westminster Abbey.

19. Katharine Hillard (ed.), *op. cit.,* pp.318, 319.

20. *Ibidem*, p.320.
21. Harriett Low in a letter to her father, written in London on 5 June 1837. See Harriett Low, *Letters*, Washington D.C., Library of Congress, Manuscript Section, Low-Mills family papers, box no. 2, folder "General Correspondence 1836 to 1870".
22. In a letter to her sister Ellen (Nelly), written in London on 31 March 1842. *Ibidem*.
23. This is another quotation from the same letter.
24. In a letter to her father, written in London on 28 June 1837. *Ibidem*.
25. See Elma Loines (ed.), *op. cit.,* pp.18 and 315.
26. Harriett in a letter to her sister Ellen, dated 10 and 11 February 1848. See Harriett Low, *Letters*, Washington D.C., Library of Congress, Manuscript Section, Low-Mills family papers, box no. 2, folder "General Correspondence 1836 to 1870".
27. Harriett in a letter to her father, written in Manchester, on 2 March 1845. *Ibidem*.
28. *Ibidem*.
29. Sarah kept a diary while staying with Harriett in England and Paris, which can be found among the Low-Mills family papers, in the Library of Congress.
30. Harriett in a letter to her sister Ellen, written in Manchester, on 17 March 1846. *Ibidem*. Ellen Low described the marriage in detail, in a letter to her brother Edward in Canton. Quoted in Elma Loines (ed.), *op. cit.,* pp.252, 253.
31. Harriett in a letter to her brother Josiah, written in Edinburgh on 10 April 1840. See Harriett Low, *Letters*, Washington D.C., Library of Congress, Manuscript Section, Low-Mills family papers, box no. 2, folder "General Correspondence 1836 to 1870".
32. Harriett in a letter to her sister Ellen, written in Manchester on 24 February 1848. *Ibidem*.
33. Harriett in a letter to her sisters, written in London on 8 April 1848. *Ibidem*.
34. See Elma Loines (ed.), *op. cit.,* p.59.
35. For more information on the A. A. Low & Brothers' Fleet, the history of the ships, and the reasons why the Lows gave up the China trade, see Elma Loines (ed.), *op. cit.,* pp.285–291.
36. See Nan P. Hodges and Arthur W. Hummel (eds.), *op. cit.,* pp.14–15.

Bibliography

Manuscripts and Transcriptions

Hillard, Katharine (ed.), *My Mother's Journal. A Young Lady's Diary of Five Years Spent in Manila, Macao, and the Cape of Good Hope from 1829–1834*, Boston, George H. Ellis, 1900.

Hodges, Nan P. and Arthur W. Hummel (eds.), *Lights and Shadows of a Macao Life. The Journal of Harriett Low, Travelling Spinster*. 2 parts, Woodinville (WA), The History Bank, 2002.

Hummel, Arthur W. (ed.), *The Journal of Harriet Low. Annotated Transcription*, Washington, D.C., Library of Congress, Manuscript Section, Low-Mills Family Papers, Boxes 22 and 23, Unpublished Typescript (1075 pages).

Loines, Elma (ed.), *The China Trade Post-Bag of the Seth Low Family of Salem and New York*, Manchester (Maine), Falmouth Publishing House, 1953.

Low, Harriett, *Journal*, Washington, D.C., Library of Congress, Manuscript Section, Low-Mills Family Papers, Boxes 13 and 14; indication, in brackets, of the page numbers as in Hummel's transcription: Vol. I: 24.5.1829–18.12.1829 (pp.1–111); Vol. II: 1.1.1830–3.9.1830 (pp.112–266) with the following title given by Harriett: *Eight Months in Macao by a young lady in the year 1830 by the author of a Journal at Sea published in 1829;* Vol. III: 1.3.1831–15.12.1831 (pp.267–402); Vol. IV: 25.1.1832–31.7.1832 (pp.403–505); Vol. V: 1.8.1832–22.3.1833 (pp.506–633); Vol. VI: 19.3.1833–23.8.1833 (pp.634–740) with the following title *The Lights and Shadows of a Macao Life by a Travelling Spinster. Dedicated to Her Beloved Sister;* Vol. VII: 24.8.1833–17.11.1833 (pp.741–790) called *Continuation of the Lights and Shadows of a Macao Life by a Travelling Spinster. Containing the Grand Finale and an Affectionate Farewell to China;* Vol. VIII: 19.11.1833–1.8.1834 (pp.791–935); Vol. IX (not bound and written in pencil): 2.8.1834–21.9.1834 (pp.936–947). The 520 footnotes added by Hummel continue on pp.948–1075. One volume of the *Journal* was lost at sea, dating from September 1830 to February 1831.

Harriett Low, *Letters*, Washington, D.C., Library of Congress, Manuscript Section, Low-Mills Family Papers, Box 2, folder "General Correspondence, 1836–1870" and Box 11, folder "Material Concerning the Far East, 1829–1831".

Printed Works

Adams, Sandra, "A Woman's Place in the West and East: Corset versus Bound Feet", in *Review of Culture* [English edition], Macau, Instituto Cultural de Macau [Macau Cultural Institute], ser.2, no.24, July to September 1995, pp.62–93.

Amaro, Ana Maria, *O Traje da Mulher Macaense. Da Saraça ao Dó das Nhonhonha de Macau*, Macau, Instituto Cultural de Macau, 1989.

American Unitarian Association, *One Hundred Scriptural Arguments for the Unitarian Faith*, Boston, Bowles and Dearborn, 4th ed., 1827.

Argyle, Michael, *Psychology and Religion. An Introduction*, London and New York, Routledge, 2000.

Bathalha, Graciete Nogueira, *Glossário do Dialecto Macaense. Notas Linguísticas, Etnográficas e Folclóricas*, Coimbra, Faculdade de Letras, Instituto de Estudos Românicos, 1977. (Separata da Revista Portuguesa de Filologia, Vols. XV, 1971; XVI, 1974 e XVII, 1977).

Boxer, Charles R., *The Great Ship from Amacon*, Macau, Instituto Cultural de Macau, 1988.

Boxer, Charles R. (ed.), *Seventeenth Century Macau in Contemporary Documents and Illustrations*, Hong Kong, Heinemann (Asia), 1984.

Buck, Claire (ed.), *Bloomsbury Guide to Women's Literature*, London, Bloomsbury Publishing Limited, 1992.

Cabral, João de Pina and Nelson Lourenço, *Em Terra de Tufões. Dinâmicas da Etnicidade Macaense*, Macau, Instituto Cultural de Macau, 1993 (Colecção Documentos & Ensaios, 6).

Cheng, Christina Miu Bing, *Macau, A Cultural Janus*, Hong Kong, Hong Kong University Press, 1999.

Clinton, Catherine, *The Other Civil War. American Women in the Nineteenth Century*, New York, Hill and Wang, 6th printing, 1992.

Coates, Austin, *A Macao Narrative*, Hong Kong, Oxford University Press, 3rd ed., 1993.

Coates, Austin, *Macao and the British; 1637 to 1842. Prelude to Hongkong*, Hong Kong and others, Oxford University Press, 2nd impression, 1989.

Conner, Patrick, *George Chinnery, 1774–1852. Artist of India and the China Coast*, Woodbridge, Antique Collectors' Club, 1993.

Couling, Samuel, *The Encyclopaedia Sinica*, Hong Kong and others, Oxford University Press, 2nd impression, 1991 (first published by Kelly and Walsh, Shanghai, 1917).

Cremer, Ralph D. (ed.), *Macau — City of Commerce and Culture*, Hong Kong, API Press, 2nd ed., 1991.

Crespo, Joaquim Heliodoro Callado, *Cousas da China. Costumes e Crenças*, Lisboa, Imprensa Nacional, 1898 (Contribuições da Sociedade de Geographia de Lisboa).

Crossman, Carl L., *The Decorative Arts of the China Trade, Paintings, Furnishings, and Exotic Curiosities*, Woodbridge, Antique Collectors' Club, 2nd impression, 1997.

Dauphin, Cécile, "Single Women", in Geneviève Fraisse and Michelle Perrot (eds.), *A History of Women in the West. Vol. IV. Emerging Feminism from Revolution to*

World War. Cambridge (Mass.) and London (UK), The Belknap Press of Harvard University Press, 1995, pp. 427–442.

DeQuincey, Thomas, *Confessions of an English Opium-Eater*, Harmondsworth, Penguin Books, 1986 (edited with an introduction by Alethea Hayter).

Downs, Jacques M., *The Golden Ghetto, The American Commercial Community at Canton and the Shaping of American China Policy, 1784–1844*, Bethlehem, Lehigh University Press, 1997.

Druett, Joan, *Hen Frigates, Passion and Peril, Nineteenth-Century Women at Sea*, New York, Simon & Schuster, 1998 (A Touchstone Book).

Forbes, Robert Bennett, *Personal Reminiscences*, Cambridge (Mass.), John Wilson and Son, 1876.

Forbes, Robert Bennett, *Remarks on China and the China Trade*, Boston, Samuel N. Dickinson, 1844.

Forjaz, Jorge, *Famílias Macaenses*, 3 vols., Macau, Fundação Oriente, Instituto Cultural de Macau, Instituto Português do Oriente, 1996.

Fraisse, Geneviève and Michelle Perrot (eds.), *A History of Women in the West, Vol. IV, Emerging Feminism from Revolution to World War*, Cambridge (Mass.) and London (UK), The Belknap Press of Harvard University Press, 1995 (Georges Duby and Michelle Perrot, general editors).

Goldstein, Jonathan, *Philadelphia and the China Trade, 1682–1846, Commercial, Cultural, and Attitudinal Effects*, University Park and London, The Pennsylvania State University Press, 1978.

Gunn, Geoffrey, *Encountering Macau. A Portuguese City-State on the Periphery of China, 1557–1999*, Boulder (Col.), Westview Press, 1996.

Hosford, Stacilee Ford, *Gendered Exceptionalisms: American Women in Hong Kong and Macao, 1830–2000*, Hong Kong, The University of Hong Kong, Ph.D. Dissertation, 2002.

Hoe, Susana, *The Private Life of Old Hong Kong: Western Women in the British Colony, 1841–1941*, Hong Kong and others, Oxford University Press, 1991.

Hsu, Immanuel C.Y., *The Rise of Modern China*, New York and others, Oxford University Press, 5th ed., 1995.

Hummel, Arthur W., "The Journal of Harriet Low", *The Library of Congress Quarterly Journal of Current Acquisitions*, vol. 2, nos. 3 and 4, 1945, pp.972–989.

Hunter, William C., *Bits of Old China*, Shanghai and others, Kelly and Walsh, Limited, 1911a.

[Hunter, William C.,] *The "Fan Kwae" at Canton before Treaty Days 1825–1844 by an Old Resident*, Shanghai and others, Kelly and Walsh, Limited, 1911b.

Hutcheon, Robin, *Chinnery, the Man and the Legend*, Hongkong, South China Morning Post, 1975.

Jorge, Cecília, "Rebecca Chase [Kinsman]: An American in Macau", in *MACAU*, no.11/ 2002, pp.38–53.

Kenyon, Olga (ed.), *800 Years of Women's Letters*, Harmondsworth, Penguin, 1994 (with a Foreword by P. D. James).

Lamas, Rosmarie Wank-Nolasco, "The Diary of Harriet Low in the Context of North

America's Women Travellers of the Early Nineteenth Century", in *Review of Culture* [English edition], Macau, Instituto Cultural de Macau [Macau Cultural Institute], ser.2, nos.34–35, Jan./June 1999, pp.261–275.

Lamas, Rosmarie Wank-Nolasco, *History of Macau. A Student's Manual*, Macau, Instituto de Formação Turística, 2nd ed., 1999.

Ljungstedt, Anders, *An Historical Sketch of the Portuguese Settlements in China and of the Roman Catholic Church and Mission in China & Description of the City of Canton*, Hong Kong, Viking Hong Kong Publications, 1992 (complete version of the first edition of 1836).

Macau. A Invenção da Paisagem. Chinnery, Watson, Borget, Smirnoff. Colecção do Museu Luís de Camões, Galeria de Exposições Temporárias do Leal Senado, 9 a 30 de Março, Macau, Leal Senado, 1996 (trilingual edition, Portuguese, Chinese, English).

Mackerras, Colin (ed.), *Sinophiles and Sinophobes. Western Views of China*, Oxford (and others), Oxford University Press, 2000.

Mitchell, Tom, A Foreign Affair, in *South China Morning Post* Features, 15 April, 2002.

Montalto de Jesus, C. A., *Historic Macao*. Hong Kong, Oxford University Press, 1984, (reprint of the 2nd edition of 1926, with the title *Historic Macao. International Traits in China Old and New).*

Um Museu em Espaço Histórico. A Fortaleza de S. Paulo do Monte, Macau, Edição Museu de Macau, 1998.

The Norton Anthology of English Literature, Vol. 2, Meyer Howard Abrams, (general editor), New York and London, W. W. Norton & Company, 6th ed., 1993.

Oleiro, Manuel Bairrão and Rui Brito Peixoto, *Museu Marítimo de Macau*, Macau, Museu Marítimo de Macau, s.d.

Paiva, Filipe Emílio de, *Um Marinheiro em Macau – 1903. Álbum de Viagem*, Macau, Museu Marítimo de Macau, 1997 (Composition by Jorge Abreu and Raul Leal Gaião).

Pereira, Fernando António Baptista, "A 'Acrópole' de Macau. O Complexo Religioso, Cultural e Militar da Companhia de Jesus", In *Um Museu em Espaço Histórico. A Fortaleza de S. Paulo do Monte*, Macau, Edição Museu de Macau, 1998, pp.14–58.

Perrot, Michelle (ed.), *A History of Private Life. Vol. IV. From the Fires of Revolution to the Great War*, Cambridge (Mass.) and London (UK), The Belknap Press of Harvard University Press, 1990 (Philippe Ariès and Georges Duby, general editors).

Petroski, Catherine, *A Bride's Passage. Susan Hathorn's Year under Sail*, Boston, Northeastern University Press, 1997.

Pickowicz, Paul G., "William Wood in Canton. A Critique of the China Trade before the Opium War", in *Essex Institute Historical Collections*, no.107, January 1971, pp.3–24.

Pittis, Donald and Susan J. Henders (eds.), *Macao. Mysterious Decay and Romance*, Hong Kong and others, Oxford University Press, 1997.

Porter, Jonathan, *Macau. The Imaginary City. Culture and Society, 1557 to present*, Boulder (Col.), Westview Press, 1996.

Quincy, Josiah (ed.), *The Journals of Major Samuel Shaw, the First American Consul at Canton*, Boston, Wm. Crosby and H. P. Nichols, 1847.

Ride, Lindsay and May, *An East India Company Cemetery. Protestant Burials in Macao*, Hong Kong, Hong Kong University Press, 2nd ed., 1998 (edited by Bernard Mellor).

Scharlau, Winfried (ed.), *Guetzlaff's Bericht ueber drei Reisen in den Seeprovinzen Chinas, 1831–1833*, Hamburg, Abera Verlag, 1997.

Schriber, Mary Suzanne, *Writing Home, American Women Abroad, 1830–1920*, Charlottesville and London, University Press of Virginia, 1997.

Teixeira, Manuel, Monsignore, *Macau no Século XIX Visto por uma Jovem Americana*, Macau, Direcção dos Serviços de Educação e Cultura, 1981.

Teixeira, Manuel, Monsignore, *Toponímia de Macau*, 2 vols., Macau, Instituto Cultural de Macau, 2nd ed., 1997 (vol. I, Ruas com Nomes Genéricos [Streets with Generic Names]; vol. II, Ruas com Nomes de Pessoas [Streets Named after Persons]).

Tillotson, G. H. R., *Fan Kwae Pictures. Paintings and Drawings by George Chinnery and Other Artists in the Collection of The Hongkong and Shanghai Banking Corporation*, London, Spink and Son Ltd., 1987.

Trollope, Fanny, *Domestic Manners of the Americans*, Harmondsworth, Penguin Books Ltd., 1997, (edited by Pamela Neville-Sington).

Waley, Arthur, *The Opium War through Chinese Eyes*, Stanford (California), Stanford University Press, 1968.

Watts, Ian E., "Bi-racial identity, bi-racial status: Two Chinese orphans raised by the Canossian Sisters in Macao", in *Review of Culture,* ser.2, no.31, April to June 1997, pp.77–88.

Wood, William W., *Sketches of China; with Illustrations from Original Drawings*, Philadelphia, Carey & Lea, 1830.

Index